Coaching Youth Football

2nd edition

by
John T. Reed

342 Bryan Drive
Alamo, CA 94507
510-820-6292
fax: 510-820-1259
Area code will change to 925 in March, 1998
e-mail: johnreed@johntreed.com
www.johntreed.com

Dedicated to my son, Daniel, who got me into football coaching

About the author

John T. "Jack" Reed coached offense, defense, and special teams for the San Ramon, California Bears youth football program from 1990 through 1994 and in 1996. He was J.V. defensive coordinator in 1994 and varsity assistant coach at Miramonte High School (Orinda, CA) in 1995. In 1996, Reed was the freshman offensive coordinator and special teams coordinator at Granada High School in Livermore, CA. Reed played sandlot football as a kid in the fifties and sixties. He played tackle football off and on in junior high school, high school, college (intramural), and in the army. His playing career is generally without distinction except that the army team on which he was a starter won the Fort Monmouth "Superbowl" in 1971.

Altogether, Reed has coached over twenty teams including baseball (tee ball to semi-pro), volleyball (high school boys varsity and junior varsity), and youth soccer. He is a member of the American Football Coaches Association, California Coaches Association, National Youth Sports Coaches Association, the National Federation Interscholastic Coaches Association, the Football Writers Association of America, and the American Baseball Coaches Association.

He holds a bachelor of science degree from West Point and a master of business administration degree from Harvard Business School.

Other football books by John T. Reed

- *Coaching Youth Football Defense*
- *Football Clock Management*

Thanks to

My sons, Daniel, Steven, and Mike for agreeing to my recommendation that they try football for a year before deciding whether they wanted to play soccer or football...my wife for being a football widow to an extent during coaches meetings, scouting trips, practice, and games...the San Ramon Bears for taking my oldest son in after he was cut by another team and for giving me the opportunity to coach...Pat Elliott...Steve Noon...Jim Monroe for his expert advice...Kathryn Steele, Bears trainer, and Shannon Pablo, Miramonte trainer, for their counsel on injury prevention and treatment...my fellow coaches for putting up with my foibles and faults...our cameramen without whose videotaping of games we coaches wouldn't know what the heck happened out there...my players, who also put up with my faults and foibles as we struggled together through their early years as players and my early years as coach...Miramonte High School coaches Richard Blaisdell, Floyd Burnsed, Paul Yriberri, Vince Dell'Aquilla and Granada High School coaches Aaron Gingery, Bob Turnbeaugh, Ken Nelson, Brad Morosoli, Hank Stephens, T.J. Thomas, John Glover, and Doug Pederson for their instruction and encouragement...Roger Theder, NFL and college coach, for his advice and encouragement...Dana Bible, Stanford offensive coordinator for sharing his thoughts and experiences with me...Holly Newman, referee for reading the book and straightening me out on high school rules...Ace Cacchiotti of NFL Films for his generous assistance...NFL team public relations men: Bob Moore of the Chiefs, Harvey Greene and Neal Gulkis of the Dolphins, Frank Ramos of the Jets, Greg Gladysiewski of the Cardinals, Rich Dalrymple of the Cowboys, Lee Remmel ofthe Packers, Pat Hanlon of the Giants, Todd Starowitz of the Eagles...John Aldrich, Erv Hatzenbuhler, Ken Keuffel, and Ed Racely for consulting we me and helping me design my single-wing offense...Hugh Wyatt for helping me design my double-wing offense.

Published by John T. Reed
342 Bryan Drive
Alamo, CA 94507
510-820-6292 Area code will change to 925 in March, 1998
fax: 510-820-1259
e-mail: johnreed@johntreed.com
Web site: www.johntreed.com

Cover photography by David Fischer, San Francisco, CA
Hand model: Steven Reed
Manufactured in the United States of America
Library of Congress Catalog Card Number 97-069472
ISBN: 0-939224-40-2

Table of contents

1 Overview 1
2 Special teams 17
3 Kickoff Team 19
4 Kick return team 41
5 Punt team 51
6 Punt block/return team 61
7 PAT/FG kick team 65
8 Defense 69
9 Offense 105
10 Videotape 222
11 Minimum-play players 226
Appendix A What to teach your players 229
Appendix B For more information 232
Appendix C Practice schedules 237
Index 244

1

Overview

A lot to coaching youth football

Youth coaches too often feel they can show up with their equipment bag and good intentions and they are entitled to the eternal gratitude of the community for their efforts. That's not good enough. True, we are unpaid. But the job of coaching a football team is difficult and complex and the age of the players or compensation of the coaches does not change that. Coaching a youth football team is one of the most rewarding, if not **the** most rewarding, job in all of coaching. But it is also a responsibility.

On several occasions, we have played against new teams. Their coaches obviously thought their good intentions, long-ago playing experience, and watching football on TV were all they needed. They were wrong. We invariably blew such teams out of the stadium. Their players worked hard but failed miserably because their coaches did not know what they were doing. Even experienced coaches too often go only on faded memories of what their high school coach did, modified by garbled recollections of the wisdom of football color men.

I congratulate you on your decision to educate yourself about the responsibility you have taken on as a youth football coach. I am excited for you because I know how rewarding your season can be.

Simple but thorough with oomph

I see three main things lacking in most youth football programs: simplicity, thoroughness, and oomph.

Most youth football coaches have far too many plays and too many defenses. The consequence is that their kids could not pass a simple quiz on any of them. In fact, their **coaches** could not pass a challenging quiz on **their own system**. I'll demonstrate that later in this chapter.

The players do not **know** what they are supposed to do in each situation, let alone have the practice time needed to **master** doing the job. By confusing the kids, those coaches nullify their natural athletic ability and rob them of their aggressiveness. Confused players are tentative. And he who hesitates is lost in football.

The complexity of most youth football systems also prevents thoroughness. My players know what to do with a kickoff that only goes one yard. They know that a deflected punt means nothing. They know how to take a safety. They know how to execute a two-minute drill—or to waste clock time.

The vast majority of youth football players, on the other hand, have only a narrow knowledge of the game. That knowledge is what they have to do **if all goes exactly**

according to plan. When it does not, they are lost. You cannot do that to your players. You must prepare them for all situations. To do otherwise is incompetent coaching.

Finally, youth coaches generally do not understand how much **oomph** is required to produce a disciplined, competent football team. They practice far too many things far too few times when they should be practicing far fewer things far more times. In this book, I will draw your attention to those things that require zillions of repetitions—like long snapping and passing and defensive linemen staying low.

Five documents

Coaching a football team revolves around five documents:

- Play book (Special teams, offense, and defense)
- Scout report
- Practice schedule
- Depth chart
- Game play lists.

The relationship between these documents is **circular**. That is, they are interdependent. Consequently, all the decisions you make regarding the five documents must be constantly **revisited** throughout the pre-season, regular season, and playoffs. In other words, you draw up tentative versions of your play book, scout report, practice schedule, and depth chart the first week. Then you continually modify them as the various aspects of your team, coaching staff, and opponents come into clearer focus.

Play book

All **pro** teams have written play books. I suspect most **college** teams do as well. But the head varsity coach where I first coached **high school** football, Floyd Burnsed, does **not** produce or hand out play books. He said he tried it in past years and found it to be a waste of time.

Play sheet

I prefer play books, play **sheets** actually, that are handed out to the kids. I agree that many kids ignore them. But most study them. And when a kid does not know his job, he has fewer excuses if he was given a play book. Also, I've had high school players ask me for play sheets because they felt it was the only way they could learn their jobs.

I should note that Floyd Burnsed is one of the most successful coaches in our area. His career head coach record at Miramonte High School in Orinda, CA as of 10/3/97 is 115-51-1 with six league championships and one state championship. Miramonte was ranked eighth in California in their division in 1994, so I hesitate to deviate from Floyd's formula.

Details

I am trying to read almost every book and article ever written on football. I have not done that but I have read a lot. One theme that has emerged from my study is that the best coaches know their plays in incredible detail. Ohio State's Woody Hayes was probably the most famous off-tackle play coach of all time. I've read that he would talk to young coaches about the nuances of the off-tackle play in hotel lobbies at conventions until the wee hours of the morning. Similarly, Vince Lombardi was famous for the Green Bay sweep and he was said to have done all-day clinics on just that one play.

Here are the things you need to know about each of your offensive plays:

- formation
- ball carrier

- hole
- likely cutback or bounce-outside opportunities
- quarterback's footprints until after exchange if he's not keeping
- ball carrier's footprints until receiving ball
- blocking rules for every no ball carrier versus every defense you may face
- each blocker's target on the body of his assigned defender
- duration of any delays like jab steps or delayed receiver releases
- which hand or hands the quarterback uses to exchange the ball with a running back
- the first step of every player on the team versus every possible defense
- plan if play is disrupted before exchange is complete
- the identity of the defender who is the focus of any fakes
- how the ball is to be hidden from that defender
- any options built into the play like "taking the defender whichever way he wants to go," pulling the ball down and running with it, outlet receivers, option pitch, and so forth
- necessary modifications to the play in adverse weather
- purpose of the play
- past performance of the play
- best personnel to execute the play
- best and worst defenses for this play
- blocking technique to be used by each player
- key coaching points for the play (what must and must not happen for the play to succeed).

Once you recognize what it takes to design and teach and master **one** play—just **one** play—the absurdity of handing kids a 30-play play book should become apparent. In fact, most coaches do **not** realize what it takes to design, teach, and master a play, which is probably why their plays don't work very well on game day. The vast majority of youth play books are just bare sketches showing only the movement of the backs and receivers. There are few blocking rules, players always step with their favorite foot first and so forth. If you want to see what a proper play book should look like, get Hugh Wyatt's *Dynamics of the Double Wing* play book (360-834-3868).

I suspect one of the main reasons many coaches do **not** do a written play book is that they do not know what should be in it. Putting it down on paper would reveal what the coach knows, and does not know. That's not the case with guys like the above-mentioned Floyd Burnsed, who has over 25 years of successful coaching experience. But guys like Floyd are a minority at the high school level and are near non-existent at the youth level.

I estimate that about 90% of youth coaches are too complex. The youth football **playoff finalists** are almost all teams with very simple systems.

Staff only

You might compromise and produce a play book for the coaching staff only. That way you'll all be on the same page literally and figuratively.

Keep it simple, real simple

Bob LaDouceur is the head varsity football coach at De La Salle High School in Concord, CA, which is near my home. In a newspaper article during the 1994 season, he said his team only has a total of **nine** running and passing plays. His team wins the North Coast Section championship almost every year. In 1994 they were ranked #1 in the U.S. by ESPN. They have a longest-in-the-U.S. winning streak of 64 games as of the start of the 1997 season.

The offensive coordinator of the Fairfield Suisun Indians team that won the 1993 California Youth Football League Championship at the junior pee wee level was Sam Roberson. He told me that he only had **four** plays, total. My 1993 youth team, which arguably was second best to the Indians, had about seven plays, but when I looked back on the season, I concluded that only three were productive. We would have been better off if we had never run the others.

The leagues I have been involved with go from age eight to 14 or 15. But I have been contacted by coaches who coach younger kids, six- and seven-year olds, in tackle football. I have never coached that level but from talking to those coaches and my experience with eight-year olds, I would suggest the following: Teach the line to do one run-blocking scheme, like a wedge, and one pass-blocking scheme, probably a quick block where they fire out at the knees of the defense to make them get their hands down. The backfield players could vary what they do somewhat, especially if they are among your oldest players.

In contrast, the **typical** youth coach puts in 30 or more plays over a season.

Self quiz

I suspect that the majority of coaches **do not know their own system**, which suggests that their players know even less. Here is a self-quiz to check. You must be able to answer these questions within seconds, like a player in the field has to do. And you should not be thinking about any of them for the first time.

1. Which of your offensive plays are not likely to succeed against a 4-4 defense?
2. If the flanker in a pro set I goes in motion, stops behind his right guard, then after all have been set for one second, the tailback motions out to the right, what do your defenders players do to adjust in each of your defenses?
3. What is your left tackle's first step—direction and distance—on your favorite play against a 5-3 defense?
4. When you are in a man-to-man defense, who has the quarterback after he pitches or backward passes the ball?
5. How does your regular defense line up against a stacked trips left formation?

6. What blocking rules does your tight end employ on your off-tackle play to his side?
7. What does your right wideout do when he has completed his pass route but his quarterback is still scrambling with the ball?
8. What is your defensive line's wide split rule?
9. What does your left wide out do on your sweep right?
10. Who is your contain man on the side where there is a tight slot formation, where does he line up, what is his stance, and what technique does he use?

Competent high school, college, and pro coaches can answer these questions instantly. The fact that they are paid and you are not does not change the fact that all coaches must be able to answer these questions, or at least the ones that pertain to their coaching assignment. The proper response to the fact that you must devote less time to football than higher-level coaches is to reduce your number of plays and defenses, not to excuse poor execution of a college-size play book.

Scout report

Before the season, see some video of past seasons to find out what your opponents typically do. Sure, it changes from season to season at a couple of teams. But there is generally a sort of standard approach in most leagues.

In our local high school Tri-County Athletic League, relatively refined passing games are prevalent. California Youth Football featured primarily **sweeps** by the fast teams and dives and blast plays by other strong teams. You occasionally meet a team that can burn you with a pass. But the completion percentage of the average CYF team is probably around 20%—exceeded only by an interception percentage of 40%.

Use the general idea of what you're up against to make your preliminary pre-season plans. Then, as the season approaches, scout your **specific** upcoming opponents and draw up specific practice schedules accordingly. You **must** scout. Failure to scout is to football coaching what failure to x-ray is to orthopedic surgery.

The scout report is basically the other team's play book—as best you can determine it from watching them play. The scout report also contains information about the other team's personnel like notes about strong or weak players, squad size, and so forth. And the scout report should reveal play-calling tendencies of the opposing team.

Practice schedule

The practice schedule is what it sounds like. But most youth coaches don't organize their practices enough, nor do they do it correctly. In general, your practice schedule covers teaching your **play book** and the **scouting report** to your team. It also provides time for your **evaluations** of your own players. And it provides time for players to perfect their **skills** and to get used to **working together**. Finally, it shows them all the **situations** they might encounter in a game and gives them practice responding to those situations.

Depth chart

The depth chart lists all the positions on your team then shows the first-, second-, third-, and fourth-string players at each position. This is extremely important—maybe the **most** important thing a coach does.

Mark Twain said the difference between choosing the right word and the wrong word is like the difference between **lightning** and a **lightning bug**. The same is true in your depth chart. You must have your absolute best guy at each position—not your second-best guy or your fourth-best guy or the best guy of the kids willing to play that position.

Nepotism and 'Central Casting'

Most coaches give the plum positions to the various coaches' sons and do what I call 'Central Casting' with the rest. That is, the coaches' sons are offensive backs and receivers. Then the rest are assigned according to whether they **look the part**—fat guys on the line, skinny guys at receiver, and fast guys in the backfield. That's a formula for failure, especially in the playoffs, when every little thing takes on great importance.

Youth politics is another pernicious influence. Some parents are more politically active in the youth organization than others. If their son does not get the position or playing time they want, they often try to put political pressure on you to bend to their wishes. I have no idea how to deal with that stuff, or why you should care. But to do a proper job as coach, for all the players and everyone else associated with the team, you must resist basing your depth chart on political pressure.

Personalities and legacies

Coaches may other personnel mistakes. One common one is to mistake a pleasing personality or rapport for performance. Young coaches, especially, are prone to blindness toward the performance **shortcomings** of the kids they **like** as well as blindness to the performance **strengths** of the kids they **don't like**. Whether you like a kid or not is irrelevant. All that matters is performance when it comes to making your depth chart.

Legacies is another common problem. Coaches often attribute to players the performance characteristics of their **older brothers or fathers**. Sometimes, the characteristics are there. Often they are not. Get unbiased opinions from people whose football judgment you trust on kids whose older brothers' or father's football career may be clouding your judgment. Let the expert view the kid at a game or on film and don't tell him about the older brother or father.

Get quality linemen or lose

If you want to run an off-tackle play, you must have excellent athletes blocking at the point of attack. I will have my four best players in that off-tackle alley. My best running back will carry the ball. The other three top players will be the blocking back and linemen. I will have, on the line, guys that the vast majority of coaches will put at first- and second-string offensive backfield positions. More about that later.

Most youth coaches are well aware of the dramatic drop in performance between their first-string quarterback and their second-stringer, between their first-string place kicker and their second-stringer, between their first-string long snapper and their second-stringer. What they do **not** know is that same dramatic drop applies to **every** position. But they are not aware of it at the line positions because they treat the line as a sort of six- or seven-man blob. In fact, there are individual performances taking place there the same as in the high-visibility positions.

Having the wrong guy or even the second-best guy playing left tackle, or other line position, will **kill** your offense. On one team I coached, a persistent second-string lineman would sneak onto the **first**-string offense in practice. All of a sudden, our first-string offense would grind to a screeching halt against the scout team, which is mostly **second**-string defensive guys. The head coach would start yelling at the offense. Finally I would figure out that the second-string tackle had sneaked into the lineup and replace him with a first-string player. The offense would immediately resume making big gains against the scout team.

Most coaches probably have the right guy as their main running back—although coach's sons sometimes get that job instead of the right player. But the vast majority of youth coaches probably have, at key line positions, guys who should be fourth or fifth on the depth chart and the guys who should be playing line are misused in prima donna positions like wide receiver and backup quarterback or running back.

Season practice organization

The season has three segments:

- pre-season
- regular season
- playoffs.

The pre-season starts on the first day of practice and ends on the last day before the first day of practice for the week before your first game. In most teams, the pre-season ends with a scrimmage against another team or two or three. The pre-season is a time for putting in **generic** special teams, offensive, and defensive plays. By generic I mean they are applicable to **all** your opponents. If there is a dominant opponent in your league, pre-season would be a good time to practice against their offense and defense.

The pre-season is also your main **evaluation** time. You should never stop evaluating all season long and into the playoffs. But you do the **most** evaluation the first day of practice and progressively less with each passing day. This diagram shows what I mean.

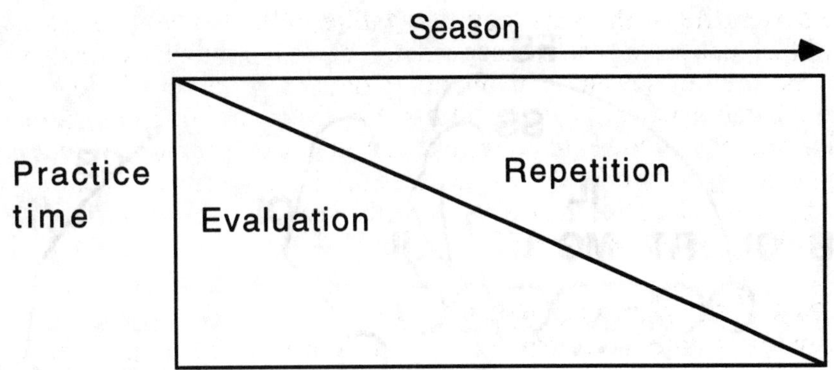

Game play lists

You should go into each game with a list of situations and the plays you will call when you get into those situations. My approach is influenced by a book by Minnesota Vikings offensive coordinator Brian Billick, *Developing an Offensive Game Plan*. Although I found as a high school freshman offensive coordinator, I had to modify his approach.

Here are the categories I used for the last game of the 1996 season (which we lost 8-6 to the undefeated league champion): 1st & 10, 1st & 5, 1st & 10+, 2nd & 7+, 2nd & 2-6, 2nd & 1, 3rd & 11+, 3rd & 7-10, 3rd & 4-6, 3rd & 2-3, 3rd & 1, 4th & 1, backed-up (inside our own 10), 2-minute drill, 4-minute drill (slowdown) and "nothing's working plays." You generally need a separate shorter list for red zone or goal line because most defenses change in that area.

I had injured players stand next to me and keep stats during games. After the games, I would enter the results for each play into a computer spread sheet. As the season progressed, a pattern emerged. Some plays were very effective; others, not. My game day play list reflected what plays were most likely to gain the necessary yards. This strikes me as obvious, but my impression is that most coaches, even including many high school teams, do not figure out which of their plays are working and use them. Rather they have an idea of which they **think** should work and they behave as if they **are** working in spite of all evidence to the contrary. These coaches have teams good enough to win their games, but they keep stopping their own team with passes that are incomplete or are intercepted, when their running game is averaging four yards a carry!

As a general rule in youth football, **if you pass, you punt**. Because passing wastes a down about 80% of the time, which forces you to get a first with only two plays and if you are averaging four yards a carry, which is enough to get a first down with three downs, you find yourself with 4th and two instead of first and ten. I will talk about how to optimize your passing game in this book. But I have enormous respect for the difficulty of succeeding with the pass, especially at the youth level.

Theory and reality

Football coaches are the biggest bunch of theoreticians I know. Yet virtually all of them would vehemently deny that they were any such thing.

Why do I say that? Try working backwards from your film to your play book once. That is, diagram one of your plays based on what actually happens on the field when your team runs it in a game, rather than on what's supposed to happen.

Here's an actual play my junior pee wee (ages 8 to 10) team ran at the beginning of the game against River City on 10/23/93.

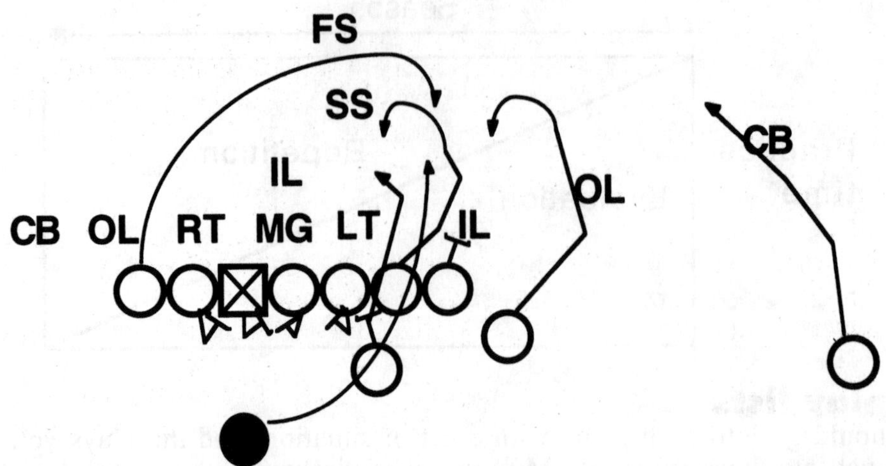

The way we coaches would describe it is, "We had 3rd & 4 at the River City 37. We called a seam buck. It only gained 1 1/2 yards, but we went for it on fourth down using the same play and got the first." Another day at the office for us coaching geniuses, right?

In fact, the only block thrown on the play was by the right tight end, Artie Cervantes, whom I believe is the best lineman ever to wear a San Ramon Bears uniform. He hit his man and drove him outward and to the rear out of the play. The flanker, wing, and super tackle (player between the right end and the right tackle) just sort of wandered downfield tentatively and when no defender showed any interest in being blocked by such a slow moving offensive player, they turned around to watch how the tailback was doing with his ball-carrying activities.

The guards, center, and right tackle hit no one. They got hit and driven back about a step where they regained their footing and stopped the defender. In effect, they each did a pass block. Thank God for the zero line splits. The upback or blocking back banged into the driven-back right tackle bounced off and ran upfield looking for someone to block.

The tailback (ball carrier) seemed slow to start, but he hit the hole and managed a gain before he was tackled by the strong safety. The super tackle ran right by the strong safety on his way to blocking no one. The blocking back might have blocked the strong safety had he not been knocked backward and passed by the ball carrier. The backside tight end might have blocked the strong safety had he not rocked back on his heels at the snap, standing up slowly, then taking a deep circle route to the path of the ball carrier.

You should also note the alignment of the defense. I suspect River City's defensive play book had no such defense. Here's the **play book** version of this seam buck play.

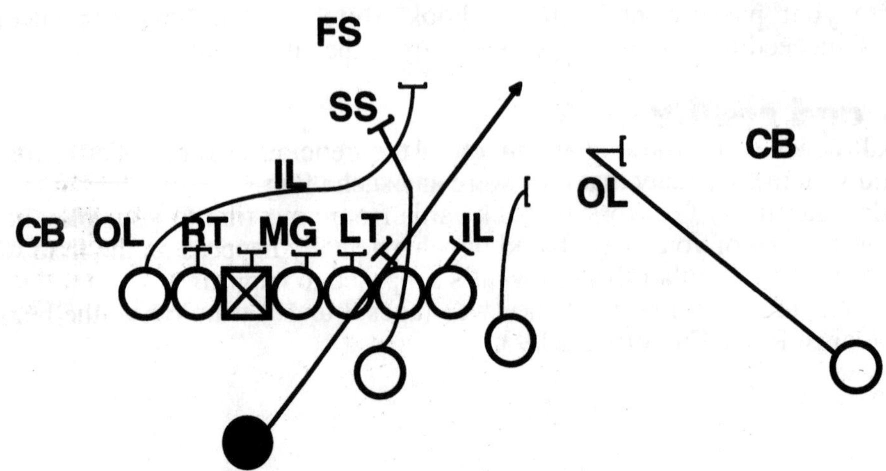

As you can see, this was mere theory. The players, or most of them, did not execute this play. By the way, we won this game, 25-6. Like I said, coaching geniuses.

Get real. Diagram what your players are actually doing in games. Don't kid yourself that they are doing what your play book diagrams say.

'We'll run 26 power all day'

A high school coach I once worked for saw a scout video, laughed out loud, and predicted, "We'll run 26 power all day against that defense." We didn't. Rather it was yet another tough victory on our way to the league championship.

I, too, have laughed at the "stupidity" of my opponent when scouting, only to find that we had trouble beating them, or even lost the subsequent game.

You often hear coaches say something like, "22 blast is there all day." They mean there is something unsound about the opponent's defense, thereby making it easy to run a particular play against it.

I have on occasion, spotted something unsound in the opposing defense, and exploited it for a play or two. We gained 14 yards on a sweep against Berkeley when I noticed their defensive end was crashing in at too steep an angle to discharge his contain responsibilities. We have on a number of occasions, put a receiver out wide, noticed that he was not covered by a defender, and thrown to him successfully. But even if the opposing **coaches** are too dumb to fix the problem, their **players** almost always are smart enough to make an appropriate adjustment to patch the hole.

'The story of today's game will be...'

Both coaches and announcers decide before a game what the story of the game will be. Announcers are useful for instruction because you can see them on your TV. Pay attention to the next several pre-game shows you see. The studio announcers and the game site announcers will say what the story of today's game is expected to be. "It's gonna be Young and Rice against Aikman and Irvin."

Then, as the actual game progresses, each defense stuffs the other's passing game and the only thing working is Young's pulling the ball down and running and Emmit Smith's swing pass catches and runs.

Yet the coaches continue to call the passes that are not working and the announcers continue to talk as if they were right about deep passing being key in the game. Often, these expert, former-player or former-coach announcers, get all the way into the fourth quarter before they figure out they were simply wrong.

It happens to youth coaches even more. It is **very** hard to see what's happening right before your eyes in a game. The game video is almost invariably a surprise. You must make extraordinary efforts **during** the game to figure out during the game what is **really** going on out there.

Unsportsmanlike conduct

We had no unsportsmanlike conduct penalties on the three teams where I was either head coach or acting head coach. That is no accident—especially in this era of NFL and college players displaying tons of unsportsmanlike conduct. I do a ten-minute chalk talk with my players on conduct. I cover each type of unsportsmanlike conduct (Rule 9-5), describe it, and demonstrate it and tell them, "There will be none of that on this team. In fact, my policy is to take **out of the game** anyone who draws an unsportsmanlike conduct flag." That apparently made the desired impression.

What you demand

The following are some of the most important lessons I've learned. In fact, they are lessons I've learned over and over in my life every time I've managed people in a different situation. I'll state it in the form of sayings I've seen in coaching books.

You get what you demand.
What you tolerate, you encourage.
Discipline is something you do FOR someone, not TO them.

Indiana basketball coach Bobby Knight also teaches a course at Indiana University. On the first day, he asks his students to write the five **best** teachers they ever had on one side of a piece of paper and the five **most demanding** teachers they ever had on the other. He says the lists are usually identical.

Do it right or do it over

There is a right way to do things. If people did things the right way on their own, you wouldn't need coaches or managers or leaders. In fact, people do **not** do things the right way much of the time. When players screw up, they either deny it happened at all or, if you don't buy that, they say you are asking the impossible or didn't make yourself clear or some other excuse.

When I was a company commander in the army, my mess sergeant said we were always out of milk because the army didn't give him enough. At first, I accepted that excuse. Then I noticed other mess halls weren't out. Upon investigation, I learned that the mess sergeant was not preventing early diners from hogging the milk.

Excuses, excuses

In my early years as a landlord, tenants gave me sob stories about why they couldn't pay the rent on time. The stories sounded reasonable. But by talking to other landlords and experiencing 23 years as a landlord, I learned tenants will pay on time if you insist and will pay late if you let them. In my **last** years as a landlord, I would lower the boom on all delinquents the first day after rent was due.

I can tell you similar stories about employees, baseball players, my kids, and so forth.

In football, the kids tackle lousy and swear it's the only way they could have done it in that situation. They drop passes because of lack of concentration, but claim it was a bad pass. The defensive linemen stand up but swear they didn't or that they had to. And on and on.

Calling a competent football coach a perfectionist is redundant

The difference between the good coaches and the bad coaches is that the bad ones **accept** the excuses, while the good ones demand perfection. I used to be a bad coach in that respect—because I was too inexperienced to recognize that the players were wrong.

But as time goes on, you notice that some of your opponents are getting **their** players to tackle properly. **Some** of your own players always hang onto passes even when not perfectly thrown. Some members of your d-line **do** stay low. And as you notice and investigate those performances you inevitably come to the conclusion that everybody **can** do it right, but that most will only if you **insist** on it.

Players do not realize what they are capable of

It's not that the players are lying. Sometimes they are. But more often they are making the same mistake the bad coaches make. They have little experience doing things the right way, and the right way is often harder than the wrong way, so they assume the right way is **impossible**.

One of the main things coaches do is get people to do more than they thought they were capable of. In fact, that is the great glory of coaching. Getting a kid to do more than he thought he could is the greatest gift you can give him. But it does not seem so at the time. Great coaches get people to do more because their years of experience have shown them what people can do when they give it their all.

Best tacklers in the league

In 1992, my defense had the best tackling technique in the league. Why? For the previous two years I had **taught** correct tackling, **urged** correct tackling, and **pleaded for** correct tackling. But I had not **insisted** on it.

But in '92, if a player tackled incorrectly in practice, I took them out of scrimmage and made them tackle correctly five times against a dummy. The players hated that and you could literally see them bear down and concentrate on tackling correctly so they would not have to do one of my doggone remedial tackling sessions.

In our semifinal playoff game, we missed a total of one tackle. We lost 19-7. But we did not lose because we missed tackles. When we touched a guy, he went down and went down where he was touched.

Insist

Sometimes, you can demand what you need by creating a punishment drill. Sometimes, a well-placed butt-chewing will do it. Sometimes, you have to demote a player to get his attention. If you have enough depth, I've found that demotion usually works.

A couple of my 1994 high school players were drifting away from correct technique as the season progressed. I had a heart-to-heart talk with them and warned them in somber tones to get back to the technique they had been taught or risk losing their jobs. Apparently they had heard that before and nothing happened because they were shocked the following Monday when I told them they were demoted to the bench. When I put them back on the field two weeks later, their technique was just fine.

Both carrots and sticks

The bottom line is that you **must** get the players to do what they're supposed to. You start by teaching and encouraging and positive feedback and all that. But you're naive if you think that's all you'll ever need. There will come a time when you have used all the carrots. When that time comes, you need to get out the sticks.

Tough love

In modern pop psychology terminology, that's called **tough love**. It appears to be the most effective parenting technique as well as the most effective management and coaching technique.

My background as a West Point graduate causes some people to jump to an incorrect conclusion. They think all West Pointers are hard asses. In fact, if you could have watched my first week as a West Point plebe, or my own approach to welcoming new plebes as a senior three years later, you would be impressed by the extremely demanding standards cadets are held to, but also the dignity with which they are treated and the amazing example the upperclassmen set.

Here is an exchange that made a big impression on me thirty years ago. During my first two minutes at West Point, an upperclassman asked me if I knew how to salute. I said I did and he asked me to demonstrate. He then said something that seemed incongruous amidst the chaos of shouted commands and ass chewings that was going on all around me. He said, "Mister, may I touch you?" I said, "Yes, sir," and he rotated my salute hand to the proper position.

There were many other such incidents during my four years at West Point. The same guys who were always chewing you out for an inadequate shoe shine themselves had impeccable, far superior shoe shines.

One of my classmates complained that it was impossible to perform a tricky maneuver called "inspection arms" with an M-14 rifle. The upperclassman asked for the rifle and executed it perfectly. The plebe then complained that we were wearing cotton gloves while the upperclassmen were not during that particular drill period. The upperclassman took the plebe's cotton gloves, put them on, and promptly executed another perfect inspection arms. As I recall, the upperclassman said nothing at all during this incident except, "Give me your rifle" and "Give me your gloves." But his approach could not have been more effective.

On forced marches, the upperclassmen sternly demanded that we keep up, but they periodically made us stop and take off our boots and socks to inspect our feet to make sure we had no blisters.

When hot food was delivered to the field, the plebes always ate first, then the upperclassmen, then the officers. Frequently, the cooks gave the plebes at the head of the line portions that were too large and some upperclassmen and officers had to go hungry. That is precisely why they always went last.

We thought, "Jeez, these guys are incredibly demanding. But the SOBs are not asking us to do anything they are not doing along with us, or did do several years ago. And they clearly have our best interests at heart." That's a good model for football coaches.

Running out of gas

Discipline is not just for West Point. Civilians are disciplined when they have to be. Civilian **human** authorities in the '90s are very lenient. But the **inanimate** objects in our lives, like gas tanks, often impose harsh discipline, with excellent results.

If you run out of gas, you suffer a painful penalty. You have to hike to a gas station or phone. It is extremely inconvenient and a very effective punishment. As a result, normally undisciplined civilians are extremely disciplined when it comes to running out of gas. They run out about once or twice in their lives.

The East St. Louis Flyers

One of the most inspirational football coaching books I ever read is *The Right Kind of Heroes* by Kevin Horrigan. It's about Bob Shannon, coach of the East St. Louis, IL Flyers high school football team. East St. Louis is a disaster that was profiled in *Sixty Minutes* among other places. The neighborhood is so bad that the players' parents won't attend home games. Nevertheless, Shannon's record was 152-21 last I heard. He had also won six Illinois state championships and been named *Sporting News* High School Coach of the Year five times. His favorite expression is, "Get it done." He judges everybody and everything by that standard.

The notion that you can mold youth football players into a competent team with nothing but positive words is a '90s fantasy. Successful coaches I have observed and read about all use the **full** range of motivating methods, including both positive and negative.

Skills

In organizing your practices, you need to understand the different nature of the various skills. Some skills can be picked up with just one or two repetitions, like how to do a correct fair-catch signal. You might think you could just **tell** them about a fair catch signal or tell them and demonstrate it with your own arm. Nope. You must make **them do** it. I require the hand higher than the helmet and two distinct waves.

Some skills run counter to the way the players are inclined to do it if left to their own devices, like a defensive lineman's charge. They will stand up and look around when the ball is snapped. That will have disastrous effects on your team's defense. They must keep their shoulder pads lower than the shoulder pads of the guy who is trying to block them.

Coaching is teaching?

Some people say that coaching is teaching. To an extent it is. But getting players to do uncomfortable skills right is more akin to brain washing than teaching. **My** youth defensive linemen **did** stay low. But only because we made them do it ten minutes a night **every** night and we absolutely insisted that it be done right every time. We replaced them in a New York minute if we found them standing up. "If you stand up, you'll sit down," is our motto. At least one opposing coach asked after a game, "How do you get your line to charge low like that?" It ain't easy.

Oomph

Another lesson I have learned in life, as well as in football, is what I call the Oomph Principle. Often I have tried to accomplish something and failed. I reanalyzed my technique and could find no fault with it. Then I consulted with an expert and found I was right about my technique being correct. All I lacked was enough oomph.

I've tried to fix things around the house or in my car only to have a mechanic come and do the exact same thing I was doing, only much harder than I did. I was afraid to use that much force for fear I'd break it. The expert knew from years of experience that it would **not** break from that much force and that no **lesser** force would work.

Putting a baby's head under water

When my first son was an infant, we got him swimming lessons to drown-proof him at the earliest possible age. Clearly, to accomplish that, the baby has to learn to put his face under water, hold his breath, paddle toward the side of the pool, and reach up and grab it. His instructor, who does nothing else and was a former Olympic hopeful, gave him two "walk-throughs" of this process. After his first face-under-water experience, he came up coughing, spitting up water, and screaming as if he were on fire.

The instructor did it again and again for fifteen minutes a day, four days a week for months. He screamed his head off.

At age fourteen, he swam so fast that he set records not only in his age group, but in the next higher age group as well. He broke the league record in the breast stroke by 2.88 seconds in the summer of 1994. His infant swimming instructor did nothing I would not have done. But she used far more oomph than I would have dared.

I have watched youth football coaches try, and fail, to put in a passing game year after year. Then I joined the Miramonte High School football coaching staff. Miramonte is known for its great passing game. Our '94 quarterback, Matt Kroger, had the highest passing efficiency rating in the league. How does Coach Burnsed do it? Pretty much as you would expect. The quarterbacks and receivers drill on their footwork and mechanics. And they throw passes in practice.

250 passes a day

One day I asked Floyd **how many** passes each of his quarterbacks threw in the average practice session. "250." "250!" Our youth coaches did similar drills for their quarterbacks. But they only had them throw about ten or twenty passes a practice. Not enough oomph.

As of this writing, De La Salle High School, which is near my home, has a 67-game win streak going—the longest current streak in the U.S. They run the veer triple option. Have you ever wondered how much oomph it takes to run the triple option? I talked to a young man who quarterbacked De La Salle's freshman and J.V. teams. Here's what they do on just the pitch portion of the option. There is a standard drill in which two option quarterbacks run along respective yard lines from one side of the field to another and pitch to each other. They are five yards apart. The drill is well known and is in virtually every drill book or option book. At De La Salle, each quarterback is required to do ten round trips a day of that drill. Any round trip in which the ball hits the ground does not count. That's oomph.

When you plan your practices, recognize that many skills take enormous oomph on the part of the coaching staff and allocate time accordingly. That is, they require a tremendous number of repetitions and those repetitions must all be correct. Close attention must be paid to how the players are performing the technique and correction of poor technique must be instantaneous. Examples in football include:

- long snapping
- passing and receiving
- tackling
- low line charges
- backpedaling
- option reads
- option ball handling
- field goal holding
- getting off on the correct snap count
- correct stance.

Working together

Football is a team sport—more so than any other sport I know of. In many cases, two players have to work **together**. Each such skill must be practiced by the **same** players who will have to perform it in the games. For example, if you have your quarterback receive the snap with his hands in the center's crotch, like virtually all teams do when they're not in a shotgun formation, the center and quarterback must practice that at **every** practice session. Furthermore, they must practice it **with each other**. A center snapping to someone other than the first-string quarterback is of little value and may even be harmful. They **must** get used to working **together**.

I have seen many a youth team that fumbles a dozen or more snaps per game—even at the end of the season! That's such bad coaching it makes me mad just to be in the same profession with the guy who is responsible. The same is true of handoffs, pitches, passes, long-snapper-to-punter exchanges, long-snapper-holder-field-goal-kicker execution.

Second string

It is important that you get your second-string players plenty of working-together reps as well. Unfortunately, it's easier said than done. But you must structure your practice so that the first-string center and first-string exchange snaps, the second-string center and the second-string quarterback, and the third-string center and quarterback.

You may want to substitute them as a unit. Baseball pitchers often have, and are allowed to use, a favorite catcher who is not otherwise first-string.

If you cannot substitute them as a unit, you must get **cross reps**. That is, the first-string center must snap to the second-string quarterback and vice versa. But that's when the mathematical possibilities start to bang into the reality of only so much practice time.

Same number of reps

If you watched me coach, you would often be hard pressed to tell which of my players were starters and which were bench warmers. That's because I try to get the same number of reps for each.

I have seen many coaches focus on their starters and totally ignore their subs. That's unfair to the subs and just plain bad coaching. Rare is the football team that gets through a season without absences due to injury or discipline or family matters. Also rare is the team where no one gets demoted during a season.

Because you will inevitably need them, you must prepare your subs. Many a crucial failure in games I've coached was due to a sub playing a position poorly simply because he did not get enough reps in practice. Your practice schedules must constantly rotate subs in. It won't happen if you don't organize it that way and monitor it to make sure it's happening.

Like riding a bike

Some skills must be practiced **every day**. Others need only be learned **once**.

For example, I am big on picking up fumbles and running with them rather than falling on the ball. I recognize that there are times to fall on the ball. But there is no doubt that most non-professional players fall on balls they should have picked up. I have found this to be a riding-a-bike type skill. Actually it's more of a habit than a skill. Any idiot can pick up a ball and run with it. Once learned, there is little need for additional reps.

Deliberately kick badly to practice pick up

However, I have also learned that it takes a fair number of reps to acquire the habit initially. At every punt-return team practice, I tell my punt-team kicker to deliberately kick the ball into a lineman's butt so we could get practice on dealing with a blocked punt.

I had told my players emphatically that they were to pick up the ball and run **always** on fourth down since the possession is predetermined by the down. I even did a drill where I threw the ball down and each player on the team took a turn picking it up and running with it. Nevertheless, when the punter's punt was blocked in special teams practice, kids would fall on the ball.

I would go nuts, in a good-natured way, ranting and raving about what a waste it was to fall on a ball that was already ours when it was so easy to pick it up and run for a touchdown. I would invariably toss the ball down five successive times and make the boy who fell on it pick it up and run five times. While doing that I would tell him over and over, "Pick it up and run!"

Brain washing

This is brain washing. This is theatrically making a scene. It also works. During the season, our players blocked many punts, but they never fell on a single one. They always picked them up and ran with them.

In our 1994 varsity Miramonte High School game against San Ramon Valley High School, we lost a fumble way behind the line of scrimmage on fourth down. The quarterback was on the ground under a San Ramon player. No fewer than six San Ramon Valley players, unaccompanied by any Miramonte players, frantically chased the ball as it bounced away from the line of scrimmage. Then they fell on it.

San Ramon Valley **lost** that game by a score of 20-14. If they had picked that fumble up and ran with it there is about a 90% probability that they would have **won** the game 21-20.

Our 1994 J.V. high school team fell on two bad punt snaps deep in the opponent's territory in one game late in the season. Why? I was not the punt-return coach. The guy who was never practiced what to do with blocked punts. It doesn't take a lot of reps and they don't have to be done all season. But you **do** have to rep this around six to twelve times with your punt return team to get the players to react correctly to the situation when it develops in a game.

Short drills

One of the most important things you should keep in mind when making up your practice schedule is to limit **drills** to **five or ten minutes** each. In my first year as a youth football coach, the head coach would give me some second-string players and tell me to do such-and-such drill.

After about twenty minutes, I'd find my players getting bored stiff and misbehaving. I would then start snapping at them because of their misbehavior. Fortunately, about that time I read in a football coaching book that you should change what drill you're doing every five minutes—ten at the most. I have found that to be correct. You can do some competitive things like **scrimmage** for as much as 45 minutes without the kids misbehaving. But I suspect there are too many different things to accomplish for you spend 45 minutes on **anything**.

I must add that I stood next to DeLaSalle High School's Bob LaDouceur at his 1993 spring practice and watched him run his center and first- and second-string offensive backfields through veer option plays for 45 minutes straight. No one got bored. No one misbehaved. No one lost concentration.

Note that LaDouceur has charisma. I don't. Rare is the coach who does. 45-minute-long drills without boring his players. Maybe it only works for the charismatic. Although Vince Lombardi, whom I thought had charisma, also said to limit drills to "short periods" in his book *Run To Daylight.*

Set routine

I used to believe that you should constantly use different drills as the season wore on to prevent the players from getting bored. My current thinking is that you should have such new drills **in reserve** in case you need them. But I would not **assume** that your drills are boring the team just because you have used them many times.

I am now a great believer in the **set routine**. That is, it is good to do the same thing every night. One reason is it is very **efficient**. It is a thing of beauty to see a well-drilled team move smoothly and quickly from one activity to another. I went to three college spring practices in 1994: Stanford, St. Mary's College, and Diablo Valley College. They toot an air horn and two hundred guys go tearing off to their next practice station.

Introducing new drills wastes time because you have to teach the new drill and the kids have to get used to it. In many cases, the drill will not work. Whereas the old drills are time tested.

The set routine gives the players a sense of comfort, lets them get into an efficient, productive rhythm. Change it only when forced.

Practice discipline

Football teams have to practice a long list of things every week. Once the season starts, there is a temptation to **panic** when things don't go well. After a loss, poor coaches abandon a sound practice schedule and overfocus on one aspect of the team's play. For example, if the team made a lot of poor tackles in a loss, the coach may spend half the next week's practices on tackling. That will result in those things that are **not** being practiced going to heck in a hand basket.

You must maintain practice discipline. That is, you must draw up a sound schedule in the pre-season and stick to it no matter what. I recommend that you put **ten minutes** a day of what I call **emphasis time** into the schedule. When a weakness is discovered, that ten minutes, **and no more**, will be used to fix it. Time and time again head coaches have told me, "Jack, we're going to cut back on your time this week to spend more time on offense or whatever."

One-crisis-allocation-of-resources

When I was in the army, I called that the one-crisis-allocation-of-resources approach to management. When a motor-pool inspection was coming up, the battalion commander would order everybody to the motor pool for months at a time. Other things would get neglected. Then there would be a VIP demonstration and everybody would be ordered to the demonstration site for months at a time. During that period, the motor pool and everything else would get neglected.

This is incompetence. Do **not** do that to your players and fellow coaches. I recommend the following daily schedule:

6:00 Stretching
6:10 Specialty skills
6:20 Special teams
6:50 Emphasis time
7:00 Defense
7:30 Offense
8:00 End

Big picture

The typical youth coach has a system which he simply does not fully understand. In fact, if that typical youth coach were forced to answer detailed questions about his own offense, defense, or special teams, you would find he would draw a blank on **most** of the questions. The typical youth coach has only the sketchiest understanding of the implications and details of his own systems.

And his players know far less. And if you judge their performance by the only legitimate test, their actual game execution of the plays in question, reality falls laughably far short of the fantasy land in which the coach plots and teaches his grand strategies.

What youth coaches need to do to make real their coaching theories is to reduce their offensive, defensive, and special teams systems to much simpler versions. They must dramatically increase the number of reps they get of each and they must video their practices and games and analyze what their players are actually doing.

They must **know** what they want, in all its details, **teach** what they want, and once it is clear that lack of understanding by the player is no longer the problem, **insist** that the players do it.

They must also assign their payers to the positions which are best for the team. The best eleven athletes should be on first string. The best eleven should not be lined up in three or four layers of offensive backs and receivers while boys whose only talent is pie eating occupy crucial line positions. They must resist political pressure and nepotism pressure to violate the best interest of the team when it comes to the depth chart. They must look beyond personality and the careers of older family members to see the actual performance of each player and place him accordingly on the depth chart.

2

Special Teams

Lip service

Special teams are important. Almost every coach **says** that. But actions speak louder than words. When I got my first special-teams position, I told the head coach I had would take it only on three conditions:

- special teams will be practiced **every day**, not just once a week
- special teams will be the **first** team practiced every day
- special teams will get **no less than 30%** of total teams practice time.

Why special teams are important

Special teams plays comprise 20% of the plays in a typical game according to George Allen in his book, *Guide to Special Teams*. In some youth games I analyzed, 15% of the plays were special teams (kickoff, kickoff return, punt, punt return, PAT/field goal kick, PAT/field goal kick defense).

But special teams plays are **more important** than just 15% to 20% of the game. That's because the average special teams play results in a **bigger change in field position** than the average scrimmage play. In our 1991 Vacaville playoff game, the average scrimmage play resulted in a 1.65-yard change in field position. The average change on **kickoffs** was 11.75 yards. The average change on **punts** was 18 yards.

Punts are dangerous

From the standpoint of the punting team, punts are an extremely dangerous play. If the punt does not get off for whatever reason, the play typically **loses** at least ten yards. If the ball is loose because of a bad snap or blocked punt, the receiving team may pick the loose ball up and run it in for a touchdown most of the time. It blows my mind that coaches don't recognize what a dangerous play the punt is and spend much more time perfecting it. It also blows my mind that teams which cannot protect their punter nevertheless go ahead and punt.

20% of kickoffs returned for TDs

When my oldest son was in his first year as a youth football player, about twenty percent of his team's kickoffs were returned for touchdowns! I was merely a father watching from the stands that year. That's one of the reasons I got into coaching. I was appalled. I was kickoff team coach for four years. **No** kickoffs were returned for touchdowns in three of those years. The other year, two were returned for touchdowns. As a high school J.V. coach, **two** of my kickoffs have been returned for touchdowns. More about those touchdowns later.

Retain possession

All special teams plays are **supposed** to result in a change of possession. The **unexpected** is when the kicking team **retains** possession. My youth teams were probably the league best at that. We recovered our own kickoffs all over the place. An unexpected loss of possession is the equivalent of a 50-yard change in field possession according to the book, *The Hidden Game of Football*. That book is based on **NFL** statistics. 50 yards represents the typical combined total of the additional yards the team **would have** moved the ball with scrimmage plays and a punt if they had not lost possession. In youth football, where the legs are not as strong, the average loss of possession is probably the equivalent of a **thirty**-yard change in field position. That's still a lot.

Scouting

You need to scout opposing kicking teams to see how far their kicker can kick. It is a **disaster** if the kick gets **behind** your returner. Returners tend to be too close to the line of scrimmage on punts. In 1990, we had a punter with a strong leg. He frequently kicked the ball behind the returner and we pinned them against their own end zone as a result. You must scout the kicker's distance and then tell your kick returner to get to the necessary depth. If you have no scouting report, get them back to the maximum for the age group.

You should also note whether their punter is a side winder or is left-footed. Your punt blockers need to know that so they know where the ball will leave the foot.

You need to know where they kick on kickoffs and punts and the trajectory of the kick.

If they put on a particular return for kickoffs and punts, make note and have your scout team do that return in practice.

Steal games

Don Shula, head coach of the Miami Dolphins, said,

> *Special teams are still a very important part of winning or losing a game. The difference now is most all coaches and teams realize it. You can't steal a game anymore the way we could in the early sixties.*

He's talking about the NFL. You still **can** steal games with special teams in youth football—and in high school and college in my opinion. My youth team beat Napa in 1991 in the playoffs as a result of their muff of a punt deep in their territory. If you have any experience at all, you probably have your own stories of games won and lost on special teams plays.

Special team practice schedule

I assume that you will allocate the 30 minutes I recommended each day. I suggest the following detailed schedule:

Tuesday	kickoff and kick return
Wednesday	punt and punt return
Thursday	PAT/field goal kicking and PAT/field goal kicking defense

3

Kickoff Team

Kickoff team goals

• Touchback percentage:

your kicker's on-the-fly range	% touchbacks
30	0
35	0
40	10
45	20

• average return of five yards
• no touchdown returns
• strip ball and gain possession 10% of time
• strip ball and run for touchdown 5% of time
• average opponent starting point = 1.2 x max on-the-fly range - 5 yards from kickoff yard line (e.g., if your kicker can kick 40 yards on the fly, 1.2 x 40 - 5 from normal 40-yard line kickoff point is the receiving team's 17-yard line)
• onside kick successful 30% of the time

Touchback

A touchback is when the kick goes into the end zone. By rule, the ball is dead the moment it touches the plane of the front edge of the goal line and the return team may **not** run the ball out of the end zone in high school. The ball automatically gets put on the 20-yard line (the receiving team can choose a spot anywhere between the hashes, Rule 8-5-4). Youth leagues generally use high school rules.

Few, if any, youth kickers can kick the ball 60 yards on the fly. But the ball will roll after it hits the ground—especially on Astroturf. A kick that **rolls** into the end zone is as much of a touchback as one that goes in on the fly. We had two touchbacks by us and two against us in JV high school play in 1994. All reached the end zone on the bounce.

In youth football, a touchback is most likely after a penalty against the receiving team permits the kickoff team to kick from closer than 60 yards to the goal line. Touchbacks are a good deal for the kicking team because forcing the other team to start on their 20-yard line is pretty good field position. But more importantly, there is no return.

Ball stripping

Anyone who has watched pro or college football lately has noticed that defenders try to strip the ball far more frequently nowadays. They also frequently succeed. You should coach that on defense in general and especially on kick returns.

Most kick return tackles are **gang tackles**. A gang tackle gives your players several seconds during which they have hold of the ball carrier, but the play is not yet blown dead. It is pretty much impossible to hold onto the ball for that long when several guys are trying to strip it.

Stripping is done by slapping at the ball, grabbing at the ball, exploding a shoulder into the ball, and pulling the ball-carrying arm away from the body. Putting the tackler's **helmet** on the ball works, too, but it's so dangerous that it would be criminal to teach kids to do that. The current goal in the football world is to **take the helmet out of hitting**.

Missed tackles are bad, but strips are really good

Old school coaches fear a would-be ball stripper will, in his efforts to get the ball, miss the tackle altogether. Most youth coaches are old school. That is, they played thirty years ago and consequently are thirty years behind the times.

The bottom line is that missed tackles are bad—but turnovers are good—**really** good. You can afford to give up a few more yards in return for an improved turnover margin. In other words, the risk of a player getting a few more yards because of your stripping efforts is worth it because takeaways are really valuable.

Kickers' range

I have coached kickoff teams at the jr. pee wee, pee wee, midget, freshman, jr. varsity, and varsity high school levels. From that experience, I'd say the maximum on-the-fly range of the typical kickoff kicker is:

jr. pee wee (10-year olds)	30 yards
pee wee (11)	35 yards
jr. midget (12)	40 yards
midget (14)	45 yards.

My JV high school players, generally 15-year olds, could kick to around the ten yard line or 50 yards. The best varsity high school kickers can kick to the goal line.

No return

Kickoffs are **very dangerous** for the kicking team. A famous call from the end of 1994 has been run over and over again on national TV. Plano East High School was in the semifinal game of the state championship tournament in Texas made an unbelievable comeback using three consecutive, successful onside kicks. Then, when they finally took the lead, they kicked off **deep** to a star athlete on the other team. He ran the ball back about 98 yards for the winning touchdown. There is a detailed account of that sequence of events in my football clock management book.

Your kickoff strategy is determined by your personnel and your offensive strength (points scored per game, time of possession, etc.) and your defensive strength. Our kickoff strategy was determined by the confidence we had in our ability to stop any team, anywhere on the field. We held several teams to negative yardage and the defending state champion to only one net yard in the playoffs in 1991. We did similarly well in 1992.

How do you achieve no return?

There are a number of ways you can prevent a return. You must create a **fair-catch situation** if the ball is in the air or, if the ball is on the ground, you must make sure the opposing team does not get to it until your players have arrived at the ball as well.

Ground balls

I told my kickers to kick **all ground balls**. One kicked a number of traditional fly balls deep down the middle in spite of my instructions. We were lucky none broke for a touchdown. To prevent further fly balls, I switched to a different kicker who could not kick as far, but who always kept them on or near the ground.

In high school, I and my varsity counterparts have had the same problem. We tell the kickers to keep the ball on the ground and they still kick fly balls. The only way I've been able to stop them is to **replace** them. The deal I had with my 1994 youth kicker was that if his kick was caught in the air—or could have been—he owed me ten pushups.

No interference

Another advantage of the grounder is that you **cannot interfere** with a receiver who hopes to catch it. With a **fly** ball, you must avoid getting close to a member of the receiving team who is trying to catch the ball until it touches the ground or a member of the receiving team—even if the receiver does **not** signal a fair catch. Failure to signal a fair catch gives you the right to hit him **after** he catches the ball. But you can never touch him **before** he catches a **fly** ball, fair catch signal or not.

In **college** and **NFL** rules, the ball needs to go ten yards, but it does **not** need to touch the ground. College and NFL kickoff team players can catch the ball in the air after ten yards. You can**not** do that under high school rules. It's interference. Once the ball touches the ground, you can block any receiving team players.

The kick my teams had the most success recovering was kicked from one hash to the other side of the field, **over** the front row of receivers, **not** to them, like this:

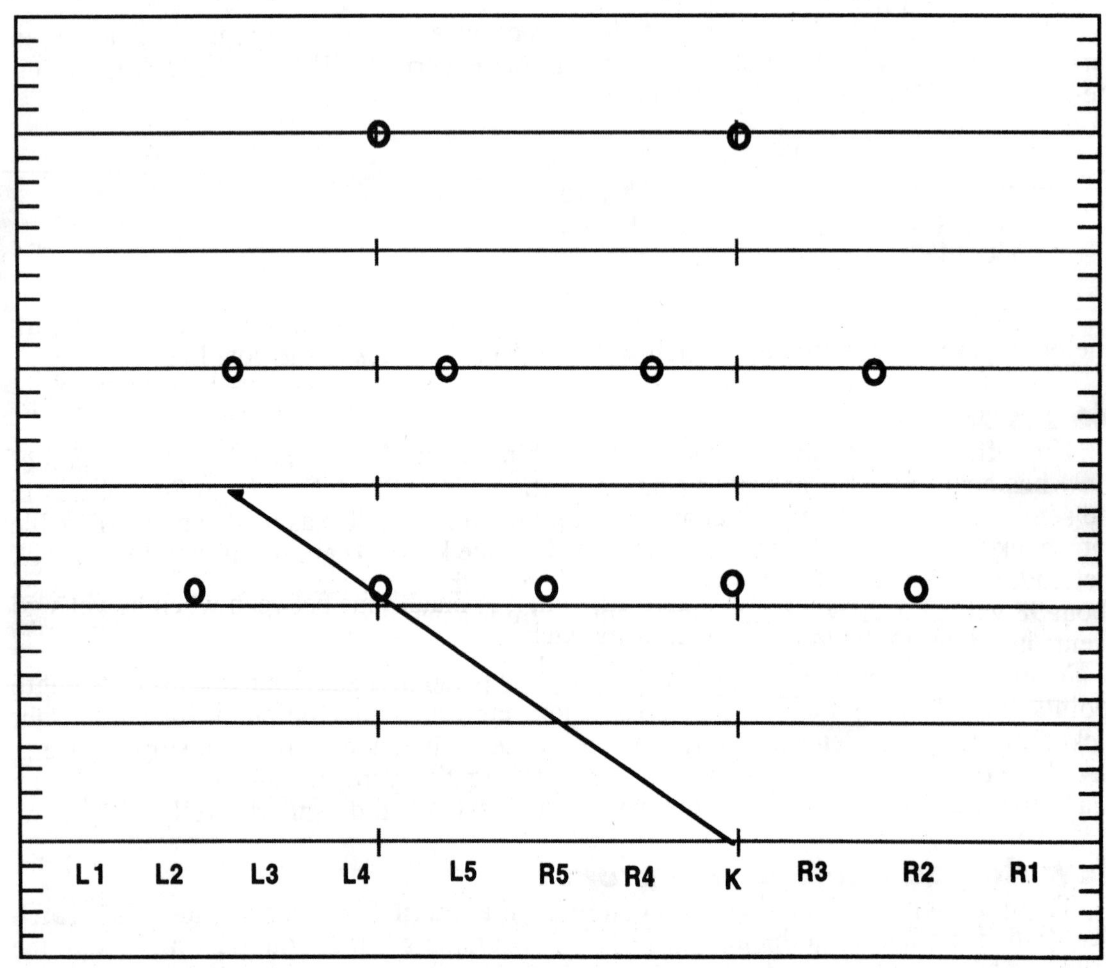

Try to keep the ball in bounds, but don't try too hard

You should try to avoid kicking the ball out of bounds. Although it's not a fate worse than death. The rule allows the receiving team to make you kick over from five yards further back or to take the ball where it went out or to take the ball 25 yards from where it was kicked. That's usually the receiving team's 35-yard line. Most teams take the ball where it went out or on the 35—which means no kick return. Whew!

Your L1 and R1 should bat the ball like basketball players if necessary, to keep it in bounds, after it touches the ground and goes ten yards.

Where to align

It is important that each of your players memorizes exactly where to align for the kickoff. It seems to me that all youth teams but mine kind of wander in a general vicinity.

When I say exactly, I mean **exactly**. The special teams coach must also know exactly where they go so he can make sure they are in the right place in practice and at games. Here are the distances we used in 1994:

Position	Alignment
L1 and R1	5 yards from the sideline
L2 and R2	5 yards inside L1 and R1
L3 and R3	3 yards outside hash (high school)
L4 and R4	2 yards inside the hash (high school)
L5 and R5	5 yards inside L4 and R4
kicker	anywhere he wants between or on the hashes

Sometimes, youth football teams practice on fields marked for college games (my youth teams played at Napa Community College, Laney College, and Los Medanos College) during his youth playing days, Diablo Valley College is the home field of the Pleasant Hill, CA youth team) or even pro games (the California Youth Football championship was played at Sacramento State when that was the home field of a Canadian Football League team, a New Orleans youth team rents the Superdome for an annual Christmas tournament). Those hash marks are different and require different alignment of your players in relation to the hashes.

Depth depends on running speed

The depth of the tacklers varies according to their running speed and is worked out by trial and error in practice so that they are going **full speed**, but do not encroach, when the ball is kicked. Generally, the fastest players are about at our 32 and the slower ones at about our 33. These alignments give even spacing of 5 yards between each non-kicker player and 5 yards from the sideline.

The kicker raises his hand then drops it yelling, "Go!" to signal the other players to start running full speed. In practice, he learns the proper time to give that signal. Encroachment is caused by the **kicker** allowing too much time between when he yells go and when he kicks the ball. The rest of the kickoff team is not to even look at the ball on the tee as they run. When the kicker says "Go!," they are to go. Any offside penalties are **entirely the fault of the kicker** once we have the proper starting point for each member of the kickoff team.

The kicker hangs back as a **safety** after the kick. He must always stay on line with the ball carrier. For example, if the ball carrier runs to the right hash, the kicker must slide over to the right hash.

I have no clue why many coaches have their kickoff team members facing inward and starting to run when the kicker passes them. They have barely gotten moving when the ball is kicked. That approach is quite common, and, as far as I can tell, quite a bad idea. I suspect it's just one of the many triumphs of choreography over common sense that you see in football. (Want examples of some others? The clap-and-slap pre-game warm-up. The slapping of thighs by offensive players in response to the quarterback's yelling "Ready!" The huddle break.) You want your kickoff team guys at absolute full speed when the ball is kicked.

Once the ball is whistled ready for play, no member of the kicking team other than the kicker or the holder, if any, may be beyond the free kick line. In other words, during the 25 seconds or less between the ready-to-kick whistle and the kick, nobody but the kicker and holder may cross the yard line you are kicking from. (Rule # 6-1-3)

Beware the backward bounce

Coaches generally assume that the **worst** thing that can happen on an onside kick is that the receiving team gets possession of the ball. Wrong. I **saw** the worst thing in a '91 San Ramon Bears-Tri-Cities midget playoff game and in my '93 Oakland Saints game.

The Tri-Cities ball went about eight yards, then bounced **backward** toward the kicking team. The members of the kicking team jumped sideways out of the way as if the ball was a hot rock. They should have treated it like a punt bouncing the wrong way. Unfortunately, the receiving team guy had no qualms about grabbing it on the bounce and running untouched for a 45-yard touchdown.

In my 1993 game, the opponent put their best ball carrier on the left side of the front row of kick returners. The main failure was that we failed to spot him and kicked right to him. The boy who should have tackled him used poor technique and lost him. The kicker failed to hustle over to perform his safety responsibilities.

Don't touch until it goes ten yards and hits the ground

If a member of the kicking team touches the ball before it goes at least ten yards **and** touches the ground or is touched by a member of the receiving team, the receiving team gets the right to have the ball at the spot where the kicking team touched it. (Rule # 6-1-7)

Equivalent of a punt for the first ten yards

On the other hand, if they do **not** touch it, it may go even further toward the goal line the kicking team is defending. A kickoff which has **not yet gone ten yards** and touched the ground or been touched by a member of the receiving team is the **equivalent of a punt**. The kicking team should surround it and let it bounce untouched as long as it is going **toward** the receiving team. But as soon as it starts bouncing **backwards**, they should down it to prevent it from going any farther in that wrong direction.

By the same token, the **receiving** team need not touch a ball which has **not** gone ten yards or touched one of their members. Just like a punt which is untouched by the receiving team, it is their ball where it becomes dead.

Kickoff team cannot advance the ball

The kicking team can recover, but cannot advance an **untouched** or **muffed** ball. (They can only advance a kickoff if the receiving team gets **control** of the ball **then** fumbles it.) So tell your players **not** to pick up and run with an untouched or muffed kickoff. The refs will whistle the play dead as soon as a member of the kicking team gets possession of the ball which has gone ten yards and touched the ground or touched a member of the receiving team.

Once the ball goes **beyond** ten yards and touches the ground or has been touched by the receiving team, the kicking team members must immediately fall on the ball just as they would fall on a punt which had touched a member of the receiving team. The only difference between the behavior of a **kicking** team and a **punt** team regarding falling on the ball is the ten-yards-and-touched-the-ground rule.

Kicking technique

In spite of the fact that I was a part-time place-kicker, I have given up trying to teach kick-off technique at the youth level. Doing so makes the kids mechanical and ineffective. I just let them do it their way and find the best kid.

The kick-receive team you face

There appear to be just two variations on the kick-receive teams you will face: normal and expecting an onside kick.

Front line

The normal alignment has five or six guys on the front line. Those guys typically are supposed to be **blockers** and are typically taken from the ranks of the **linemen**. They usually have jersey numbers in the 50 to 79 range.

Their mindset is to **block**. They often step aside when a ball is kicked to them because they do not see carrying the ball as their job. They are **nervous** about carrying the ball because they rarely, if ever, do it. They generally do not **want** to carry the ball once they have accepted their role as linemen. They usually have "hands of stone." As a result of all of the above, they are likely to **muff** a ball kicked to them.

If they have been coached regarding kicks which come to them, they were almost certainly told to just **fall on the ball**.

In short, these are the guys we **want** to kick the ball to if we want to recover the ball or at least prevent a return.

Rear ranks

The second rank has three or four guys who are typically first-string ball carriers but not stars. They are probably ends, defensive backs, and a running back. These guys can handle the ball, they expect that they have a good chance to get the ball on the kickoff. Some probably hope it comes to them. Others probably hope it doesn't because they're nervous. They are good runners. They are probably all between the hash marks and may be even closer to the center of the field.

The **rear** rank has one or two guys. One is the team's **biggest star.** The other is their **second biggest star**. They are the team's best athletes. They **want** the ball. They can break it for a touchdown on most teams if they get some daylight and a block or two.

Not to the their best runners

Now it's obvious to me that you do **not** want those rear rank guys to catch the ball. The **opposing coach** wants them to catch the ball. That's why he put them back there. Yet the vast majority of the kickoffs I've seen in youth football are high and deep down the middle—right to **the guys the opposing team wants to get the ball**.

If your goal is to visually imitate pro, college, and high school teams, that's the way to do it. But I thought the goal was to score more points than the other team. And that's why we do **not** kick the ball to those guys.

A lot of coaches have the presence of mind to tell their kicker to kick away from the best runner on the other team. But that generally means to just make that best runner trot ten or 15 steps to one side to catch the ball. Or it means kicking to the second best runner on the other side. Neither is enough of an improvement for me. I don't want **either** of those guys to **touch** the ball, let alone to touch it when my tacklers are still ten or more yards away.

'Hands' team

If the opposing team expects an onside kick, they will put **good-hands** guys in all eleven spots. That is, first- and second-string receivers, running backs, and defensive backs. These good-hands guys are like the second-row guys on a normal kick-receive team. But because of how close your tacklers are, these guys will probably fall on the ball if you keep the kick within ten to 20 yards from your kickoff line. In short, the good-hands guys being on the front line don't scare me too much. I'm still scared of the guys in the rear row, though. Actually, you'd better keep your eyes open. Some teams put their best runner on the front line if they expect an onside kick. And guys like him are dangerous wherever they are.

The world's greatest zone defender

Every football field has the world's greatest zone defender. His name is Out-of-Bounds. He tackles every single ball carrier who ever steps in his zone—instantly. They don't drag him for five more yards. They never break his tackles. They never fall forward and get an extra yard or two. He never misses. He's never out of position. And he covers one entire side of the field from end zone to end zone. Use him.

How do you do that on the kickoff? Keep the kickoff as near the side line as you can. Kickoff **from** the hash mark itself and aim at a spot halfway between the hash mark and that same side sideline.

True, if the ball goes out of bounds, the other team can make you kick over from five yards farther back. But my experience is that they are usually so delighted with the great field position they got from the squib kick that they decline the penalty.

Which side?

Does it matter which side? Yes, I think it does.

Most people are **right handed**. And at the youth level, right handers like to run to their right. In fact, in six years in youth football, I don't think I ever saw a kickoff returner run anywhere **but** to his right. Note on your scouting reports which direction the kickoff returner ran.

Let him try to run to his right when the ball in lying on the ground seven yards from the **sideline** to his right.

Force him to run to his left

In that case, he'll probably try to run to his **left**. But now we have a good chance to knock the ball loose. If he's right handed, he'll either carry the ball on his right side—which is the side where our tackler will hit him—or he'll carry it in his left hand—which is not as dexterous as his right. Either way, we have increased the chances of a fumble.

If he runs straight up the sideline, we have three or four guys to meet him. Plus we have the world's greatest zone defender just a few steps away. The world's greatest zone defender will make one of his instant, 100%-sure, right-here, right-now "tackles" if only you will nudge the ball carrier into his zone.

TGS

Kick return teams often do things in their alignment that should cause your kicker to call an audible. We used the acronym "TGS" to check for those things. Here's what it stands for:

T	Is the front line of the receiving team **T**en yards away from the ball as they should be?
G	Is there a **G**ap in the front line of the receiving team?
S	Is there a **S**tar running back on the front line?

Ten yards

Amazingly, youth football receiving teams often line up on their own 45-yard line, or even their own 40, instead of the 50, where they are supposed to be. About once a game in my experience, the refs tell the receiving team front line to move up.

The receiving team is especially likely to line up too far from the ball when a penalty is enforced against the kicking team on the kickoff. In that case, the kicking team lines up on their own 35- or 25-yard line. The front five of the receiving team is supposed to be ten yards away. If they are not, your kicker should kick an onside kick that only goes about 12 yards.

As dumb as the receiving team's behavior sounds, I have found that my kicking team invariably does a **dumber** thing, they accommodate the receiving team by kicking to where they **are** rather than where they should be, **unless I coach them otherwise**. I do. We deliberately set up this situation and work on recognizing it and taking advantage of it in practice. When we coaches see it, we yell, "TGS. Watch the T!" That's our code for "The receiving team is too far back. Kick it twelve yards only."

Gap

Probably because of lack of special-teams practice, and failure to teach the kids where they line up in relation to the sidelines and hash marks, youth kick-return teams often line up unevenly. That is, their front line has a gap that's **wider** than the eight to nine yards it **should** be if they were evenly spaced. The most common gap is on what I call the "friendly" side, that is, the side of the field where our bench is. As the kick-receive team members wander out after our team has scored or at the beginning of a half, they tend to be screwed up and not go far enough from **their bench**. It looks like this.

Receive team lined up with gap on front line

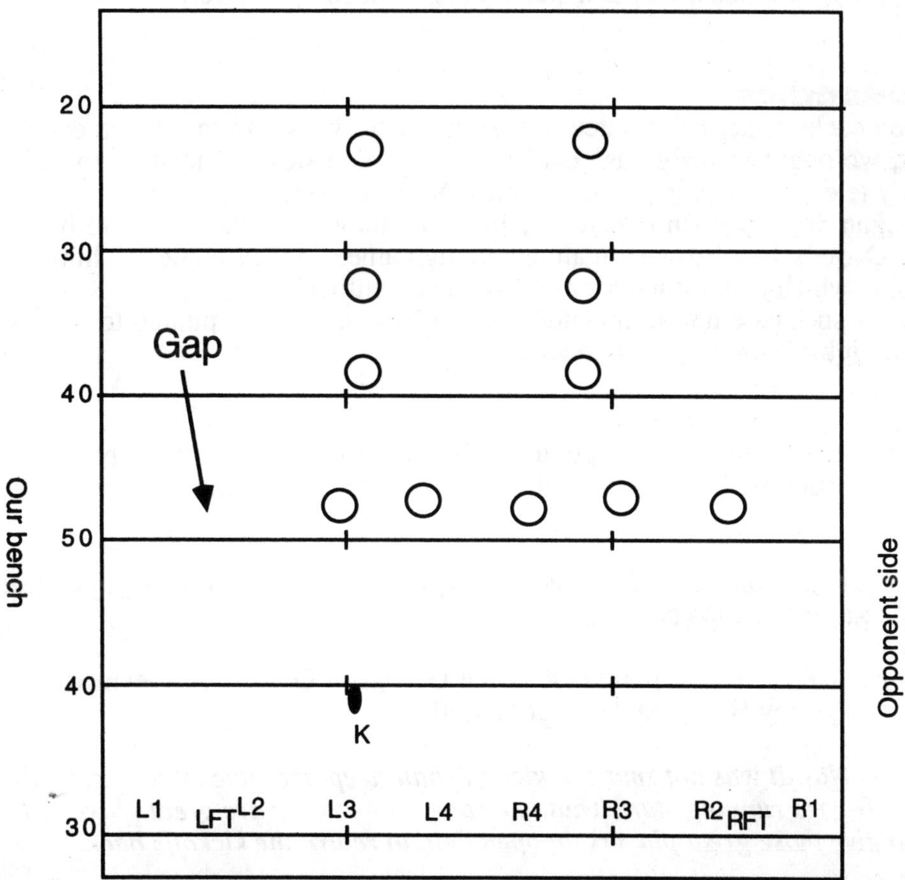

Furthermore, they often rely on their coaches to yell out alignment corrections. Coaches have trouble **seeing** the alignments on the far side of the field—our side—and they have trouble yelling **loud enough** when they do.

Don't wait until they fix it

If the kicking team dilly dallies, the receiving team will usually get straightened out. We practice getting lined up **quickly**. We waste little or no time getting proper spacing because our kids know how far to pace off from the various field marks. If you saw one of our games, you'd see our kickoff and kick-receive team members trot to the hash marks or sidelines then deliberately pace off their alignment.

When there is a gap, we want our kids to kick an onside kick **to** the gap. We alert them by yelling, "TGS. Watch the G!"

Star

Teams that scout us see that we do a lot of onside kicks. Often, they put a star receiver or two on the front line. Once (Oakland Saints 1993), we did not see that and the guy ran it back for one of the only two touchdowns ever scored against my youth kickoff teams. On another occasion, the opponent's biggest star was trying to sneak up to the right front. We yelled, "Watch Number 12! Watch number 12!" You could see the air go right out of him and he pulled up and stayed where he was.

We regard anyone with a jersey number that's not between 50 and 79 as a star. We do **not** kick toward those players. (On the other hand, both **my** youth and high school kick-return teams always have non-linemen on the front line. Because I do so many onside kicks as a coach, I am extremely conscious of the weaknesses of linemen on the kick-return team, and I **always** have my hands team on the field.)

Our code yell when we spot a star on the front line is to yell his number or, "TGS. Watch the S!"

Macho coaches

Some coaches may be tempted to take a macho view. As in, "If we can't stop their best guy, we ought to resign as coaches." I urge you **not** to succumb to that. Here's a cautionary tale from Michigan State's coach Norm Parker.

Michigan State's coaching staff decided that they were "not going to be intimidated by Notre Dame's Tim Brown" in an upcoming game. So they punted to him—a 55-yard, high, punt—which he returned for a touchdown—untouched.

But they still were not intimidated by Tim Brown. So they punted to him again. This time he ran it back for a 75-yard touchdown.

Tripped

Bloodied but unbowed, they punted to him a third time. This time he did not score a touchdown—but only because the last man who had a shot at him managed to trip him.

Parker now says,

> *"If the other team has a guy like Tim Brown back to return punts, you are nuts if you kick him the ball."*

Parker makes a similar point discussing Georgia's Gator Bowl team which had Tim Worley and Rodney Hampton deep for kickoffs.

> *"Now it was not smart to kick the ball deep and give either one of those backs a 30-yard running start. That is insane. Those guys are great players. It is insane to give those great players an open field to return the kickoffs back."*

Who's afraid of Lem Barney?

When he was with the Rams, George Allen decided he would squib kick to the Detroit Lions because their returner Lem Barney was too good to risk a deep kick. But just before the game, he let the team captains talk him into a deep kick.

Allen told the team, which had practiced the squib kick all week, about changing his mind in the locker room and he said they yelled loud enough to lift the roof off the building. They were psyched. Apparently so was Barney. He returned the opening kick 92 yards for a touchdown. The Rams squib kicked the rest of the day and won because Barney's kickoff return was the only touchdown the Lions scored.

No Lem Barney in your league?

You may say, "Yeah, but we aren't up against Tim Brown, Tim Worley, Rodney Hampton, or Lem Barney."

Maybe you are. Once upon a time, some youth football coach probably **did** coach against those guys. Nobody could tell him at that time that they were going to star in college or the pros. The opposing teams' kickoff-return runners in your youth league are, in many cases, the high school, college, and pro stars of tomorrow.

Besides, running with the ball is largely instinctive. While tackling and kickoff coverage is largely technique and experience. So the kickoff-return **runners** have a big advantage over the kickoff-team **tacklers** in youth football. That's why the percentage of kickoffs run back for touchdowns appears to be so much higher in youth football than in higher levels.

What about field position?

The argument I had with some of our rookie coaches about my always-squib-kick approach to kickoffs was about **field position**. The coaches who didn't like the squib kicks said I was giving the other team too good of a field position.

How far can they kick it?

At the junior pee wee level, field position after a kickoff is pretty much determined by the league's age and weight limits. Eight-, nine-, ten-, and eleven-year olds who weigh 85 pounds or less can only place-kick a ball about 30 to 35 yards. And it takes them longer to run that far than it takes the kick to travel that far. If you kick 30 to 35 yards, the receiver has time to field the ball in the air or on the ground and run. So at best, your coverage isn't going to tackle him until he has run about ten yards—that is, to his own 40 or 45.

If you kick off from your 40, a 30-yard kick will generally be fielded at the opponent's 30. With good coverage, he should be tackled at the opponent's 40. With poor coverage, he gets farther—maybe even all the way to a touchdown.

Same starting point

Now where do they get the ball **my** way? I want the kick to go 15 to 20 yards if I'm not trying for a recovery. If the receiver falls on it—which is what they almost always did against us—they get the ball on their 40 or 45. So what's the big-deal field position difference between kicking it as far as you can and squib kicking it?

True, you can get a lucky break at times if the receiver muffs a deep kick. He or his teammate will probably recover it. But they could be on their own 10-, 20-, or 30-yard line. Now we're talking some meaningful field position compared to my 40 or 45.

Line drive it

If you insist on kicking deep, my advice is to kick a **line drive** about half way between the sidelines and the hash mark. A line drive is less likely to be fielded in the air and more likely to take crazy bounces. I'd kickoff **from** the hash mark, too. I really know of no reason to kick from the middle of the field. Iowa State's Coach Jim Walden always kicks from the right hash mark.

I must add that my main field position opponent on our coaching staff told me by the end of the season that I had "made a believer out of him." One thing that convinced him was I let them kick high and deep in our mid-season intra-squad game. My son, Dan, ran one such kick back for a touchdown (called back on a clipping penalty). But even if he **had** been tackled, the receiving team would have had the ball first and ten on about the **kicking team's** 25-yard line. Now, **there's** field position!

Lining up for squib kick

This diagram show how the kickoff team lines up for a 20-yard squib kick from the left hash mark.

Line up for squib kick from left hash mark

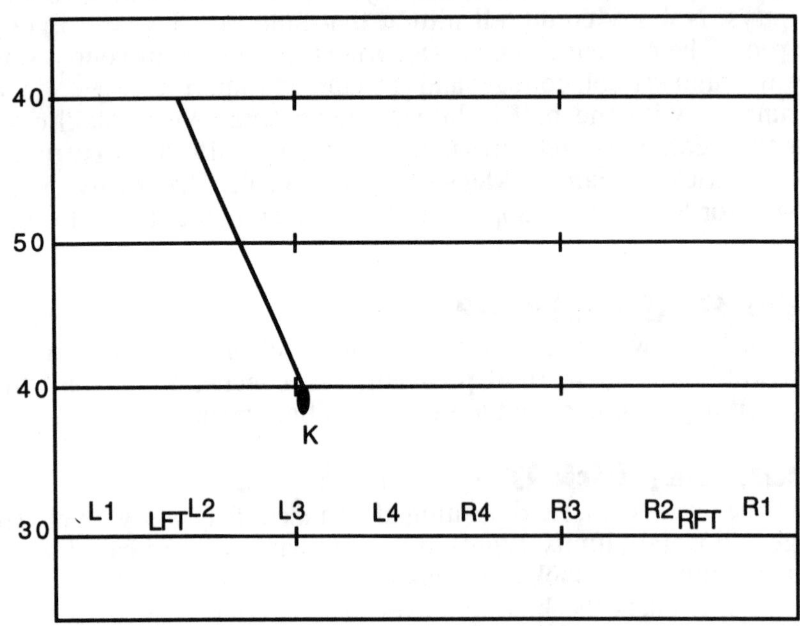

Stay in your lanes

The field is 160 feet wide. There are eight guys I call **lane tacklers.** Each is assigned to cover a 20-foot wide lane directly in front of him. When the ball is kicked, he is to run straight down his lane no matter where the ball is kicked. As he approaches the depth of the ball, he is supposed to get under control and only then move toward the ball. That move should be made about 6 yards before he reaches the depth of the ball. The kickoff team **ends'** first responsibility is to prevent the ball carrier or any blocker from getting **outside** them.

Bust the wedge

If the receiving team intends to return up the **middle**, and they are well-coached, they will drop back and form a line of blockers in the middle of the field. That line is called the wedge. The first kickoff team guy to get to the wedge has to break it up. He does that by running into it full speed. He must hit the blockers **high**. Hitting **low** is against the rules. Few players at any level have the physical courage to do this. Find one who does.

Other teams

Most of the teams we played against did **not** stay in their lanes on kickoffs. Rather they all converged on the ball carrier. That's extremely bad and very dangerous technique. Unfortunately, we never were able to capitalize on it. I guess because of our lack of speed. Toward the end of one season, we tried to institute a wall-of-blockers return on one side of the field. But we never able to make it work. Our best kickoff return of the year went up the middle in 1992.

Contain

When I played in junior high school, I was once right end on a kickoff. I converged toward the ball which was in the middle of the field and the receiver ran around my end for a 70-yard touchdown. No coach had ever told me to stay in my lane or to make sure the ball carrier never got around me. In fact, I don't think we had ever practiced kickoff coverage at all. They just threw us into positions willy nilly when the game arrived.

We drum "stay in your lanes" into our kids weekly and remind them just before kickoffs in games. In 1996, one of my freshman ends, in spite of being told repeatedly not to let any blocker or ball carrier get outside him, suddenly made a move to the inside of a blocker. The ball carrier went around his end for a touchdown. All the end did was momentarily get his head on the wrong side of the blocker, like this diagram shows, but it was enough to give up an 80-yard touchdown.

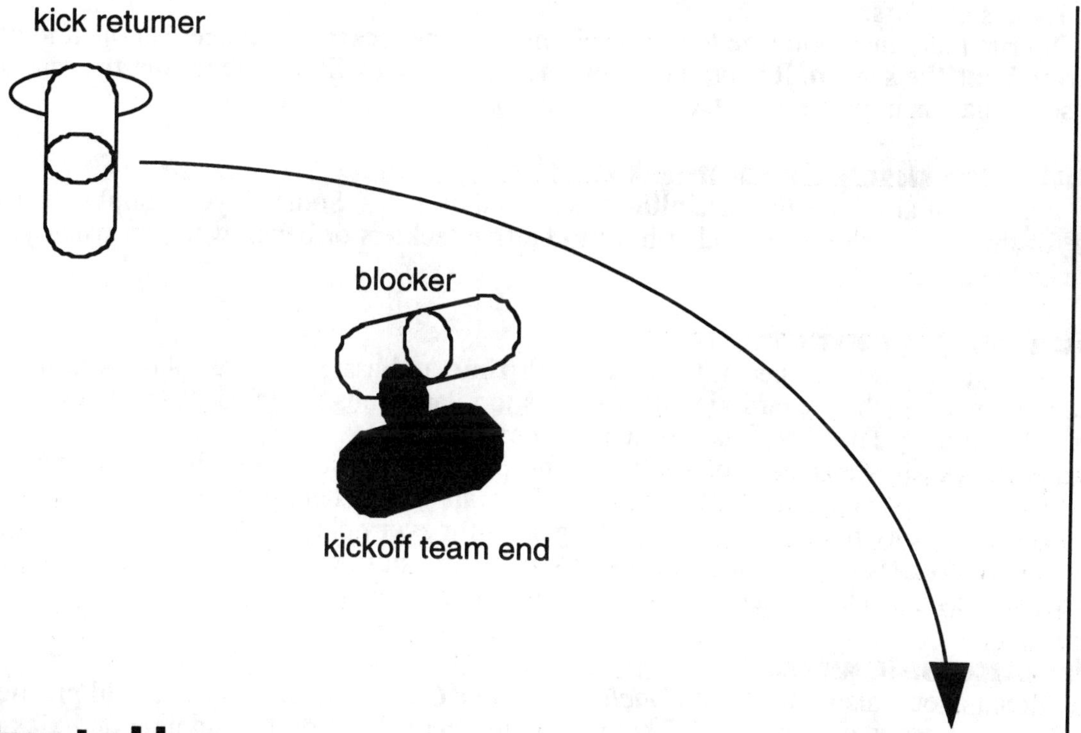

Free tacklers

I got the idea of free tacklers from Bud Wilkinson's book on defense. He didn't call them free tacklers. But he has two guys who go straight to the ball.

These guys have no lanes. They line up **outside** L2 and R2 to confuse the blockers on assignments. For example, the next to last guy on the left side of the **receiving** team may tell his neighbor, "I've got number 85." He says that because number 85 is the next to last guy on his side of the kickoff team. But number 85 is the right free tackler. He is probably not going to get anywhere near the next to last guy on left side of the receiving team. Rather number 85 is going to head straight for the ball which we usually kick to our left side of the opponent's 30-yard line.

I think you need free tacklers because the lane tacklers may interpret their lane too literally and run past the ball carrier. Or the ball carrier may hit the seam between two lanes thereby confusing each lane tackler as to who should tackle. They both should, but confusion is always possible. In any event, there is no confusion as to the duties of the free tacklers. They are to go straight for the ball carrier and tackle him.

Free the best

The free tacklers should be your **best** kickoff team tacklers. How do you determine who they are? Count how many tackles each player makes on kickoffs in practice and in games. The guys with the most become free tacklers. You may say, "Heck, that's a self-fulfilling prophesy. Obviously, the free tacklers will get most of the tackles because they are allowed to go everywhere."

Actually, it did not work out that way on our team. I moved several lane tacklers up to free tacklers because they made more kickoff tackles than the original free tacklers. (One year one of the free tacklers I demoted to lane tackler was my son. No nepotism here.)

Kickoff team personnel

First you have to find your **best eleven kickoff team tacklers**. The only way to do that is to run kickoffs and see who makes the most tackles. The guys who do best in tackling **drills** are not necessarily, or even probably, the best kickoff tacklers. The only true test is kickoffs.

So run them in scrimmage to see who's making the tackles. And keep an open mind **throughout the season**. It is probable that the best eleven will change during the season as some players improve more than others and some decline in desire or hustle.

Only the disciplined need apply

They must also have the **discipline** to stay in their lanes. Some players simply always go for the ball. Such players either have to be free tacklers or bench warmers when you are kicking off.

Dumping grounds

Some teams regard special teams as **junk time** and assign weaker players to those teams. Some coaches regard kickoff teams as too dangerous for their star athletes. You gotta be kidding. The kickoff is extremely important.

The kickoff is also part of football. The players on your team signed up to play football. Their parents **paid** for them to play football. So let them play. If kickoffs are too dangerous for **any** player, they are too dangerous for **every** player. Not letting a boy play on the kickoff team because you did not want him hurt would be like not letting a baseball player run bases (the most dangerous part of baseball).

Practice sideways

I read about this in the 1990 *Coach of the Year Clinics Manual*. You should practice kickoffs **sideways** on your field. That is, you tee the ball up on the sideline and kick it sideways across the field. The reason for this is the yard lines help your kickoff lane tacklers see their lanes clearly.

The sideline would be the kicking team's free kick line. The receiving team would line up ten yards away. The hash marks are 53' 4" or 17.78 yards from the sidelines. So the kick receive team front line would be 7.78 yards from the hash marks. One goal line would constitute one sideline and the other sideline would be at the 47-yard line of the opposite end of the field. Here's a diagram.

How to practice kickoffs

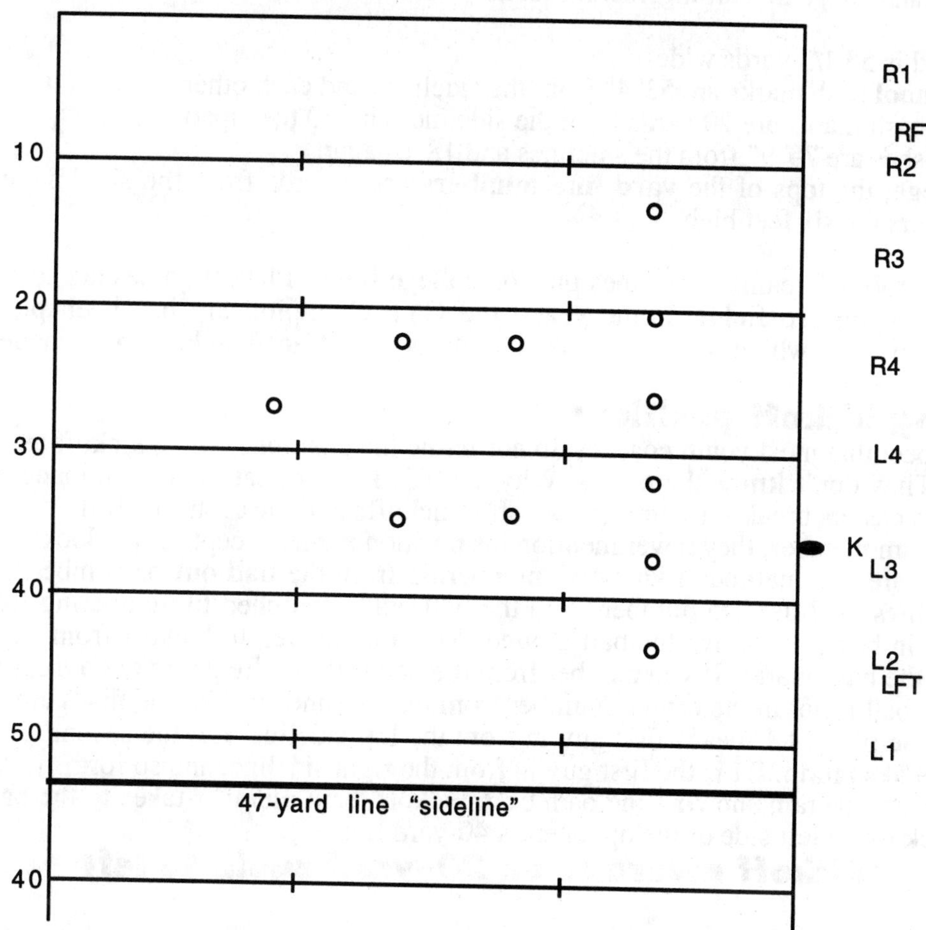

Know your position

I spent a lot of time in games telling kickoff team members to spread out or get closer to the next guy. Apparently the players cannot see that they are improperly spaced just by looking. The best thing is to teach the players to pace off the distances from the sidelines or hash marks to their positions.

Here are the distances in yards for the kickoff formation diagrammed above. These are slightly different from the ones earlier in this chapter because that kickoff did not use free tacklers. You'll have to get the player in question to pace off these distance to see how many paces they need to take on game day.

L1	6 yards from left sideline
LFT	close enough to L2 to hold his hand on outside
L2	6 yards outside left hash mark
L3	on left hash mark
L4	6 yards inside left hash mark
K	anywhere on or inside hash marks
R4	6 yards inside right hash mark
R3	on right hash mark
R2	6 yards outside right hash mark
RFT	close enough to R2 to hold his hand on outside
R1	6 yards from right sideline

Hash measurements at different levels

You can change this arrangement. Just keep in mind these basic principles:

- The field is 55 1/3 yards wide
- **high school** hash marks are 53' 4" from the sidelines and each other
- **college** hash marks are 20 yards from the sidelines and 40 feet apart
- **NFL** hashes are 70' 9" from the sidelines and 18' 6" apart
- In college, the tops of the **yard line numbers** are 9 yards from the sideline and the numbers are six feet high.

Youth football teams sometimes play on college fields. Playoff games are sometimes even played on pro fields. Some years, the CYF championship has been played at Sacramento State, which was marked for its role as a pro Canadian Football League field.

Naming kickoff positions

I suspect that most youth coaches do not **name** the positions on the kickoff team. The reason? They don't **know** the names. Why not? You never hear them mentioned on TV. TV sports casters break for commercials after kickoffs and kick returns. If they discuss a kickoff team member, they never mention his position name, except for the kickers.

There are two methods I know of: numbering from the **ball out** or numbering from the **sidelines in**. I used to number from the ball out. I switched to numbering from the sidelines in because I move the ball around. You are allowed to kickoff from anywhere between the hash marks. If you number from the ball **out**, you're going to **confuse** people when the ball is not in the center. Number from the sidelines in. The sidelines are always in the same place. L1 means first guy in from the left sideline; L2, the second guy from the left; and so forth. R1 is the first guy in from the right sideline, and so forth.

Here's a diagram showing the path each kickoff team member takes to the ball on a squib kick to the left side of the opponent's 40-yard line.

Kickoff coverage on 20-yard squib to left

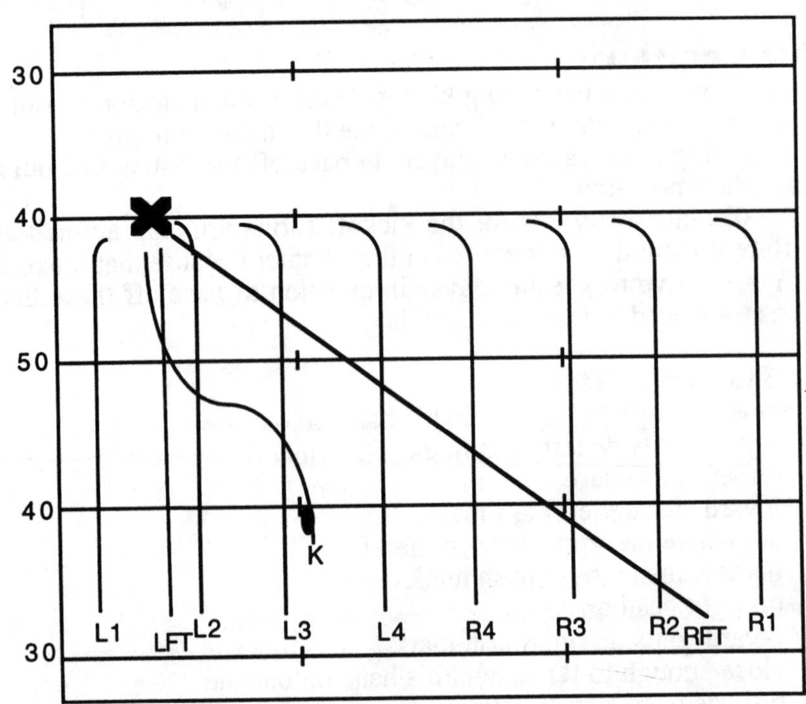

Kicker must be a tackler

After you have picked the best eleven kickoff team tacklers, you audition those eleven only for the jobs of kicker and backup kicker. There may be a better **pure** kicker among the guys who were **not** the eleven best kickoff tacklers. But unless he can kick the ball 60 yards and get a touchback, who cares?

The job of the kickoff team is to prevent a return and to get the ball if possible. The kicker is, after he kicks the ball, a **tackler**. If he's a **lousy** tackler, you have a ten-man kickoff team. That's dumb. Especially when kickoff **distance** is actually a bad thing. The goal is **not** to kick as far as possible. It is to make sure the **return is as short as possible**. That takes tackling skill, not kicking leg strength.

Accuracy, not distance

What you are looking for in a kicker is **not** distance, but **touch and accuracy**. You are going to want to kick the ball to spots which just about all of your kickoff team members can reach with their foot. You want the guy who is most accurate. And if you want to bloop the ball over the heads of the opposing front line, you need a kicker who can consistently do that.

Test your kickers by laying a pad out as a target. Then see who comes closest the most often. To test for bloops, put a line of players between the target and the kicker and tell him to hit the target after going over the outstretched arms of the leaping players.

Ends

Ends must be more disciplined than the other lane tacklers. The other lane tacklers can wander all over the width of their lane chasing the ball carrier. But the ends must always stay outside the ball carrier and his blockers. If they make the kickoff team as tacklers, your normal defensive ends or outside linebackers are probably the best kickoff ends because they are used to containment responsibilities.

Other lane tacklers

If you are going to kick to the spot in front of L2 as I recommend, he should be your best kickoff tackler other than the free tacklers. L1 would be your second best; R1, third best; and so on down to R4, who would be your weakest kickoff team tackler.

Backups

You actually need to identify your **13** best kickoff team tacklers. You need about two backups in case of injuries or other absences. If the need for a backup occurs during a game, you'd best put him in the spot of the injured player so there is no confusion as to who's playing what position on the kickoff team. The only exception to that would be if the injured player is the kicker. You ought to use your second best kicker as injury sub for the first-string kicker.

Loafing

There is a lot of loafing on the football field if you don't work on eliminating it. That's especially true of special-teams plays like kickoffs because the action is so far away from most players. You must tell the players **not** to loaf. Rather they must go at full speed until the whistle just like they should on a scrimmage play.

Here's a drill you can use. When a ball leaves a kicker's foot or a passer's hand, yell, "Air!" The players then must run at top speed to wherever they're supposed to go. On a pass, it would be back downfield to tackle the receiver—rather than stopping to watch the rest of the play. On a punt receive, it would be to whatever return position they were supposed to go to. On a kickoff, it would be down their lanes then turning in toward the ball carrier.

Instead of wind sprints

This could be done instead of wind sprints. I have never liked wind sprints as a coach. The players hate them. By substituting this "Air" drill, you could have them run as much, but at least they could see how it relates to the game better. And they would learn to react properly and instinctively to the word "Air!" and/or the situation of the ball going into the air.

This would probably work well with a stopwatch. For example, you could put a dummy at the kickoff receiver's spot in the middle of the field. The kicker would kickoff and you'd yell, "Air!" At the moment of the kick, you'd start your stop watch. You would stop it when the last of the eleven players had touched the dummy. Then you'd have group two do the same. The losing group has to put away the equipment. Run it several times because the losing group will want a rematch after the first one. And if group two wins the second time, group one will demand another chance and so forth. Players demanding to do it again is generally **not** what you get when you do regular wind sprints.

Odd surfaces

Kickoffs on odd surfaces are different. **Mud**, for example, tends to retard bounces. On the other hand, it also makes the ball hard to secure, like a greased pig.

In our 1994 playoff game against Berkeley, I told my kicker to kick the ball right into a puddle which was behind the middle of the receiving team's front line. I also told him to huddle the kickoff team and tell them to expect it so they would be in the proper frame of mind about diving in the water to get it. I figured the Berkeley players would hesitate when they saw the ball in the puddle.

The ball stopped dead when it hit the puddle—no bounce at all. The Berkeley players **did** hesitate. But they regained their senses fast enough to recover the ball before we could. We did, however, win the game 28-0.

Astroturf

Another odd surface I coached on was **Astroturf** at Berkeley High School in 1994. We lost that game and I believe the turf was the reason. The ball bounces crazy on Astroturf. For one thing, it bounces **much higher**. If you have to play on Astroturf in an upcoming game, try hard to arrange to practice on it beforehand. If you cannot, practice fielding kicks on asphalt. That'll give you a good preview of the bounces.

The ball not only bounces higher on Astroturf, it also bounces in new directions. Sometimes, a ball will go backward on the first hop as if it were shot out of the spot where it landed. It seems to catch in the turf and not roll over as it would on grass or even asphalt. If you cannot get a full practice session on turf before a game on it, try to get as much pre-game warm-up on it as possible. I kicked a zillion little kicks to our kids before the Berkeley game to get them used to the crazy bounces.

We did not lose the game because of a bad bounce. Rather our kids seemed to be afraid of the surface. They played as if on asphalt. That is, they were extremely reluctant to leave their feet. Normally, we'd welcome that. Youth football players spend far too much time leaving their feet. I've even considered practicing tackling on asphalt to cure them of it. But when our guys played on Astroturf, I saw that idea can be carried too far.

Kickoff after safety

If the other team scores a safety against you, you have to kick to them from your 20-yard line. At higher levels, where the coaches know what they're doing, they generally punt. You can punt, place kick, or drop kick the ball after a safety. Punting is preferred because you can get enough hang time to cover it well. Punt from the right hash mark over to the left side of the field. This gives your players a better chance to get down the field and cover the kick.

You'd better practice this at least once a month so your boys aren't confused if it happens. You could lose a close game in just this one play. We returned a punt kickoff after a safety for a touchdown in that 1992 Pittsburgh game after we scored a safety.

Targets of opportunity

The opposing team may line up in an unusual way. If so, you should notice and take advantage of it.

Whole front line between the hash marks

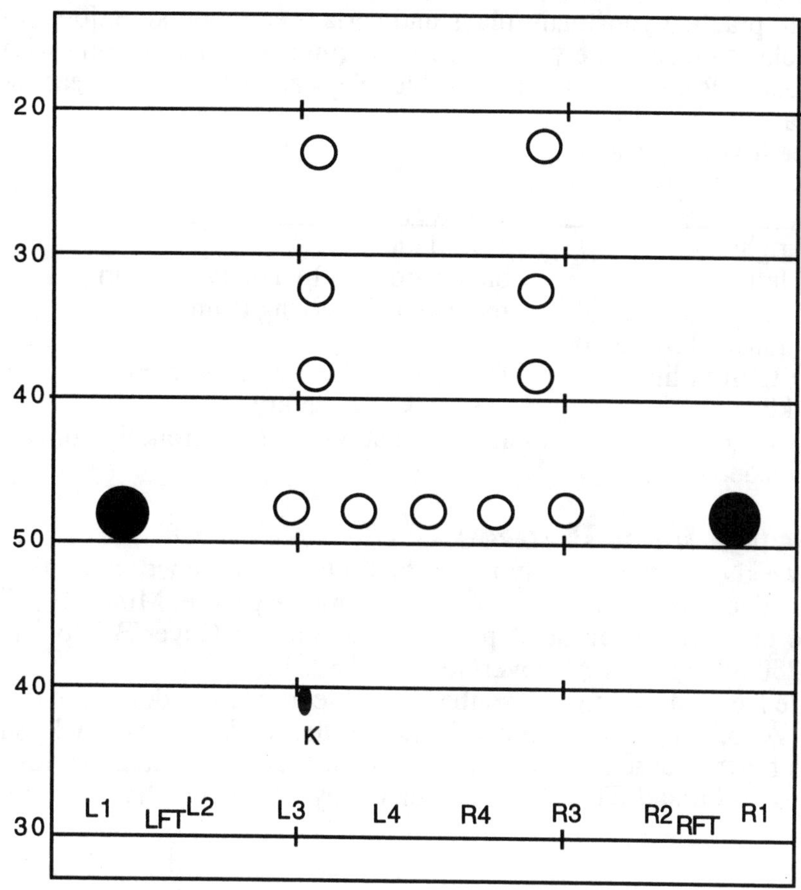

We know what the opposing coach had in mind when he set up this kick receive formation—a return up the middle. And it's pretty good for that purpose because the entire receiving team **is** concentrated in the middle. And no doubt, in practice, the scout team kicked the ball high and deep straight down the middle and it worked just fine. But no kickoff team coach in his right mind is going to kick deep down the middle against this formation. You onside kick that sucker out to the end of the 50-yard line where I've put the big black dots and your ends or free tacklers should be able to recover it unopposed. This is one case where you would **not** want to use the spin kick.

Pittsburgh lined up like this in our 1992 game with them. We onside kicked every time. We recovered **all six** of the kicks, although one of our players touched one before it went ten yards and another was awarded to Pittsburgh in spite of our guy having possession in a pile. By that time we were up by about four touchdowns to zero and the refs thought we were out of line to onside kick at all. Had it not been for the one player's mistake and the ref's charity, we would have recovered all six kicks.

Periodic kickoff team practice schedule

With 30 minutes a week allocated to kickoff and kickoff return, you obviously have 15 minutes for kickoff alone. In general, you will have a scout team opposing the team you are focusing on during this period. That essentially means that someone, first or second string, is working on kickoff for the whole 30 minutes.

I break the kickoff agenda into two categories:

- things that should be practiced **weekly**
- things that should be practiced **monthly**.

You need to practice your main plays and certain common situations or kick return team plays weekly to make sure your players are quite skilled at dealing with them. And you need to practice less common, but possible, plays and situations at least once a month so the players are not surprised.

Here are the lists I suggest:

weekly	monthly
onside kickoff right	1-yard kickoff
onside kickoff left	backward pass by receiving team
8-yard kickoff untouched	reverse by receiving team
8-yard kickoff touched by receiver	
pop-up kickoff to front line	fake reverse by receiving team
25-yard squib kick	free kick after safety
walk-through stay in lanes	kickoff that bounces off front line of receiving team
TGS recognition and response	

Diagram on 8 1/2 x 11 cards

Both the weekly and the monthly plays should be diagrammed in Magic Marker on 8 1/2 x 11 cards. You can buy them in a paper or stationery store. Mine have the following printed on the package, "Wausau Papers Exact® Vellum Cover/Bristol White 8 1/2 x 11—23.34M 250 Sheets—Bs. 65 cover/80 Bristol 82511."

You shuffle the cards each week so the kickoff team players don't know which play is coming when. Also, you insert the monthly card of the week into the stack. Save the other monthly cards for the subsequent weeks. The scout kick return coach holds the cards up one at a time to his huddle. Then his scout team players execute the play on the card they just saw.

Scout report in season

That's the **preseason** routine. Your card plays in the preseason are **generic**. Once the season begins, you should have **scout reports** on the upcoming opponent. At that time, you should modify the cards to show the specific upcoming opponent's kick return alignment and plays and the jersey numbers of their stars. If they have dangerous returners—most teams do—get your team's game jersey with the stars' numbers and have scout team returners wear those jerseys. This is to help the kicker learn where **not** to kick the ball.

8-yard kickoff

An 8-yard kickoff is a screw-up. But screw-ups happen—fairly frequently in my experience. So your players have to be ready. Practice this by having a coach toss the ball to the required 8-yards. Do not have the kicker try to kick it eight yards. For one thing, you don't want him to practice that. For another, it'll take him all night and you'll waste practice time.

Remember that a kickoff that does not go ten yards is like a **punt**. The kickoff team players should form a tight cup around their side of the rolling ball and follow it. They should be crouched low and quite close to the ball. If a member of the receiving team touches the ball, your kickoff team members should instantly explode their shoulders down on the toucher's wrist and try to get possession of the ball. I used to tell them to "amputate the receive team guy's hand at the wrist." At the beginning of the 1994 season, I had several veterans of my 1993 team demonstrate with me being the receiving team player who touched the ball. They almost took my hand off.

In a 1993 game, we accidentally kicked an 8-yard kick. Our team did exactly as trained. They formed a tight cup and followed the ball. A member of the receiving team panicked and tried unsuccessfully to grab the ball. He almost certainly did not know the rule, i.e., that the ball belongs to his team even if they do not touch it and if it does not go ten yards. We recovered the kick. The ref told me, "You were lucky your guys didn't touch it first." "Luck my foot," I told him, "We practice that every Tuesday."

Remind your players of the rule as you practice this.

Pop-up kickoff

A pop-up kickoff is another **mistake**. The receiving team front line can and should signal a **fair catch** in this situation. But I have never seen a youth football player signal a fair catch in a game. Other than my team, there probably are no front-line players who **know** they can signal a fair catch on a kickoff. Most people think it's only allowed on punts.

Coach **tosses** the pop-up. Having a player kick it will waste time and teach him bad habits. Have a scout receiving team member signal fair catch. Have him catch one and deliberately miss one. Your players must give him room to catch a kick that is on the fly and has not touched the ground, whether he signals fair catch or not.

Replace the scout team player with a stand-up dummy. Toss the ball to the dummy. Have the players surround it giving it room to make the catch, then hammer it hard as soon as the ball touches it. This is practice for a kickoff-receive team player who catches the pop-up with**out** signaling fair catch. Do **not** use a **real** player for this because of the danger of injury. Have the players ignore the fact that the ball is not caught by the dummy. They should behave as if it **were** caught when it touches the dummy.

25-yard squib kick

This can either be a mistake in an onside kick attempt or a deliberate play. Because of the increased probability of a return, your players must stay in their lanes. Assign your assistant coaches to watch certain members of the kickoff team to see if they are staying in their lanes and making tackles. For example, if you have six assistants, assign them like this:

Coach A	L1 and L2
Coach B	L3 and L4
Coach C	L5 and R5
Special teams coach	Kicker and R5
Coach D	R4 and R3
Coach E	R2 and R1
Coach F	Scout kick receive team and line judge.

Coaches who have **two** players should watch **one** on one play and the **other** on the next. They should report to the special teams coach on what they saw. They may coach their player between plays but they must do so **on the run**, that is, while walking along side the player in question, so as not to delay the start of the next repetition. And they must speak in a **whisper** so as not to interfere with the special teams coach who will typically be urging the teams to line up for the next repetition.

Coach acts as line judge

After he lines up his kids and tells them what return to run, the scout-kick-receive team coach should station himself on the yard line where the ball is teed up to make sure no member of the kickoff team is **off sides** (crosses the line before the kick—Rule 6-1-4).

When first teaching this, and whenever there is a general problem with lane discipline, have the team do a **walk-through**. That way the coaches can focus on keeping the players in their lanes and make sure they understand lane discipline. I have them start out then yell, "Freeze!" as soon as I see a breakdown in lane discipline. I point out to the errant players their incorrect spacing, then move them to correct spacing and yell, "Go!" for them to resume closing on the scout team kick returner.

Actually, the way I do it is to go full speed one direction then reverse direction and do a walk-through on the way back.

1-yard kickoff

This is a **big** mistake. The kicker's foot touches the ball but it only falls off the tee or travels a yard or two. Virtually no one realizes it. But this is a **live kick**. It is the same as an 8-yard kick. It cannot be recovered by the kicking team unless the receiving team touches it first. Treat it like a punt. Form a cup on the kickoff team side of the ball and hope the other team touches it. They probably will just stand there until the ref blows the whistle. Practice this once a month so the players know what to do. It gets more interesting when you are the **receiving** team. More about that later.

Backward pass

Unless this is one of your plays, you need to have your **coaches** play the role of kick returners. The kids will take the whole 15 minutes trying to figure out what you want. A backward-pass kick return is one in which the initial returner suddenly turns and throws across field to a teammates who is at the **same** yard line or **behind** that yard line. A **forward** pass on a kick return is **illegal**.

Mix this in with a couple of regular returns so the players can't tell it's coming. Let the kickoff players see both a **caught** pass and a **dropped** pass. Teach the players the pertinent rules. Namely, you can recover, but you cannot advance a muffed kick. (Rule 6-1-6) However, once the receive team **gets control of the ball**, and fumbles or muffs or throws a pass that is dropped or untouched, they create a **live ball** which the kickoff team can not only recover, but also **pick it up and run with it**. (Rule 2-22-2) Make sure your players pick up the dropped or missed backward pass and run with it unless an opposing player is close to recovering it.

It is important that your players see this play once a month so they recognize it as soon as possible in a game and to impress upon them yet another reason for lane discipline.

Reverse and fake reverse

Treat a reverse and fake reverse pretty much the same as a backward pass. Have **coaches** serve as kick returners. The kickoff team players try to **two-hand touch**, not tackle, the coach returners.

Do not try to use **players** unless your kick return team has this play. They will take forever to learn it, thereby wasting practice time. Even my high school kids wasted incredible amounts of time saying, "Huh?" when I asked the scout kick return team to run a reverse. Then they start running screwy reverses with pitches and fumbles. It's a regular hand-off in which the two deep returners run past each other on paths parallel to the yard lines. One forms a pocket, the other either gives him the ball or fakes it.

The **fake** reverse can be more dangerous than the **real** reverse. The Oakland Saints came from behind to beat us with a fake reverse (from scrimmage) in 1994.

As with the backward pass, deliberately **fumble** one of the hand-offs. The kickoff team members should try to **pick it up and run with it** if no opposing player is close to recovering it.

Free kick after a safety

If your team gives up a safety, either deliberately or accidentally, you need to kick off to the other team afterwards from your own 20-yard line. (Rule 6-1) Unlike a regular kickoff, you can **punt** the ball on the free kick after a safety. Most coaches, and some referees I've had, assume that because you **can** punt, you **must** punt. Wrong. You can place-kick, drop kick, **or** punt. (Rule 2-22).

I do not have a preference. We've done both. **Punts** give you more **hang time** thereby reducing the possibility of a return. **Place-kicks** generally give you **more distance** and are more reliably deep. You should practice **both** and see which your team seems to do better with. If you decide to use the punt, you will have to relearn the timing as to when the tacklers start running full speed. This is one circumstance where I'd probably kick deep rather than onside. See my book *Football Clock Management* for a more complete discussion of when you kick onside and when you do not at the end of a half.

The main thing is to practice the free kick after a safety once a month so, if and when you have to do it, your players execute smoothly and confidently. Most teams never practice this and their coaches and players stumble around a lot as a result when the situation arises

Kick that bounces off front line receiver

Kicks sometimes bounce off a front line member of the receiving team right back toward the kickoff team. Since they are moving full speed the other way, they can run right by the ball leaving the return team free to pick up the ball and run it for a touchdown. As I said earlier, I saw that happen in the 1991 Bears-Tri-Cities playoff game. In 1994, one of our kickoffs bounced off a Berkeley front line guy—right back to the kicker who caught it and went down on one knee (because he knew you cannot advance a muff).

Tell your scout kick-return team to bat the ball right back toward the kickoff team and that same receive team should try to pick it up and run. (The **receive** team **can** advance a muff.)

Success

I coached youth kickoff teams in 1991, 1992, 1993, and 1994. In 1994, I also coached a high school J.V. kickoff team. In 1996, I was special teams coordinator of a high school freshman team.

In 1992, I believe we recovered 30% of our kickoffs. There were virtually no returns at all, and none for touchdowns. The opponents almost always fell on the ball if we didn't. In 1993, I had a much weaker, almost all rookie team and less consistent kickers. They still recovered about 20% of their kickoffs.

In one of my Miramonte High School games, Mt. Diablo ran a routine return. My players stopped him for an unremarkable return. I was starting to write down the jersey numbers of the tacklers when I heard a big cheer from the other side. My players also assumed the play was over, but the refs did not blow the whistle. The returner broke free and ran for the touchdown. Assumption is the mother of all screw-ups.

In high school, we cannot run full-speed kickoff plays in practice because of the danger of injury. So I fixed the problem revealed by that touchdown by chewing out the team and replacing the players responsible. Thereafter, I reminded the team to gang tackle until the whistle before every kickoff. We had no further big returns.

4

Kick return team

Kickoff return

After years of trying different approaches, I finally had some success on kickoff returns with my 1996 freshman high school team. Before that, the only one we ever returned for a touchdown was a punted free kick after a safety in our 1992 Pittsburgh game. Our returner caught the ball in the air and one player threw a key block. Other than that, I don't know why it worked.

Gordon Wood is the winningest coach in Texas high school football history. In his book, *Game Plan to Winning Football*, he said, "I had never been sold on a kick return until the last two years I coached." He then explained the return and diagrammed it. I used it on both my pee wee and high school J.V. teams in 1994. I was happier with that return than with any other I have used, but we still had no touchdown runbacks.

Man-to-man blocking

The key thing about Wood's kick return is all but two receive-team players are assigned a particular kickoff team player to block. That is extremely important because it **makes it crystal clear what each player's assignment is**. In the confusion of most kickoffs, kick return players aren't sure what to do, so they do nothing or they make a half-hearted effort with predictable results. The **kickoff** players, on the other hand, all know exactly what to do: tackle the ball carrier.

For years, my fellow coaches and I yelled, "Block somebody!" before every kickoff. If you've ever seen players pair up for a drill, you know what "somebody" they're going to pick to block when you leave it up to them—the wimpiest looking guy on the other team. Three or four of your players may hit him. Then there's the notion of what is a block. Generally, if you just say, "Block somebody!" they will pick a weak looking opponent and administer a hit and quit. When you complain about their performance, they will protest, "But I hit a guy just like you said."

Full effort

When I went to the man-to-man blocking on kick returns, all that changed. It was a thing of beauty to watch at the game and on the video. Each of my players homed in on his man like a heat-seeking missile. Furthermore, they did not hit and quit. Rather they persisted, chasing the guy all over the field.

The big difference was that I said, **"Keep your guy from tackling our ball carrier."** That's a far cry from "Hit somebody" when you think about it.

After a kick return, we would immediately tell the guilty parties, "That was your man that made the tackle. What happened?" The kid knew if that happened again he was likely to lose his position.

In practice, we made the kids who missed their block, and their targets, run the play over while the successful blockers went down on one knee. That is, we would run a kickoff return play. The ball carrier would be tackled. We would ascertain who made the tackle.

Instant replay

Then we would run the play again. Only this time we would tell everybody on both the kick return team and the scout kickoff team to take a knee except the guy who carried the ball on the previous play, the guy or guys who made the tackle on the previous play, and the kick return team members who missed their blocks. A coach would throw the "kick" to the ball carrier and he would have to take the same path as on the previous play. Then, all eyes would be on the one or two guys who previously missed their blocks. On this replay, we could see the technique used by the blockers and their persistence or lack thereof.

In fact, some kick return team members were totally unsuited for the job. This practice of making the kick return team members who failed re-execute their assignment in an isolated situation quickly smoked out the boys who did not belong on that unit. My impression is that most youth and high school teams never grade their special teams performance and therefore **never** find out that they have guys on the kick-return team who haven't made a block all season.

Often, we found new **kickoff** team starters from this drill as well. Sometimes, this drill would reveal improper blocking technique, like blocking too soon or lunging from too far away. We corrected the technique and gave the blocker in question another try.

The most gratifying thing about this kick return was that finally everyone on the team was at least **trying** to do the right thing.

But I'm getting ahead of myself. First let's go over the names of the kick return members and their alignment.

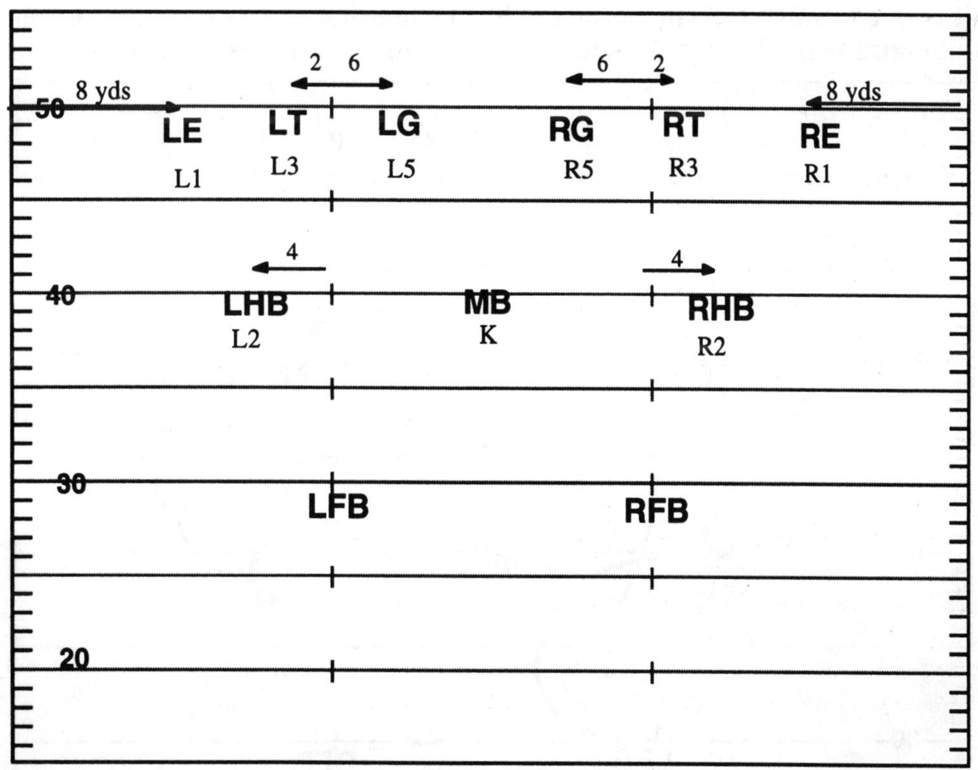

Position names

There seems to be no standard way of naming kick return team members. The most common, and the one I used, was to name them like offensive positions.

The diagram on the preceding page is actually part of an 8 1/2 x 11 card I carried to each game. Only I had player numbers instead of position names. The L1 and so forth are the kickoff team members who are the blocking assignments of the players. The card enabled me to compare the on-field alignment with the correct alignment at a glance. It also shows the distance from hash marks, etc. so I can yell out corrections when necessary. The position names and alignments are:

Position	Alignment	Blocking assignment
Left and right ends	8 yards from the sideline at our 49	L1 and R1
Left and right tackles	2 yards outside the hash at our 49	L3 and R3
Left and right guards	6 yards inside the hash at our 49	L5 and R5
Left and right halfbacks	4 yards outside the hash at our 40	L2 and R2
Middle halfback	middle of field at our 40	kicker
Right and left fullbacks	on the hash at our 30	non-ball carrier lead blocks

How far can he kick?

Note that the depths of the halfbacks and fullbacks vary according to the scouting report. If the opponent's kicker can kick deeper than normal, you **must** move both your halfbacks and fullbacks back farther. If his leg is especially weak, you can sneak them closer to midfield. When in doubt, keep them deep.

Letting a kick get **behind** your fullbacks is **cardinal sin** of kick returning. It can spell disaster and has for me. We never touched two kickoffs that were recovered by the other teams at about our 15. On another occasion, we had to go back to our ten for a ball and got tackled in that vicinity.

In this return, the kick returner runs toward the middle of the field after he gets the ball, then breaks out to the same side he came from. The other fullback needs to run to that side and, if all goes according to plan, he should block either L4 or R4. In reality, he blocks the first guy he encounters. Here's a diagram of this kick return where the left fullback received:

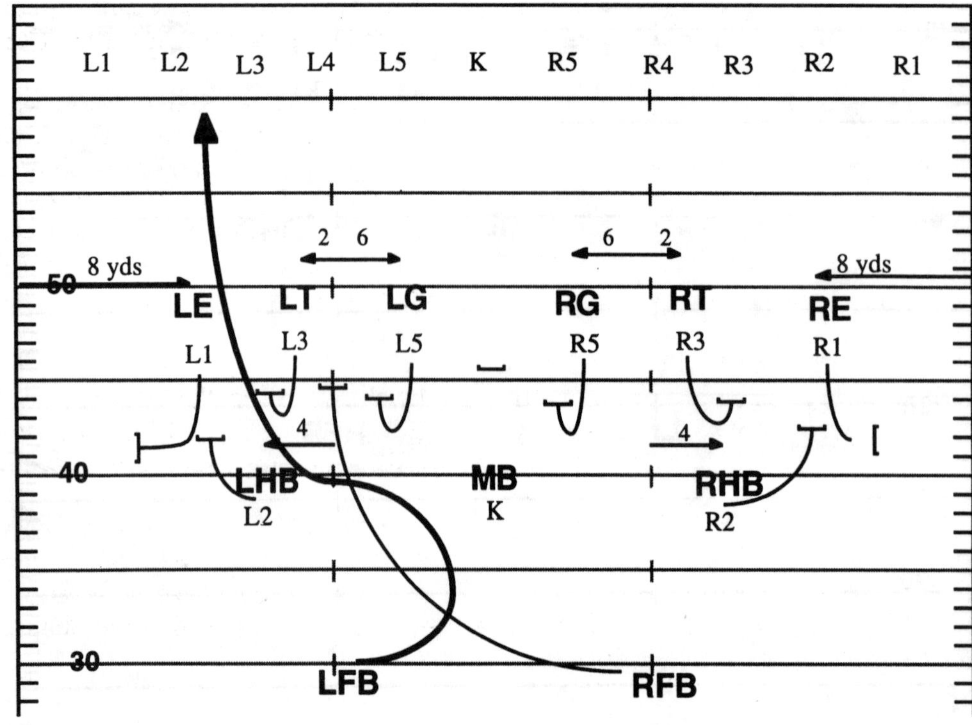

Six-man front

I use a **six**-man front on my youth return team. In high school coaching, I used **five**. Five is sort of standard. You used to have to have at least five men on the front line by rule. Six is appropriate when you fear an on-sides kick.

I have observed that coaches tend to design their teams to stop their **own** approach. For example, a team with a great passing game will tend to use a defense which is designed to stop the pass. That's not logical. You should stop what your **opponent** has, not what **you** have. But we all tend to be very conscious of our own approach and sort of paranoid that the opponent might use it. That may be why I use a six-man kickoff return front.

Catch the ball in the air

Another cardinal sin of kick returning is letting the ball hit the ground. As a general rule, the kids want to let the ball hit the ground before they get it. That way it's easier to catch and if they miss they can blame the crazy bounces footballs take.

You must **insist** that they catch the ball in the air. Letting the ball hit the ground takes many yards off the return at best and can be disastrous at worst.

You must give your kick returners lots of practice at catching kicks in the air. I always had a kick returner behind the goal posts for our nightly PAT practice.

You must constantly harp on the need to catch the ball in the air and punish the returner if he lets a catchable ball hit the ground. If he persists in letting catchable balls hit the ground, you must replace him, no matter how good a runner he is. The line I repeated over and over at both the youth and high school levels was, "If you do not catch the kick in the air, you are not a candidate for the job of kick returner."

In my early years as a coach, I had kick returners who **never** caught a kick in the air all season. Now, as an experienced coach, I am eagle-eyed about whether my kick returners show reluctance to catch kicks in the air and I am very quick to replace anyone who shows reluctance to catch on the fly. I usually start with my best runners at kick returner. But let a few balls hit the ground on my team and you'll be on the sideline watching the second- or third-best runners doing your job.

Consequences of a muff

Part of the problem is **coaches** who tell players to get away from punts. That gives players the notion that muffing a kick is the worst crime imaginable. Not true. The worst crime is anything that delays getting control of the kickoff.

In punts, the ball belongs to the receiving team no matter where it lands if the receiving team does not touch it beyond the expanded neutral zone. That is true for kickoffs only for the kick's **first ten yards**. After that, muffs matter not. The kicking team needs no help from the receiving team to gain possession. So there is **no risk** in trying to catch the kickoff ball in the air. I encouraged kick returners to catch even on a dead run. If they are coming toward the kickoff team, a muff on a dead run would typically knock the ball back where it came from. Even if we lost possession, we would still have good field position.

'My son should be on the kick return team'

Occasionally a player would tell us he thought he should be on the return team. Or his father would. We would try him in our everybody-but-one-take-a-knee drill. If he was right, the player in question would succeed. If not, it quickly became apparent. It was an excellent argument settler.

I took a coach's son off the kickoff team one year and caught hell for it. I was ordered to put him back on the team. Instead, I ran a drill in which a kick returner went one-on-one with a kickoff team member or would-be member in a ten- or fifteen-yard-wide alley. Most players would be unable to even **touch** the kick returner. That drill ended the debate about that player being put back on the kickoff team.

You must also analyze your game films to see whose man made the tackle. Then scrutinize that player's performance in subsequent practices.

No clipping

The majority of long runs in youth football are called back for clipping. Kickoff returns are intended to be long runs. To the extent that you succeed, you must avoid having your success nullified by a clipping penalty.

We did that by constantly emphasizing it in practice. I carry a penalty flag to all practices. I throw it liberally. The kids hate it—which is good. I sure hate it when a touchdown or long run is called back in a game.

I also yell, "No clipping!" over and over in all kick return and other long run situations. It has worked. The kids now have a Pavlovian response to all long run situations. Whenever a play lasts longer than about three seconds, they start thinking about clipping avoidance. You **must** achieve that clipping avoidance habit.

Throw a clip, go to the bench

I also have a rule that if you clip, you are off the team in question. For example, if a member of the kick return team clips on a return during the second game of the season, he is immediately taken off that team **during the game**.

I don't make a scene. It's done quietly. But all players know the deal. I treat it as if he had been injured and put the next guy on the depth chart in his place. The boy may be restored to the kick return team later in the season, say after four weeks.

Words and even penalty flags often have no effect on a boy. But losing his job invariably makes a big impression on both him and his surviving teammates. It also gets him off the field, which solves the problem as well.

Policy led to my resignation

But I must tell you that I did this in a 1996 youth game and it resulted in my mid-season resignation as head coach. In our Fair Oaks game, we ran a kick return back for a touchdown. But it was called back for a clip, the first time any of my teams had ever had a touchdown called back on a clip in my nine-team career. I quietly told my assistants, "Whoever it was is done for the day." We then got the jersey number from the referee and sent in a substitute.

A rebellious assistant coach went to the president of our association after the game and depicted my substituting for the clipper as the youth coaching crime of the century. She ordered me to eliminate that policy and I resigned rather than do that.

I actually got the idea for that policy from the husband of the woman who ordered me to change it. His team committed three unsportsmanlike conduct penalties in one game in 1991 and he got chewed out by league officials as a result. The next practice, he announced that anyone who committed unsportsmanlike conduct would be done for the day. I adopted that policy and extended it to **safety** penalties like clipping.

The policy is in the best interest of the team, the opposing players, and the player in question. I suspect that the player whose day ended when he clippped will not soon clip again. As Lou Holtz said, "Discipline is not something you do **to** someone, it is something you do **for** someone." I sure didn't bench him for me. He was first string. Benching him weakened us in the game, which we lost 8-0.

Be positive—most of the time

The phrase, "No clipping!," is stated in the **negative**. Generally, it's not a good idea to state athletic admonitions in the negative. The **positive** version is, "Only block when you can hit the front jersey numbers of the opponent."

Another related problem is illegal use of the hands. Tell the players they must keep their hands in front of their chest. They tend to reach out toward a defender when they miss the block.

Game-day evaluation

You need to evaluate on game day as well. Some players come ill or injured but don't tell anyone. Others play poorly in unusual conditions like in mud or on Astroturf. The way I tracked that on game day was to rapidly write down the jersey numbers of the kickoff team on my game kick return diagram card.

Then when the tackle was made, I would write down the jersey numbers of the tacklers to see who blew his blocking assignment. You have to be very **fast** to do this. Talk to the boy or boys who failed and ask why. If it happens repeatedly in a high-scoring game, you should probably replace him right then. Especially in playoff games, you cannot wait until next week.

Backward pass

In 1992, I put in a backward-pass kick return for the playoffs. We practiced it for three weeks. We intended to use it the first time we needed it. But we won the first two playoff games by the same score, 26 to 0, without it.

In the third, the semi-final game of the league championship, we needed it. We put our first- and second-string quarterbacks at halfback on the kick return team. Our best returners were back at fullback. The plan was for the halfback who caught the ball to tuck it away and simulate a return for a few steps, then stop and pass backward to the fullback on the opposite side of the field. The fullback was instructed to always keep at least one yard line between his depth and that of the halfback with the ball.

15-yard return

We executed the play perfectly in the game. But we only got a 15-yard return out of it. That was better than normal. But not the touchdown we had hoped for. Our scouting indicated that their team converged on kickoffs. That is, their lane discipline broke down. I suspect their lane discipline was good that day because they heard **us** yelling, "Stay in your lanes!" when **we** kicked off. It reminded them of what their coaches had told them in practice. In any event, they stayed in their lanes and one guy was in front of our backward pass receiver.

If you are going to use the backward pass or any other tricky return like a reverse or fake reverse, make sure you practice it enough times to be competent at it. Whenever you try to confuse the other team, there is a great danger that you will confuse **yourselves**.

My most successful return play

As I said earlier, I finally discovered a successful kick return in 1996 on my freshman team. The March 1996 issue of *Scholastic Coach and Athletic Director* magazine had an article called, "Getting the most in returns" by Jason Mooney, Special Teams Coordinator of Galena (KS) High School.

Mooney said,

> *In 1993 and 1994, our three deep return men led the league (finishing 1-2-3) in total yardage, average yardage per return, and return touchdowns.*

I decided to try his return. As promised, it worked. The very first return we did in our first game of the season went for a touchdown.

Hand-off kick return

It has a backfield like a full-house T formation: quarterback, fullback and left and right half backs. A left, right, or middle return is called. The front 7 guys line up in wall left, wall right, or wedge to block.

Step one is to get the ball to the **quarterback**. If he catches the kick, that takes care of it. If one of the **other** backs catches the kick, he runs by the quarterback first and gives it to him—unless he is the designated ultimate ball carrier, in which case he **fakes** handing it to the QB and keeps going. If the ultimate ball carrier did **not** catch the kick, he waits until the quarterback gets the ball then runs by him and receives a hand-off. All three backs take care to twist or bend at the waist after the fake or hand-off so the enemy cannot tell who has the ball. The **fullback** has to **spin** 360 degrees as he goes by the quarterback. Our opening-game kick return for a touchdown was return left. It looked like this.

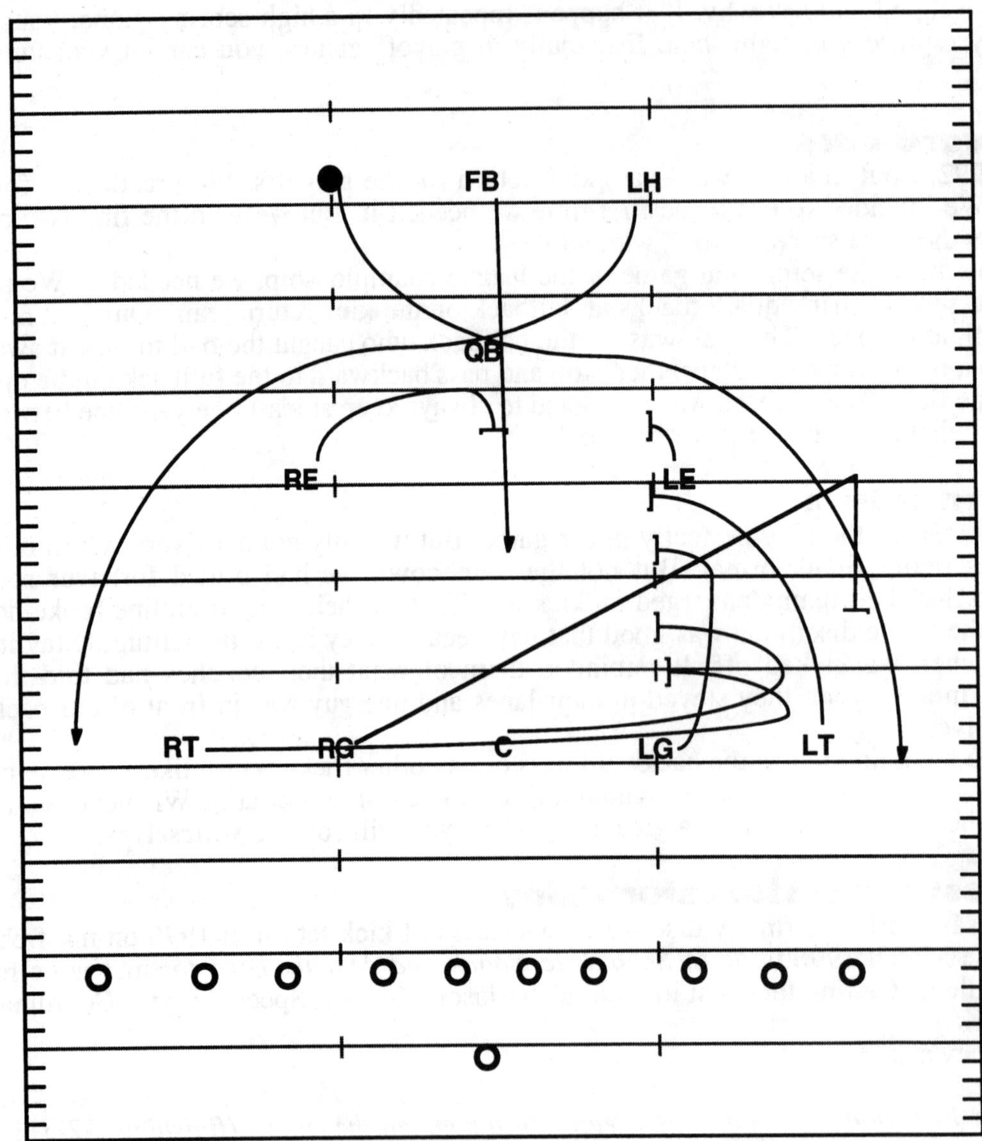

We had to have a set sequence. Ours was as follows:

If the ball went to the rear three backs, the **guy who caught the ball** went by the quarterback **first**. Obviously, nobody would fall for any of fakes before the guy with the ball went by the quarterback.

If a **halfback** caught the kick, the **fullback** went **second** then the other half back. If either of the **middle** players, the quarterback or fullback, caught the ball, the half backs would go in **left-to-right order**. The identity of the player who was to end up with the ball was irrelevant to the order in which they ran by the quarterback.

Ball kicked to:	Sequence of passing quarterback:
quarterback	LH, FB, RH

left halfback	LH, FB, RH
fullback	FB, LH, RH
right halfback	RH, FB, LH

In addition to the opening-game touchdown return, we also had one that went to the other team's 5-yard line and a bunch that got past midfield. I had more success with this return than with any other I've used over nine seasons.

I practiced this return by standing about ten yards in front of the quarterback, calling out a direction for the return, then throwing the ball to one of the four backs. They would then execute the necessary hand-offs and fakes. Meanwhile, another coach threw grounders, line drives, and pop-ups to the front two rows. We then had the front two rows run to their blocking spots for each type of return. Finally, we ran live 11-on-11 kick returns against a scout kickoff team.

We never had a fumble until the next-to-last game of the season. Both our quarterback and our fullback were hurt and out for the kick return. A substitute quarterback expressed misgivings about executing the return. I told him to "Just keep it yourself if you're not comfortable." He decided to go ahead and execute the return and he and the substitute fullback fumbled the exchange to the other team. With the first-string in, we never had a problem with the exchange.

Mooney said the backs should practice their part of the play **every day**. We only practiced it **once a week.** Mooney said the play seems to work best to the **right or left, not the middle**. We had the same experience. I generally planned to go up the middle once we had run a couple of returns left and right. But we rarely received that many kickoffs in a game.

I must comment on our freshman quarterback, Chris Peart. He had never played football before. Yet he caught the kickoffs on the fly week after week, turned his back to the onrushing kickoff team, and coolly executed his hand-off and fakes as the opponents thundered toward him. On a couple of occasions, the play was so well executed that he got tackled, hit from behind by full-speed kickoff team members.

Also deserving note is the right halfback who scored the touchdown and got most of the big returns, Justin Gonzales, whom I converted to tailback from wide receiver (after I told him how many times per game each position got their hands on the ball).

Short kicks

All of the above discussion of kickoff returns pertains to when the kickoff team is dumb enough to kick **deep** to your best returners. Amazingly, that happens most of the time. In our 1996 freshman season, virtually every kick went right to our quarterback. But not always. Sometimes they kick to your middle or front row.

Kick to middle or front row

If they kick to the middle or front row, I just have the guy who catches it run straight toward the goal. The enemy will arrive momentarily so there's no time to get fancy. You also are missing two blockers in the case of a middle row kick; ten in the case of a front row kick. The blockers still block their assigned man. The block just has less meaning.

Virtually all coaches teach their front line kick return guys to fall on the ball if it's kicked to them. I even saw an NFL hands-team player catch an on-side kick chest high then throw himself to the ground untouched by any opposing player. That's only appropriate during the end-of-game take-a-knee period. See my new book *Football Clock Management* for a detailed discussion of when the leading team can take a knee.

Fair catch a pop-up

I told my guys to fair catch a pop-up kicked to them on the front line. That never happened in a game, but we practiced it weekly.

If the kick was a line drive or grounder that was sure to go ten yards, I told them to catch it and **run** with it if **possible**, and to **fall** on it if **necessary**.

If it was not **sure** to go ten yards, they were to get near it to make sure it did not go ten yards, but not to touch it if it was going to come to rest after going less than ten yards. The only exception to that was if the kickoff team failed to gather around the less-than-ten yard kick.

Snatch it and run

Generally, the kickoff team will recover the ball after it goes two or three yards because they don't know any better. But if a kicker just grazes the ball with his foot and it dribbles only a yard or two, they might stand there bewildered assuming it is a dead ball. I taught my kick-return team guards to casually stroll up to such a ball, and, if it was unguarded, snatch it up and run.

You don't have to fall down to get possession

The proper mindset is, above all, to **get possession** of any ball that has or will go ten yards. However, that does not mean you fall on every kick.

For one thing, falling on a ball does not necessarily increase your chances of gaining possession. You can maneuver better on your **feet** than on your **knees** or **side**. If you fall on a moving ball and miss, you're in big trouble.

Another reason not to fall on the ball is that the onside kick is not necessarily on the ground. If it bounces on one hop to your chest, like that NFL receiver on the hands team, you should catch it standing up. And once you've done that, why would you ever tackle yourself? Isn't that the opponents' job?

Practiced every week

I have, for years, taught my front line players to catch and run with line drives and grounders to them. Furthermore, we practiced it every week. It only took a minute. I'd stand in the spot where the kicker was and hurl grounders and line drives underhanded at several of my front-line kick return guys. For emphasis, I'd yell, "Pick it up and run!" each time.

They caught it and ran straight north. And that's exactly what they did in **games**. We got some of our best post-kickoff field positions from line drives to our front line. My kids, who had done it dozens of times in practice, calmly caught the ball and charged straight ahead. In one game, the opposing kicker kicked a one-hopper to one of my guards. He caught it and ran straight ahead for a small gain.

There was a penalty against the kicking team. They kicked again—the same kick to the same player with the same result. The only on-side kick we ever lost was when one of my front-line guys—an 8-year old—shied away from the ball.

In our 1996 freshman season, one team kicked an onside kick to one of my front line guys who was big, fast, and had great hands. He caught it matter of factly on one hop and ran it right down their throats like the fullback he was.

Huddle return

A kick return that intrigues me is the huddle return, We tried to run it for about half the 1993 season. Basically, the kids never executed it correctly in games. Even so, it worked great once. We got a 23-yard return. I still suspect it will work even though the only video I have of it is from a blooper video. And that was from an old movie of a pre-war college team.

Basically, you have the halfbacks and fullbacks, including the guy who got the ball, go into a huddle. The fullback who did not get the ball or designated fullback in charge stands in the back of the huddle facing the oncoming kickoff team. The guy you want to end up with the ball stands directly in front of the captain with his back to the enemy.

The other players form a huddle with their backs to the enemy. If a player other than the guy you want to run with the ball has the ball, he takes a position right behind the intended ball carrier with his chest against the intended ball carrier's back. He reaches around and places the ball in the stomach of the intended ball carrier. This insures that it is a backward hand-off.

Go when you see the whites of their eyes

When the captain can see the whites of the kickoff team's eyes, he yells, "Go!" Every member of the huddle explodes out to one sideline or the other pretending to hold a ball. They keep twisted at the waist so their chest faces away from the enemy players and toward the goal we are defending.

The problem with this return was that one or two kids would inevitably not go to the huddle. Even so, we still got a great return in Benicia in 1993. The Benicia players tackled the wrong guy at first and the guy with the ball went 23 yards. That proved to me that this was a great play. But I just couldn't get the kids to stay cool enough to pull it off. The pressure of the game and having your back turned to onrushing players seemed to unnerve some of them.

Kick return practice schedule

The kick return practice schedule is almost a mirror image of your kickoff practice schedule.

weekly	monthly
grounder to front line	1-yard kickoff
line drive to front line	any trick return you plan
8-yard kickoff untouched	
pop-up kickoff to front line	
25-yard squib kick	free kick after safety
deep kicks to fullbacks (standard return)	

Spend most of your time on the most common kickoff in your league. In our league it's the deep NFL style kick. We only spend a few seconds on the front line stuff, hurling balls in rapid succession at different players.

You only have about 15 minutes for all this so you have to keep everyone moving and you have to keep your assistant coaches from delaying the next repetition. They must coach on the run and quietly. They cannot speak loud enough to force you to stop talking to wait for them to finish and they must not prevent the player they are focusing on from lining up promptly for the next repetition.

If the head coach will not give you at least 15 minutes a week exclusively for kick return team practice, do not take the job of kick return team coach.

Grade your video

Tell your videotaper to zoom out so he gets all eleven members of the kick return team in the picture. You must grade at least one kick return for each game. That is, you run the tape eleven times focusing on one player at a time so you can grade his performance. If you have a **kick return team coach** (and a weak defense that gives up scores), and you can make multiple copies of the game film, he should grade **each kick-return play** of the game. But grading film is time-consuming so it would be tough for the **head** coach to grade more than one kick return a week.

Players who grade low should be given remedial practice and replaced if you believe you have a better player for the position.

5

Punt team

Punt

Most coaches seem to treat punts as a necessary evil. That's a big mistake. The punt can be a potent weapon—or a fatal weakness. It is an extremely dangerous play—for **both** teams. You have to focus on it and master it like any other aspect of football.

Punter technique

I don't want to spend much time on punter technique. There are books and videos by great punters on that subject. (*How to Kick the Football* by Edward J. Storey and *The Art of Place-Kicking and Punting* by Jennings, Bahr, and Danmeier. These books are probably out of print. To get them, go to your local library and ask them to do an **interlibrary search**. This almost always results in my getting the book in question.)

Here are the basics of the punt. The **drop** is crucial. The ball should be dropped, not tossed upward, with the laces up and the ball parallel to the ground. One drill has the punter just drop the ball and not kick it. If it bounces straight up, he did it right.

He should pick a distant **target**, like a light standard, to aim at. Do **not** pick a **person** because they may move.

He should step straight toward the target and point his kicking toe toward the target as he punts. Do **not** let them step to the side and kick off the side of their foot. That's sandlot nonsense.

The kicking foot swings **straight up**, not across the body. The non-kicking foot does **not** leave the ground. The common photo of the punter up in the air in the follow-through is an indication of incorrect technique.

The punter must keep his **head down** and eyes focused on the point of impact throughout his kick and follow-through.

He must **not** catch the snap **against his body**. It takes too long to get it back out. Rather he must catch it with his **hands** out away from his body. If he has to move to his side to catch a bad snap, he must **not cross his legs** to do so.

Distance between punter and snapper

Except when the ball in inside the five-yard line, **NFL** punters stand about **15 to 18 yards** behind the long snapper to receive the snap.

Augustana College coach Bob Reade and Dan DeMonbrun, a **high school** special teams coach, each wrote a book in which he recommends the punter stand **13 yards** behind the long snapper.

The *Boys Club Guide to Youth Football* says the punter stands **12 yards** behind the long snapper. In the book *Youth League Football*, authors Tom Flores and Bob O'Connor say

The depth of the punter should be ten yards behind the line of scrimmage in a tight punt formation, 12 to 14 yards for a high school spread punt, and 15 yards for a college spread punt. Youth teams, of course, should shorten the distance relative to the age of their players.

In his book, *A Parent's Guide to Coaching Football,* Jack McCarthy says,

At the youth level, [the punter lines up] ***7 to 10 yards*** *[behind the line of scrimmage] and that's still quite a hike for a young center.*

We were about **five** yards back in 1993 with our single-wing, quick-kick approach. I recommend no more than eight yards for youth football. It's true that a deeper position gives the punter slightly more time. But the weak link in youth football punting is not time, it's the long snapper. Make his job as easy as possible. It's easier to learn to protect the punter than it is to learn to snap the ball ten yards.

Not caught in the air

Kick the punt so the punt returner can**not** catch it in the air. Just as it is a cardinal sin for a kickoff returner or punt returner to fail to catch the ball in the air, it is a cardinal sin for the kicker to **let** the returner catch it in the air.

You must kick it **away** from the returner. I go nuts, in a kidding way, when one of my kickers allows a returner to catch a kick in the air. I require the kicker to give me ten pushups if the ball is caught in the air, or could have been. Kicks that hit the ground are returned for short yardage, if they are returned at all. Kicks that are caught in the air are almost always returned for significant yardage and often touchdowns.

Punt it out of bounds

The best way to prevent a return is to kick the ball out of bounds. Most snaps are from the hash mark. So you can and should punt the ball out of bounds, except when you do a **quick kick** and no one is deep to receive it.

Long snap

The long snap is more difficult than the punt. Virtually all teams have a dozen guys who can punt, some farther than others, but they can all punt. However, a great many youth football teams have **no one** who can long snap. Or so they think.

I have seen many a youth football team that **never** punted. Indeed, at the Pop Warner Super Bowl in 1993, virtually no team punted—ever—no matter what the down and distance. I suspect it was because they were afraid of a bad snap or blocked punt. I must add that I was appalled by such bad coaching at that level of success.

Audition everyone

You must audition **everyone** on the team, except an obvious first-string punter or place kicker, for the job of long snapper. That includes the star quarterbacks and running backs. Do **not** make this a fat kid's job. Make it a top athlete's job—or you will pay the price—most likely in a crucial playoff game.

I personally conducted this audition as head coach to emphasize its importance, while my assistants held "glamour" auditions like those for running speed and passing accuracy. And I made sure I did it the very **first day** of practice to get the long snapper started on practicing.

1,200 snaps

I figure the long snapper needs about 1,200 long snaps before the first game. There are about 21 practice days before the first game in the leagues I have been in. If you work backwards, you'll find that's about 1,200 ÷ 21 = 57 snaps a day. You can only do about 20 at a time. The players get tired. So you need to send your long snappers—you need at least two—off to practice their long snaps **three** times a practice. Take every opportunity to get long snapper practice. When the punters practice punting, have them start with a snap. Ditto the field-goal kickers.

Earlier in the book, I talked about "**oomph**." This is an example of it.

My 1993 long snapper, Richard Chinn, was the subject of a two-page spread in the May 1994 issue of *Sports Illustrated for Kids*. He snapped 402 straight long snaps without an error in games. The reasons were that we chose him carefully, his father happened to be the long-snapper coach (selected for that job before the long snapper was chosen), he worked hard, and we gave him tons of repetitions. The reason our opponents either are afraid to punt or suffer bad long snaps when they try is because they only give their long snapper a chance to practice about 50 repetitions before the first game. Their long snappers don't have 1,200 reps by the end of the **season**.

Punter audition

Give **everyone** on the team a punter tryout. Identify the top two or three then designate them the punters. They need lots of repetitions, although not near as many as the long snappers. They generally do **not** improve their kicking distance over the course of a season. Rather they practice to get used to catching the snap and kicking away from the returner. They also need to learn to get the kick off rather **quickly**. They already have the punting skill. What they need is the **comfort level** to pull it off in game conditions.

I generally do **not** use the best pure punter as my game punter. Rather I try to use my single-wing tailback when I run that offense. We do a "fourth-down quick kick" and having to substitute a punting specialist would eliminate the element of surprise inherent in the "quick kick."

Time

The total time from when the snapper starts to move the ball until the punter's foot hits the ball should be no more than 2.00 seconds.

At first, your kids will take longer. Don't worry too much about it initially. Let them get comfortable. Then start timing them and telling them it needs to be 2 seconds or less.

In a typical practice, I stand next to the punter and long snapper and time every punt, yelling out the result after each one. If they are too slow, I point out the need to speed up. Your kids will have no trouble getting their time down to two seconds. But it won't happen unless you push them. The punter should take no more than two steps.

If you fail to get the time down to two seconds, your punts will be blocked at times. That's a disaster.

Coverage man

You need one boy to go immediately downfield when the ball is **snapped**, not when it's punted. He makes the tackle if the ball is caught. He recovers the muff if it's dropped.

Most teams use a wide receiver. I don't like that because I don't **use** a wide receiver in the double wing or wing T formations. Furthermore, many punt-receive team coaches double team the wide out to prevent him from going downfield. I like to use a wing back or other player coming out of the backfield. He will generally get out untouched.

In the NFL, no more than two punt team guys can go downfield before a ball is punted. Most youth coaches assume the rule is the same in high school and youth football. It is **not**. There is **no limit** on the number of men who can go downfield on a punt before the ball is kicked. However, somebody better block.

Punt formation

I have used three punt formations: the double wing, the single wing and a through-the-quarterback's-legs wing T. The double wing gave the best protection. The single wing and wing T gave adequate protection, but had the element of surprise in that the receiving team did not know we were punting. In a 1994 game against Napa, our best play of a bad day was our fourth down, through-the-quarterback's-legs punt out of the wing T. Here are the three formations.

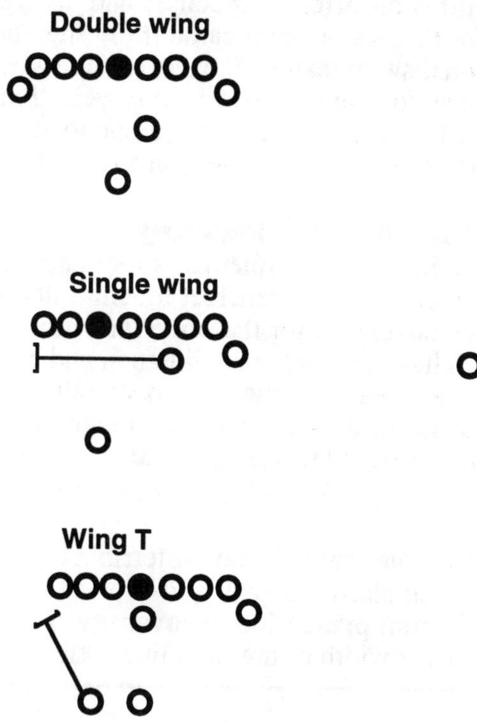

Protection

Protection is crucial. I prefer to use the normal offensive line to minimize substitutions. When I am in the quick-kick mode, I generally can**not** substitute because the substitution would give away the plan to punt. Substitutions also get fouled up and cause penalties or force you to use timeouts. However, sometimes the offensive line coach and I disagree on who the best linemen are and I will not allow my punts to be blocked to avoid substituting.

'Where did you come from?'

I find out who belongs on the line by simply running punts against a scout team in practice. A punt will get blocked.

We ask the kid who blocked it, "Where did you come from?" The player shows us where he was lined up and we identify the blocker who failed. Then we run the play again and focus our attention on that blocker. Most times, the punt blocking team guy gets through again. We admonish the blocker to stop him or lose his position and run it again.

If he fails again, we replace him, generally with the guy who was beating him. We do that every week throughout the season. Basically, the punt team linemen are the guys who won that week's competition. Same is true for the blocking backs.

Substituting

If you have to make a substitution when you punt, you must make **extra marks on your game card**. It should show the jersey numbers of each of your special teams players in a diagram of their formation so you can compare what you see on the field to your card at a glance. The extra marks will help you remember to get the sub in.

You also must make a note to get the guy he goes in for **off** the field. For example, if 58 normally plays right tackle and you want 60 in on punts at that position, write 58 OUT! and 60 IN! in big red letters on your punt card. When the punt team goes in, turn to the bench and yell, "60 get in there at right tackle! Punt Team!" Then turn to the field and yell, "58 out!"

Line up special teams in pre-game warm-up

I like to line all my special teams up on the field during the pre-game warm-up. I also write each player's positions on offense, defense, and special teams on their hands with a black felt-tipped pen before the game. You can tell my stars because they have six positions. I got that idea from my sons' swim teams. They write the swim-meet events on the hands.

The common mistake is for the coach to simply yell "Punt team!" and assume the kids will get it right. They don't even get it right in **high school.** You have to specifically remind players who are doing something unusual to get on and off the field.

Zero line splits and area blocking

The line split (distance between one lineman's foot and his neighbor's) should be zero on punt teams. That is, the linemen have their feet touching the guy next to them. They cannot interlock them before the snap except for the center and guards.

We area block punts. That is, we tell each linemen and back to block the area where he is standing. If no one comes to their area, they are to stay there and block no one. If you assign them to block a particular **man**, they are liable to lunge out after him and open a fatal gap. Man assignments also make you vulnerable to **stunts**.

Fan out

This next principle is simple, but kids have a terrible time getting it right for some reason. Consequently, you have to emphasize it over and over all season. Once the ball is kicked, the nine blockers must switch from **protection** to **coverage**. To do that, they must fan out across the field so that they cover the width of the field like a kickoff. Here's a diagram:

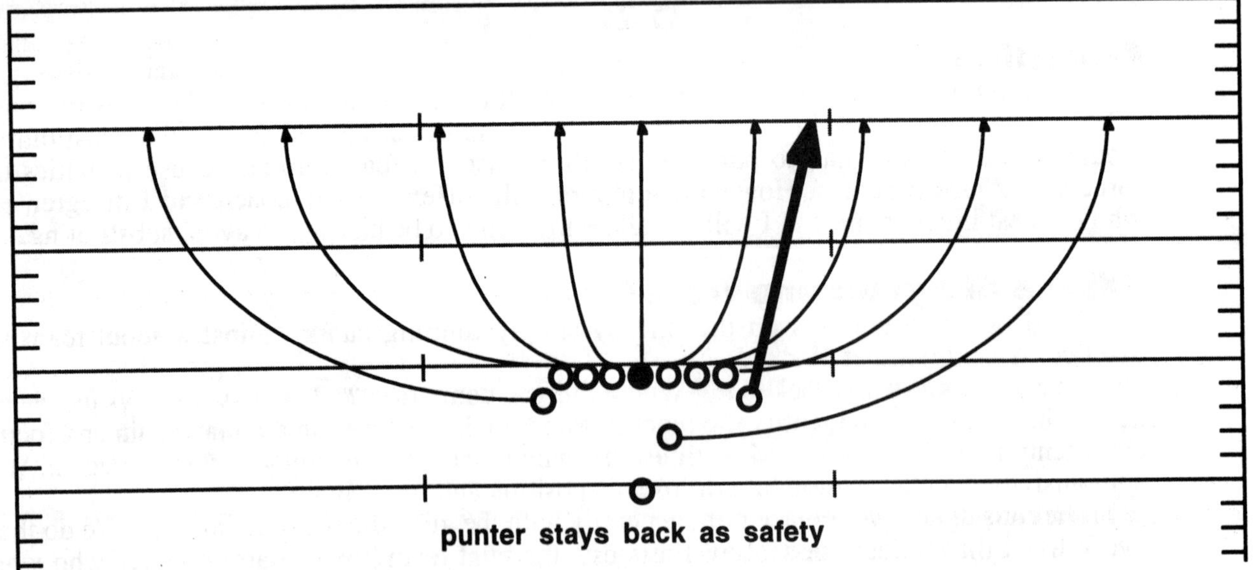

The thick line represents the path of the one player who releases on the snap and goes straight to the football. Obviously, they must converge on the ball carrier and make a gang tackle once he commits to a path as with a kickoff.

Never follow your own color

Tell the players they must never, "Follow their own color." That is, they must not run along behind a teammate. Following behind a teammate would mean one lane has **two** guys and another has **none**. A player who finds himself behind a teammate must slide **out** to the next empty lane.

You teach this by **walk-throughs**. Have the long snapper snap and the punter punt. Yell "Air!" when the foot hits the ball. Then the players walk in a fan out pattern until you yell, "Freeze!" You yell that as soon as you see a player out of his lane or a player following his own color. Point out what's wrong. Move one boy to fix the problem then tell them to start walking again. Do this until they have fanned out then converged correctly on the ball carrier. Do this weekly.

I like to have them punt one direction and fan out and go **full speed** to the ball then punt back the other direction, this time **walking** through to make sure the fan out is correctly spaced. In other words, you emphasize the speed when you go one direction and emphasize the spacing when you come back the other direction.

The coverage men must **not** penetrate beyond the depth of the ball.

Full speed

The lack of a fan-out pattern bothered me throughout every season. But lack of hustle drove me nuts. In the 1994 season, there were several times when we executed the punt perfectly, the punt was on the ground far from the punt return man deep in his own territory, but our players loafed down the field and the guy was able to pick the ball up and get a good return.

The fix, although I'm not sure I ever completely fixed it, is to run the fan-out drill at **top speed**. I sometimes do it instead of end-of-practice wind sprints. Line up the punt team in punt formation, execute a punt, yell, "Air!" when the foot hits the ball, and have your entire coaching staff pursue the players down the field yelling, "Full speed! Full speed!"

Reverse direction and do it again. Keep doing that until their fatigue is causing them to slow down. Do **not** continue when they are too tired to run at full speed or they will get into the habit of ignoring the admonition to run full speed. Doing the walk-through fan out in one direction and the full-speed fan out the other enables them to catch their breath while still practicing and learning.

Do not tolerate loafing

This worked for me on sweep defense drills. I know of no reason why it would not work on punt coverage. Players who loaf should be punished, for example, by making them run an extra punt coverage drill on their own.

Chronic loafers must be replaced. A chain is only as strong as its weakest link. If you practice the long snap, punt, blocking and fan-out pattern to perfection, but the players loaf getting down field, you have wasted all that effort. They must get there ASAP to recover a muff, cause a fumble, or at least stop a return before it gets started.

You are striving for a Pavlovian response to the situation and the word "Air!" Then in **games**, yell, "Air!" and, "Full speed! Full speed!" during the actual play.

Situations

What I have described above relates to when everything goes according to plan. Everything does **not** always go according to plan. You must practice for the screw-ups.

Bad snap

If the snap is so bad that your punter cannot get the punt off within two seconds, he needs to throw a pass or pick the ball up and run for the first down. You need a code word to yell to alert the backs to go out for a pass. For example, "Red!"

If the punt is abandoned because of a bad snap or whatever, the coaches and punter yell, "Red! Red!" Two backs then flare out into the flat staying behind the line of scrimmage so that rules like ineligible receiver downfield and blocking during the pass do not come into effect. The punter then throws the ball to one of them if he is open. If they are not open, or if he has a clear running lane, he tucks it away and runs for the first down. Here's a diagram:

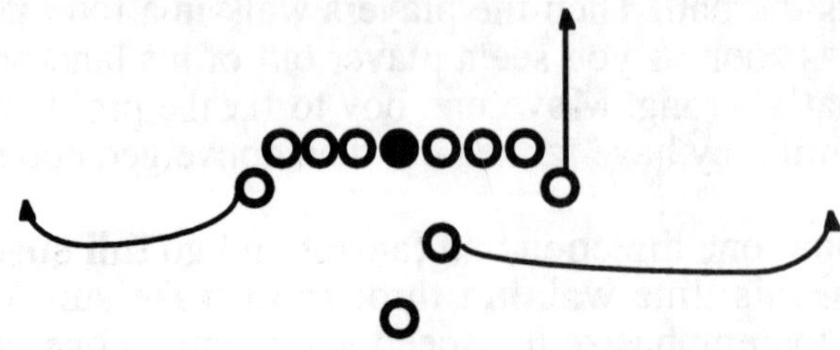

We practiced this, but never used it because our long snaps were all good. But in 1992, we had great success with a deliberate fake punt pass to the blocking back on a similar pattern. You practice this by telling your snapper to deliberately snap badly during punt team scrimmage against a scout punt receive team. It should be done at least once repetition per week. Do it over if they do not do it right.

Blocked punt

Your players should be coached to **pick up a blocked punt and run with it.** Falling on the ball accomplishes next to nothing. It only prevents the punt blocking team from picking the ball up and running with it.

On **fourth down**, falling on the ball has nothing to do with **possession**. It's the receiving team's ball no matter who falls on it. The only way to help your team in the event of a blocked punt that you get to first is to pick it up and run with it. If you get a **first down**, great! But if not, at least you've given them worse field possession.

Practice this by telling your punter to deliberately punt the ball into a player in front of him. Inevitably, the players will fall on the ball. When they do, make the player in question pick it up and run five times in rapid succession. Tell them over and over that possession is preordained by the down. They must **not** fall on the ball. I've found that it takes about the first month to get it ingrained in them that you do not fall on a blocked punt.

Punt touched by a member of the receiving team

Virtually everyone knows that a punt touched **downfield** by the receiving team can be recovered by the punt team. Most do not realize that such a **muff cannot be advanced**.

You should tell your scout team punt returner to deliberately drop at least one ball per punt practice. In the case of a muff, the players should either fall on the ball or, if they recover it standing up, drop to one knee or run out of bounds to avoid being tackled unnecessarily. There is no reason to stay in bounds even if you are in a clock-wasting mode because the clock will stop on change of possession anyway.

Fumble on the return

A fumble after the receiving team **gets control** of the ball can be picked up and **advanced**. Tell your scout team returner to deliberately **fumble**, as opposed to muff, one ball after catching it per punt practice. Make sure the coverage guys pick it up and run with it if they can rather than just fall on it.

By the way, if the receiving team gets control of the punt, then fumbles back to the punt team, it's **first down** for the punt team even if the new possession spot was not enough to get a first down based on where the chains were before the punt.

Touch inside expanded neutral zone means nothing

Hardly anyone knows the rule about the receiving team **touching the ball in or near the punt team backfield**. The rule is punts touched by the receiving team within the expanded neutral zone or in the punt team's backfield mean **nothing**. (Rule 6-2-6) Treat them as if they had not been touched at all. The expanded neutral zone extends two yards into the punt receiving team's side of the line of scrimmage from the forward point of the ball.

To practice this, have a coach catch the punt snap then **throw the ball straight up** as if it were a punt. I tried having the punters punt it straight up. They were too inaccurate and wasted too much time.

Catch it and run

The correct behavior in this situation is for **all members of the punt team** to try to **catch the ball in the air or pick it up off the ground and run with it**. (Rule 6-2-3) The ball has to be caught in or on the kicking team's side of the neutral zone in order to be advanced. The **expanded** neutral zone only has meaning regarding touching by the receiving team.

In practice and in games, every coach and player who is aware of the errant kick should yell, "Straight up! Straight up!" Do this once per punt practice. Repeat only if they do the wrong thing. The only risk is referee ignorance of the rule. Our refs are high school refs and they generally know the rule.

Kick to your teammate

By the way, you can actually kick a sort of forward or backward "pass" to any member of the punt team, even a lineman, as long as he catches it **in the neutral zone or behind** the line of scrimmage. He can catch it in the air or pick it up off the ground, and run with it, as long as he is not on the receiving team's side of the neutral zone when he gets it (Rule 6-2-3). It is treated the same as a backward pass even though it is punted. If he muffs it or fails to touch it, it is a live ball.

Let it bounce, if it's going the right direction

Most people have seen punt team members hovering over a ball that is bouncing the way they want it to. You have to practice that. Do a little drill where coaches lob a ball about ten yards in front of a player and he follows it down the field. He must immediately down it as soon as it bounces the wrong way. Do this just once in preseason unless the team screws it up in a subsequent practice or in a game.

The only exception is when you are in a time-wasting or time-conserving mode. There often comes a time in close games when you are less concerned about **field position** than you are about **time**. In that case, you down the ball immediately, even if it's going the right direction, if you are trying to conserve time, and you let it bounce, even if it's going the wrong direction, when you are trying to waste time.

Don't 'down' it, recover it

It is common for players to just touch the ball to down it. Technically, that's correct. But as a practical matter, it is **dangerous**. Have them recover it like they would recover a fumble to make sure there is no doubt that it was touched by the punt team. Otherwise, the punt team may touch it, then start to leave the field, while a punt returner notices that no whistle was blown, picks it up, and runs for a touchdown.

Down it on the one

Have the payers practice keeping it out of the end zone once a month. The first player down should sprint past the ball and wait for it at the one. He must not let any part of his body be in the end zone when he gets the ball or it will go out to the 20. Drill this by punting the ball against air (no scout team). The punt team members should understand that downing the ball on the one only applies to balls that the receiving team is **not trying to catch.** If a punt returner is chasing the ball, you must stay away from him until he catches the ball or muffs it. Getting too close is interference (Rule 6-5-6). Just stop the return.

Fair catch

I have never seen a fair catch in youth football. This in spite of the fact that my punt returners have to fair catch **every other ball in practice**. Nevertheless, you must prepare your players for a fair catch by the returner. If he signals a fair catch, you may not tackle him after he catches it. Of course, you may not get near him **before** he catches it, even if he does **not** signal a fair catch.

First man sprint past the fair catcher

The first man down should **sprint past** a fair-catch-signaling returner. Smart returners sometimes signal fair catch to trick coverage men into thinking they are under the ball and planning to catch it when, in fact, they have decided not to catch the ball and want it to bounce into the end zone for a touchback.

For example, it is standard practice not to attempt to catch any punt coming down inside the ten-yard line, but the punt returner in that situation is supposed to stand out at the 15 or 20 and signal fair catch to decoy the coverage men away from downing the ball on the one.

Fair catch means nothing if he muffs it

The fact that a man has signaled fair catch means nothing as far as possession goes if he does not catch the ball. If he **muffs** it, recover it. If he doesn't even touch it, you must let it bounce toward your goal as long as possible, but stop it immediately from bouncing the wrong way unless you are in a time-wasting mode.

Drill this once a month by tossing a high ball to a scout team put returner. Have him signal fair catch and catch one, muff one, and decoy one. The punt team players need to get within four yards and be ready to pounce on a muff. The first man down must sprint by the fair catch signaling returner then look up and find the ball and try to keep it out of the end zone. Have a coach play referee during this drill.

No fair catch, but imminent tackle

You should also drill once a month on how to treat a punt returner who fails to signal fair catch when he should. That is, he will be hit immediately after catching the ball. Practice this, which is also a defensive back drill, by tossing a high ball to a tall free-standing dummy. The players must practice their timing to make sure they do not arrive until **after** the ball hits the dummy. We called this our Ronnie Lott Drill.

Late pick up

Punt team players usually let their guard down once they believe the punt team will make no attempt to return the punt. There have been cases, Herb Adderly of the Green Bay Packers did it once in the NFL, of punt returners hanging back as if they have no intention of returning the ball, only to suddenly sprint in, scoop it up and go. Adderly scored a touchdown.

Have your scout-team returner try this once a month. Make sure your **entire** punt team covers the ball until the whistle. Pounce on any player who lets his guard down before the whistle and make him do it right five times. Do it right or do it over.

Pass if uncovered wide receiver

In 1996, I was special teams coordinator of the Granada High School freshman team in Livermore, CA. One of our assistants had coached there the year before and said we should have a receiver out wide on the punt team because the defense never covered him. So I did.

As it turned out, he exaggerated. They generally **did** cover him. But **sometimes** they did not.

There is a pertinent, but little-known, rule. Rule 7-2-1 says,

> *After the ball is ready for play, each player of Team A [offense] must have been, momentarily, within 15 yards of the ball before the snap.*

The Granada **J.V.** team tried to run this play in 1996 at a game I attended and they failed to comply with this rule. The play was successful, but brought back for illegal formation.

We taught our friendly side (near our bench) wing to wait until the ready-to-play whistle, then trot out to a flanker spot about five yards from the sideline. At that flanker spot, he stood facing inward with his hands on his hips as if he were a member of the players standing off the field on our sideline watching the game. We practiced this every week, including the ready-to-play whistle. In our weekly practice we invariably had the defense cover the receiver for some plays and ignore him on others. In games, we were never flagged for violating the 15-yard rule.

Problems with the fake punt pass play

We had a couple of problems with the first receiver we used. On one occasion, he did not go out far enough. He was only about eight yards from our tight end. The punter saw that he was uncovered and threw him a pass. But the defenders easily got to him while the ball was in the air and tackled him short of the first down. We ended up turning the ball over on downs,.

On another occasion, he was out wide enough but simply dropped the pass, and again we turned the ball over on downs. We fixed the problem by changing receivers from the friendly-side wing to the punter's personal protector, a boy who understood the need to be near the sideline far from any defender. He also had the best hands on the team.

In our game with Miramonte, punter Justin Gonzales saw that MVP fullback Mike Kukahiko was uncovered, called for the snap, threw Kukahiko the ball, and we got the first down. That game ended in a tie so every little bit helped.

In our game with undefeated league champion Foothill, the opponent also failed to cover Kukahiko. But Foothill's coaches, who happened to be Fox TV analyst John Madden's sons, saw the uncovered man and frantically yelled for a timeout, which they got before the snap. We lost that game 8-6.

Fifteen minutes a week

You should practice your punt and related plays like bad snap, blocked punt, fake punt, and so forth at least fifteen minutes per week. Do not take the punt team coaching job if you cannot get that much practice time from the head coach.

Grade your punt team performance

You must also grade at least one punt off your game video each game. If you have a punt-team coach and the capability of making a copy of the video for each coach, he should grade every punt. Give any low graders extra practice or replace them.

6

Punt block/return team

Punt receive team

I call the punt receiving team the punt **block** team because that is mainly what I want my punt receive team to do. But that is hard to do so they need to be ready to return the ball as well. In fact, the labor is divided. The punt returner is only one interested in returning the kick. The other players are interested in blocking it first, and helping the returner second. Of course, all have to worry about the **fake punt**.

Punt block

The blocked punt is, on average, **the best play in football**. That is, the average blocked punt changes the field position more than any other play.

A punt in youth football generally goes ten to forty yards beyond the line of scrimmage. A blocked punt generally goes ten to twenty yards in the **other direction**, for a total difference in field position of 10 + 10 = 20 to 40 + 20 = 60 yards. Furthermore, if you train them to do so, they can pick up and run with 80% to 90% of blocked punts with few, if any, punt team players able to stop them.

Bad snap as good as blocked punt

You get much the same result from a bad snap with no need to block anything. It almost makes sense to spend more time practicing the punt block than any other offensive, defensive, or special teams activity. The problem is that it is difficult to succeed with a punt block if the punt team is reasonably well staffed and coached.

We had tremendous success blocking punts in 1992 at the San Ramon Bears jr. pee wee team. I can only attribute it to my 8-2-1 defense and a bunch of talented kids. I got much smarter about blocking punts in subsequent years, but we had less success.

Born, not made

One thing I believe, and I have seen in many football coaching books and heard from fellow coaches, is that **some kids are born to block punts**. The rest are not. You can and should train the blockers to avoid roughing the kicker. But the basic **desire** to block the punt must be there.

Most players don't **want** to block the punt. They won't admit it. But they physically fear being hit by the punt. In 1994, we had guys in the punter's backfield time and time again. But they shied away from getting in the way of the punt.

How to find them

How do you find them? Run punt scrimmage plays and see who blocks the punts. You can also do one-on-one drills where a would-be punt blocker gets a clear shot at the punter. Start that drill either by having your long snapper snap the ball or by a coach shoveling the ball to the punter. The would-be blocker comes from his normal defensive position and tries to block the punt. Use a Nerf football or a partially deflated regular football to soften the blow.

With no blockers, the receive-team guy should block every one. But you'll see that they hardly block any because they deliberately miss.

From the side

If the player in question comes in from the side, put dummies on the ground for him to land on since he should dive parallel to the ground. There should be no dummies for blockers coming from between the tackles because they need to jump straight up and come back down on the same spot they left from.

Roughing the kicker

You must **not** rough the kicker. The penalty is awful—fifteen yards and an automatic first down. Some coaches are so traumatized by past roughing penalties that they virtually never put a punt block on. That's a mistake.

We **always** tried to block the punt rather than return the kick in my five years as a youth coach. I recall no roughing-the-kicker penalties. Although I suspect there must have been some. If so, they did not happen at important moments.

I remember that we had some roughing in practice because I made a very, very big deal out of it when it happened. And that is part of the reason why we had so few in **games**. I told my players that if you roughed the kicker, just once in a game, you were **off** the punt block team. I believe I only had to enforce that once. If the player in question makes no such mistakes on scout team in practice in the ensuing three or four weeks, you should put him back on the punt block team, assuming he's still one of the top eleven guys for that team.

Beware the long count

In a fourth-and-less-than-five-yards situation, the punt team will often try to draw you off sides with a long count, hard count, or non-rhythmic count. Accordingly, you should have your scout team do that in punt-block practice.

Inside the ten-yard line

Your punt returners must be trained **not** to catch punts that land inside their ten-yard line. They should pretend to fair catch such punts at the 15 or 20 to decoy the punt coverage men away from the ball so that it will bounce into the end zone untouched for a touchback.

Free rein

I told my punt-block specialists that they could line up **wherever they wanted** when the opponent was punting. They were highly motivated and would experiment with different starting points. I felt it was not especially a coaching issue. I just wanted to encourage those guys to take as much responsibility as possible.

Books I have read on blocking punts says you should overload one side or the middle. Some recommend having a pair or trio of players work in tandem. One or two players focus on moving the punt team blocker out of the way while the other flies through the gap to block the punt. Another technique is to stack two players who each explode to opposite sides of a punt team lineman. That can confuse the offensive linemen as to whom to block.

In 1996, my oldest son was one of my youth assistant coaches and was in charge of the field goal blocking team. He and I read the scrimmage-kick-blocking section of every football book and clinic manual we could find and developed this play as a result.

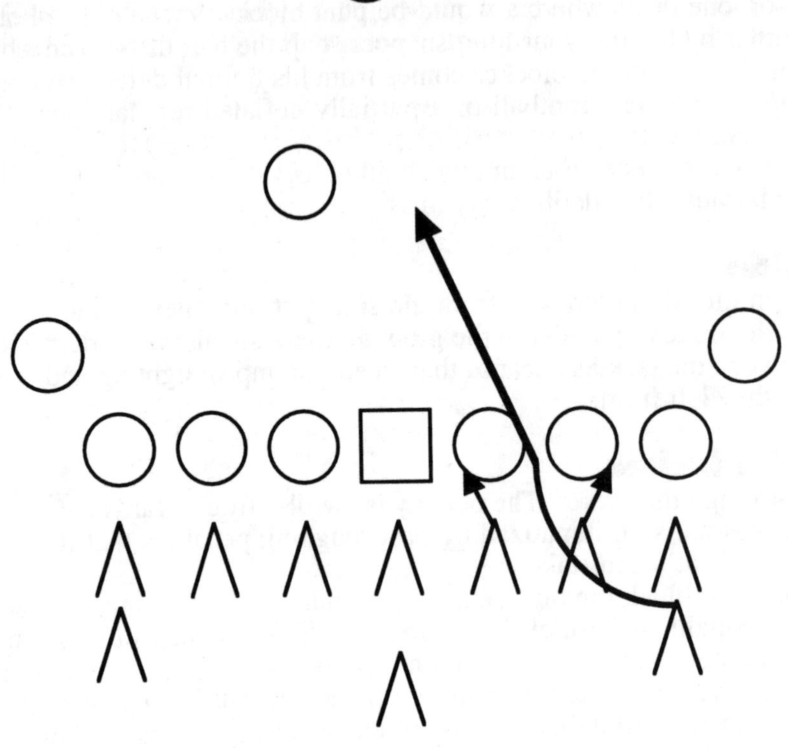

The play is for the right defensive guard to attack the inside shoulder of the left offensive guard and for the right defensive tackle to attack the outside shoulder of the left offensive tackle. We hope they will each step away from the B gap to meet the repsective defenders thereby opening the B gap for the hidden linebacker to loop through and block the kick.

In this play, the player at right linebacker would be your best kick blocker. Before the snap, you want to keep the kick blocker away from the immediate area of the offensive linemen between whom you want him to go. When the offensive linemen get set, they will observe the only defenders in their area are the defensive linemen and assume that's who they have to block. If, on the other hand, the punt blocker shows blitz in the B gap before the snap, the offensive linemen will stay home and block him.

Beware the fake punt

As I said earlier, we had great success with a fake punt pass. Many teams snap the ball to the blocking back who plunges through the line. In fact, there is a whole offense known as the short punt offense. It was popular in the early part of this century. So you can run practically any play from a punt formation including reverses to the wings and passes.

So the punt block team needs to be mindful of the possibility of a fake punt and be ready to stop it. I always have the scout punt team snap the ball to the blocking back at least once per punt block practice. I also have the punter run a sweep once and throw a pass at least once. As always, if the punt block team screws up, we run that particular play over until they get it right.

Normal defense—with a deep safety instead of a middle linebacker

We try to run our normal defense with one safety deeper than normal. His depth is based on the scout report on how far the opposing punter usually kicks. Of course, my normal youth football defense is a ten-one. More about that later. Suffice it to say that it is a good punt block formation.

It is also a sound defense. Pass defense is man-to-man cover one. That is, the punt returner/safety has zone coverage on the entire field. The linebackers and corner backs, although up on the line of scrimmage, have man-to-man coverage on particular potential receivers. The interior defensive line men charge through the interior gaps and the defensive ends contain any sweeps. We have never been burned by a fake punt.

Successful block

I tell the scout team punter to deliberately kick the ball into a player to simulate a blocked punt (unless the scout team is managing to block them without this help). The punt blocking team is required to pick the ball up and run, not fall on it. I've discussed that at length earlier.

Suffice it to say that you would **never** see one of my teams fall on a blocked punt. We scored at least one touchdown on a blocked punt (in 1992 against Napa). And we have run many others part way to the end zone before being tackled. We have never been burned by trying to pick up rather than fall on a blocked punt.

No punt team member ever tried to advance the ball, let alone succeed at it. Picking up blocked punts as a member of the punt blocking team is risk-free. Falling on a punt your team has blocked is nothing less than idiotic.

Catch the ball in the air

OK, let's say your block attempt failed and they got the kick off. Now you need to do the best return you can. That starts with the punt returner **catching the ball in the air**.

One season, I was the punt return coach and I realized in our final playoff game that my punt returner had **never** caught a punt in the air all season. He **always** concluded this one was too risky and skittered away allowing the punt to bounce toward our goal.

Insist that they catch it on the fly

I have since made a very big deal of insisting that the punt be caught in the air. And I've noticed that every book on football that discusses the matter says the same thing.

Ideally, I want my punt returner to catch the ball in the air **on a dead run**. Most coaches have the punt returner walking on eggs, terrified that he will muff the ball.

My attitude is that muffs happen. I try to minimize them by getting the best punt catchers in the punt returner position. And I only have about one lost muff per season. But I don't want my punt returners pussy footing around scared to death of a muff.

Excellent field position after running muff

If they try to catch the ball on a dead run going toward the goal line we want to cross, I figure a muff will probably bounce 30 yards toward that goal. And if the other team recovers it, at least we have good field position.

You must insist that your punt returners catch the ball in the air if at all possible. If the ball hits the ground, it generally rolls ten to twenty yards toward the wrong goal. Any player who repeatedly lets that happen needs to be replaced. As does any **coach** who repeatedly lets that happen. Do not put your best ball carrier at punt returner if he will not catch the ball in the air. Instead, use the best ball carrier **of those who catch the ball in the air**.

Fair catches

You have to give your punt returners lots of practice. We do it during PAT kicking and during punt and punt return practice. We require our punt returners to make **every other catch a fair catch** in practice.

During punt return practice, let your punt returners catch a couple of punts in a crowd of players who are running around them and verbally harassing them. Make sure you tell your players **not** to do that in games. It is unsportsmanlike conduct and interference. But other teams do it so you want to prepare your punt returners and sort of overtrain them so they are able to handle situations that are even worse than they will encounter in games.

Get out of the way

One of the common problems I see in punt returns is never discussed in coaching books—punts that fall on unsuspecting return team players thereby enabling the punt team to regain possession. Punt return team members need to look up and find the ball when it is punted. Coaches and players should yell, "Straight up!" to alert them. They must either fair catch the ball or get out of the way so it does not touch them.

You have to practice this. Have the scout team punter catch the snap and throw the ball almost straight up so it comes down just beyond the expanded neutral zone. Have those who can catch, **fair catch** it, and those who can**not** catch well get out of the way. When they get out of the way, they must keep their **eye on the ball** in case it follows them. It has to bounce somewhere. If it bounces **at** a player who is trying to get out of its way, he must recover it so it does not touch him and get recovered by the opposing team.

Punt-return blocking

My emphasis is on punt **block** so my punt return players will be late in setting up blocks. Consequently I just want them to block the closest punt team player whose front jersey numbers they can see. Those who have no handy target should peel off and set up a wall for a return to the punter's right.

You should practice this by walking through it. If they are too slow in games, do like the punt coverage fan out: alternate walk-throughs and full-speed run-throughs. In youth football, I strongly recommend against the straight punt return where one guy stays back to keep the punter honest while the rest of the punt return team peels off to set up a return.

No clipping

You must discipline your players to refrain from clipping on the punt return. It seems to me that most open-field plays in youth football involve a clipping penalty. As I said earlier in the book, I immediately replace any player who draws a clipping penalty and he will be lucky to get back on the return team before season's end.

In practice, I keep an eagle eye out for clips, ask my fellow coaches to do the same, and make a big deal out of it when one occurs. Such players should be punished. Making them block a sled five times correctly is one suggestion. You could have a coach spin a one-man sled or blocking dummy while the offending player chases it until he gets a legal front shot.

In games, I yell, "No clipping!" whenever an open field situation like a punt return occurs. It works. We rarely have clipping penalties on my teams. Our opponents have tons.

Grade this team weekly

Grade at least one punt block/return play a game (assuming your defense is good enough to force at least one punt per game). Give players who grade low extra practice or replace them.

7

PAT/Field goal kick team

PAT kick

In youth football, a PAT **kick** is generally worth **two points**; a run or pass, **one**. So you should make every effort to create a competent PAT kicking team.

This is very much a function of the age group. I have only seen one successful PAT kick at the jr. pee wee (8 to 10) level. An Elk Grove boy did a kick that hit the cross bar and bounced almost straight up before falling behind the bar in our 1992 26-8 defeat of that team.

Leg strength

The key factor is the leg strength of the boy you have available. But there are a couple of tricks I have discovered over the years.

First, you must have a **prolonged tryout** for the PAT kicker position. If your tryout is too brief, you will likely overlook the best kicker.

We almost did that in 1994 at the pee wee (9 to 11) level. An adequate tryout would be every day for half the season. No kidding. I did an extensive tryout with about three rounds for the finalists in 1994 and still came up with the wrong boy. Fortunately, the right boy kept fiddling around with it and we discovered him. He had been eliminated in the **first** round of the try out.

Our pee wees lost a playoff game by one point in 1993 when they missed a PAT kick attempt. They had previously won a regular season game by one point at the last second with a PAT kick. In 1994, we deliberately took a safety and thereby won a game over Benicia by one point. Earlier in that game, we had kicked a two-point conversion or else we would not have had the luxury of taking that safety.

In 1996, my Granada High School freshman team got the ball at our own 38 with 2:01 left in the game. We had no timeouts left and we were trailing 14-12. We drove down the field and with the clock around :05 after one play which took us to the opponent's nine, we spiked the ball to stop the clock at :01. We then attempted our first field goal of the year. It was good and we won 15-14.

A week later we attempted our second from the opponent's four. It was wide right. We had tried kicking extra points early in the season, but we missed several and the head coach ordered me to stop kicking extra points. The 1994 pee wee coach had also gotten discouraged and told me stop practicing the PAT kick but I talked him into letting me continue and we won the above-mentioned take-a-safety game as a result.

Not enough coaches

In 1996, I was the Granada special teams coach but because of a lack of coaches and over forty players, I could not devote much time to the field-goal team. At the beginning of practice, I sent the punter, place kicker, a kick returner, and the long snappers off by themselves to practice kicking. I stayed on another field to work with the quarterbacks.

In contrast, in 1994, I had an assistant named Cy Doerner who worked with the field-goal kicking team every night. It was he who discovered that we had selected the wrong place kicker and it was during his time with the players that they discovered that the key to eleven-year olds succeeding at field goal and PAT kicking.

Practice kicking

Our PAT kicker in 1994 was Kenny Hendricks. The trick with him was he needed the ball tilted way back at about a **45-degree angle**. Don't ask me why. And don't tell me that's not the right technique. We had the best pee wee level PAT kicking team in the league in 1994. We even kicked one on a super rainy, muddy day in a 26-0 playoff victory against Berkeley.

I do not believe your PAT kickers will increase the distance they can kick the ball with practice over the course of the season. Rather they will learn by experimenting during practice the proper angle for the ball, when the kicker should start his approach, where he should plant his foot in relation to the tee, and so forth. So the purpose of practice is to find the right combination of steps, impact point, angle of approach, and all that.

Light touch

You should coach pee wee and jr. pee wee PAT kickers with a very light touch. Let them do their own thing. About the only fundamental I taught was to keep your head down.

I was a place kicker myself and tried to teach my technique, including a step-hop approach. I found the kids need to take more steps to build up momentum. I also tried to teach the straight ahead toe-kick technique. I was born in 1946 and that's the only way it was done when I was a kid. PAT kicking is so difficult for jr. pee wee and pee wee players that the normal techniques don't work. Let them figure out their own way to do it.

A lot of oomph

You must practice PAT kicks, with a snapper, holder, and kicker, **every day for about ten minutes**. Use both first- and second-string snappers, holders, and kickers. Alternate so they all have a chance to work with each other. You should also have your punt/kickoff returners catching the kicks on the other side of the goal posts.

'Punt' your PAT kicks

I'm not sure what style Hendricks used. I didn't care. But I think he was sort of **punting** the ball. That is, he was striking the ball like a punter, only the ball was on the kicking tee.

His approach was almost straight ahead. But I don't think he struck it with his toe. Rather he hit it with the top of his foot. He had previously been a soccer player and was playing football as a ten-year old rookie.

There is no doubt that both jr. pee wees and pee wees can **punt** the ball through the uprights from the ten or so. But if you tee it up on a kickoff tee, virtually all of them have great difficulty consistently kicking it through the uprights—and that's without the complications of a snap, hold, and rush. Try the ball-at-a-45-degree-angle "punt" place kick with your younger players.

Holder

Speaking as a former place kicker, the holder has the most difficult job—at least once you got above the level where the boys have the leg strength to kick it far enough. Accordingly, you must select your holder very carefully.

When I kicked for the Headquarters Company team that won the Fort Monmouth Super Bowl in the army in 1971, the **only** player we could get to hold the PATs successfully was our premier running back. In 1994, I tried everyone on the team out for the job of holder, held a second round of tryouts, and ended up using our premier running back, Will Sykes. He was an important, albeit generally overlooked, factor in the success of our 1994 PAT kicking team. (I pointed it out at the post-season awards banquet.)

He, too, must get lots of practice. That's why you have the three members of the PAT kicking team, and their backups, practice every day for ten minutes plus during PAT special team practice so they get used to the rush as well.

Distance to holder

The **standard** distance between the ball and the holder throughout football is **seven** yards. Forget that at the jr. pee wee and pee wee level. We were able to put the tee as close as **four** yards from the ball and still get the kick off. As I recall, we were at about **five** yards with our 1994 PAT kick team. Don't be afraid to move closer than seven yards, especially if you are right at the limit of your kicker's range.

Protection

I recommend a double-wing formation the same as described above in the punt team section. You should use the same kids and coach it the same way. If someone on the scout team breaks through, either improve the boy who should have blocked him or replace him.

Mud

We practiced in some lousy weather in the 1994 season. It was very cold, very wet, and very productive. We needed to learn how to kick PATs in mud.

Some coaches and players are not aware of the fact that you can place the ball **anywhere between the hashes** for points after touchdown. (Also after scores, touchbacks, fair catches, and safeties. Rules 6-1-2, 6-5-4, 8-3-1, 8-5-4) When conditions are good, you place the ball in the middle of the field. As a result, there is a worn spot there. When it rains, that spot becomes a puddle. Place the ball to one side or the other of the puddle. That makes the kick slightly harder. But kicking out of a puddle is crazy.

During our rain practice, our kids learned to move the ball out of the puddle and that they could still make the kick. That Saturday, we had to do it on our home field at the same end where we had practiced. And we did.

Be patient

At the lowest two levels, it takes a long time to get your act together on PAT kicks. Be patient. Our 1994 head coach wanted to stop practicing it after a while. We persuaded him to let us continue. It took us until the fifth game of the season in 1994. And we won that game with our first two-point conversion.

Field goals

If your kicker has the leg, you can also kick field goals. That is most likely at the jr. midget (10 to 12) and midget (11 to 14) levels. Our pee wee kicker was able to kick successfully if the line of scrimmage that was about five yards further back than the PAT spot, in other words the LOS was the eight-yard line. But we never encountered a situation where we thought that was the percentage play.

Short field goal attempt can be returned or recovered

If you kick field goals, or your opponents do, remember that if a field goal attempt does not go into the end zone it is treated like a punt. That is, it **can be returned** by the defense or recovered by the kicking team after being touched by the defense, and it belongs to the receiving team if not touched by them.

Leon Lett's bonehead snatching of defeat from the jaws of victory

One of the most famous plays in recent football history was the Cowboys' Leon Lett's touching of a failed field goal, thereby giving the opponent Miami Dolphins a second opportunity to kick. Thanksgiving, 1993. Cowboys 14, Dolphins 13 with :15 left in the game. Dolphins at the Cowboy 24.

The Dolphins field goal attempt was deflected, landed in fair territory and rolled around. All the Cowboys had to do was let it roll then take a knee on the subsequent snap to win the game. But for some reason, Cowboy defensive tackle Leon Lett came flying down the field and tried to recover the ball. He only managed to **touch** it, whereupon the Dolphins recovered it at the Cowboy one-yard line with :03 left in the game. They again attempted a field goal and it was good, winning the game 16-14.

Essentially, Leon Lett created an **artificial muff** of a scrimmage kick. The Dolphins wisely had no one back to return the field goal—or at least they thought they didn't until Lett arrived. As with a muffed punt, the kicking team can recover the ball and gets first and ten. The pertinent rule in high school (6-2-4), and therefore youth football, is the same as the NFL rule (9-1-6). A loose failed field goal attempt rolling around in fair territory is the same as a loose punt rolling around.

Grade this team weekly

As with the other special teams, grade at least one PAT/field goal kick plays per game if there were any. Upgrade or replace weak players.

8

Defense

The big picture

Defense is **reaction** football, in contrast to **offense** which is **assignment** football. Your defensive players must react to the offensive **formation**, any pre-snap changes in that formation (i.e., **motion** and **shifts**), and to the offensive **play** itself. That's not my philosophy. That's a fundamental principle of football. Coaching defense therefore is teaching your players how to react to formations, shifts, motion, and offensive plays.

This is not your old high school team

Most youth football coaches give me the impression that they design their system based on:

- the system their high school coach used
- the system they think colleges they see on TV use
- the system they think NFL teams use.

There are probably many youth football coaches trying to use former NFL coach Buddy Ryan's 46 defensive system, since it has been described as the state of the art by TV football analysts in recent years.

Youth football is a different game

Do **not** design your defense that way. You must take into account the age and size of your players. That, should immediately alert you to the fact that you are playing a different game.

The varsity head coach where I coached high school football in 1994 and 1995 had field passes to a San Francisco 49ers summer camp practice in 1994. He said it was hard to get much he could use in high school football because the NFL is so pass oriented. "Their whole game is like a seven-on-seven drill," he said. A seven-on-seven drill is a pass defense drill in which you leave out the down linemen. The defensive linebackers and defensive backs oppose the offensive center, quarterback, and eligible receivers.

Pass versus run

The percentage of passes and runs is the main difference between the higher levels of football you may be tempted to imitate and youth football. As you would expect, the NFL has the most pass plays. Here are the pass, completion, and interception percentages for the various levels:

Level	% pass plays	% completion	% intercepted
NFL 1996	54%	57.6%	3.39%
NCAA IA 1995	42%	54.7%	3.77%
NCAA IAA 1995	39%	51.3%	4.27%
NCAA II 1995	39%	50.1%	?
H.S. varsity my area 1996	35%	48.6%*	5.13%*
4 J.V. HS teams '95		31%	8.89%
My '96 freshman team	16%	39%	9.09%

* Tri-County Athletic League (San Francisco Bay Area) passers with 30 or more passes. The **overall** completion percentage including passers with **less** than 30 passes per season would almost certainly be lower.

Do you see a pattern developing here? My experience in youth football is that teams pass once or twice a game at the 8-10-year old level, out of a total of about 40 plays. So that's 5% passing at that level. You can draw a rough continuum.

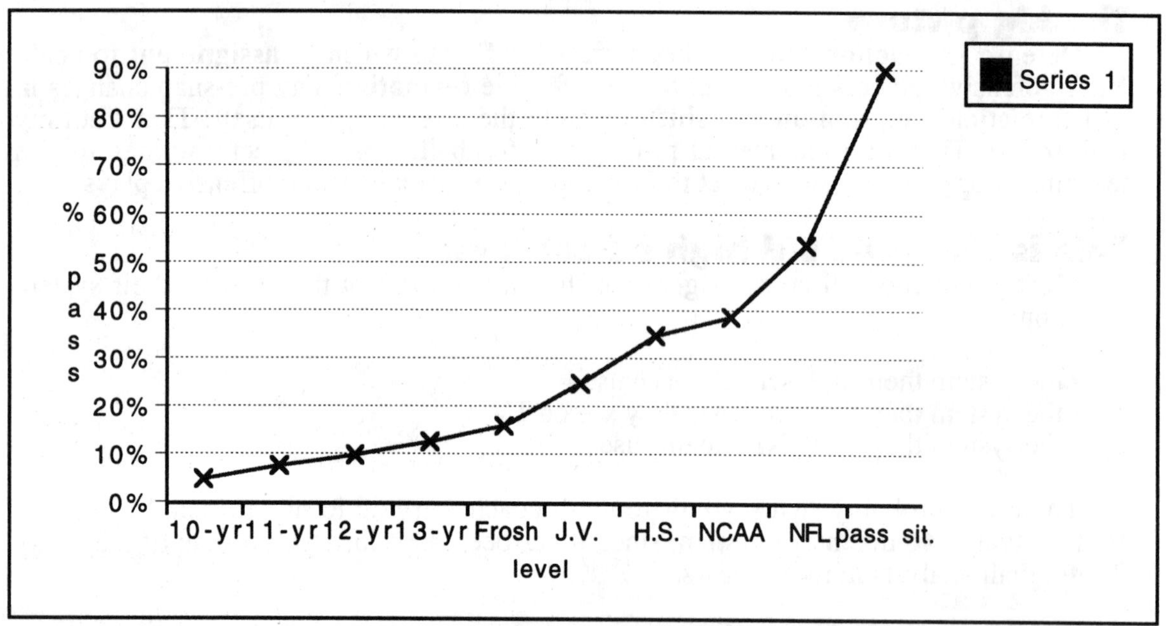

The most common defense in high school is a 5-3. Many high school teams run a 4-4, but they almost always send at least one of the linebackers, which results in a five-man rush. College teams love the 4-3. NFL teams often rush three men, as few as two in sure passing situations.

Do you see a pattern developing here? The lower the threat of passing, and therefore the greater the run threat, the more players the defense rushes—**at the levels where the coaches are competent**. This pattern is so consistent that you can state it as a rough algebraic formula:

The number of rushers = 10(the percentage of running plays)^2.

So in the NCAA where the percentage of running plays is 60%, the formula would be $10 \times .6^2 = 10 \times .36 = 3.6$ rushers. In fact, the 4-3 is the most popular defense in college.

Gap-8 makes sense

If you interpolate to youth football, you should be running a gap-eight, which I did with great success. But the most common defense in youth football is the 5-3. The gap-8 is rarely seen. How come?

Youth coaches are generally incompetent. They run what their local high school runs, or what they ran in high school, or what everybody else runs. Part of it is timidity. Many youth coaches suspect that a gap-8 would work better, but they are afraid to be different. If you run the **same defense as everyone else**, you can **blame the players** when you lose. But if you run an **unusual defense**, like the gap-8, it's the **coach's fault** if it fails, as in, "It can't be our defense. We used the same 5-3 as the league champions."

The league champs in most youth leagues are league champs because they have the best personnel and their coaches are not dumb enough to nullify the effectiveness of those kids. The team with the best personnel can run just about **any** defense and it will work because the speed and athletic ability of the kids will compensate for the stupidity of the scheme. But this book is for the 90% of the coaches who can't win just by putting superior athletes on the field. This book is for coaches who need to **coach** to win.

Stop the run

As you can see, youth football is predominantly a **running** game. At the lowest levels, it is almost **entirely** a running game. Even at the midget (13-14-year olds) level, it's about 80% run. So your defense should be one that is best suited for stopping the **run**.

I am constantly amazed to see youth football defenses arrayed on the field as if they were playing the Buffalo Bills and it was third and long. If you're using the "nickel" (five defensive backs) or "dime" (six defensive backs) defense in youth football, you're probably watching too much TV.

'Just like your defense, coach'

I suspect that there are thousands of youth coaches who are using a defense that mimics some higher level team they admire. For example, they might be running Buddy Ryan's 46 defense. Suppose Buddy Ryan were to show up at one of their games, to watch his grandson or some such. I suspect a meeting between Ryan and the youth coach would go something like this:

Youth coach: "Coach Ryan. It's a real honor. I hope you noticed we're running your 46 defense."

Ryan: "That's my 46? No, I didn't recognize it. Besides, why in the heck would you run a 46 in this league? These kids can't pass. You ought to be running a gap-8."

Youth coach: "But Coach Ryan, **you** didn't run a gap-8. We're tying to use the same defense as you used in the NFL."

Ryan: "I understand what you're trying to do. I just don't understand **why**. I used that defense to stop Joe Montana and Jerry Rice. You have a totally different situation here. Look at what you're up against: sweeps and dives. Put 'em in a gap-8 with man coverage."

I hasten to add that Buddy Ryan never said this as far as I know. Furthermore, I cannot be sure what he would say in such a situation. But I suspect that any competent coach would recognize that the almost-all-running game at the youth level warrants a gap-8 defense and that emulating a defense from a higher level, where they face a very different offensive threat, is a bad idea.

Thank God middle-aged men don't coach youth **medical** teams. A youth medical coach who admired Dr. Christiaan Barnard might perform a heart transplant on a kid with a strep throat. Here's how that conversation might go:

Youth medical coach: "Dr. Barnard. It's a real honor. I hope you noticed I performed the heart transplant operation you pioneered."

Dr. Barnard: "That's my procedure. I thought it was a ritual sacrifice. Besides, why in the heck would you perform a heart transplant on a ten-year old boy with no symptoms other than a sore throat? You should just give him antibiotics."

Youth medical coach: "But Dr. Barnard, **you** didn't prescribe antibiotics. I was trying to perform the same procedure you performed on Louis Washkansky in 1967."

Dr. Barnard: "I understand what you're trying to do. I just don't understand **why**. I used that procedure to try to save the life of a terminally-ill patient whose heart could stand no further repair efforts."

High school, college, and pro coaches only take SOME ideas from other levels

Is NFL football different from college football? Yes, somewhat. Are college defenses different from NFL defenses? Yes, somewhat.

It is clear to the average fan that high school, college, and pro football **games** differ from each other. And it is clear to serious fans that each of those levels use different **defenses** from the other levels.

But when you get the **youth** level, which is even **more** different from high school than the higher levels are from each other, you find youth coaches using the **same** defenses as high school, college, and pro teams. There's no way that's anything other than blind imitation of higher level coaches by youth coaches who don't know what they are doing.

It is smart to study other coaches, at all levels, to see what you can learn from them. But before you can learn from other levels, you must first understand the basic principles of football. Once you do, you will not make the mistake of taking a higher level defense whole hog and applying it to a level for which it was not designed or intended.

Goal-line defense

At the higher levels of football, it is almost universally acknowledged that goal-line defense or red-zone defense are different from other defensive situations. The reason is that there is no longer a vertical threat of a deep pass.

Guess what other aspect of football has little or no threat of a deep pass? **Youth** football. There is little or no threat of a deep pass because the kids' arms are not strong enough to throw that far, their practice is too limited to complete the pass, and their pass protection is too inept to permit them that much time.

The first several days of practice I put my players through a series of tests. Among other things, we test their ability to throw the football for distance and accuracy. Here are two of my results so you can see the ranges of youth-football-player arms. These are **first day of practice**. You could expect the range would increase slightly over the season as the player's arm got in shape.

14	40 yards
13	35 yards
12	31 yards
10	27 yards

These ranges are sort of average. Exceptional players can throw farther. I had one 12-year old who could throw 40 yards. These ranges also establish the relatively small semi-circle in which youth football is played. Here's a diagram of a football field showing the 40-yard radius and the 27-yard radius.

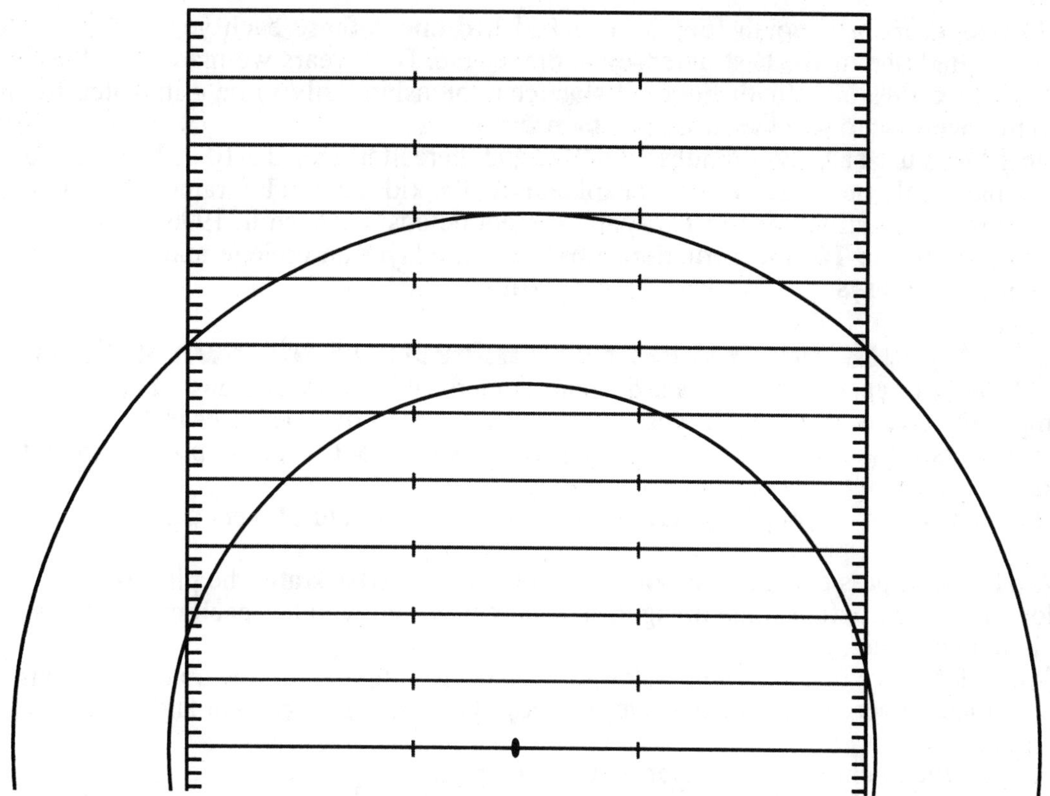

Remember that the line of scrimmage is about five yards in front of where the quarterback sets up to pass. So the maximum range of a 13-year old who can throw 40 yards is really just 35 yards beyond the line of scrimmage; that of a ten-year old who can throw 27 yards, just 22 yards beyond the line of scrimmage. In the above diagram, the coach of a ten-year old team need only defend the inner semi-circle.

This is one of the reasons why I marvel at youth coaches who time their players in the 40-yard dash. (I time them in the 10-yard dash and the 20-yard dash.) Youth quarterbacks generally cannot throw the ball 40 yards. So exactly what game situation is the 40-yard dash measuring? Kickoff coverage ability?

Youth football is short-range football

So not only is youth football largely a running game, it is also generally like goal-line situations at higher levels, no matter **where** the ball is on the field, because of the lack of a deep threat. Every football team at all levels needs a goal-line defense. The difference between youth football and the other levels is that goal-line defense is about the **only** kind youth teams need.

In 1993, I had the second best offense in our league, right behind the state champion. But we had trouble running PATs in. My star tailback, Will Sykes, had 21 touchdowns, but only four PATs. (We had no one who could kick PATs, which count two points in youth football as opposed to one point for a run or pass.) But at the end of the season, we did better because we started running end sweeps and throwing passes for PATs. Fortunately for us, the opposing coaches never figured out that they were able to stop us in general with their **goal-line** defense and that it would work all over the field.

Keep it simple

You must keep your defense as simple as possible. That applies to all levels of football. Virtually all coaches agree with that—at least in words. But actions speak louder than words. And by their **actions**, most coaches love complexity.

In five years as a youth football coach, I had **one** defense each year. In 1991 and 1992, we had one of the best defenses in the league. Both years we made it to the final four in the California Youth Football state championship, only to be eliminated by the team that went on to win the state championship.

In 1991, I used an 8-2-1 defense. In 1992 and thereafter, I used a 10-1. I strongly urge you to have only one defense. I will explain how the kids should be trained to apply that defense to all situations. When I was an assistant defensive coach in 1990, the defensive coordinator put in **16 different defenses**. He had played in college and was probably using his college system. We were 3-7 that year.

Typical youth coach does not understand his own defense

I'll bet the typical youth coach does not understand his own defense. Here's a quiz. Competent coaches can answer these questions about their own defenses instantly. So can their players. Remember, it's not what the coach knows but what the players know that matters.

See if **you** can answer these questions instantly. See if your **players** can.

- Who has man pass coverage responsibility on the quarterback after he pitches?
- How does your defense line up against a stack trips and who has each man in the stack in man coverage?
- If your defensive linemen or outside linebackers are supposed to line up **on** an offensive lineman, under what circumstances do they abandon that alignment and line up in the **gap**?
- Who has the pitchback if the offense runs the option?
- What do your defensive backs do in man coverage if receivers cross?
- What is your linebacker to do if the offensive backfield flow is away from him?

You gotta believe

You and all your coaches and players must **believe in** your defensive system. That starts with **you** believing in it. You must consider all the defenses that make sense. I'll make a strong pitch for my defense in this chapter. But if you still believe another is better, you must use that one and **not** mine.

If you don't understand and believe in the defense that you use, both your coaches and your players will sense that and it will destroy their confidence. If you have strong assistant coaches, you may find one or more that have their own strong beliefs. You must hear them out privately. If they convince you, change, but if not, **they** must change. And you must keep a keen eye out to make sure that they have. They must enthusiastically sell as well as teach **your** defense. If they do anything less, fire them.

I have seen teams where assistant coaches undermined the head coach to the players behind his back and it was very bad. You cannot just **teach** the players your system, You must **sell** them on it. You must convince them that your team has the best defensive system for your team.

Strength against strength

Above, I told you two of the basic principles of football: defense is **reaction** football and offense is **assignment** football. Here are two more crucial principles:

- The basic principle of **offense** is strength against **weakness**.
- The basic principle of **defense** is strength against **strength**.

Offensive coaches probe your defense looking for weak points. They may do it intellectually like coaches assuming my 10-1 is weak against the pass and trying to throw.

Inevitably, they also probe for weakness by trying all their different plays at the beginning of a game and going back to those that worked best.

Take away their best plays

As a defensive coach, you must take away their **best** play **first**. That's another way to state the principle of strength against strength.

In 1993, I had a lousy defense. As far as I can tell, it was because I only had one defensive veteran on the team. Everyone else was a rookie.

In the second game of the season, we were playing the team that eventually won the state championship: Fairfield Suisun. Scouting indicated that their big play was the tailback crashing straight ahead through the right side B (guard-tackle) gap. I told my kids, we must stop that play first. I put my strongest defensive lineman and linebacker there and we **did** stop him. He got nothing all day on that play. After the game, their offensive coordinator Sam Roberson said to me, "Boy, you really shut down my tailback."

Couldn't stop everything

Unfortunately, it was about the only thing we shut down. Our second priority was to stop their **sweep**. We stopped all but one. And our third priority was to stop their **reverse**. My defensive end had to see one reverse go for a touchdown before he understood the importance of trailing a sweep to the other side through the backfield.

I **ignored** the pass because they were two of 11 for 15 yards passing in their previous game and pre-season scrimmage and I had to ignore **something** to muscle up to stop the tailback dive.

Turned out they were the best jr. pee wee passing team I ever saw and they threw two touchdown passes against us that day. (And one interception) The basic problem was they were a state champion team with strength in every category. It's hard to put strength against strength when they have six strengths and you only have two.

Sweep and blast

The two main plays in youth football are the sweep and the blast. Some teams don't have the speed to run the sweep. My San Ramon Bears organization was generally one of those.

In 1993 my tailback, Will Sykes, could turn the corner for big gains. But all other years it looked like the opponents' faster defensive backs simply ignored the sweep until it was underway then sprinted out and tackled our guy for a loss by sheer speed superiority. If you face a team with a back who has the speed to turn the corner before your defense can stop him, that will be the main play you have to stop.

Isolation play

The other highly successful play in youth football is the blast or isolation play. That is simply a dive with one or two lead blockers. I have also seen a similar play, the power off tackle with a lead blocker, succeed in youth football, although not as consistently. Youth teams that lack superior speed—and which have competent coaches—rely on blast or blast-like plays.

In 1990, Vacaville knocked us out of the playoffs and went on to win the state championship. We were amazed to learn that they beat the perennial champion Oakland Dynamites and asked their coaches how. "We never ran outside the tackles," was their answer.

Stalemate until the blast play

I have seen many a youth game where both teams knocked heads scorelessly until one team figured out they could move the ball with the blast play. In 1993, our pee wees were down 6-0 against Napa. At half time, the offensive coordinator said he had no ideas. His assistant said, "I know what to do." They let him try.

He took the two best blocking linemen and but them in the backfield in a power I. My son, Dan, was the tailback. They then proceeded to run the tailback blast right and left over and over. We gained 6, 8, 10 yards a carry. The Napa public address announcer referred to my son as "The workhorse" after yet another big gain. Dan scored the tying touchdown on a 25-yard blast play and was taken out to rest. The extra point run failed.

Napa adjusted

When we got the ball back, they again ran the blast to my son over and over. Now the Napa players began to adjust and the gains were held to three and four yards. But they were overplaying the blast. I was on the sideline and suggested to the assistant offensive coordinator that it was time to **fake** a blast to my son and throw a pass. He said, "That's exactly what I just sent in." The quarterback faked the blast hand-off and threw a slant pass to the tight end on the back side of the play. Touchdown. We won, 12-6.

The following year, our pee wees played the Fairfield Falcons in the playoffs. We scored easily on the third play of the game. But we couldn't score anymore. We tried to kick the PAT and failed. (I was not a coach on that team.)

Another team discovers the blast

In the second half, Fairfield discovered the blast and began to move the ball methodically down the field. They actually scored on a throwback pass but should have, and could have, stuck with the blast. They got the game winning extra point with a quick-count blast play.

In a midget game I scouted in 1993 at Los Medanos College, both teams knocked heads without scoring for the first half. In the second half, one team discovered the blast and rolled methodically down the field to score the winning touchdown.

In 1991, when I was defensive coordinator for the first time, we held the defending state champ Vacaville team to no first downs and beat them 6-0. Vacaville was a double-tight-end, full-house-T, run-between-the-tackles team. We stopped them because I had many good players that year and because my defense is geared mainly to stop the sweep and blast play.

Slant or look-in passes

I generally do not fear the pass much at all in youth football. We **wanted** the other team to pass because we intercepted about half of them. But when I worry about the pass in youth football, one pass I worry about is the slant or look-in pass. It looks like this.

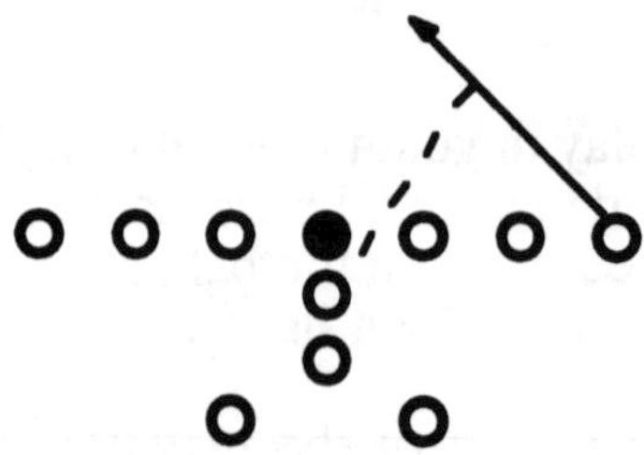

In 1990, when I was assistant defensive coach, the Tri-Cities Cowboys beat us with three slant passes, all of which went for touchdowns. Their right tight end slanted at a 45-degree angle to the middle of the field and their quarterback threw to him instantly from a one-step drop. Our normal safety had a fever at game time and had been replaced by a nine-year old second stringer.

'Fool me twice'

Fortunately, we got to play Tri-Cities a **second** time that year. The defensive coordinator was away on business that week and I took his place. We practiced stopping that slant pass over and over. I put my best player on that receiver and put my tallest linemen at defensive guard. The line had instructions to raise up with their hands high at the slightest hint of a pass. Tri-Cities only completed one pass in that second game, to another receiver, for little gain. We won three touchdowns to one.

In the above-mentioned 1993 win over Napa, we did it with a slant pass.

Dynamites discover the slant pass

In 1994, I scouted the Oakland Dynamites-Vallejo Generals pee wee playoff game. It was even until Oakland discovered the slant pass. They threw it again and again ultimately scoring the winning touchdown. We were eliminated the next day so I did not get to see if we could have stopped them. (Although I think it's an easy play to stop.) The Dynamites went on to win the state championship that year.

My defense is designed to stop the best plays

My 10-1 defense is designed to stop the slant. There is a large pass rush of at least six guys. The receivers are being blocked as they try to release. And I have a middle linebacker standing about where the tight end would like to catch the pass.

The years I had my best defenses, slant passes were just about the only ones completed against us. But they went for little or no gain.

Halfback passes

The other youth football play I fear is the halfback pass. That's where the ball is handed off or pitched to a running back who starts to run then pulls up and throws deep.

The defensive backs tend to abandon pass defense once the ball is handed off or pitched. I call that the **"one-exchange" mentality**—the subconscious notion that there can only be only one hand-off, pitch, or pass per play. There can be two or more.

Lob to wide open guy

In the halfback pass, the receiver is typically wide open and the back just throws it high so the receiver can run under it.

Oakland completed a half back pass for a touchdown against us in 1991. My son was the defensive back who decided it was a run and came up leaving his man wide open in the end zone.

His 1994 midget team executed a halfback pass perfectly to a wide open receiver in a game against the eventual league champion. Unfortunately, the receiver (not my son) dropped the ball.

'See it enough times'

In his book, Game *Plan to Winning Football*, Gordon Wood says, "A defense can stop any play, if it sees it enough times in practice." Wood is the winningest coach in Texas high school football history.

The key to stopping the halfback pass is to have your scout team run it over and over in practice so your defensive backs get into the habit of considering all apparent running plays to be halfback passes **until the ball crosses the line of scrimmage.** Youth football players, especially halfbacks who get little passing practice, tend to always throw regardless of whether the receiver is covered. So a defensive secondary that stays home on a halfback pass can have a field day intercepting those lobs.

Stunts

Most coaches want to be aggressive. When defensive coaches think of aggression, they think of **blitzing**. In fact, blitzing is very problematic in youth football.

The problem is narrow line splits. In high school and higher levels, the line splits are two to three feet. A linebacker can blitz through those gaps. But in youth football, the line splits are from zero to about eight inches. You can**not** blitz through those gaps. We used zero splits in 1993. The eventual state champion team tried to blitz against us. Their blitzer just disappeared into the mob at the line of scrimmage. He never got into our backfield.

OK if big splits

Sometimes, you run into a youth team that has line splits of one foot or more. Berkeley had one-foot line splits in our league once. When we had our scout team take those splits, our defense got wide-eyed. "Do they really get that far apart?" they asked. "That's what the scouting report indicated," we told them. Berkeley did, indeed, split that wide and our line had a field day.

I use a gap-charging defense so, in a sense, I blitz everybody on every play. But that's not really the definition of a blitz, which is an intermittent stunt. I recommend that you **not** blitz unless you know before the snap that a ball carrier will be at a particular spot **outside the tackles.**

For example, when I scouted Elk Grove in 1992, I noticed that every time they lined up in a slot, the quarterback rolled out to where the slot was and threw a pass. I told my safety to blitz to that spot whenever they came out in a slot. In the event, he forgot. Had he done it, he almost certainly would have sacked the quarterback.

Formations, shifts, and motion

Whatever defense you choose, it must have rules for how to line up versus all the formations the offense might show. Furthermore, the players must know how to apply those rules to shifts and motion.

You cannot stubbornly line up a particular way every time regardless of how the offense lines up. For example, my 1993 offense had a flanker out wide to the side where our bench was. We had a standing rule that the tailback would immediately throw a pass to the flanker if the defense did not cover him. That happened in games and we completed the pass and gained yards. We would have thrown it sixty times in a row if they had never covered that flanker.

Less likely to adjust to lack of balance

There are more subtle things. Most youth teams put someone out on a wide receiver. Lou Holtz says if you flank out a wide receiver with no arms the defense will cover him. But they are less likely to adjust properly to things like an **unbalanced line** or a **strong** (unbalanced) backfield.

We did both in 1993. We had a four-two unbalanced line, that is, two guys on one side of the center and four on the other. We also had three running backs in the backfield, all on the side where the four linemen were. That gave us eight guys on one side of the ball, two guys on the other, and one flanker out wide to whichever of those sides was our bench.

Outnumbered them

The defense would typically line up in a balanced formation with five and a half guys on each side of the ball. So we had them outnumbered 8 to 5.5 on our long side. Furthermore, our guys were concentrated in a small area with zero splits. The defense was typically spread out horizontally and vertically. They did not adjust properly to our offensive alignment. As a result, we were able to overpower them at the point of attack.

Shifts and motion are simply changes in formation. You must change with them for the same reason you must line up with proper respect for the strength of the offensive formation to begin with.

'It worked in the video game'

Here's a story that could only have happened in the nineties. One guy who called to order my defense book told me he was already running the gap-8 with great success. He said he switched to the gap-8 for his youth team because it worked so well in a video game he played with his son. According to the caller, the Sega Genesis game *College Football National Championship I* has a defense called the "Bear Defense" which is a gap-8. Whenever his son ran that defense against him, he could not run the ball.

Learn basic defensive theory

For starters, I believe you must learn basic football defensive theory. I get highly annoyed at post-game pizza party discussions talking about football fundamentals. Most youth coaches feel they know all they need to know from just being TV football fans and former high school players.

In fact, most youth football coaches literally do not know the first thing about defense. When I became a high school coach, I was surprised at the many basic principles I did not understand. In high school, if you used an unsound defense, the opposing coach would almost always see it and recognize its weakness and immediately try to call appropriate plays to exploit that weakness. Youth coaches, on the other hand, would look at the defense all night and not recognize either the weakness or the way to exploit it. And if they recognized a weakness and knew how to exploit it, they probably would not have the ability to exploit it because of lack of the necessary plays or lack of the ability to execute them.

Please read at least one basic book on defensive theory. The best one I've seen—and it covers offense and special teams as well—is *Football: the Violent Chess Match* by Tom Flores and Bob O'Connor. It was published by Master Press in 1994. I met the publisher at the Chicago booksellers convention in 1997 and commented on what a great book that was. He expressed surprise and said it was out of print for lack of sales. So you'll have to get it by interlibrary search.

Two other books that I recommend would be Fritz Shurmur's *Coaching Team Defense* (1994 Harding Press) and Bud Wilkinson's *Football Winning Defense* (1987 Time, Inc.). These are all generic defense books that do not push a particular defense.

You really need 17 guys to play defense.

In *Football, the Violent Chess Match*, Tom Flores says,

> *With equal material a team should be able to stop the eleven with 17 men. If the defense ran a gap eight alignment to stop the run and had defenders in all six short zones and in all three deep passing zones, the offense would me hard pressed to move the ball.*

Notice the phrase, "If the defense ran a gap eight alignment to stop the run..." Coach Flores, who spent 33 seasons in the NFL and won five Super Bowl rings as a player, assistant coach, and head coach, is taking it for granted that the gap-8 stops the run. It sure does. But I have a heck of a time convincing youth coaches. They are all worried that someone will break through that thin line. Here's a diagram of Flores' hypothetical 17-man zone defense:

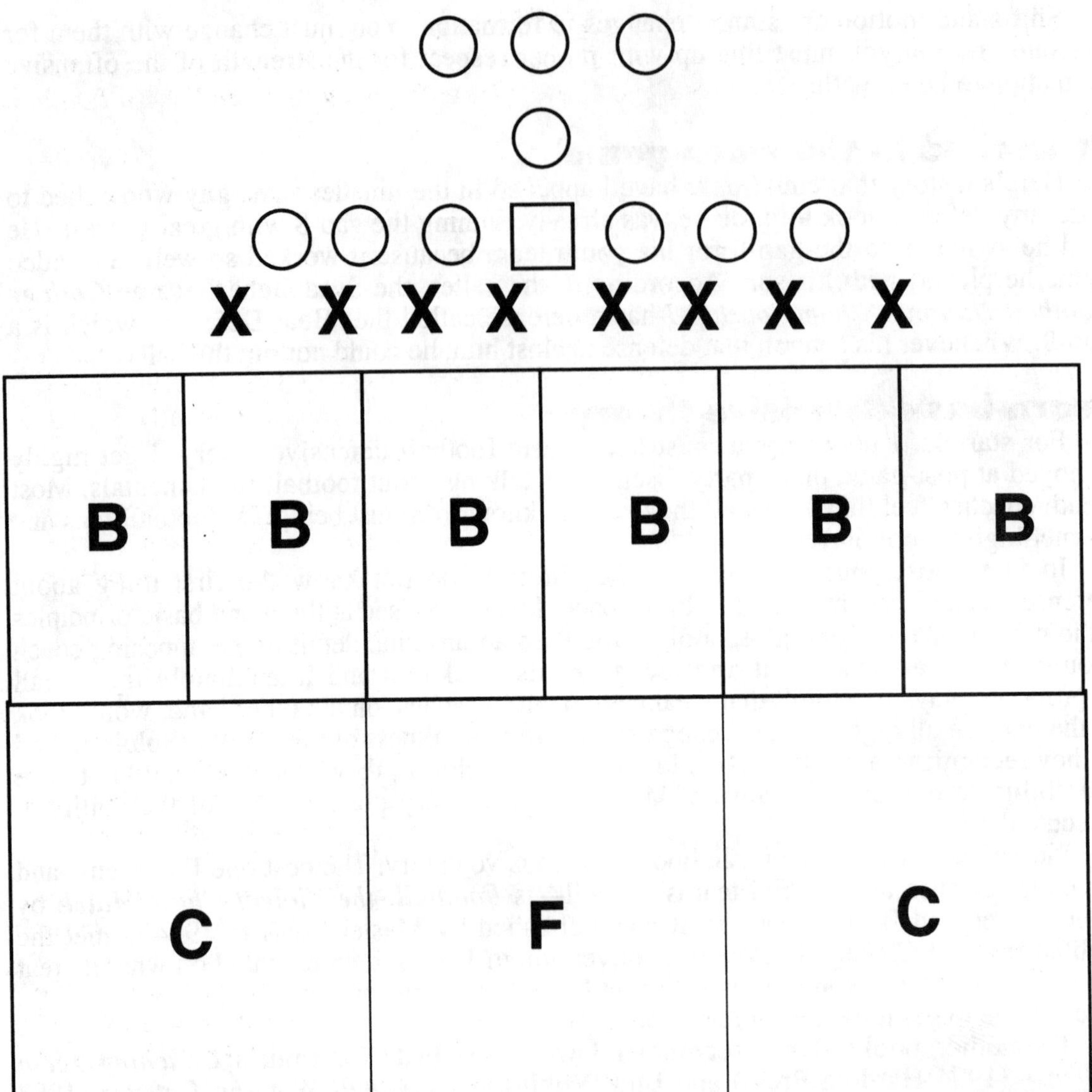

Of course, the rules prevent the defense from having 17 men on the field. So the defensive coordinator has to decide **which six to remove**. In youth football, I think it's obvious that you remove the six linebackers and switch to a man pass defense rather than zone.

College and NFL football defensive coordinators have a less obvious decision because of all the passes at their level. They generally remove the players that are less needed for the **down-and-distance** situation in question. For example, they tend to put in more pass coverage guys in passing situations—actually, it's not the situation but the report of the opponent's down-and-distance **tendencies**.

The tricky part of college and pro defense is trying to **conceal** which of the 17 defenders has been removed. That's why you hear TV announcers talking about **disguising coverages**.

In youth football, you do **not** need to disguise coverages because the opposing offenses are not capable of exploiting defensive pass coverage weaknesses.

What the gap-8 does to the offense

You just read what Tom Flores said about the gap-8. Here are some other comments on the gap-8 from the book *The Smorgasbord Offense for Winning High School Football* by Joe Blount:

Page 107: *There are certain plays that we will not run at a gap-8 defense. For instance, we will not use a play that necessitates a pulling guard.*
Page 136: *It is not a good idea to run 'power' at a gap-8 defense.*
Page 153: *The majority of the time we will bypass the 2-hole when the defense is gap-8.*

One of the principles of war is the **initiative**. although defense in football is reactive in nature, some defenses take more initiative than others. The gap-8 defense, because it is so aggressive, takes much of the initiative away from the offense. Specifically, it has, or should have, the following effects:

Effect	Reason
• Forces the offense to narrow its line splits	Defenders in middle of gaps
• Discourages pulling	A pull lets **two** guys penetrate
• Discourages trapping	No pulling = no trapping
• Eliminates double-team block unless option	Defender for every lineman
• Eliminates running between the tight ends	Defender in every gap
• Generally forces the offense to down block only	Standard response to gap
• Forces the offense to try to sweep or pass	Inside running lanes clogged
• Renders fakes or counters irrelevant	No linebackers are keying
• Prevents releasing more than two receivers	QB + 2 receivers leaves 8 blockers
• Prevents use of the hot pass	plugging prevents fast release

I say "should have" because in youth football, opposing offensive coaches almost never recognize that they have to stop running inside or that they should not bother with fakes against the gap-8.

One year when we played the Manteca Delta Rebels at their field, you can hear their father on the audio of our videotape yelling out sarcastically to their team's head coach, "Quit running up the middle, coach. It's locked tight. Shut down. Hermetically sealed." He had run numerous zero-gain dives against the middle of our gap-8.

Picking a particular defense

Once you have a basic understanding of football defensive theory, you should pick a particular defense. Note that I said **pick, not create**.

I enjoy brainstorming new defenses and offenses as much as the next guy. But I do **not** have my team use some cockamamie defense that **I** dreamed up. I only use **proven** defenses that have been created and tested over decades by successful coaches.

Goal-line run defense

I strongly recommend that you pick a defense that is designed for **goal-line** situations and is biased toward stopping the **run** rather than the pass. I urge you to pick only **one** defense. I will explain my gap-8 and 10-1 in the pages that follow. Partly I want to sell you on those defenses. But I also want to show how you set up a defense in general.

'It's been sung'

Judy Garland's daughter, Liza Minelli, was once asked to sing *Somewhere Over the Rainbow*. She declined saying, "It's been sung."

I say they same thing about football defenses. The world does not need some crackpot youth football coach designing a defense. Defenses have already been designed. Not only designed, but tested, retested, and tested again, over decades of play at the most competitive levels. The notion that a youth football coach, with virtually no training or experience, can come up with a defense that is superior to the defenses designed by Knute Rockne, Vince Lombardi, Bear Bryant, and so forth, is absurd.

Pick one

Pick one from among those that have already been invented and proven. Hundreds of books have been written about defenses. Here is a list of many of the defense books I have read. If you see one with a title that interests you, have your librarian or a book-finding service get a copy then adopt a **pared-down version** of the defense. The defenses in the books are written for high school and higher levels and are therefore too complex for youth football. But it is important that you get a **book** on the defense that you use so you have an integrated, tested version of it. Otherwise, you are reinventing the wheel.

Book	Author	Publisher
Directory of Football Defenses	Drew Tallman	Parker Publishing
Missouri Power Football	Devine & Onofrio	Lucas Brothers
Ara Parseghian and Notre Dame Football	Ara Parseghian	Men-in-Motion
Football Coaching	John McKay	John Wiley&Sons
Multiple Monster Football	Warren K. Washburn	Parker
Modern Football	Fritz Crisler	McGraw-Hill
Vince Lombardi on Football	Vince Lombardi	NY Graphic Soc.
Coaching Football's Split 4-4 Multiple Def.	Pete Dyer	Parker
Building a Championship Football Team	Bear Bryant	Prentice-Hall
Hot Line to Victory	Woody Hayes	Ohio State
Championship Football	D.X. Bible	Prentice-Hall
Football's Fabulous Forty Defense	Jack Olcott	Shane Co.
The Slanting Monster Defense in Football	Dale Foster	Parker
Coaching Football Successfully	Bob Reade	Human Kinetics
Game Plan to Winning Football	Gordon Wood	Summit Group
Football's Super Split Underdog Defense	Bill Siler	Leisure Press
Coaching Team Defense	Fritz Shurmur	Harding Press

The old days

In the early days of football, the game was mostly **running**. Does that sound familiar? Accordingly, I suggest that you look to some of the **older** (pre-1960s) books on football for a 1990s youth football defense. More modern defenses are designed to stop the balanced passing-running game. For example, a defense you don't see much anymore is the seven diamond. It looks like this:

The seven-diamond defense

S

CB CB

ML

OL RT RG N LG LT OL

◐ ◐ ○ ⊠ ○ ◑ ◑

The seven-diamond is rather strong against the run while paying moderate respect to the pass—about what you want in youth football. There is also a seven-box.

The seven-box defense

QB HB

FB HB
OL RT RG N LG LT OL

Note that the names of the backs in the seven-box are the same as the names of an **offensive** full-house T-formation. That's because the seven-box was used back in the one-platoon days before unlimited substitutions were allowed—back in the days when players went **both ways** the whole game.

Old books less helpful

If you want information on the seven-diamond or seven-box, you'll need to find some **old** books. Unfortunately, few books that I am aware of discuss these defenses much. And the old books were written before the modern format of a football book developed. In modern defense books, you generally get the theory of the defense, the kind of player you need at each position, the alignments versus various offensive formations, and the job descriptions of each player against the various initial movements and plays of the offense.

I have a rare book called *Missouri Power Football* which discusses the seven-diamond at some length. I know of **no** book that discusses the seven-box in any detail. Although Bud Wilkinson, in his *Football Winning Defense*, says that his Oklahoma 5-4 was a "logical adjustment from the 7 box." There is plenty of information about the Oklahoma 5-4. I have considered using the Oklahoma 5-4 in youth football because it seems to put two guys against the sweep on each side. Here's the Oklahoma 5-4:

Oklahoma 5-4

S S

CB LB LB CB
RE RT N LT LE

Lots of guys on the line

I favor the 10-1 for youth-football defense. I might favor it for high school. I'd have to try it there and have not yet done so. Let me tell you how I arrived at the conclusion that the 10-1 is best.

In 1990, when I was assistant defensive coach, the defensive coordinator used 16 defenses. His favorite was the "60 read." That featured a six-man line with two linebackers and three defensive backs. The players were to generally hold their position and read the offensive play before springing into action to stop it. We were powerless to stop the sweep with this defense.

Other teams doing better

I noticed some other teams were doing better at stopping the sweep. They had cornerbacks on the line of scrimmage out wide. That put eight men on the line of scrimmage with two linebackers and a safety. I persuaded our defensive coordinator to try it and it had the desired result.

One of his 16 defenses was one he called the "80 Gap." He said it was for goal line and short-yardage situations. It seemed to me that it would work for **everything** we were seeing. After all, no one ignores the pass in goal-line defense. They just worry less about it, which was appropriate for us. Over time, we had more and more experience with the 80 gap and I became more and more convinced it was the way to go in general, not just near the goal line.

The 8-2-1

In 1991, I got my chance. I was named the defensive coordinator. The previous defensive coordinator had moved up to the pee wees. I immediately decided to use the 8-2-1. It looked like this:

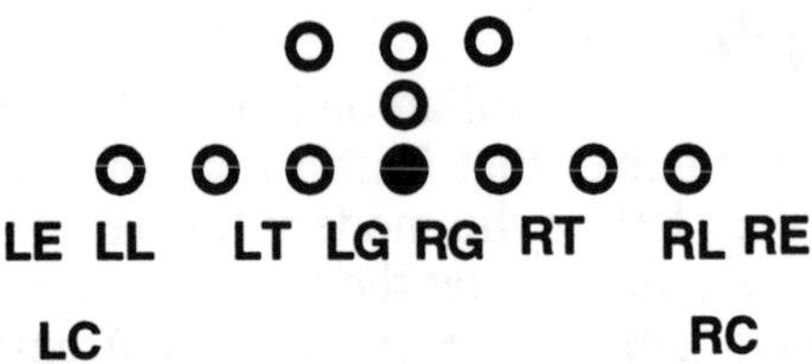

Kent State's idea, not mine

My details on that type of defense came from a magazine article written by an early-seventies Kent State coach, Trevor Rees, who used it everywhere on the field, not just in goal line. (Ironically, the defensive coordinator I coached under in 1990 played football at Kent State.)

I had mentioned my notion that putting as many as **ten** guys on the line would make sense in youth football to Jim Munroe, a San Ramon Bears coach, who had coached 150-pound football at the U.S. Naval Academy. He told me it was not so crazy an idea and offered to send me some articles he had on the subject. In the Kent State article, Rees said they began using the 10-1 only for goal line and short yardage but,

> *...it achieved so much success that we began employing it on any down anywhere on the field.*

In other words, his experience at the college level paralleled mine at the youth level.

Tested version of the defense

From that article, I got an integrated, field-tested version of the defense that I only had a vague notion of. That was crucial. For example, it alerted me to the fact that my linebackers had to plug the offensive tight ends. That means to hold them on the line of scrimmage so they cannot go out for a pass.

The article also said the pass coverage should be **man-to-man**. That's basic football to a high school coach. But most youth coaches do not understand principles like the advantages of using man-to-man pass coverage near the goal line. Man is dangerous at the college and pro levels when there is lots of field because the receivers can break away from the man who's covering them. But in goal-line situations, they cannot go far because they run out of field.

Furthermore, when you load up the line of scrimmage with rushers, you have fewer guys in the secondary to cover the passing zones. Fewer coverage men forces you into man coverage because there are more zones to cover, nine, than there are receivers (five).

The 10-1

In 1992, my second year as a defensive coordinator, I started with the 8-2-1 that had been so successful the year before. (In 1991, we shut out six of our ten opponents, held our opponents to an average of 6.2 points per game, scored 3.2 points per game on defense, and held four opponents to negative yardage.)

But as the 1992 season wore on, we noticed two things: our left side was doing better than our right and our left-side cornerback had moved up to the line of scrimmage on his own initiative. He was one of the 2 in the 8-2-1.

Move the 2 up

Being no dummy, I told the right-side cornerback to do the same. Thus was born the 10-1—at least at the San Ramon Bears jr. pee wee team. As I said above, it was born in similar fashion at Kent State. And, I was to learn later, at a high school in Texas.

Celina, TX High School

In 1994, I received a flyer from football coaching guru Bob Rexrode (1408 N. Ricketts, Sherman, TX 75092). One video advertised had the following description:

> **Excellent pressure defensive video from Texas' winningest active coach**
>
> "The 10-1 even pressure defense" by G.A. Moore $34. The 10-1 is an aggressive, attacking defense that is simple to teach and fun to play. Celina, Texas High School Coach, G.A. Moore, the winningest active coach in Texas (280-62-11, and *Texas Football Magazine's* Coach of the Decade for the 1980s) went to the 10-1 pressure defense 15 years ago. Since that time, the 10-1 has led Moore's teams to a 162-14-2 record and 3 state championships (unscored on in the 3 state championship games). Moore says the 10-1 even pressure defense is a great equalizer which can use average- to below-average-sized personnel. It limits what offensive opponents can do because constant penetration will kill most offenses. It will make other defenses more effective because opponents will have to spend so much time preparing for the 10-1. In Coach Moore's 30 years of coaching, he has coached in schools from A to AAAAA in Texas and has never had a losing season. He loves the 10-1 even pressure because his players can "just lay back their ears and get after it." According to opponents, the 10-1 even is the ultimate penetrating, pressure defense.

I called Coach Moore

When I read that, I called Texas information and asked for the phone number of Celina High School in Celina, Texas. I talked to Coach Moore for about an hour. It turned out he had come to the 10-1 about the same way we did. He was desperate for something that would work, tried a goal-line defense against an opponent they figured they had no hope of stopping anyway, and were surprised to see that it worked.

As I asked Coach Moore how he handled various situations, it became apparent that he had run into the same problems that we did, and that he had solved them in similar fashion. We both recognized the importance of a low line charge. We both plugged the tight ends. And so forth.

I offered to trade my 10-1 book, *Coaching Youth Football Defense*, for his 10-1 video. He agreed and we traded. Turns out that his 10-1 is more complex than mine, which is to be expected since he is at a higher level.

Buddy Ryan's 46 defense

Here's a brief 9/1/97 *Sports Illustrated* description of Buddy Ryan's 46 defense, which has been all the rage for a decade or so.

> *The Chicago Bear' 46 defense, which was at the heart of their 1985 Super Bowl season, was based on six to eight players' rushing the quarterback, who theoretically would be buried before he had time to find a receiver.*

Hmmm. Six to eight rushers. Does that sound familiar? By the way, *Sports Illustrated's* Paul Zimmerman says that the 46 defense was named after Bears strong safety Doug Plank, whose jersey number was 46. I wonder how many coaches who admired Buddy Ryan have lined their team up in a 4-6—four-man line and 6 linebackers—because they thought the 46 stood for the number of players in the first two rows of the defense.

Zimmerman further describes the 46 as

> *...the ultimate in pressure: eight men stacked near the line, every gap covered, incessant blitzing.*

He further said that teams without Ryan's talented players found it was vulnerable to outside runs and that the defensive backs grew tired from playing man the whole game. In youth football playing man is not more tiring than playing zone. Indeed, it may be **less** tiring because coming up from zone coverage to stop the **many** runs in youth football is probably more fatiguing than covering the **occasional** pass route.

Zone blitz

That 9/1/97 article was about the success of the zone blitz in the NFL in recent years. The zone blitz, like my gap-8 and 10-1, sends a lot of guys. But they manage to stay in a zone behind the blitzers because some of the apparent linemen drop back into pass coverage instead of rushing. One NFL lineman said he normally blocks two or three different guys over the course of a game. But against the zone blitzing Steelers, he blocked five or six different guys in one game.

Says Zimmerman of the zone blitz,

> *Again pressure is the main feature, only this time it comes from an intricate blitz package featuring linebackers and defensive backs firing in from all angles, with defenders—sometimes linemen—dropping into zones behind them.*

I do not think the zone blitz would be as effective in youth football as it is in the pros. The pros are trying hard to fool each other. In youth football efforts to fool the opponent are often for naught because the opponent is too dumb to knew how they're supposed to react to begin with. And when you start trying to fool the opponent, you frequently fool yourself. Prime example? Varying the snap count in youth football.

The 'press' defense

The 10/28/96 issue of *Sports Illustrated* contained an article about the "press" defense ("Under Siege"). It's named after the basketball full-court press.

> *...the hottest and most effective weapon in the college game. At its roots the press is a heavily blitzing 4-3 defense with the cornerbacks locked in man-to-man coverage. Most teams using the scheme fill almost every gap by bringing all three linebackers, plus an eighth man, usually a safety, up tight. Five of the top six teams...and seven of the top nine, play some form of the press.*
>
> *The press does two things: First, it denies an opponent a running game by putting at least eight defenders in the "box," an imaginary rectangle on and just off the line of scrimmage. Second, having forced the opponent to throw, it sends in such a horde of blitzers that quarterbacks have no time to exploit the inherent weakness of the press, its dependence on [man] pass coverage.*

Note the phrase "denies an opponent a running game..." In youth football, if you deny an opponent a running game you have generally denied them an offense. Furthermore, I believe youth football players are better at man coverage than they are at zone because it is easier for them to understand. As I say elsewhere in the chapter, I once tried zone defense and abandoned it the same day because my players were so awful at it.

Penn State's Joe Paterno says his team ran the gap-8 in 1968.

My youth football 10-1

Here's a diagram of my 10-1 versus an offense with double tight ends and a full house backfield.

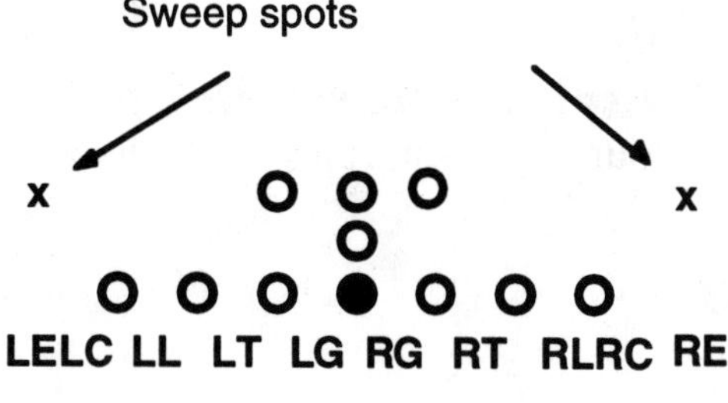

Stances and alignments

The guards and tackles are in **four-point stances** in the middle of the A and B gaps. All other players are in two-point stances.

The four-point stance has the back parallel to the ground, the head up, the toes under the butt, and the hands under the shoulders.

I prefer the hands to form a teepee with the player's weight on his finger tips. The players seem to find that difficult. They prefer to either make a fist or put their palms on the ground. Both the fist and the palm slow the players' movement. The fingers are springier. I suspect the problem is strength. If you insist on the fingers, they should build up the strength over the course of the season.

Middle player, not where ball is

The linemen treat the middle player of the seven offensive linemen as if he were the center regardless of whether he has the ball. That's how you deal with **unbalanced** formations. If your guards always line up one gap from the ball regardless of whether the offensive line is balanced or not, you create a weakness in your defense.

Wideouts

The cornerbacks and linebackers are to line up on their man (1 through 5 as discussed below). With double tight ends and a full house backfield, the 1 and 5 backs line up on the tight ends. If there was a wider receiver, the 1 or 5 back would line up on him.

The defensive ends are to line up one yard outside an end and two yards outside a wingback.

Middle linebacker up close

The middle linebacker or 3 back lines up half way between the widest offensive players. I originally called him a safety and had him eight yards back. But I found he almost never made a tackle when he was that far back.

In 1992, the safety moved up closer to the line on his own. When I noticed, I decided to leave him there because he seemed to be doing well. He led the team in assists that year and was second in tackles. So I recommend that your middle linebacker position himself about three yards behind the defensive guards.

Number your backs

In 1996, I figured out that I should number my defensive backs and linebackers to simplify teaching how to line up against strange formations. The backs are numbered from 1 to 5. 1 and 5 are what I used to call cornerbacks, 2 and 4 are what I used to call linebackers, and 3 is what I used to call the safety or middle linebacker.

The offensive eligible receivers are numbered from the defense's left to right and the defensive back aligns on and has man pass coverage responsibility for his corresponding numbered offensive back. If the offense uses a stack such as a wide receiver stack or an I formation, where players are behind one another, the front most guy gets the lower number.

Alignment against various formations

Here are examples of how our alignment rules would be applied to various formations both common and unusual.

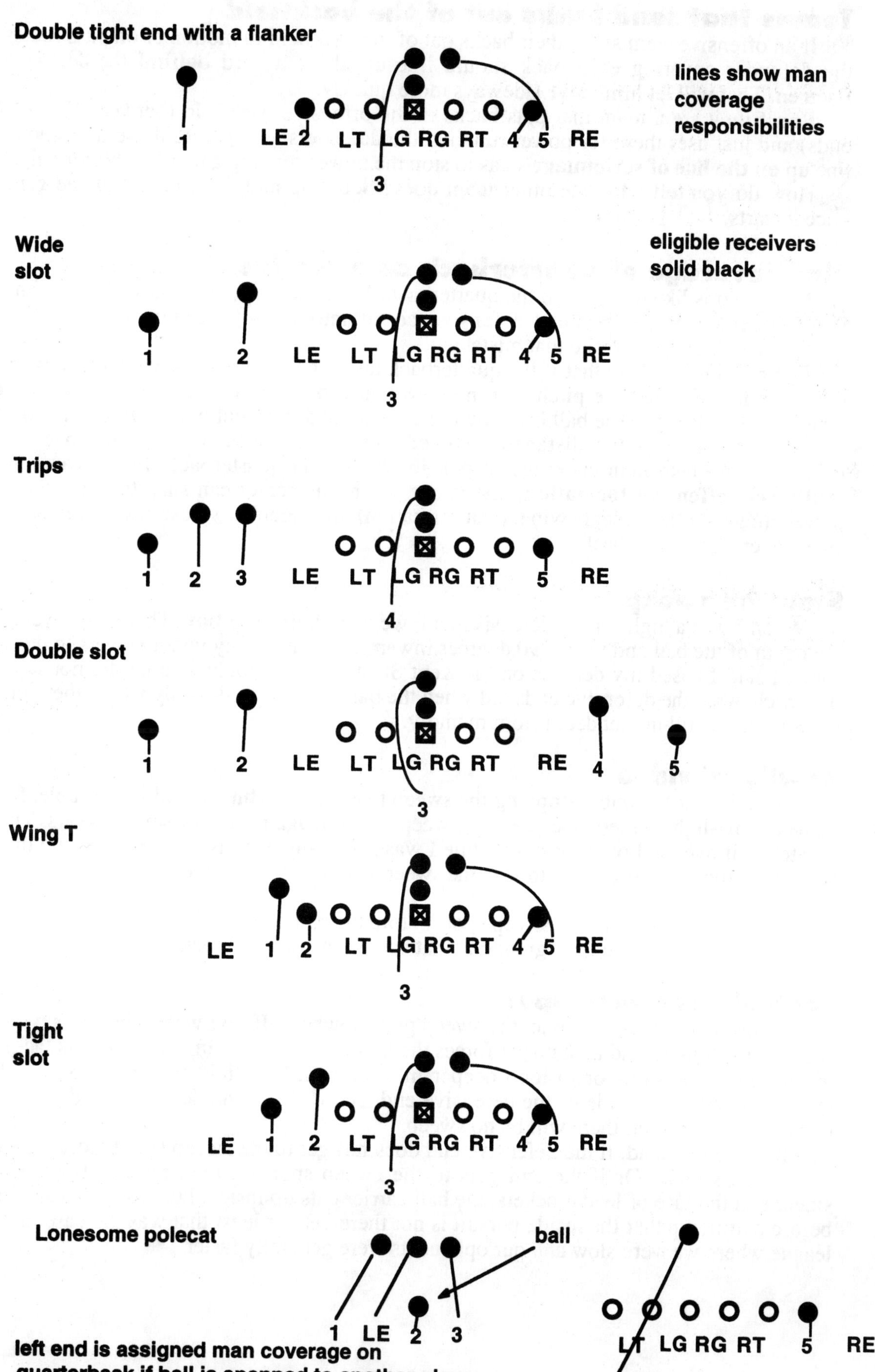
Double tight end with a flanker
lines show man coverage responsibilities
1
LE 2 LT LG RG RT 4 5 RE
3
Wide slot
eligible receivers solid black
1 2 LE LT LG RG RT 4 5 RE
3
Trips
1 2 3 LE LT LG RG RT 5 RE
4
Double slot
1 2 LE LT LG RG RT RE 4 5
3
Wing T
LE 1 2 LT LG RG RT 4 5 RE
3
Tight slot
LE 1 2 LT LG RG RT 4 5 RE
3
Lonesome polecat
ball
1 LE 2 3
left end is assigned man coverage on quarterback if ball is snapped to another player
LT LG RG RT 5 RE
4

Teams that send backs out of the backfield

If an offensive team sends their backs out of the backfield in motion or on pass routes, the defender covering each back should line up about a yard **behind** the defensive linemen. That will let him move sideways more quickly.

But if they are a team that puts backs in the offensive backfield (between the tight ends) and just uses them for power running, the defenders assigned to those men should line up **on the line of scrimmage** so as to stop the power running game for shorter gains.

How do you tell what the other team does? Scouting and the conduct of the game once it starts.

Man coverage of quarterback as a receiver

Many teams like to throw to the quarterback. I like the play, especially if the defense is in **man** coverage, because defensive coordinators rarely assign anyone to the quarterback. Don't you make that mistake.

Our rule in 1996 was that if the quarterback takes the snap under center and **pitches**, the defender who had the pitch man now switches to covering the quarterback. If the quarterback gets rid of the ball by throwing a **backward pass** out wide, switching would not work because of the distance involved. So in that case, we have the backside defensive end take man coverage responsibility for the quarterback. In the case of a **multicycle offensive formation**, that is one where the center can snap to two or more players (e.g., shotgun, single wing, punt formation), the defender whose man received the snap covers the quarterback.

Stop the sweep

When I was a high school defensive end, we were trained to **box**. That is, we went to the depth of the ball and turned 90 degrees inward. So I taught my youth players to do the same. I said I based my defense on the Kent State coach's article. But he did not say in the article what the defensive ends did when the ball was snapped—only where they lined up. So I had to fill in that detail from memory.

'Lowlight' video

We had far less trouble stopping the sweep than before. But we still had trouble. So I made a "low-light" video tape of every sweep ever ran against us for several years. Then I watched it over and over for days while I was riding my exercise bicycle. I found there were two crucial requirements to stop the sweep with the box technique:

- The ends must get to the sweep spots before the ball carrier.
- The ends must hold their ground at that spot in the face of blockers.

Control the sweep spot

If those two things are done, the sweep goes nowhere. If you watch the films, you'll see that a defensive end at that spot forces the ball carrier to turn in where he gets tackled by the inside pursuit—or to loop deeper into his own backfield thereby allowing the pursuit to arrive out wide of the defensive end. Basically, if the defensive end makes a pile at the sweep spot, there will be no sweep.

On the other hand, if the defensive end does **not** get to the sweep spot before the ball carrier, he's gone. Or if the end gets to the sweep spot but then retreats toward the sideline in the face of lead blockers, the ball carrier cuts up inside, but has gotten so wide before cutting up that the inside pursuit is not there yet. At least that was the case in our league where we were slow and our opponents were generally faster.

Or you can be fast

If you have the faster players, it may not matter how you play the sweep. I used to joke that when our slow kids tried to run a sweep, the opposing defensive backfield players would play scissors and rock to see who would have to run over and tackle the kid for a two yard loss.

Wide side

Another thing I learned from the sweep "low-light" tape was that almost all successful sweeps go to the wide side of the field. In other words, if the ball is on the right hash mark, the sweep will be run to the left. So in 1993, I designated my cornerbacks, ends, and linebackers as **wide** or **short** side and **flip-flopped** them. I then put my best three guys on the wide side and my second best on the short side.

Kids A, B, and C (the wide-side three) would always go to the wide side and kids D, E, and F would always go to the short side. When the ball was smack in the **middle**, the wide trio would go to the defensive **left** side on the theory that the offense probably is right-handed and therefore prefers to run to its right. The defensive captain makes the call on which side is wide if the ball is in the middle.

The wide side and short side approach seemed to work much better and I recommend it. My head coach/defensive coordinator on the Granada High School freshman team complained once in 1996 that one of his outside linebackers was doing a good job but the other was not. I recommended designating them wide and short side outside linebackers and flip-flopping them. He did and it worked much better.

The high school approach

In the fall of 1994, I became the defensive coordinator of the Miramonte High School junior varsity football team. Position-wise, I was the outside linebackers and running backs coach. Outside linebackers are the current terminology for what was called the defensive end when I played in high school. The varsity head coach taught me how to train the outside linebackers. He said the boxing technique I used in youth football was **unsound**. In high school, if the outside linebackers box, they are susceptible to cross blocks and trap blocks like these diagrams show:

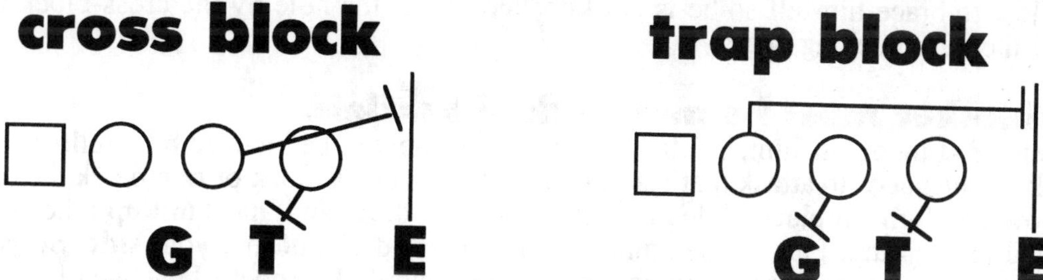

Too vulnerable to off-tackle plays

It is easy for the blocker to run the boxing end out of the picture on an off-tackle play which wants to go between the defensive end and defensive tackle. So the boxing will stop the sweep in both youth football and high school football. But it cannot be used as part of typical high school defenses because it makes you too vulnerable to power off-tackle plays with cross, trap, or kick-out blocks aimed at the outside linebacker (defensive end).

Youth football presents different challenges

I will note that in youth football, I have seen almost no trap blocking or cross blocking. Although Napa did it to our 1994 team. I was not the defensive coordinator. But our ends were boxing. Napa ran a power off-tackle play all day using a sort of trap block by a running back, better known as a kick-out block. In 1993, I had the best offense in our organization's history. One of our best plays that year was an off-tackle play in which an upback or blocking back, instead of a pulling guard, did a trap block.

Here's how the high school varsity head coach taught me to train our outside linebackers.

Outside linebacker training

They line up on the outside shoulder of the tight end on the strong (tight end) side and the tackle on the weak (no tight end) side. If the guy they are lined up on blocks **down**, that is, blocks the next defensive player to the inside of the outside linebacker, the play is an off-tackle play.

The outside backer was to do what I called "Hip and dip." That is, he was to step to his inside at about a 45-degree angle, put his hands on the outside hip of the offensive player who was blocking down, and shove him hard into his own backfield. Then the outside backer was to immediately dip his shoulders low, staying parallel to the line of scrimmage, and brace himself for the block that will soon come from his inside.

Blocking progression

There is a **blocking progression** that you should teach. The blocking progression tells you who is can block you first; who, second; and so forth. The outside backer's blocking progression is:

1. the man he is lined up on
2. the next man to the inside (offensive tackle or guard)
3. the next man inside #2 (offensive guard on the strong side)
4. the near back

If the man he is on blocks down, he steps inside closing the off-tackle hole and getting low to brace himself so he is not knocked out of the hole by the cross-blocking tackle or the trap-blocking guard.

Lead blocker must be met in the backfield

If neither of them hits him, he almost certainly is about to be blocked by a fullback or halfback. So he needs to attack that lead block. With the cross block or trap block, he can dig in low and fight in place. A lead blocker, on the other hand, has built up a head of steam and momentum. Plus he is coming from your inside **front**, not your **side**. So you have to get your own momentum going toward him or you'll be knocked backward.

Hook block

A sweep generally calls for the tight end to **reach** or **hook** block the outside linebacker. That is, the tight end tries to throw his helmet and inside shoulder across the outside linebacker's outside hip.

When our outside linebackers see the tight end's helmet head for their outside hip, they were to put their hands on the tight end's shoulders and extend their arms to a locked-at-the-elbows position. That is, they held the tight end as far away from their body as possible. At the same time, they run sideways along the line of scrimmage staying a step ahead of the ball carrier—running all the way to the sideline if necessary. It is a **cardinal sin** for an outside linebacker to **penetrate** across the line of scrimmage on a sweep to his side—the opposite of the boxing technique, where it is a cardinal sin to **not** penetrate to the sweep spot.

Cannot even be touched

In youth football, I have found that if the defensive end is so much as **touched** by the offensive tight end, he will be taken out of the play. I told my defensive ends that I wanted them to get to the sweep spots **untouched**. They were to line up just far enough from any offensive players to make sure that happened.

Will the high school approach work in youth football? I think it will surely work on the **short** side. It's worth trying on the **wide** side.

In our last pee wee playoff game of 1994, we got eliminated by the Oakland Saints. But they never ran a successful sweep against us. I noticed during the game that our wide-side defensive end was using the high school outside linebacker technique.

I was not the defensive coordinator of that team so I did not tell him what to do. He seemed to figure it out on his own. But it worked during that game. No sweep gained yards. In our experience in youth football, a game, especially a playoff game, where we were not beaten by a sweep was rare. (They beat us with a look-in pass that went about 85 yards, among other things. Our 1994 pee wee defensive coordinator did not use a 10-1 defense.)

Knocked-down 50 versus 10-1

I must also note that all defenses are integrated systems. The outside linebacker techniques described above were for the Miramonte High School defense, which was a knocked-down 50. ("Knocked-down" refers to the fact that the defensive tackle and outside linebacker slide in one gap on the weak or non-tight-end side.) Miramonte had five guys on the front line. With only five guys on the whole front line, the outside linebacker had responsibility for **both** the C (tackle-end) and D (end-sideline) gaps. He had to stay in the vicinity of both gaps to carry out both responsibilities.

In the 10-1, there are **twice** as many guys on the front line so the defensive end has **no** dual responsibility. His job is to stop the sweep, period. The linebackers (and cornerbacks if no wide receivers) stop the off-tackle play.

So the Miramonte outside linebacker technique is not better in all cases. But it most definitely is better than boxing if you are in a five-man front defense. On the other hand, if your wide-side defensive end can handle the sweep using the slide-along-the-line-of-scrimmage technique, it gives you added strength for stopping the off-tackle play, which is potent at **all** levels of football.

Stop the reverse

In 1990, we played Vacaville in the playoffs. The first half ended with the score 0-0. We had won the half in terms of field position because we had the better punting game. In the second half, more of the same, until Vacaville ran a reverse. It went 60 yards for a touchdown. They did it again later in the second half with the same result. I had put a **new guy** at defensive end. I trained him to pursue sweeps that went away from him through the enemy backfield. He peeled back on a deep pursuit angle instead. Vacaville went on to win the state championship two games later.

Defensive ends **must** be trained to trail sweeps that go away from them through the backfield at the depth of the deepest offensive player.

An alternative technique is to just stay at their starting point until the ball crosses the line of scrimmage. Staying at their starting point is a better technique if the opponent has an **inside**-handoff reverse. An inside handoff means the running back receiving the handoff, usually a wing, is between the quarterback and the line of scrimmage so the quarterback is handing the ball **toward** the line of scrimmage. If the backside defensive end penetrates several yards, he will be too deep to stop the inside-handoff reverse.

All other defensive players must take backward pursuit angles. Here's a diagram of a sweep to the offense's right showing the proper pursuit angles including the backside (away from the way the ball is going) defensive end's path of going to the depth of the deepest offensive player and trailing the play through the offensive backfield.

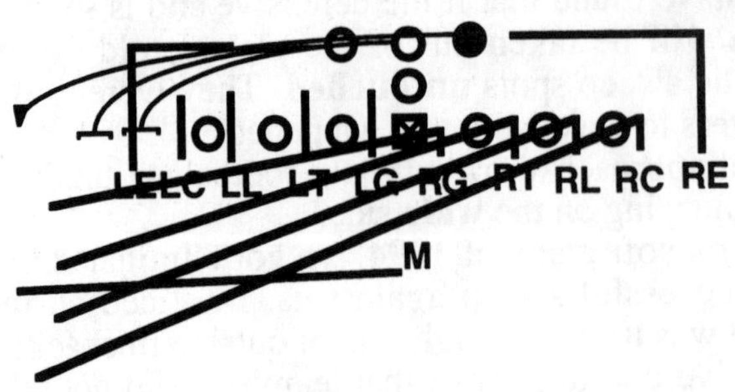

Note that the right end in this diagram goes to the depth of the deepest offensive player then trails the play through the backfield. Our defensive ends were so well drilled on this point, the 1990 playoff end being the one exception, that I loved to see opposing offenses run reverses. We generally threw them for a five- to seven-yard loss. I also found that most **new** defensive ends have to get burned at least **once** before they take the anti-reverse training to heart.

Skill sprints

We had great sweep pursuit with a couple of exceptions when I was defensive coordinator. The reason was one simple drill we did about once a week. Our team was running wind sprints at the end of practices. Some coaches call them gassers. I hate them. The players hate them more. Because they hate them, the players usually loaf *en masse*. That disturbs me profoundly.

To make the gassers more interesting, I asked the head coach if we could do what I called "Skill Sprints" instead. These were actual running efforts that players could expect to make in a game. The drills were run so that they were conditioning drills. But they were also designed to teach the kids the correct route to take and to inculcate in them the habit of reacting instantly and correctly to the situation and of going full speed.

Coach ball carrier

It was me, the coach, versus the entire defense. Another coach did the same thing behind me going the opposite direction with the second-string defense. I would hold the ball as if I were the opposing quarterback, simulate receiving a snap, and retreat to either a sweep, reverse, or drop-back pass. As I did, I yelled the word the players were supposed to yell, namely, "Sweep!" "Reverse!" or "Pass!" over and over.

In the case of a reverse, I would yell "Sweep!" at the outset of the play then yell "Reverse!" when I changed direction. Every player on the defense was required to touch me with two hands. Once the play got under way, I would yell "Full Speed! Full speed!" at the pursuing players. We rarely had a loafer. Anyone who did would be sent over to the second-string side or made to run the drill over all by himself. Plus each player was required to touch the coach so any lack of speed had to be made up as greater distance to run. In all, our players did not loaf either in he drill on in games.

You can also do skill sprints with kickoff and punt return teams.

Watch the cutback

I now believe that drill should be done with **two** ball carriers: one to run the sweep and one to cut back. In our 1992 semi-final playoff game against the Fairfield Falcons, they ran a sweep. Our pursuit was textbook. No one loafing. No one lagging. Our entire team ended up aligned in front of the sweeper down the sideline he had headed to, except, of course, for the backside defensive end who was trailing the play through the backfield in case of a reverse.

So diligent and fast were our pursuers, that they overran the ball carrier and he cut back against the grain and went untouched for about a 60-yard touchdown. You have to designate **some** of your pursuers, like the backside tackle and cornerback, to protect against the cutback by staying a step or two **behind** the ball carrier.

Everyone was containing outside-in. No one was pursuing inside-out. You must assign some players to each of those responsibilities.

In the two-ball version of this drill, the outside-in guys would be required to two-hand touch the sweeper and the inside-out guys would be required to two-hand touch the cut-backer.

Pass pursuit

I also did this drill with a drop-back pass. In that case, everyone had to rush with their hands high, then, when I threw the pass, I would yell, "Air!" and everyone had to run full speed to the ball and touch it.

Stopping runs between the tackles

I have good news and bad news for you. The **good** news is that you can use even your **weakest players** on the defensive line at guard or tackle and no one will be able to run the ball through there—even your minimum-play players.

The **bad** news is that you will get killed between the tackles if you do not discipline those players to **stay low**. In fact, you must require them to keep their hands on the ground until they are in the opponent's backfield.

I have had one player in most years who could be trusted to not get blocked out of the hole even though his hands were not on the ground during his charge across the line of scrimmage. But the vast majority of kids will, if you let them, stand up as soon as the ball is snapped so they can look around and see what's going on. If you let them do that, they will get blocked out of the hole and the opponent will have no trouble running between the tackles against you.

'The Drill'

To teach this, and more importantly, to make it an ironclad habit, we did a daily drill named, "The Drill," by our 1992 head coach. We simply had the defensive down linemen, guards and tackles, go one against two like this diagram:

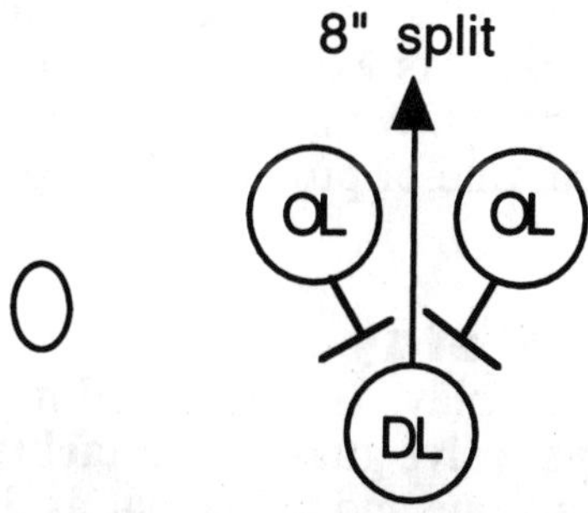

A coach starts the drill by calling the cadence of the upcoming opponent and moving the ball. The defensive lineman is in a four-point stance (both hands on the ground). The offensive linemen are in three-point stances (the standard football stance with one hand on the ground and the other on the thigh or held in front).

The defensive lineman explodes forward on all fours on ball movement. The offensive lineman, who are being played **by** defensive linemen generally, try to double-team block the defensive lineman out of the gap either backwards or to either side.

Stalemate OK if it's in the gap

We do not mind if the defensive lineman is stalemated in the gap. In fact, that's the usual result. But if he gets pushed **back** or **sideways**, we insist that he do it over correctly, that is, that he keep his shoulders lower than the shoulders of the offensive linemen. We did this ten minutes a day every practice. If the defensive player is stalemated in the gap, he has done his job. No dive or blast or any other kind of play can get through there.

One exception may be the very lightest players allowed in your league. Players who weigh 60% more and who are quick can move out even a low ultralightweight.

If you **insist** that they do it right, they learn that the only way to avoid being moved out of the gap they are defending is to stay low. We also drilled them occasionally by having them do their gap charge on air, that is, against no opposition. In that drill, they have to keep their hands on the ground and they scramble two yards forward.

Like aeronautical engineering

In automotive engineering, if a car you design has its fender fall off, you are embarrassed. But in aeronautical engineering, if a plane you design has its wing fall off, that's a disaster.

The gap-8 and 10-1 defenses are like aeronautical engineering. All defensive coordinators tell their linemen to stay low. But the kids don't like to stay low so they largely ignore the coach. Fortunately for the coach, he's using a 5-3 defense so the three linebackers can clean up the mess caused by the sloppy technique the coach tolerates on the front line.

When you go to a gap-8 or 10-1, you are forced to **coach** the defensive line. You have to do what you were supposed to do to begin with, teach a correct technique then insist that it be executed that way. On my defenses, our insistence that the linemen stay low is hammered into them nightly and we keep a chart in games that instantly tells us if a defensive lineman stood up.

Point-of-attack success chart shows it works

In games, this worked. I keep a point-of-attack success chart during games. I chart every play by drawing a line at the point of attack showing how many yards the other team gained. In one game, against Vallejo in 1992, the chart showed several five- or six-yard gains up the middle against us. That was extremely unusual.

We watched the down linemen. As expected, we found that two new guys were standing up when the ball was snapped. We immediately replaced them with two veterans whom we knew did **not** stand up. End of problem. We went on to defeat the previously undefeated Vallejo Generals 13-6.

Stops the blast—IF they stay low

I said I was scared of the blast play. So I designed my defense to stop it. The 10-1 stops it cold—**as long as your defensive guards and tackles do not stand up**.

I sometimes refer to this technique and alignment as the "Coffee Table" defense. If the defensive guards and tackles stay on all fours, they are like four coffee tables. It's tough to run through coffee tables.

During the 1994 season, when I was special teams coach only, our defensive linemen frequently stood up, with the predictable result. I used to observe that it we could shoot them with tranquilizer darts just as the ball was snapped, we'd be better off. Instead of standing up, they would then slump down on all fours, thereby clogging their gaps.

So good it's illegal in some leagues

I'll give you one more piece of evidence that the low gap charge by the defensive linemen is highly effective. Many youth coaches who called after my book, *Coaching Youth Football Defense*, came out, told me that it was **illegal** in their league for defensive linemen to line up in the gap. I smiled when I heard that because my local Little League has been outlawing tactics of mine and my son's for years.

When my son, Dan, played tee ball, he figured out that he should just keep running all the way around to home on every hit. He ignored the adult coaches, including me, telling him to hold up, because he correctly figured out that his opponents were very unlikely to make a good throw and tag. Runners in our tee ball league are now artificially sent back to the last base whenever the ball reaches the infield.

Another manager in our Little League had his kids master stealing home. They got so good, the league outlawed stealing home unless a throw was made to a base to try to make a play on a runner.

When I became a manager at higher levels, I made extensive use of first-and-third double-steal plays. They use the runner at first to draw a throw so the runner at third can steal home. Our batters were told never to stop at first base on a walk if there was a runner at third, even with two outs. And they were drilled in the proper way to execute the play. The next year when I moved up to another level, they outlawed stealing second on a walk at the lower level.

The football rules against more than one guy being it motion at the snap and requiring everyone to get set for one second before the snap were passed to stop Knute Rockne's Notre Dame shift.

Gap-8 and 10-1 defenses and blitzing are often illegal in pre-season and all-star games at all four level- of football (youth to pro).

Stopping the pass

Most people scoff at my gap-8 and 10-1 as being absurdly vulnerable to the pass. Baloney.

In 1992, we played the Delta Rebels twice. The first time, we ran the 10-1 and beat them 19-0. They threw one pass as I recall. Then we met them again in the playoffs. They had apparently studied their video of the first game and decided, "No wonder we couldn't run the ball against San Ramon. They have ten guys on the line and the eleventh right behind the line. They're giving up the pass."

So in the second game, they called six pass plays.

One was incomplete. And that was the highlight of their passing game that day. We intercepted four passes and knocked one out of the quarterback's hands as he was getting ready to throw. We then picked that ball up and ran it in for a touchdown.

We won the second Delta Rebels game 26-0, in spite of our star running back being sidelined with a cracked rib. Vacaville was there to scout us and offered the comment, "You guys are as good as they say you are," in the snack bar line afterwards. We beat Vacaville 26-0 the following week.

I must add that as recently as two years before that, our Bears teams were the doormats of the league.

Three ways to stop the pass

There are three ways to stop the pass:

- sack or interfere with the quarterback
- prevent the receivers from going out for a pass
- cover the receivers closely enough to intercept or bat down any passes to them.

The gap-8 and 10-1 are biased in favor of the first two. But, of course, all defenses try to do all three. I have four down linemen coming between the tackles. They are trained to scramble into the backfield on all fours. But once they clear the offensive linemen, they are to rush a passer with their hands high (if they can see his eyes). The hands are raised high mainly to obscure the quarterback's vision and to force him to throw at a high angle. They are **not** held high to deflect the pass, because the quarterback is presumed to be smart enough not to throw the ball into someone's hand.

Stay on the ground

They are trained **not** to leave their feet trying to bat the ball unless they are sure the ball has left the passer's hand. We try to pump fake them up into the air, both to show them why you must not leave your feet during a pass rush and to train them to ignore the pump fakes.

The defensive ends are also rushing. They must do a **contain** rush. That is, they box as normal to stop the sweep, then they rush the passer from the side so he cannot scramble out and run around end.

Broken play must be stopped

One of the best plays in youth football is the broken play. A scrambling quarterback is a prime example. The defensive end should rush with his hands high if he can see the quarterback's eyes and should not leave the ground to bat a ball unless he is sure it has left the quarterback's hand.

You might also rush a linebacker or cornerback, if he has no quick receiver to cover. A quick receiver is a receiver who is on or within a yard of the line of scrimmage. backs in the backfield are receivers but they are not "quick" receivers if they are between the tight end positions. That's a lot of pass rush, six to eight guys, especially for youth football players who are generally not good pass blockers or poised pocket passers.

Plug the tight ends

Defenders assigned to cover tight ends should bump them That is, they hit the receiver as soon as the ball is snapped trying to stop him from releasing. They hit him again and again, driving him back or to the sideline if possible. They must stop hitting him if he

> *...is not attempting to block or has gone past or is moving away.*
> Case 9.2.3A of the National Federation of State High School Associations Case Book.

And they must refrain from holding and other illegal blocks.

High school rules, not NFL

Many youth coaches mistakenly think NFL rules apply to youth football. In this case, the misapplied rule is that you cannot bump a receiver more than **five yards** downfield. That is true in the NFL, but **not** in youth football where high school rules are used. In high school you can bump the guy all day anywhere on the field as long as the receiver is attempting to block you or could be.

Nobody there

If the quarterback has no receiver to whom to throw, he cannot complete a pass. I have seen many times when our opponent's quarterback immediately brought the ball up to pass, only to pull it down again because there was no player with his color jersey downfield.

In a 1991 playoff game against the defending state champion Vacaville team, they tried to throw a quick look-in pass to their right tight end. He couldn't get off the line and the quarterback was sacked as he stood there waiting for the tight end to appear.

The bump and run

Bump and run is a misleading phrase. I got the Colorado Bump and Run video and the actual technique involves little or no bumping. In fact, one of the principles of the technique is that you let the receiver make the first move then you hit him if you hit him at all.

If you want to employ bump-and-run technique, get that video. It's sold by the various coaching catalogs that are listed in the back of this book.

In general, bump-and-run is difficult to do on **wide** receivers. It's kind of standard on tight ends. Bump-and-run is also difficult to do if the athletic ability of the receiver is much better than the athletic ability of the defensive back. Finally, it is generally a technique that is only employed by defensive backs who have "help." That is, they are backed up by a safety who is in zone coverage.

Cover the receivers

I use **man-to-man** coverage in youth football. I urge you to do the same. At our spring high school football practice one year, I asked the defensive coordinator if he would run various zone and man coverages against us in practice so my receivers could do a coverage recognition drill. The head varsity coach heard the request and said, "We can't. The defensive backs haven't mastered cover three yet."

Cover three is the most common **zone** defense with a free safety covering the middle third and the cornerbacks covering the side deep thirds of the field. So you can see that zone coverage is the more difficult to teach and master. I tried it briefly in youth football and it was such a disaster in practice that we abandoned it that same day. Maybe more oomph would have fixed the problems. But there's only time for so much oomph in a youth practice schedule.

The man coverage I use is actually "cover one," that is, there is a middle linebacker or safety who is in zone coverage. His zone is the whole field, an easy zone to recognize the boundaries of, a zone with no "seams."

Stay with your guy

In man coverage, the defenders simply stay with their man if he escapes their bump-and-run efforts. You practice that with one-on-one (one receiver goes out for a pass and one defender tries to cover him) and seven-on-seven drills.

Covering someone man-to-man is pretty straight-forward. You learn by practicing it in game-like conditions. The technique is to focus on the **man**, **not** the quarterback. Don't look for the ball until the receiver does.

It's good to practice man coverage **without a ball** some of the time to emphasize focus on the man. The other main thing you need to teach is avoidance of penalties for encroachment, interference, clipping, blocking below the waist, striking a player in the head, tripping a player who does not have the ball, contacting an eligible receiver who is no longer a potential blocker, and holding.

Personnel

You must put the right kids in each position. This is fairly simple. The problem in youth football is that virtually all youth sports teams are highly political. Think about it. They typically have an **elected** board. Head coaching jobs are much sought after. If you antagonize the wrong parent, you can find yourself out on the street.

The team closest to where I live, the San Ramon Valley Thunderbirds, is **not** the one my oldest son played on. He tried out there and got cut as an eight-year old. I had no quarrel with the cut, but he and the other boys who were cut were almost totally ignored for a month, apparently in the hopes that they would quit. We did not go back there while the same people were in charge. They later had a palace coup—sweeping out the board and all but one head coach. We went back in 1997, but my youngest son was cut and I later resigned as offensive coordinator of a different team because the head coach directed me to change my offense in response to "pressure" from parents and board members.

The San Ramon Bears, where I coached for six years, was a splitoff from the South Valley Knights formed by some parents who were unhappy with that program and who were unable to change it to their liking. The whole California Youth Football League is apparently a long ago split-off from a Pop Warner program where two factions of parents couldn't get along. The Diablo Valley Youth Football League, where I coached for part of 1997, I apparently a split off from the California Youth Football League, again, as a result of disputes between adults.

The bottom line is many youth sports coaches, in all sports, put kids in the wrong position to stay on the right side of their parents. You should **not** do that. It's dead wrong and unfair to the players who worked for and deserve the positions. If the job requires that, you don't want the job. Here's the right way for defense.

Rookies on the line

You can put rookies on the defensive line. That is, at guard, tackle, and end. The **ends** must be extremely **disciplined**. I regard the position as extremely important in youth football and had a theory that I should put my best athletes there. But I found that many of the best athletes were **un**disciplined and would not execute the job description correctly, thereby hurting the team greatly.

So I now put the best **disciplined** athletes at defensive end. That is, if I catch the guy I put there taking a short cut instead of boxing at the depth of the ball carrier, or retreating in the face of lead blockers, or failing to pursue through the backfield on a sweep the other way, or failing to contain rush on a pass, I admonish him to not do that again. If he does make that mistake again, I replace him. I have tried to "work with them" as some coaches urge. I found it a waste of time. Above all, the kind of kid you need at defensive end is one who does what he is told.

Veterans in the backfield

My experience is that only **veterans** will do at linebacker, cornerback, and safety. I had one rookie who made first string at cornerback. But he was the only one in six years.

Count tackles

I count tackles and assists in practice and at games. A tackle is the first or only guy who makes the tackle. Assists are for those who get there after the tackle has been started but before the whistle is blown.

To put the first- and second-string guys on an equal footing, I then calculate number of tackles and assists **per every ten plays played**. Basically, the guys with the most tackles and assists per ten plays are the guys I start. Ignore stuff like running speed or size or whatever. If those things matter, the players who have them will show up high in the tackling stats.

Chronic penalty flags disqualifies you

The one exception to that is players who chronically draw **penalty flags**. By chronically, I mean one or more per game. I get rid of them fast. The only exception would be a superstar. In that case, I treat his penalty flags as withdrawals from a bank account into which his tackles are deposits. If he gets "overdrawn," he sits.

Defensive personality

There is a defensive personality and an offensive personality. You don't need to think much about it. The tackles and assists statistics will reveal who has the defensive personality. But you do need to know one baffling thing about football: some guys who star on offense are lousy on defense and vice versa.

I have seen many a coach play a weak guy on defense because he assumed that the guy must be good at all aspects of football because he was good at running back. In other words, don't make your best running back a cornerback just because he carries the ball well. Check his tackles and assists stats first. You may also find some weak **offensive** players who turn into tigers on **defense**.

Offense and defense are almost two different sports. At the varsity level in high school, few players go both ways. Fatigue avoidance is part of the reason. But the scarcity of kids who can be competitive at both "sports" (offense and defense) is the main reason.

Tackling

Ultimately, the main fundamental of defense is tackling. I went through a three-year learning process on tackling. The first year, I urged the kids to tackle correctly. Although I was not sure how I wanted them to tackle.

The second year, I knew what they should do. I urged them to do it. But they had many excuses for doing it wrong. We were knocked out of the semi-final game of the playoffs that year by the Oakland Dynamites, who went on to win the state championship. That loss really bothered me so I watched the video many times to see what I had done wrong.

Turned out our defensive failures were caused by two things: Substitutes who did not know their job well enough and poor tackling. I resolved that there would be no more poor tackling.

Remedial tackling

The following season, I added remedial tackling to our approach to tackling. Whenever a player made an incorrect tackle, I took him out of scrimmage and made him do five correct tackles on a big stand-up dummy. That seems like a little thing, but it was a big motivator for the kids, especially the veterans. They started with the same old excuses ("It was the only way I could tackle him"). I ignored the excuses and made them do their remedial tackling. Pretty soon, they decided to just do it correctly.

As the season progressed, it became clear that we had the best tackling technique in the league. We again made it to the semi-final game of the state championship, this time against the Fairfield Falcons.

We got beat. But when I analyzed the game I saw that we only missed one tackle the whole game. The rest of the time, if a Falcon was hit, he went down where he was hit. The story of the game was they had a great running back who broke loose three times. The rest of the game, we stopped them. It was 7-7 at the half. But they got two more big runs for scores in the second half and we were unable to score.

Tackling drill

We taught tackling with two drills that we ran for ten minutes every night. We put a bunch of half-round pads down as a mat and put a large round stand-up dummy on its side. The ball carrier would trot along the large dummy at half speed and the tackler would come from the side and tackle him. We required the tackler to wrap the ball carrier's thighs up tight and lift the ball carrier up in the air over the large dummy. They were not to touch the lying-down large dummy. They would land on the half-round pads in this drill.

Other coaching points were to keep the head up and the back flat and put the tackler's shoulder pad on the ball carrier's thigh pad. We did this so everyone got one repetition from each side each practice. If a player did it wrong, we made him do it over until he did it right.

Slow it down

If he did it wrong again, we slowed it down to slow-motion speed. If he still got it wrong, we had the ball carrier stand still and put the tackler up against him in the correct position. Then he would execute the tackle by yanking the ball carrier's legs tight against the tackler's chest and exploding upward from a squat position.

As a general rule, you **should not do full-speed tackling drills.** We almost never do them in high school. Many football coaching books I've seen say **not** to do full-speed tackling drills. Do **half**-speed and concentrate on **form**.

Hardly ever hit at Miramonte High School

Miramonte High School is known for its hard hitting. Opposing players and coaches have commented on it after games. But, to my amazement, Miramonte never does scrimmage full speed in practice. The only live scrimmages we did were a camp we attended at a college the first week after school gets out in June and a pre-season scrimmage with several other teams.

Miramonte's head varsity coach says scrimmaging wears the players out and injures them. The way we did it, they are kind of teased by thud (half-way between two-hand touch and live hitting) scrimmages all week long and finally allowed to let it all out on Friday night.

Need to hit in youth football

I think you need live hitting scrimmages in youth football because you have so many kids who are rookies and have never hit anyone hard. Hitting is an acquired taste and takes time. A team that has not yet acquired the taste cannot succeed against one that has. I noticed that the Miramonte High School **freshman** team has a lot of full-speed scrimmages. The town where Miramonte is located has no tackle youth football league, so their frosh are generally new to hitting.

Form tackle in a game

At a coaching clinic, the speaker asked if anyone in the room had ever seen a form tackle in a game. I raised my hand. I have not seen many. But there was one I remember.

In the 1992 Bears-Delta Rebels playoff game, Delta's running back started to run to his right on a sweep. I believe they were lined up in a formation that we recognized as a sweep formation based on our scout report. The guy took about two steps when he was hit by our cornerback, Tremaine Webb. The ball carrier's legs were instantly wrapped tight and he was launched upward through the air high enough to clear the pad we used for the tackling drill. You could have made a training film out of that tackle. You could sense the stunned reaction of the other team and their coaches and parents. They seemed to let out a collective, "Wow!" We went on to beat them 26-0.

We did this same drill as a front tackle, too. The ball carrier would stand in front of the large round dummy and the tackler would approach from the front, placing his helmet on the ball side, his shoulder pad on the belt buckle of the ball carrier, and wrapping his hands under the buttocks of the runner. As with the side tackling drill, he would jerk the legs violently against his chest while simultaneously exploding his legs skyward to get the ball carrier's feet over the dummy. Here's a diagram of the way we arranged the pads for the tackling drill:

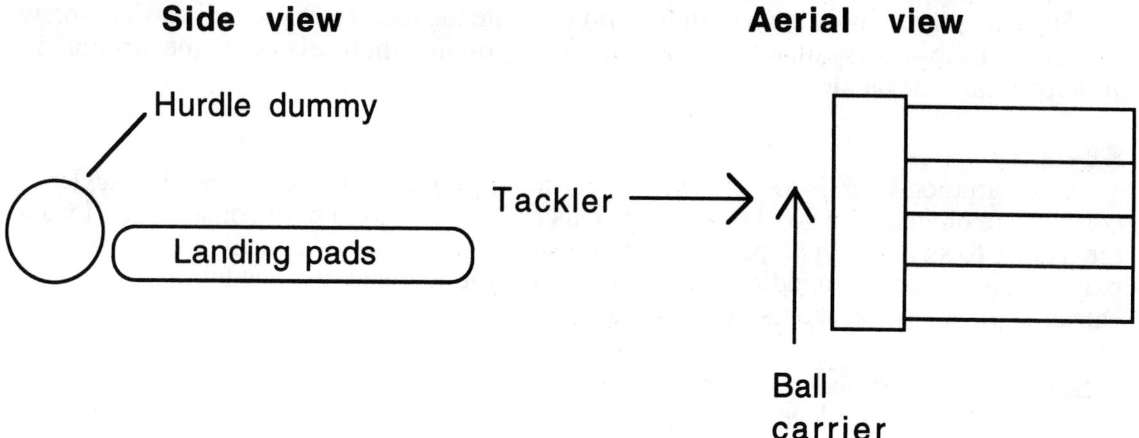

Higher level tackling

My thigh-high tackling technique comes from my own memories of what worked when I played sandlot football in the fifties and sixties. Thigh-high tackles are definitely **not** what they are doing in the '90s in high schools and colleges. I went to three college football spring practices in 1994, including a two-day visit to a clinic given at Stanford by then Stanford coach Bill Walsh. I have also been to De La Salle High School's (ranked #1 in U.S. in 1994) spring practice and to their summer camp. I have coached three seasons of high school football.

In high school and college today, the standard tackling technique is chest-to-chest with the tackler's shoulder pads lower than the ball carrier's. The tackler bear hugs the ball carrier, lifts him up, and drives him backward or sideways to the sideline.

They do **not** take the ball carrier to the ground in practice, primarily because of the danger of injury. At Stanford and at De La Salle, I saw the same drill. A ball carrier at one corner of a five-yard square runs toward the opposite corner at half speed. A tackler at an adjacent corner meets him in the middle of the square, grabs him, and runs him out the opposite corner. It looks like this:

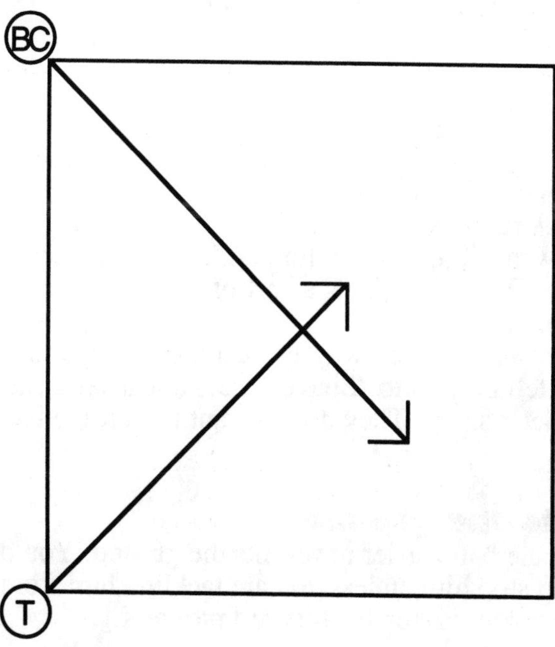

The ball carrier holds the ball in the arm opposite the tackler. Some ball carriers screw up this drill by spreading their legs or by throwing themselves to the ground in anticipation of the tackle.

Spin

One variation I like is to have the ball carrier **spin** when hit. That forces the tackler to concentrate on getting a good tight wrap. This drill is half speed until contact, then I want the tackler to switch to full speed. When you watch me conduct this drill, you see the two players jog toward the middle of the square, then after contact, the tackler drives the ball carrier explosively out the far corner of the box.

I prefer my drill

I do not like the college-high school drill I just described. My drill seems to be much sharper and more effective. I tried the high-school tackling technique on my 1996 youth team and it was a waste of time. When I switched back to my way of doing it, there was an instant improvement.

In 1995, I was watching a freshman game with my fellow varsity coaches. My son was a cornerback on the freshman team in question. He was also a graduate of my youth tackling drill. He tackled a guy using my youth technique. The varsity defensive coordinator standing next to me said something to the effect of, "Wow! Nice tackle!"

In 1996, I was sitting next to a fellow Bears coach—a guy who had been coaching two levels up from me for years. I mentioned that I had resigned after the 1993 season because I was tired of the bare minimum number of players we got every year. I had just 20 in 1993, 17 of them rookies. The coach said he remembered my resignation well and was very disappointed. I asked why and he said something like,

> *My son started football on that team the year after you quit. I wanted him to be coached by you.*

Why?

> *We've been getting players from your teams up at our level for years and we really like the way they tackle. Very crisp, sharp, and sure. I wanted my son to learn that.*

Stay on your feet

One of the most common tackling mistakes is leaving your feet when you make the tackle. Most players seem to think the way you tackle someone is by attaching yourself to him, going limp otherwise, and dragging the runner down with your body weight. That only works against weak runners.

The main reason I want lift in my tackling drills is that you cannot leave your feet and also lift the ball carrier. Requiring lift is a sort of quality control measure to insure that the tackler is not leaving his feet.

My lift requirement is a **better** way of accomplishing what coaches are trying to accomplish when they tell players to "Step on the ball carrier's shoes." Kids do not **want** to step on the ball carrier's shoes. They do not want to hurt the ball carrier's foot or twist their own ankle.

No need to go to the ground

In my ideal tackle, the ball carrier never hits the ground. You don't need to put a ball carrier on the ground to stop him, unless you are tackling him from **behind**. All you need to do to tackle the ball carrier is stop his forward progress.

Can't strip after the whistle

Furthermore, the ideal tackle is not a tackle at all, it is a **strip** of the ball. You cannot strip the ball after the whistle is blown. And if you put the ball carrier on the ground, the refs will blow the whistle. Hold the ball carrier up and dance with him in place so the refs won't blow the whistle and you can work on stripping the ball—or let your teammate strip the ball while you hold the ball carrier. You can even justify letting the ball carrier make a little forward progress while you are working on stripping the ball so you can prevent the refs from whistling the play dead.

I have considered telling the players to bring sneakers and holding tackling practice on the **asphalt** to emphasize the importance of staying on your feet. The notion that a tackle means falling down is very deeply ingrained on football players. You need to change that.

Common tackling mistakes

Here are the common mistakes tacklers make:

- head not on front side of ball carrier
- head not up (danger of neck injury)
- leaving feet
- not wrapping the ball carrier tight
- tackling too high
- face mask penalty
- hit and quit (let loose before whistle).

A kids who makes **one** of these mistakes will generally make that **same** mistake over and over. As that kid comes up to be the tackler, I remind him of his particular weakness. For example, a kid who doesn't wrap will cause me to say, "OK, Billy, remember to wrap him tight." I also urge the kids to remind themselves on game day. As the offense comes to the ball to snap it, I want Billy saying to himself, "Wrap tight! Wrap tight!"

Gang tackling

Gang tackling is very important. It is the sign of a well-coached team. You must demand and get it. There are two good drills.

Do-your-job drill

In one, we lined the entire defense up on the ball in their normal defensive alignment. There was no scout-team offense. They were lined up on air. We placed several big tackling dummies around the backfield at positions where a ball carrier might be once a play got started.

I would get the defense set and yell, "Do your job!" On that command, they were to move forward and freeze. The down linemen would scramble forward on all fours about two yards and freeze. The linebackers would charge through an invisible tight end driving him three yards into the backfield where they would freeze. And the defensive ends would sprint to the sweep spot on their side.

When all froze, there was a tight cup formed. We pointed out to them that there was no way out of the cup if they each did their jobs. Frequently, someone would foul up and create a gap in the cup. We would straighten him out.

Then, while they were frozen in anticipation, I would yell, "Gang!" and point to one of the big dummies. All eleven kids would explode onto that dummy. The kids loved the gang tackle part of this drill.

You must use a dummy rather than a player because kids can get hurt in a gang tackle.

Double-whistle drill

Whenever you do pass or sweep drills, you can run them as double-whistle drills. In a double-whistle drill, you blow the **first** whistle at the normal time, that is, when the ball carrier is tackled or touched if you are not tackling him.

On the command, "Air!" (ball has left passer's hand or punter's foot) or "Sweep!," All eleven players must break full speed for the ball. The **second** whistle is not blown until all eleven players are in a group with their hands on the ball. When the second whistle is blown, the defensive captain says, "One, two, three!" and all the players yell, "Gang tackle!" in unison. This is called "Flying to the ball" and is a necessary defensive habit. It is also an indicator of a well-coached team. In poorly coached teams, the players who are not in the vicinity of the ball just stand and watch the play from afar.

Scouting

The more unusual an offense is, the more you benefit from scouting. I believe you should have a recent scouting report on every opponent.

'Coach hustle'

Scouting is a manifestation of what I call "Coach hustle." Football coaches are always telling players to give 110%. But then I hear them all saying they can't scout this Sunday in coaches meetings. If you are going to **ask** for 110%, you ought to be **giving** 110% as a coach. Coaches who do not scout are letting their players down. We have blown teams out of the stadium because we scouted them and they did not scout us.

Scoring 16 defensive points against Benicia

In 1991, we scouted Benicia. Among other things, we discovered that they had several one- or two-play formations. That is dumb.

We taught our kids what those formations were and what play or plays were about to happen and killed Benicia. For example, whenever they were in a slot formation, they were either going to run a sweep to the slot side or a fake sweep to the slot side and a naked bootleg the other way.

We handed out a written scout report that showed that, demonstrated the play for our defense in practice, and had our scout team run it against our first-string defense over and over.

Flash cards

In the locker room before the Benicia game, we showed the players flash cards with the slot formation on one side and the sweep and fake sweep-bootleg on the other. We created code words to alert our players to the formation and its meaning. For example, when they came out in the slot, our players and coaches would all yell, "Slot!" and point to the slot side. I would yell, "It's coming at Chris or Shane!" They were our two defensive ends.

The doomed naked bootleg

There are few plays in football as ugly as a naked bootleg that does not fool the defense. As I recall, we stopped their slot sweep for a small loss every time. But when they faked the slot sweep and ran the naked bootleg, our backside defensive end, Shane Evans, sacked the quarterback for double-digit losses.

Intercepted every pass

We intercepted every pass they threw that day, running one back for a touchdown. We drove them into their own end zone for two safeties. And we picked up a fumble and ran it in for a touchdown. We scored 16 points on defense that day and held Benicia to minus one yard. Our offense, (my son was the ball carrier, it was a big day for the Reeds) only scored one touchdown and two PATs.

Walnut Creek comes in blind

In 1993, we played Walnut Creek. They did **not** scout us. Remember how I said scouting is most beneficial when the offense is unusual? Our offense in 1993 was an unbalanced line, warp-speed, no huddle, single-wing (the single wing is an offense that was popular in the early part of this century). We also ran the 10-1 defense which Walnut Creek had never seen before. Walnut Creek's coaches and players didn't know what hit them. We spent most of the game trying to avoid having our margin go over 28 points, which turns the game into a controlled scrimmage in our league. You should note that we were 3-6 that year (only one defensive veteran).

I am a pretty competitive coach as you have probably discerned from this book. I want my kids to win and we go for the jugular, figuratively speaking, to nail down victories. But when I go up against a team that lacks coach hustle, that is, no scouting, I feel sorry for the opposing players. They have talent and they are playing their hearts out, but they are doomed to ignominious defeat because their coaches were too dumb or too lazy to scout. There have been many Saturdays on the youth football field where we won, but I thought I could have beaten my team with the other team's players.

One of the famous sayings in football coaching is, "He can takes his'n and beat your'n and he can take your'n and beat his'n." I am not that good a coach yet. I did beat California High's freshman 34-12 with my Granada freshman in 1996. The Cal High stars were most of my best players from the 1991 and 1992 teams I coached to the California Youth Football semifinals. And one of my Granada players had been a player on the Manteca Delta Rebel teams we beat in those years. So there was a slight element of beating mine with yours in that game.

I have a much better chance of taking yours and beating mine if you don't scout me.

Diagram every play

When you scout, you should diagram every single play the opponent runs. Make sure you get there on time so you don't miss the first play of the game. Most teams run the same first play of the game every week—dive right actually. But some, like my teams, had another play—friendly-side sweep. Write the jersey numbers of the ball handlers down for each play.

Here's a form I made for scouting. It's pretty standard throughout football. The positions printed on the form are the ones virtually all formations have. The scout must mark the others when the team breaks the huddle. I use a felt-tipped pen and just make a dot for each player. You have to move really fast—and that's with teams that do not run a hurry-up offense. I wonder how opponents scouted my 1993 offense which operated at warp-speed. More about that later.

One play per page

I only put one play on a page now. I used to squeeze three on each page. And I have a coach friend who puts even more on a page. The reason for just one is that the page becomes a scout-team "card" during the week before you practice. That is, your scout team coach takes the binder you created when you scouted the opponent in question and holds it up in the scout team huddle to show them which play to run during practice.

The players need an 8 1/2 x 11 diagram. So if you scout with two or more plays per page you will have to take extra time to convert the plays to one-play-per-page scout team "cards." They are called cards because college and pro teams use large posters to show the play to their teams.

Offense: ________ Defense: ________ Date ________ Hash: L M R Yd line: ____ Down: 1 2 3 4 Distance: ____

Offense: V Defense: B Date: 10/4/97 Hash: L M (R) Yd. line: V24 Down: (1) 2 3 4 Distance: 10

90 12 23 11 88 -2

How to fill the scout sheets out

The center and linemen are vertical because that is usually how you see them when you sit in the stands to scout. Write down the game-situation data while the offense is huddling. Add the other players when they break the huddle, note the numbers of the eligible receivers and where they are lined up, and draw the path of the ball carrier or pass. "Yard line" is written with a letter and a number. For example, if the ball is on the Benicia 40-yard line, write "B40."

Hash is where the ball is on the yard-line in question: right (R), left (L), or middle (M) from the offense's perspective. "Distance" means yards to go for a first down or touchdown when less than 10. Note results and penalties on the play diagram. Dead-ball penalties should be treated as a separate play.

Balls traveling through the air are marked by dotted lines. Players who go in motion are marked by wavy lines. If the offense is on your right, diagram them on the right of the scout sheet. When possession or the quarter changes, diagram them on the left. In other words, diagram them just as you see them.

Put about 60 blank scout sheets for each offense in a book-report type folder or loose leaf binder to keep them in order. You can buy those cheaply at an office or school supply store. I originally used clipboards and loose sheets. That was a disaster as I frantically changed pages in the wind or rain while the game was going on.

You should also have diagrams of the whole football field in your scouting folder. You use them to scout the kicking game. A marked up scout report appears on the previous page.

Formation tendencies

After you diagram every play, go home and analyze it. First, look for formation tendencies. That is, see what plays they run from each formation. You will generally find that most youth football coaches like to use a different formation for each point of attack. They typically use the I, Power I, four-wide receivers, or full-house T for dives and blasts and the slot or a wide flanker for sweeps. The particular team you are playing probably has a favorite formation for off-tackle, passes, and reverses.

By finding out what one or two plays they run out of each formation, and teaching your players that information, you play most of the game knowing what play is coming. It's very hard for the opponent to move the ball under those conditions.

Star position tendencies

Another common tip-off is coaches who move their star running back around to different positions according to what play they want to run. The 1992 Fairfield Falcons were incredible about this. You could tell what play they were going to run by what position their star running back, Gregory Reed (no relation), was in. We stopped them about 37 times in the semi-final playoff game in large part because we knew what play they were going to run. But Reed was such a great back that he still got loose three times and we lost 19-7.

Down-and-distance tendencies

In college and the pros, down-and-distance tendencies are apparently important. In my experience, they don't seem significant in youth football. Most offensive youth coaches try to put in 30 plays. But they end up using only a handful. So they have few choices and do the obvious in most cases. That is, they dive when it's third and short. They sweep or pass on third and long.

I'm always scared of the sweep so there's nothing more I can do on third and long than I'm already doing. We sometimes yell, "Watch the pass!" in obvious passing situations. But that's about it.

Scout the jamborees

You should scout the pre-season jamboree of your first opponent. In fact, that's your **only** opportunity to scout them. In California Youth Football, there are usually several weeks of jamborees before the first game. And they are on both Saturdays and Sundays. So you can scout your butt off. Jamborees (pre-season scrimmages) are not such great scouting opportunities because there is no kicking game, the other coach is still working out his personnel and system, and coaches try not to show too much because there are at least three other teams there playing, plus scouts in the stands. But scouting jamborees is better than no scouting at all.

Scouting should generally be done by a **two-man crew**. It is also a **skilled** chore. You need to train the people who do it before you send them out. We used pre-season jamborees as a way to train our new coaches in scouting.

Regular season

During the regular season, scouting is difficult in most youth football leagues. Most games are played on Saturday. That means your scouting target is generally playing the same time you are. There are a couple of tricks, though.

Some teams play **Sunday**, usually because they are sharing the stadium with another team. Others use a **different sequence** than the usual youngest-to-oldest progression. You can scout at Sunday games if you play on Saturday. And if you have to play at one of the Sunday games, you can scout multiple games that Saturday. If you find a team with a different progression than youngest to oldest, you may be able to both scout your opponent and coach at your own game in the same day. It might be prudent for **your** organization to become one of the organizations with a different progression just so your coaches could scout on game days.

Trade with other levels

In may cases, we found the only way to scout a particular opponent was to trade scouting chores with parents or coaches from another level of our organization. For example, in 1993, I would often trade a scouting report on a midget game done by me for a scouting report on a jr. pee wee game done for me by a midget coach.

While I was coaching my game first thing Saturday morning, the midget coach was scouting my upcoming opponent. Then, in the afternoon, I would go to the same field and scout the midget's upcoming opponent while they were back our the field where we played that day coaching their team.

Playoff scouting

In California Youth Football, the playoff games are generally arranged so that you play Saturday or Sunday and your opponent for the next week plays the same weekend but on the other day. So scouting in the playoffs is generally no sweat. But in 1992, we had to play the semi-final game at the exact same time and date as the other semi-final game.

We were at he jr. pee wee level that year. The pee wee coach, whose team had been eliminated from the playoffs agreed to go scout the other semi-final game while we coached ours. He arrived at our game just as it ended. We lost 19-7 to Fairfield Falcons. He then went over to the Fairfield coaches and asked if they had anyone scout the other semi-final game that morning. They said no. He told them he had just scouted it and wondered if they wanted the scouting report. They sure did. Fairfield won the state championship the following weekend.

During-the-game coaching

Some coaches are silent at games. Others yell out instructions. I yell out instructions. In part, it's because we conditioned players in practice to respond to certain commands.

At games, I often wear a small plastic megaphone around my neck. I bought it at an Army homecoming game during my 20th reunion. When we are on defense, I position myself behind the opponent's offense. As they break their huddle, I recognize their formation. I raise the megaphone to my mouth and yell out the formation name or whatever code word we have assigned to it that week.

If I see a player not lined up correctly, I'll call his name and yell for him to cover the flanker or whatever.

Once the ball is snapped, I try to figure out what play it is as fast as possible and yell it out. "Dive!" "Sweep!" Reverse!" "Pass!" Many of these words are the same words we use in skill sprint drills and they inspire a Pavlovian response. When I yell, "Sweep!" in a game, they tear off on their pursuit angles just like they do in practice when I yell that same word. When a tackle begins, I yell, "Gang! Gang! Gang!"

Adjustment schedule

You should think about what adjustments you will make before the game. I used to make an adjustment schedule every Friday night before a Saturday youth football game. I would write down each defensive position and then write the **Xs and Os** change I would make if we were getting beat there and the **personnel** change I would make if we were getting beat there. Once the game is under way, things are too hectic to do any analysis.

Here's a sample adjustment schedule.

Position	Alignment or technique change	Personnel change
WE	One step wider if getting beat on sweep	Switch with 32
WLB	Help from WCB on block TE or off-tackle	Bring in 52
WCB	Play two steps deeper if completed passes	Switch with 22

And so on through all eleven defensive positions.

Game chart

During youth football games, I chart the opposing offense's success at the various points of attack. Actually, I have a player or assistant coach do it. I bring a diagram of an offensive formation with yard lines indicating five-yard distances. If the opponent runs a dive right for two yards, I draw a two-yard line up from the right A gap. If they then lose two yards on a sweep left, I draw a line down from the left D gap two yards. If they complete a look-in pass for a five-yard gain, I put a "P" five yards downfield at the location where the pass was caught. If they throw an incompletion twelve yards upfield on the left side, I put an "I" there. And so on.

As the first quarter progresses, patterns become apparent. If we are getting beat somewhere consistently, we talk to the key defenders about it, or change alignment or technique or change personnel.

If you do **not** chart the game in this manner, systemic weaknesses will crop up that you do not see until you are watching the video after the game—when it's too late to fix the problem. Here's an example game chart.

Defensive order of selection

Order of selection is a concept that helps coaches decide who goes where. Pretend that you have a separate position coach for each of the eleven defensive positions. The order of selection is the sequence in which those eleven coaches get to pick their player. It's a sort of importance ranking of the positions. The order in which you fill positions in the 10-1 is

Position	Type of player
1. wide-side defensive end	obedient
2. defensive back #2	experienced good athlete
3. defensive back #1	experienced good athlete

4. defensive back #3	experienced good athlete
5. short-side defensive end	obedient
6. defensive back #4	experienced good athlete
7. defensive back #5	experienced good athlete
8. left tackle	obedient, medium to heavy weight
9. right tackle	obedient, medium to heavy weight
10. left guard	obedient, medium to heavy weight
11. right guard	obedient, medium to heavy weight

'But my staff doesn't like it...'

Many of my readers have called to tell me that they believe in and want to use my gap-8 or 10-1 but that their staff thinks it's crazy. They pepper me with questions that are thoroughly answered in this book like "Will it work at the 10-year old level?"

The basic problem is the objectors have not read the book, never saw the defense in action, and irrationally have more faith in their own instant analysis and theories than in the years of experience of me and the other coaches who have successfully used the gap-8 and 10-1. People say I should do a video. Maybe I will. At present, though, I have no such plans.

If you are the head coach, try to sell the staff on the defense. If you cannot convince them, fire them. If you allow a bunch of naysaying grumps to hang around, they will undermine the confidence of your players and board in your coaching. Nothing works when the players don't believe in it.

If you are unwilling or unable to fire the staff, see if they will give you "permission" to use it in goal-line situations, then expand the definition of what is a goal-line situation.

Or, see if they will give you "permission" to use it as a surprise defense anywhere on the field.

Or, beg them to give you permission to use it in short-yardage situations anywhere on the field.

Or, put it in a figurative glass box marked "Open in case of emergency." That's how most users of the defense got started anyway. They were in a game where nothing else worked and the naysayers said, "Yeah, what the heck. It can't be any worse than what we're doing."

I did that on offense in a 1994 game against Napa. I was just the special teams coordinator. The head coach and offensive coordinator was trying to run a wing-T because that was what the local high school used. I repeatedly urged him to use the single-wing, which I had success with the previous year. Many of his players had moved up from my team.

We had not gotten a single first down in two weeks and were in the fourth quarter of a game we were losing by 20 plus points. I said, "Why don't you let me try a single-wing wedge play?" He said OK. I put it in during a timeout and we proceeded to run that same play over and over seven straight times. We gained 31 yards and three first downs in about two minutes. That head coach later became a confirmed single-wing coach.

The resistance to the gap-8 and 10-1 I have heard about is more or less politics. I am no politician and have no interest in becoming one. I coach the best way I know how. If I am a subordinate, the head coach can fire me if he does not like what I am doing. But I will not coach in a way I do not believe in just to keep my job.

If I am a head coach, I will fire any assistant who can't support my approach. I'm not saying he's wrong, just that a head coach cannot tolerate negative psychological influences on his team.

Whether you use my system or another does not concern me. But for your own sake and the sake of your players, do **not** use any system you do not believe in just because you are being pressured to use it.

9

Offense

To get the most out of your offense you must:

1. get the absolute **best player** at each position
2. use a sound offensive **system** which is optimum for your **personnel**
3. use a sound offensive **system** which is optimum for the **defenses** you expect to face
4. insist that each member of your offense execute the **correct assignment** on every play

Most youth football offenses are **too complex.** They also run the **wrong plays** and have the **wrong guys** in the important blocking positions. They have a compulsion to **pass** every three or four plays in spite of the fact that those passes almost always fail thereby killing their drives. Most coaches are **too conventiona**l in their approach, thereby making it easier for the defense to stop them.

In this chapter, I will discuss your offensive system. I will make a strong pitch for the contrarian approach. But I realize that most of you will take a conventional approach, so I will cover that, too. I have coached unconventionally, when **I** was in charge. And I've coached conventionally, in high school and youth football, when **others** were in charge.

Best player at each position

It is obvious to me that you need the absolute best player at each position to be successful. No one ever argues that abstract point. But the vast majority of coaches at the high school and lower levels make the following personnel **mistakes**:

- let **players decide** what position they should play when they first enter the program
- give players whose **parents apply pressure** the position the parent wants
- fail to correct mistakes in the depth chart because the coach does **not want to admit** he made a **mistake**
- fail to correct mistakes in the depth chart because the coach does **not want to hurt the feelings** of the players who has the job but is not doing it satisfactorily
- fail to correct mistakes in the depth chart because of fear that the **parent** of the demoted player will be **angry**
- **platooning** (prohibiting the best player from playing offense because he plays defense)
- fail to recognize players whose talents **fade as they age** (Youth players do not lose their abilities because of age-related deterioration like NFL players. Rather they sometimes mature earlier than their peers then lose their relative advantage when their peers go through their own growth spurts.)
- assigning positions by the "Central Casting" approach (he **looks the part**)

- assigning positions based on what position the player's **father, older sibling, or other close relative played.**

The correct approach is to gather as much data as you can about each player. I test **every player for every position** the first several days of practice. Kids ask me, "Can I try out for such and such position?" "**Everybody** on this team is going to try out for **every position**," is my answer. Furthermore, the tryout never ends. All season long, I keep an eye out to see if there is a better player available for any position. I make changes all season, although fewer each week.

When appropriate, I talk to the player's previous coaches to get their opinion of his talent, attitude, and performance.

I test the players scientifically for:

- 10-yard dash speed
- 20-yard dash speed
- blocking ability
- passing ability
- receiving ability
- elusiveness.

I also scrutinize videos of practice and games. And I scrutinize our point-of-attack success chart. If we are not succeeding at a particular point of attack, I conclude that someone at that point of attack is not doing his job. In 1997, my plays up the middle did not work at the pre-season jamboree. I figured my centers were the prime suspects so I did the following drill as a test.

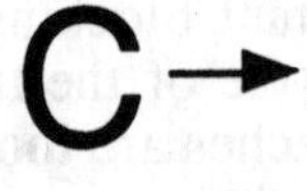

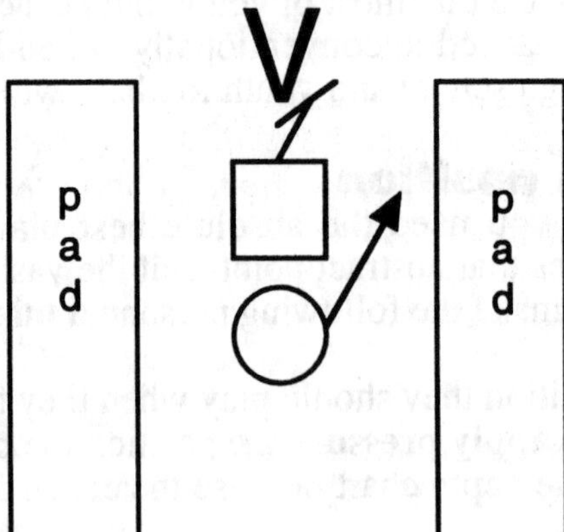

The coach stands behind the defender and points right or left. The center then snaps the ball and tries to block the defender so the quarterback can run the way the coach pointed. I tried various guys at center. As I suspected, my first- and second-string centers did not do well, generally getting blown back into the quarterback by the nose tackle. But I found one player who was able to snap and still blow the nose tackle back. I promoted him to first-string center.

Later that week, I began to suspect a number of my linemen were not the best players for their position because of scout-team defense players who kept breaking through and tackling my ball carriers for loss or no gain. I joke with the scout team defense players that if they **stop** my offense too many times, they will be made a **part of** my offense. Actually, you often see great defensive players who stink on offense. But most players who do well on defense will also do well on offense in youth football.

To test my players, I did this drill-test:

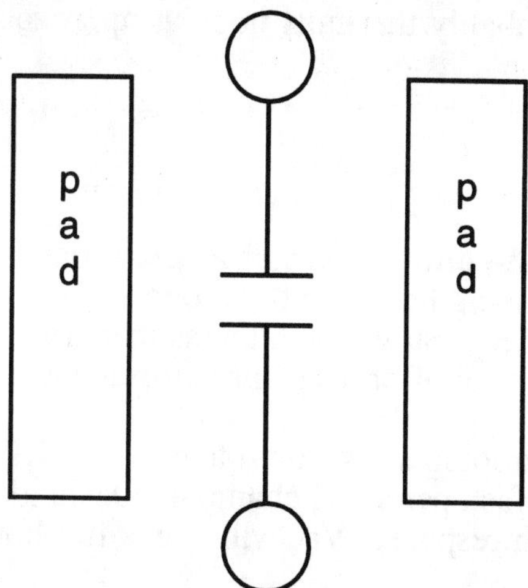

The object was to push the opponent out the other end of the narrow pad alley. We had three side-by-side stations. If you won, you moved one station to the west. If you lost, you move one station to the east.

After ten minutes or so, a pattern emerged. Some guys stayed at the winning end over and over. If they lost, they came right back after winning at the middle station. Other guys quickly went to the losing station and stayed there all or most of the time.

Whenever you test like this, there are surprises. A couple of my first-string linemen newer made it to the winning end. So I moved them down in the depth chart or switched them to a position where no line-blocking skills were required.

Emerging rookies

Rookies generally do not do well the first two months or so of practice. But every year, some rookies emerge after a month or so. The light bulb finally goes on. They get over their fear of hitting or whatever was holding them back and suddenly turn into good football players. When that happens, I move them up to first string. You should, too. You must keep an eye out for these emerging rookies. They happen every year. It is dumb and unfair to both the team and the rookie to be blind to his improvement or to refuse to promote him when he earns the promotion.

The best system

All offensive coordinators have a menu of possible offensive systems available to them. Here are many of them:

- multiple (the most common; includes I, split backs, power I, etc.)
- triple option (wishbone, veer, I)
- full-house double-tight T (middle-aged coaches recalling the offense of their youth)
- single-wing (power, spin, or buck-lateral series)
- run-and-shoot
- wing-T
- the fly
- short punt (this is a whole offense, not a special team)
- double-wing
- shotgun

Another way to look at it is what **kind of plays** you play to run. You can do:

- power running (the most successful approach for youth teams that lack speed)
- misdirection running
- speed running (sweeps, probably the most popular approach in youth football among teams with speed)
- sprint-out or roll-out passes
- option
- drop-back passing.

Another dimension is **ball-control** versus **big-play**. Fast youth teams tend to be big play (sweep) oriented. They bang heads with the opposing defense for a while then they go 60 yards for a TD on a sweep. Slow youth teams that are successful—a relatively rare breed—generally run ball-control offenses (four yards and a cloud of dust, short passes if they pass at all.)

I have only seen one champion **slow** youth team: Vacaville in 1990. We asked them how they beat the extremely fast, perennial champion Oakland Dynamites. "We never ran outside the tackles," was their response. Vacaville ran a full-house T, double-tight offense with blasts and cross bucks.

I have always coached slow suburban teams and our main problem was to beat the fast inner-city teams. My opponents generally beat us with sweeps. We simply could not run fast enough to beat them to the corner. Nor could we prevent them from getting to the corner often enough.

In 1993, I had a kid, Will Sykes, barely fast enough to run the sweep. But in general, I find I can only succeed with the sweep by setting it up with numerous inside running plays that get the opposing contain man frustrated and start abandoning his contain duties. We also used a crack-back block to help the ball carrier to turn the corner.

Strength against weakness

As stated in the defense chapter, the basic principle of the offense is **strength against weakness**. In the context of football, strength and weakness take many forms:

- physical mismatches
- outnumbering the defense at the point of attack
- superior knowledge
- better conditioning
- deeper bench.

Mismatches

One dimension of football strength and weakness is athletic ability. Things like: speed, agility, strength, and size, vary from player to player. If you can create a situation where your player of **superior** speed, agility, or whatever is matched up with an opposing player who is **inferior** in that category, and the play chosen is such that the superior ability of your player is important, you can win the play and—with more such plays, win the game and the championship.

Slow linebacker versus a fleet wide receiver

A classic example of this approach is often discussed by TV analysts. That is, the offensive coordinator trying to create a situation where a relatively slow **linebacker** has to cover a fleet-footed **wide receiver** man-to-man. You could do this by unexpectedly putting four wide receivers into a game in a non-passing situation. The defense would typically **not** have their nickel or dime package (five or six defensive backs) in, so linebackers would have to go out and cover the wide receivers. This, of course, is an NFL tactic, not generally anything that would work in a youth football game.

Size

You might try to achieve a **size** mismatch by doing the opposite. Put two tight ends and two blocking fullbacks into a game in a **passing** situation. The defense would likely have their speed-heavy nickel or dime package of defenders on the field—a poor choice for stopping a power play like a "student body right" led by NFL size behemoths.

In **youth** football, where weight limits and youthful bodies greatly limit size and strength differences, the two athletic abilities you can use to achieve mismatches are **speed** and **agility**—assuming you have boys who are superior in those categories.

The ability hierarchy

Let's rate the starting members of a typical youth football team on a scale of one to seven, where seven is best. That typical team would have a couple of weak players, a couple of strong ones, and a six or seven medium ones. It'd probably come out like this:

			4			
		3	4	5		
1	2	3	4	5	6	7
Weak		Medium			Strong	

That is, you have one weak player who rates just a one, and a similar number of 2s, 6s, and 7s. The 7 is a star and 6 is very good. Think about your own team and I'll bet you agree this fits pretty accurately.

Now think about how you array your team on the game field. In my experience, six years of watching four games a week of my own team, as well as scouting about another game a week, most youth defensive coaches do something like the diagram below.

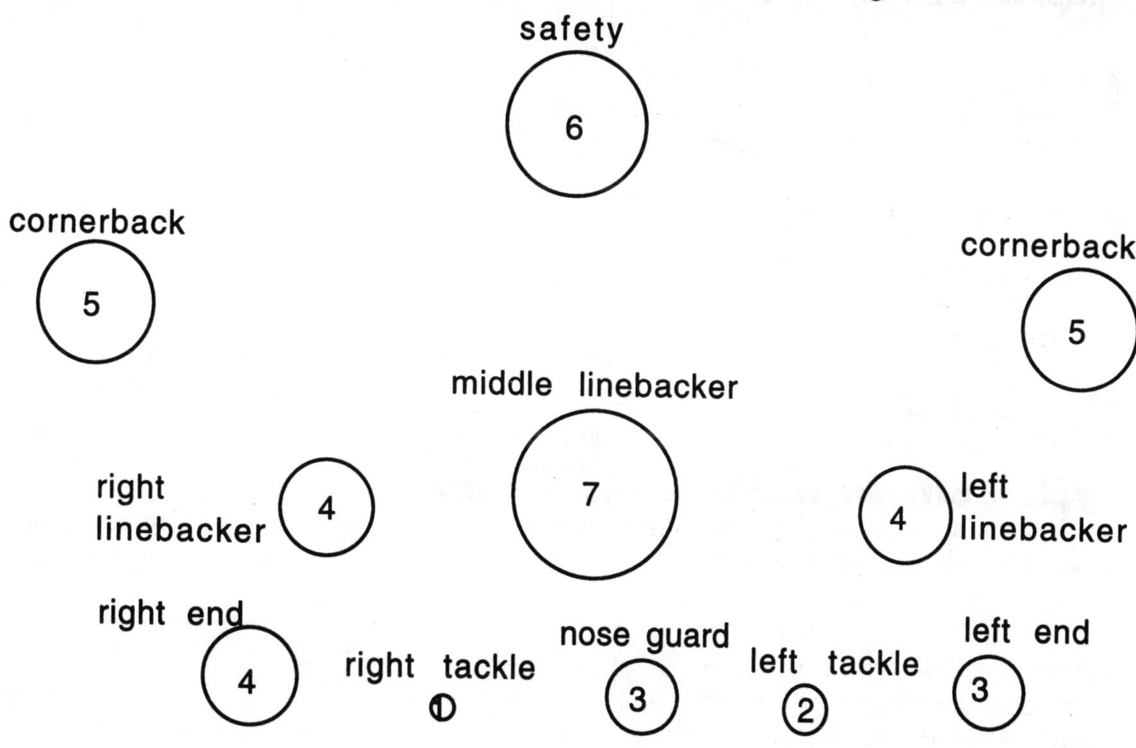

This is a 5-3-3 defense. I got it out of my scouting report on Napa for 1992. The **weakest** starting defensive player is at **right tackle**; the second weakest at left tackle and so forth. The **best** player is at **middle linebacker**. Some teams would play him at safety.

Now let's think about creating physical mismatches.

Weakest player at flanker

How's about I take my absolute **weakest** player on the **bench**, not the starting team, and put him out wide at flanker. This kid rates about a **point two** on the scale of one to seven.

Whom do you suppose the defense is going to put out on him? Their weakest player, the right tackle who scores a one on the ability scale? Nope. They probably will put one of their **fives** out on him. After all, their coaches have decided that my wide receivers are fast, good pass catchers. They watch *Monday Night Football*. They know how we offensive coordinators think.

In fact, this wide receiver is neither fast nor a good pass catcher and we will not throw to him even if he is uncovered. (The flanker is happy about this decoy role, although his father may not be. He's small and is looking forward to being a star in future years when he gets bigger. For now, he's grateful to be out of the heavy hitting in the trenches. No way does he want to carry the ball.)

Flanker, not split end

Avoid putting a young player at split end. Split ends must be on the line of scrimmage at the snap. They will draw penalty flags for not lining up correctly. It's infinitely easier to line up correctly at **flanker** (off the line). The line ref on each side signals with his arm whether the outermost offensive player is on or off the line. If he is on the line, the ref puts his offensive side arm across his chest. If he is off the line, the ref extends his offense side arm away from his body toward the goal the offense is defending.

Your flanker must look over and make sure the ref has his arm away from his body. Otherwise, the tight end will be **in**eligible and wearing an eligible receiver's jersey number.

Typical offense ability arrangement

Here is a similar ability diagram of how I believe the typical youth football coach arrange his players for **offense**. (This happens to be a power I but that's not important.)

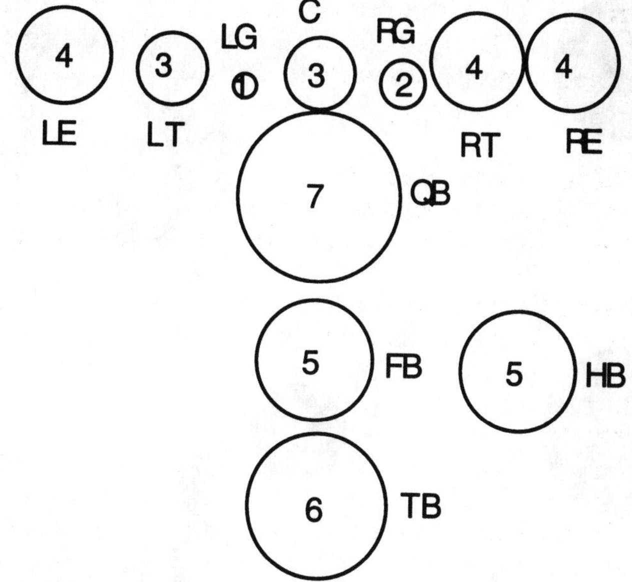

Note that the **best** player is at quarterback. That makes sense in the **pros** where the quarterback is the passer and that is a very difficult skill. But remember that youth football teams rarely pass. So why is that great athlete at quarterback? To take the ball from the center and hand it to a running back of lesser ability? I might put my best athlete at quarterback in youth football, but if I did so I would run an offense in which he kept the ball on many plays. I would not use a top athlete just to do handoffs. And it would be hard to persuade me to run a pass-oriented offense in youth football unless I had some remarkable passers and receivers.

The obvious weakness in this alignment is on the **line**. But the line is the **most important part of the offense**—especially in youth football where the fakes are rarely very good and there are few passes.

Remember also that the basic principle of football offense is strength against weakness. But this offensive formation pits **weakness against weakness** on the line.

My 1993 offense

Here is some of my preseason thinking for the 1993 season.

"We tend to be Clydesdales in a league of thoroughbreds. We have to win in spite of our lack of speed. Furthermore, we have gotten little or no mileage out of our fakes in the past. Where we have succeeded is running off tackle and up the middle—especially the isolation or blast play (one or more lead blockers ahead of the ball carrier).

"OK. I'll pick an offense that is super for running off tackle and blast plays. My research indicates the Power I (isolation or blast play) and single-wing (wedge or seam buck) are best up the middle and the short punt and single-wing are strongest off tackle. So I'll go with the single-wing."

With advice from single-wing historian Ed Racely, I threw in a reverse in order to respond to a defense that reacted too quickly to our seam buck and off tackle plays. And I knew I had to be able to go around end so I added a single-wing hook sweep to respond to a defensive end who crashed diagonally into our backfield, thereby stopping the off-tackle play.

I used a single-wing in 1993. I'll explain that in more detail later. For now, suffice it to say there is no quarterback. The center long snaps the ball directly to the tailback. Here's a diagram of my offense and the way I think the opposing defense lined up **ability** wise.

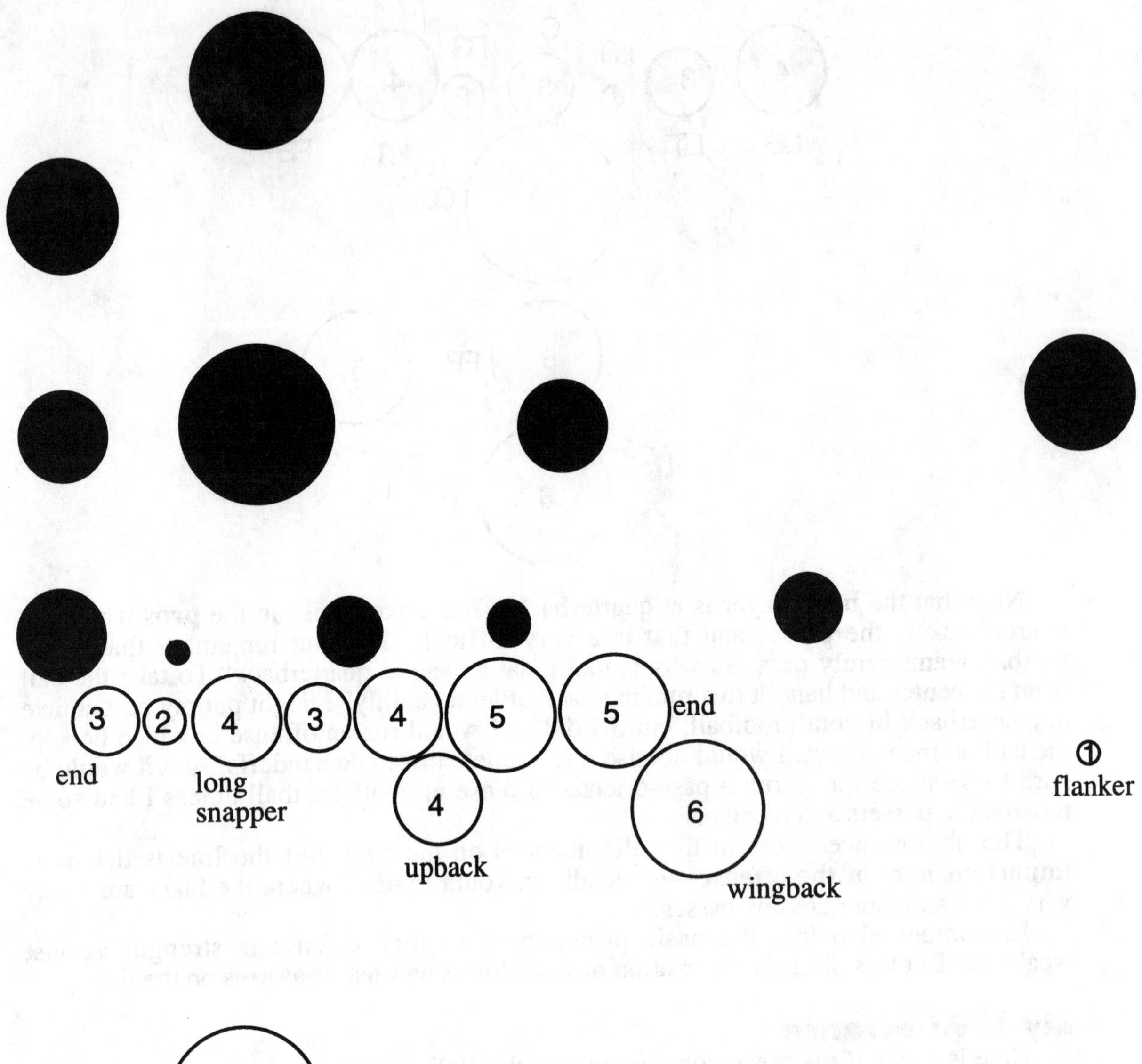

What plays do you suppose worked well? Our two best were a seam buck and an off-tackle, both of which went through the right side of the line (in the above diagram, we also made the formation strong to the **left** side and ran that way).

At the point of attack, I had a six, two fives and a four blocking a two and a three. The defense had a seven, a four, and another three **in the vicinity**. But we knew where we were going while they were reacting. We were already at the point of attack, they had to **get** to that location. We had more momentum when they arrived. In short, we got our four yards and often far more.

Decoy and talent on the line

The key difference between my offensive-talent distribution and most other youth coaches was using a weak level one player to **decoy** an opponent's five and my using fours, fives, and a six **on the line**. I also had my seven **running the ball**, not handing it off, as so many teams do.

This was not easy to do politically. My six and one of my fives wanted to be in the backfield carrying the ball. I made one a tight end and the other the wing. That gave them some opportunities to carry the ball.

My thinking was that my bread-and-butter play was going to be the **off-tackle play**. It turned out that the seam buck was better. But the basic idea was that I wanted talented players at all the key positions for the running of the off-tackle play.

Lineman of the Year

In 1996, when I was offensive coordinator of the Granada freshman team, I had a lot of talented running backs. So I took one aside, Jeff Cooley, and told him that although he was a good running back and might start on other teams, on **this** team he would be third string. I told him he had too much athletic ability to be off the field when we were on offense and asked if he would consider plying right guard. He immediately agreed. He was later elected team captain, won the Lineman of the Year award and was crucial to our very successful inside-trap running game. If you or your players are not willing to make that kind of switch, you will have trouble being successful.

Two-to-one advantage

Another way to think about mismatches is to draw a four-yard radius circle around your primary point of attack. For most youth football teams, it should be the off-tackle hole. Then try to get superiority within that circle both in terms of **numbers** of bodies as well as the **quality** of those players. A four-yard radius circle around the off-tackle hole in my 1993 **offense** in the above diagram would add up as follows: 6 + 5 + 5 + 4 + 4 = 24. The **defense**, on the other hand, would only have 2 + 3 + 3 + 4 = 12. With two-to-one superiority, we are probably going to get our four yards.

We were very successful with this approach

And indeed, we had a very successful offense with this approach. My star tailback, Will Sykes, gained 1,583 all-purpose yards and scored 21 touchdowns even though he only played in seven and a quarter 40-minute games. That's about the same yardage **total** as the typical Heisman Trophy winner. His 8.03-yards-per-carry average **exceeded** a Heisman winner's typical totals. We scored more points against our opponents than any team except the state champions. And we outscored even them against the toughest defense in the league that year, Berkeley.

Sykes was a first-string running back the year **before** and the year **after** he played for me. The year before, he scored **no** touchdowns in the regular season. The year after, he was successful, but far less so than in our system.

'Whatever happened to number 22?'

Opposing players were still talking about him at games the following year, 1994. But it was in the vein of, "What ever happened to that number 22 you had last year?" We would say, "That's him right over there. He played the whole game today." And the opponent would be surprised that he had played in the game because the 1994 #22 had nowhere near the impact he had the previous year. I think the reason was clearly the fact that he did not have the same quality blockers in 1994. High quality players were available on the 1994 team, but they were all used at backfield positions.

The order of selection

There is another, better way to think of this principle. That is, what position do you fill **first**? What position **second**? And so forth.

This approach was well explained in a book called, *Modern Belly T Football* by A. Allen Black. He says you pick your players in the following order:

1. quarterback
2. running back
3. pulling tackle
4. pulling guard
5. slot back
6. tight end
7. power guard
8. center
9. power tackle
10. fullback
11. split end.

Note that positions 3 through 9 (except 5) are linemen. The fullback and split end positions are not filled until the best athletes available for the line have been taken. This is quite different from the typical youth coach. He will hand out fullback and split end positions as plums to politically powerful players, like coaches' sons, or to the best athletes.

Best for the position

In my discussion of ones and sevens and so forth above, I implied that all positions on the football team need the same abilities. In fact, each position is unique. What you do is ask your self, "Who is the best quarterback?" Once you have answered that question, you ask, "Of the boys left other than the one I just chose for quarterback, who is the best running back?"

In many cases, the boy chosen for quarterback will be the best running back, too. That's irrelevant. He has already been taken for quarterback.

The best from who's left

After the quarterback and running back are chosen, Black chooses the best pulling tackle from among the boys left, that is, those other than the two who were chosen for the quarterback and running back positions. This is where Black deviates from the vast majority of youth coaches. Their third choice would probably be for another running back position like fullback. Indeed, Black says, "The boy we select for pulling tackle would play fullback on other teams."

This is where the rubber meets the road in being a youth football offensive coordinator. If you put a boy who expected, and whose father expected, that he would be a **fullback**, at **tackle**, you will probably get grief. The boy may quit the team. His parents may try to get you fired. He may leave the team next year.

Stick to your guns

One father threatened to remove his boy from my team if I did not take him off the line and put him in the backfield. I refused and it was one of the smartest things I ever did in youth football. The boy was a fantastic blocker and did a great job and was a key factor in our success.

You should note that Black ran a particular offense, the **Belly T**, and he did it at the **high school** level. If you use a different offense, you might change the order of selection a little. And at the youth level, I believe you should also select in a different order even if you use Black's offense, because of the relative lack of passing.

Quarterback

A youth quarterback should be a guy who can adequately hand the ball off and throw an occasional look-in pass. Since that is such a dumb job, I eliminated it altogether by running the single-wing offense. If you use a traditional indirect-snap (quarterback under center) formation, like the vast majority of youth coaches, you should not waste a great athlete at quarterback. If you plan to have the quarterback keep the ball a lot, having a great athlete at youth quarterback makes sense.

The notion that a quarterback must be a great leader and athlete stems from the passing role he plays at higher levels. In youth football, he needs a commanding voice if he calls cadence. He needs the hands and poise to complete the hand-offs competently. And he needs to complete whatever passes you intend to throw. But leadership can come from any position. You don't need to be quarterback to lead.

Hand-offs cost you a blocker

You cannot hand-off and block at the same time. So whenever you put a hand-off play in your play book, you eliminate one blocker on that play. The quarterback generally is **behind** the play after the hand-off so he cannot block. The usual thing is to have him fake a bootleg.

If he ever gets **tackled** or causes a defensive player to **move away** from or **stay away** from the ball carrier, I'll agree the quarterback is contributing to the success of the play after he makes the hand-off. But I will be very surprised if your videotapes show anybody buying the quarterback's post-hand-off bootleg fake. If you emphasize quality fakes, you can achieve success with them. But the sort of ooomph required to achieve quality faking is rare among youth coaches.

One of our secrets: ten blockers, not nine

True, the entire defense knew my tailback was going to carry the ball in most of our plays in 1993. But at least he had **ten** blockers, not the **nine** that T-formation running backs have because the quarterback is dancing around the deep backfield holding an invisible ball.

If you run a traditional offense with a quarterback, I recommend that you do at least two or three **keeper** plays so you don't risk a fumble with a hand-off, don't miss out on the services of your best athlete, and so you have all eleven players in the play.

Hand-offs cost you your best athlete

The quarterback on most football teams is their **best player**. He is **overqualified** for the role of taking the ball from the center and handing it to a running back. He should be **running** with the ball or at least **blocking** for a runner.

I won't go just on the **theory** of the play or the fact that everybody does it this way. I couldn't care less how everybody does it. I want to know what makes sense, what is really working out on the playing field—not what **ought** to work.

If the typical youth coach were to move his fullback to tackle, his split end to guard, and his quarterback to wingback, he'd probably see a dramatic improvement in his offensive success.

Practice what to do if broken play

While I was coaching high school running backs in 1994, we ran a play where the quarterback was late to the hand-off point and the running back had already gone by. The quarterback threw up his hands in disgust at his performance. I told him broken plays happen in games and that he could not react that way.

I then had him deliberately pivot late for the hand-off on the next repetition and follow the running back through the hole. We did that a couple of times. Thereafter, it was standard for us to **deliberately repeat any broken play as a broken play** to make sure the quarterback would react instantly and correctly.

Later, in the first game of the season, that quarterback was in and missed a hand-off. He followed the running back through the hole so fast that it looked like a designed play. If you do not practice what to do in the event of a broken play, your players will not do the right thing when the broken play inevitably happens in a game.

The contrarian strategy

I have a master of business administration degree form Harvard Business School. And I make my living as a real estate investment writer. One of the common approaches in the financial world is called the contrarian strategy. In that, you simply do the opposite of what everyone else is doing.

I think that approach makes even more sense in football than it does in investment. Defenses are used to defending against certain formations and plays. There is probably a conventional offense in your league.

In ours, the offenses almost all use indirect-snap (quarterback under center) formations. Typically the particular formation they use is an I, power I, full-house T, wishbone, slot, or wing T. The plays they run are generally the sneak, dive, blast, off tackle, sweep, look-in pass, and the bomb pass.

Everybody's first play is dive right. Same at higher levels, too, believe it or not. You see an occasional four-wide-receiver formation (almost invariably they run the sneak or dive out of that formation), reverse or double reverse and the occasional halfback pass.

The Wishbone triple option

In 1968, Darrell Royal's Texas team won the Southwest Conference championship and beat Tennessee in the Cotton Bowl with the Wishbone triple option. The following year, they were undefeated, beat Notre Dame in the Cotton bowl and won the national championship. The following year, they again won the national championship.

That inspired Barry Switzer, a coach at Oklahoma, that Oklahoma should also be running the Wishbone triple option. They became the best offensive team in the history of college football.

In 1971, Texas, Oklahoma, and Alabama were the three teams that ran the Wishbone and they were "...running track meets on everybody." That is, they were running up huge scores. The 1971 Sooners set the all-time season rushing record with 472 yards per game average. In 1974, they led the nation in three offensive categories including an average of 570 yards per game overall.

Why did they have this success? Because they were using a **new** offense, the wishbone triple option. Switzer says, of the 1971 rushing record, "This is a record I really believe will never be broken, because it was set at the birth of the Wishbone."

Birth of the T formation

The Wishbone did not beat the T because it was better—only because it was **different**. The T had a similar effect when **it** was introduced. The "most decisive victory" in NFL history was the 73-0 drubbing by the Chicago Bears of the Redskins in 1940. The Bears used the latest offense, Stanford coach Clark Shaughnessy's T formation with a man in motion.

Tennessee dominated with the single-wing. Maryland was dominant with the four-man I formation in the early fifties. Knute Rockne dominated with his Notre Dame box shift and the forward pass. Bud Wilkinson's Spilt T dominated at Oklahoma in the late forties and fifties. In 1956, Coach Forest Evashevski won two Big Ten Titles and two Rose Bowls with the then new wing T formation.

Try something old

The various teams that dominated briefly with innovative **new** offenses may tempt you to create a new offense. That is not my point. I don't think they succeeded because their offenses were **new**. I think they succeeded because the defenses were **not used to** stopping their offenses. That is something you can achieve with something new **or** something **old**.

I suspect there are areas of the U.S. where all the local high schools are using the wing T. A coach who moves to that area from several states away might introduce an offense that is markedly different from the wing T, like the veer triple option, and win simply because his opponents only get three days to practice against the veer all season, but they get 17 weeks or more to practice stopping the wing T—not to mention the cumulative experience of playing for several years in those leagues and even longer experience of the coaches.

So make sure you understand that I am **not** telling you to **innovate**. Rather I am telling you to be **different**. You can do that by using a **new** offense, an **old** offense, or even an offense that is **currently popular**, but not in your league.

Opponent practice time

Only about a third of the teams I've faced scouted their opponents. If your opponents do **not scout** you, they will be shocked on game day by your offense, if it is different from anything else in the league. Their coaches will have to analyze your offense, devise alignments and job descriptions to stop it, find the right personnel to staff that defense, and teach those alignments and job descriptions, all **during the game**! That is next to impossible. We have slaughtered some teams that tried and nearly beaten others who were far superior talent wise.

Suppose the opponent **does** scout you and is able to analyze your offense over the weekend. They **still** only have three days of practice to staff and teach their new defensive system before they play you.

Three days versus years

If you use a **conventional** offense, your opponents will have **months and years** of practice stopping that offense. If you use an **unusual** offense that no one else in your league uses, your opponents will have only **three days** to practice for it. If it **so** unusual that even the opposing **coaches** have never seen it, they won't even know **what** to practice during those three days.

Here are some comments from Joe Blount's book on the short-punt offense.

> *The Short Punt, with its man-in-motion, various backfield alignments and scatter stuff from the "shotgun," presents a most unusual problem to coaches of T-formation teams. For one thing, their defensive way of thinking often becomes more or less stereotyped as a result of facing similar offenses week in and week out. Confronted with the multiple direct-snap styles, they must either spend long hours studying and erecting new defenses or else reconcile their regular "T" defenses to meet the varied attack. They generally take the latter course.*
>
> *Opposing coaches prefer to kid themselves into believing that the Short Punt is old fashioned and out-of-date and feel that their "T" defenses will hold up against such an archaic style of attack. I feel that you cannot contain a good Short Punt or Single-wing running team, with their ability to concentrate men at the point of attack, with a modern T-type defense.*

I said my tailback, Will Sykes, gained 1,583 all-purpose yards in one season in our single-wing. Blount's Joby Witt set a national record gaining **2,653** yards passing and running from the short-punt formation in one season.

And here are some similar comments written by Yale University coach Jordan Olivar and reprinted in Kenneth Keuffel's single-wing book, *Simplified Single-Wing Football.*

As far as I am concerned, there is no such thing as simplified single-wing football when you are on defense. Boys today come up through three or four years of high school football and one or two years of college ball before they ever see a single-wing team from a defensive viewpoint. Then in three days, we expect them to adjust to the new tactics presented to them. It is practically an impossibility. Somehow or other our JVs on Tuesday and Wednesday never did run the single-wing with quite the same efficiency as the Varsity got to see it on Saturday afternoon from our opponents.

The timing of the single-wing is so different from the T formation that boys continually face, that the defense just gets out of position enough and is unable to react the way they do to the T.

Napa

I always got a kick out of Napa in our league. They are part-time contrarians. Play them and you'll see the shotgun, the single-wing, and the lonesome polecat. Although their main formation is the wishbone. They tend to pass more than most teams and do it fairly well. They throw a high spot pass down the left side line.

In general, Napa was well coached and they executed these unusual formations and plays well. They scored a PAT against me with the lonesome polecat and a touchdown against a team on which I was the special teams coordinator with a perfectly executed speed option.

But we generally beat them. I thought they had too much offense. And in spite of their unusualness, they were conventional most of the time.

Every play

Real contrarians run weird stuff **every play.** I did that in 1993 and we had the second most potent offense in our conference after the state champions.

Every decision an offensive coordinator makes can be made in a conventional or contrarian way. I believe you gain a tremendous advantage for your kids if you pick a sound, but unique-to-your-league, contrarian offense. Here are the various decisions an offensive coordinator makes, along with the corresponding conventional and contrarian choices.

Decision	conventional	contrarian
type of snap	QB under center	direct to running back
formation	I, wing T, etc.	single-wing, polecat, shotgun
huddle	conventional	no-huddle
cadence	down, set, hut	first sound, silent
plays	immediate hand-off	delayed hand-off, keepers, options
types of blocks	drive	double-team, trap
line splits	4 to 8 inches	zero or bigger than one foot
balance	balanced line	unbalanced line
shift	almost never	frequently
motion	rare	frequently
cycles	one	more than one

You get the idea. In 1993, I ran a warp-speed, hurry-up no-huddle, unbalanced-line single-wing. As a general rule, neither the opposing players nor their coaches had ever seen a warp-speed pace or a single-wing. Heck, **I** had never seen either before. Some had seen unbalanced lines or brief no-huddle sequences. But they had never played an entire game against an unbalanced-line, warp-speed, no-huddle.

Multiple cycles

The term "cycle" comes up in discussions of the single-wing. It refers to a series of plays started by snapping the ball to a particular guy in the backfield. You can have as many as **four** cycles if you have four different backs within snapping range of the center. All quarterback-under-center offenses are **one-cycle** offenses—with the rare exception of plays in which the ball is snapped **between the quarterback's legs** to a deeper back.

The snap through the quarterback's legs might be a safer and faster and more deceptive way to get the ball to a fullback or tailback than the usual hand-off. We did one of our punts that way on a pee wee team in 1994. It worked quite well. In one game, where we did **not** do well, our best play of the day was a punt that followed a between-the-quarterback's legs snap. The defense had no one deep to receive it.

One-cycle offenses reveal the initial ball handler to the defense

In a one-cycle offense, everybody knows who's going to get the snap because there is only one guy back there or one guy under center. We ran a one-cycle offense for most of 1993. But that was unusual for a single-wing team. Most single-wing teams have two or three guys who line up in a position where they could receive a snap direct from the center.

The point is a lack of **hand-offs** in your playbook does not necessarily mean that the same guy has to carry the ball all the time or that the defense can assume they know, before the snap, who is going to end up with the ball. We had our upback too close to the line of scrimmage and too far to the side to receive a snap because we wanted him to trap block on the off-tackle play. We could have dropped him back so that he could receive a snap and had a guard pull to do the trap block.

We also could have moved our flanker back to what single-wing coaches call the **fullback** position—slightly ahead of and to the long side of the tailback. We didn't do that because we had to use one of our offensive backfield positions for the **flanker**—a position we were forced to have because of the inability of several of our smallest, youngest players to be effective at any other position.

Punt formations are multi-cycle

But when you put more than one guy back there, you can add additional cycles to your playbook. The most common example is the **fake punt** in which the center snaps the ball to the **upback** or blocking back instead of to the punter. That punt formation with an upback is a **two**-cycle formation. Punt formations with **two** blocking backs are **three**-cycle formations. Special-teams coaches who face teams with those punt formation must warn their players to be alert to the snap to the upback(s) and have their scout punt team run those plays.

Shotgun

The **shotgun** formation is also a two- or three-cycle formation. That is, there are usually two or three guys back behind the center.

At the 1993 Pop Warner Superbowl, the winning junior pee wee team from Wilmington, CA frequently lined up in a three-backs-side-by-side shotgun formation and snapped to a halfback instead of the quarterback. They then ran a student-body sweep to the opposite side, with the quarterback blocking. They also shifted to a regular single-wing formation and ran off tackle at times.

Warp-speed no-huddle

The warp-speed no-huddle was probably the toughest thing for our opponents to adjust to. And it was no problem at all for us to inflict it upon them.

The average youth football team runs about 40 offensive plays a game. We ran 70 to 80. The Benicia head coach told me after the game that his first-string defensive players were begging to be taken out of the game because they couldn't handle the pace we were setting. Our association president was on their sidelines during the game keeping track of minimum-play players and she confirmed that we were driving them nuts.

Clock-management offense

Do you need a **hurry-up** offense?

Yes. All football teams do because they may find themselves **behind** and need to be able to run plays quickly to score before the half ends.

Do you need a **slowdown** offense?

Yes—for when you are **ahead** or for when your **defense is weak** and you need to keep the other team's offense off the field.

Does that mean you must spend scarce practice time teaching a regular offense, a slow-down, and a hurry-up?

No. The solution is obvious. Just teach the hurry-up and have a way to control the pace from the sidelines. You don't need to always run it at that breakneck pace. We didn't. In fact, we could slow it to a crawl.

We clearly had the best hurry-up **and** best slow-down offenses in our league in 1993. Actually, I was in the California Youth Football League for six years and I have never seen **any** team that could conserve the clock or waste it the way we could in 1993.

Can't waste time on the regular way

Other coaches teach their offense to always proceed at a **medium** pace and treat the two-minute drill (hurry-up) and four-minute drill (slowdown) as luxuries they don't have time to practice.

That's crazy. The luxury you don't have time for is the non-clock-conscious offense. Run **most** of your practice snaps in **hurry-up** fashion then slow things down in the game when the situation or your personnel so dictate. You should practice the slowdown offense at least once a week.

One second

The rules say you may not snap the ball until:

1. the refs blow the ready-to-play whistle and
2. all your players are set for at least one second.

Why wait four seconds? We didn't. You shouldn't either. According to some game video I timed, the average time between the ready-to-play whistle and the snap is 19 seconds. We tried to snap within two or three seconds of the whistle.

What takes the average team so long?

- huddle
- sending a play in, typically by substitute or hand signals to the quarterback
- repeating the formation, play, and snap count to the players in the huddle
- going from the huddle to the line of scrimmage
- getting set
- calling cadence.

We eliminated all of those things. ALL of them.

You don't need a huddle. Huddles are silly; a waste of not only game time but also practice time. Huddles require a play book page and teaching how to line up in the huddle. Huddle discipline (only the quarterback talks) must be taught and enforced. And coaches spend countless hours telling players to break the huddle sharply.

How we ran it

Our linemen were trained to get into a three-point stance as soon as they **got the play** or heard the **ready-to-play whistle**, whichever came **last**. In the warp-speed mode, we made sure we showed them the play **before** the ready-to-play whistle.

In 1993, we wrote the play on a 24" x 18" white board with a Sanford Jumbo Expo II dry erase marker. We could have as many as ten plays numbered 0 through 9. We wrote a three-digit number on the board. The players had to do a mathematical calculation to decode the play. In 1996 and thereafter, I used a Magna Doodle, a magnetic drawing board you can buy in toy stores. You can write four inch-thick numbers on it then erase them with a slide. I went to the Magna Doodle because I feared the white board would not work in the rain. Thus far, I have not used a Magna Doodle in the rain either.

The code

The following is **not** our code, which I want to remain secret, but it is the basic idea. You could tell your players to add the first and third numbers together and ignore the middle digit. The play is the last digit of the answer. For example, 465 would decode as 4 + 5 = 9. That means run play number 9. 239 decodes as 2 + 9 = 11 or run play number 1, and so forth.

I thought that might be too complicated. It was **not**. Our players, who were 8 to 10 years old, **never** ran the wrong play all season—not once. The other coaches in our organization send plays in by hand signals or messenger and it often gets screwed up. (My 1997 13- and 14-year olds had more trouble with it.)

Code not broken

Opposing players tried to break the code. But they invariably gave up after several plays. The opposing coaches couldn't see the numbers. They can be seen from about 50 yards—which is the farthest a player on your team would ever be away from the white board. (Signal board at the thirty-yard line and ball on the far hash at the one-yard line.)

After we played Benicia in 1993, their coach asked me how I got our players to memorize such long play sequences! He did not see us holding the white board up. Nor did he notice our players all looking toward our sideline after each play. Nor did his players mention the white board, which they could see.

Binoculars but not enough time

A coach with **binoculars** could see the board. But he would have to break the code and communicate it to his defensive players, all while we are snapping the ball within two or three seconds of the ready-to-play whistle. I doubt it can be done.

Furthermore, our tailback ad libbed just enough that the plays we called didn't always look the same. If you actually broke the code, you would then see an ad-libbed play and think, "No, it must be something else."

All players at once

Virtually all coaches tell the quarterback the play, then he tells the huddle. That's dumb. It reminds me of that party game where you whisper a sentence to one person then he whispers it to another and so forth. The last person says what they think it is out loud and it's always comically garbled. When you tell a sub who whispers it to the qb who whispers it to the huddle, you have a partial version of that game.

We told all eleven players **simultaneously** from the sidelines with the white board.

I thought we might have a problem writing on the white board on **rainy** days. We did not. If you did, you might want to create flip numbers painted on metal or plastic instead of using a white board.

Teaching the warp-speed no-huddle

To teach the warp-speed no-huddle, we had the offense run plays during the offensive team period in practice. An assistant coach would stand off to the side with the white board. A coach would act as referee, blowing the ready-to-play whistle, whistling the plays dead, and placing the ball on the ground for the next play. Our players were told to **walk**, don't run, to their places for the next play after the dead ball whistle. We told them to walk because we had time and we did not want them to waste energy unnecessarily.

In practice I added one thing we did **not** do in **games**. When the referee blew the ready-to-play whistle, I started counting out loud, "One thousand one! Two thousand one! Three thousand one!" If I got to three and the ball had not been snapped, I said, "Why haven't we snapped that ball?"

Every night

Initially, they were a bit ragged. But we did this every night all August and through the season. By the second game, it had become a habit and a rhythm. Since I had 17 rookies and three veterans, the warp-speed, no-huddle was the **only** way most of them ever knew.

In practice, we ran plays right down the field, whistling them dead after four yards or so regardless of whether the defense made the tackle. When we got to the end zone, we would reverse direction and march back the other way.

Assistant coaches had to coach **on the run**. That is, they would observe their player, walk along side of him and whisper corrections so as not to interfere with the head coach's general corrections and instructions.

False starts

One of the unexpected benefits of our silent cadence was virtually **no false starts**. I think we had **two** in the entire 1993 season. And we ran about **two** seasons' worth of plays because of our hurry-up. The two false starts we did have came from defensive players deliberately drawing our guys off-sides. I should have had our scout team defense doing that every night at practice so our offense would get used to it.

No cadence

A quarterback calling cadence is a time-honored tradition in football. We regarded it as a **time-waster** as well as a **wake-up call** for the defense. We frequently ran a play while the other team was still in their defensive huddle or while opposing players had their backs to us. If you start calling cadence, the other teams hurries to the line.

In 1996, at Granada High School, I did a silent cadence for part of the season. We had a quarterback under center. Our J.V.s, who scrimmaged against us at times, said they could tell when the ball was going to be snapped by the movement of the quarterback's forearm muscles. You could fix that by having the quarterback wear a long-sleeve, loose-fitting-shirt like a baseball undershirt.

Also, I told the center that he could delay snapping the ball after the quarterback's signal. That's what most teams do with their silent scrimmage kick snaps. The holder or punter signals the center that he is ready and the center snaps whenever he feels like after that signal. That way, any defender who jumps on the movement of the quarterback's forearm muscles will at times draw an encroachment penalty. The silent cadence with the center having the option of delaying his response to the quarterback's signal is a way of varying the "snap count" without risking a false start.

In 1997, I used a cadence because we put a man in motion in most plays and I wanted a verbal way to start the motion.

Flick of the thumb

In 1993, with our single-wing offense, we signaled the center to snap the ball with a flick of the tailback's thumb. Our other players went on ball movement, except for the wingback who could not see the ball and had to go on the movement of his teammates. To those who say, "But you lose the advantage of knowing the snap count," I say, "First year in youth football?"

Youth football teams always have to go on the **same** snap count in my six years experience. I did the same at the freshman high school level. If you vary the count, you'll have players jumping offside. And even when you always go on two or whatever, you'll be amazed at how long some players take to respond to the count. Getting off on the snap count together is important in varsity high school and higher level ball. But I have never felt it was achievable or particularly useful in youth football.

We ran play after play almost as fast as a basketball team—all in eerie silence. When our team had the ball, all you heard was referees' whistles, crashing shoulder pads, and the wind rustling the tree leaves.

Long "count"

I figured we could have a long "count" by just telling the center to delay snapping the ball a second or two after the tailback's thumb flick in short-yardage situations. I thought some defenders would figure out that the center was snapping on the tailback's thumb flick and start to go on the thumb flick instead of ball movement.

Since none of our players but the center could see the thumb flick, delaying the snap would not cause **us** to jump off sides. I figured if the center delayed, and the tailback did not rock forward anticipating the snap, some defender would jump off sides. But it never worked. Maybe the defenders did not notice the thumb flick or felt they could not rely on it. Our tailbacks said the center missed the thumb flick on occasion and they had to do it again.

Defenses did go off sides occasionally against us—but probably less than normal—a minor **dis**advantage of our silent cadence.

First sound

There **is** one advantage of an audible cadence that I missed. When you say, "Ready, set" or whatever, the defense gets into the habit of waiting for "Set" to get into a mental and physical state of readiness. By snapping the ball on first sound, i.e., "Ready," you can usually catch the defense off balance.

Suisun knocks us out of the playoffs with a first-sound play

Our pee wees, which I was not coaching, got knocked out of the playoffs in 1993 on that play. A number of times during the game, Suisun would run an isolation or blast play (dive up the middle with one or more backs lead blocking) on first sound. Their players would stand hands on knees as if waiting for the "Ready, set" commands. But the play would **start** on "Ready."

The Suisun offense never got down in a set position. We had been telling our defensive down linemen to get ready as soon as the center touched the ball for years. But the kids still wait for the opposing quarterback to get his players set.

Suisun tied the game at six late in the fourth quarter then got the game-winning PAT by running their blast play on first sound against a Bears defense that was caught off guard. During the regular season, the Bears had beaten Suisun.

If you use a cadence, be legal to go on first sound

I generally recommend that you **not** use a cadence. It slows down your hurry-up offense in a critical way. But if you insist on using a cadence, make sure you run the first-sound play at times. To do that, you must make sure your players are in a legal formation before that first sound. You must also make sure they are motionless for at least one second before your quarterback makes that first sound.

Opposing defenses

Your offensive system should reflect the defenses you expect to face to an extent. In my experience, youth football teams generally run a 5-3-3 or a 6-2-3. In goal-line situations you may see a 6-5 or a gap-8.

Youth coaches are fond of blitzing. Although there is little reason to blitz with the narrow (4 to 8 inches) line splits and lack of passing in youth football. I think youth coaches blitz because they feel the percentage of times you blitz is a reflection of your manhood and they are eager to prove how manly they are. At higher levels you would take advantage of the typically undisguised youth blitzes by tossing a quick pass to a receiver running a replacement route. That is, the receiver would replace the linebacker who blitzed by running right to the zone the linebacker abandoned.

But in youth football, the passing game is typically so weak that throwing hot passes in response to blitzes would likely result in incompletions or interceptions.

In my experience, the strength of the defense in the best teams is the speed of their linebackers and defensive backs. The weakness of those same defenses is that their **ends over penetrate**, their **linemen** tend to **stand up**, and their **linebackers** tend to react **incorrectly** to **flow away**.

Over-penetrating ends

In the defense chapter, I said I had my ends box to stop the sweep. That is, they instantly sprint to the depth of the running backs. In my gap-8 or 10-1 defenses, that's not unsound because in those defenses, other people are taking care of the off-tackle hole. But when you box with a 5-3, you leave a big gap at the off-tackle hole. Here's a diagram showing the typical youth 5-3 after the ends have boxed to the depth of the running backs.

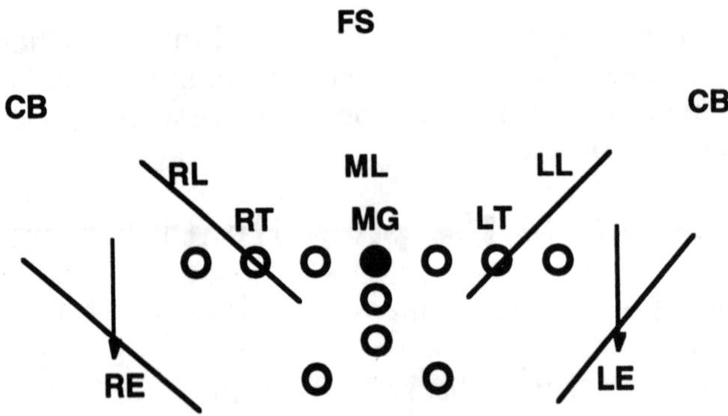

This is vulnerable to attacks at the corner. I've marked the running alleys on the diagram. You would block the penetrating end out with

- cross block or
- trap block or
- kick-out block by running back.

Then run inside him. You also need a couple of lead blockers to take care of the cornerback and nearest linebacker, although a little misdirection could get the linebacker to take a false step thereby taking himself out of the play. This behavior by the defense also is ideal for an **option** team. You would run quarterback keeps all day, perhaps pitching after you got downfield.

Nasty splits

You could enhance this effect by splitting your ends out a bit. Defensive ends or outside linebackers are generally told to line up on the outside shoulder of the offensive end or wing or to line up "on air" outside the offensive end or wing. They should have a large-split rule. A large-split rule basically says, "Keep widening out with the offensive player but don't overdo it." Here's an example of a large-split rule from the book *Missouri Power Football* by Dan Devine and Al Onofrio:

> *Play the outside shoulder of the [end] up to three yards and then head up from three to five yards. If the [end] is over five yards, return to normal position.*

As you can imagine, this defense rule, combined with an instruction to your offensive end to widen out to five yards, makes a huge hole in the defense. A split by the offensive end which puts the defensive contain man right at the limit of his team's large-split rule is called a "nasty split."

You should instruct your tight ends and wings to experiment with wider splits to see if the contain man widens out with them. You need a corresponding offensive rule as to when to move back in. If a linebacker moves up into the gap your end creates, you'd better move the offensive end back in, account for the backer with a running back, or run a quick-hitting play elsewhere so that a blitz by that linebacker would not get to the ball carrier.

'Stand-up guys'

Most youth defensive linemen are "stand-up guys." That is, they stand up as soon as the ball is snapped and look around to see what's going on. Since "low man wins" in football, all you need do to exploit this weakness is to discipline your offensive guys to stay low and to send lots of them through the middle. This is why the blast and wedge plays work so well in youth football.

Linebacker reaction to flow away

The inside linebackers in youth football are generally the best players on the field. Sometimes the safety is. Because they are so good and sort of in the open field, it is hard to block them. That's especially true if you assign relatively weak players to your offensive line and assign them to block the linebackers. The basic principle of offense is strength against weakness. Asking relatively unathletic linemen to block the best athletes on the opposing defense is weakness against strength—not a formula for success.

Inside linebackers are generally supposed to key on the running back on their side and mirror him if he flows toward the linebacker or outward like on a sweep. But inside linebackers are supposed to stay home if the flow goes away, that is, to the opposite side. The reason for that is flow away may be a precursor to a counter play coming back toward them at an angle from the far side.

The weakness is that the inside linebackers in youth football (and high school freshman and J.V. for that matter) have trouble **not** reacting to **all** flow. Their instinct is to mirror flow, which is fine when it is toward them or outward from them. But when flow is **away** from them, and the opposing offense has one or more counter plays, mirroring flow away is usually fatal to the defense.

Below are three diagrams showing the three types of flow and the correct left inside linebacker reactions.

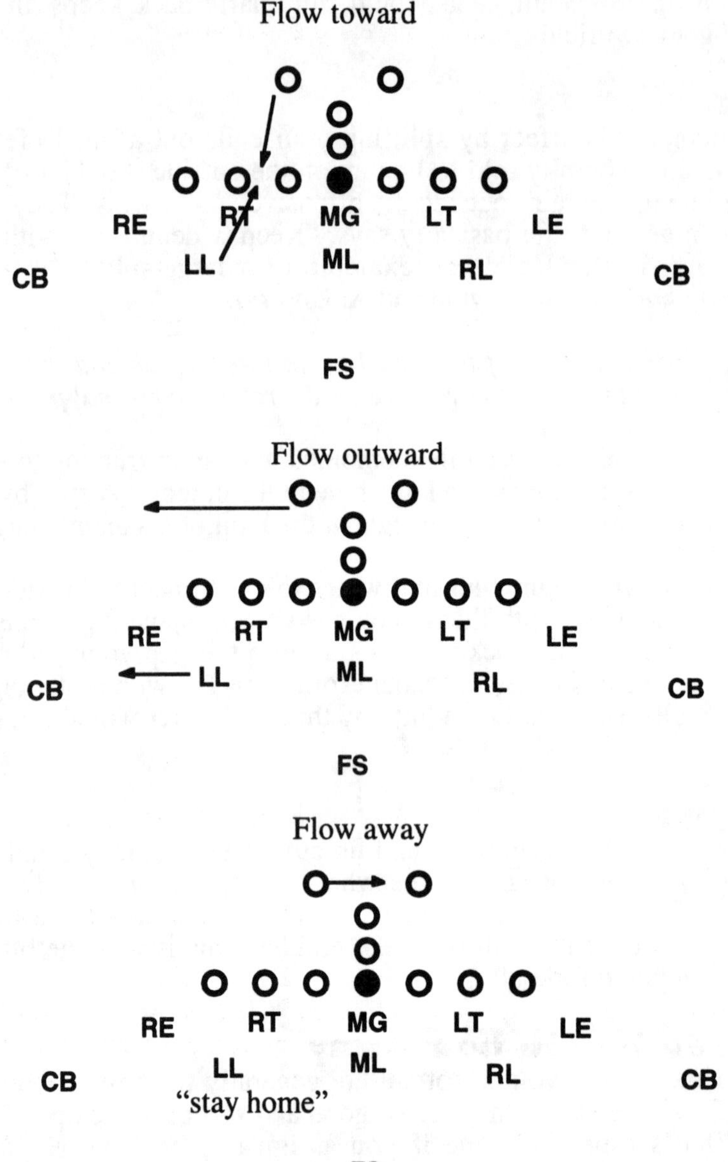

Basically, the counter play is going right where the left inside linebacker is before the play starts. But if he steps to his right to mirror the flow away, he will suddenly find the play going behind him faster than he can get back. He will typically reach out ineffectually trying to make an arm tackle as the ball carrier blows by him.

Accordingly, the ideal offense for a youth team that lacks speed would appear to be one with a wedge or blast or both, a power off-tackle play with some sort of inside-out block on the defensive end, and a counter that initially flows one way then comes back at an angle toward the other side.

Sweeps in your offense

If you have faster kids than your opponents, all you need to do is run the sweep. At our recent jamboree there were six different teams. Virtually all the scoring that day, other than by my team, was on sweeps.

Can slow teams sweep? Yes. I have done it on occasion. My current team seems to be quite good at executing two plays that end up as sweeps most of the time, although they are designed as play-action passes. Slow teams can sweep using the following:

- numerous inside running plays that convince the contain man to abandon his contain responsibilities
- crack-back blocks by wide receivers
- option pitches.

One of our 1993 opponents was Berkeley. They were much faster than we were. But we kept running the wedge and off-tackle play inside their left defensive end and he got fed up with it. I noticed he was crashing between our tight end and wing. So I called a sweep, it went 14 yards as he got blocked in easily by my wing.

That same year and since, I have been very successful with a crack-back block by the wide receiver. As we run wide, the contain main tries to get in front of the ball carrier and focuses his attention intently on him. Once he gets to where he is turning outward, the wideout has the legal right to block him from his blindside. Here's a diagram.

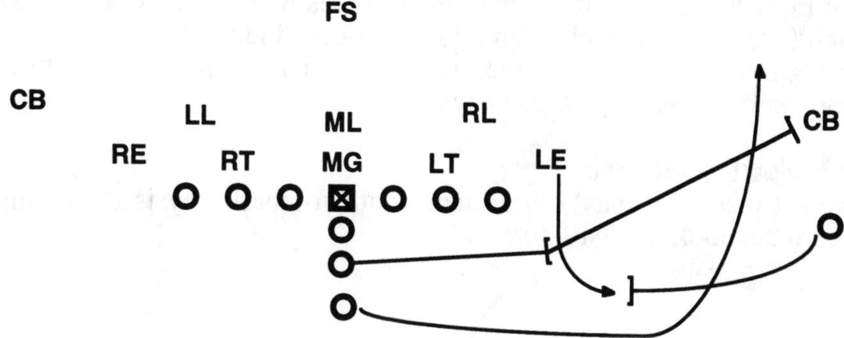

Crack-back tricks

There are a couple of tricks to the crack-back block. The biggest danger is clipping. Your crackers must be taught and disciplined to only block when they can hit the defender's front jersey numbers.

If they are approaching the defender and cannot see his front jersey numbers, they should scream, "Hey!" at the top of their lungs. That usually causes the defender to turn instantly toward the scream, whereupon he gets knocked flying. They can even yell "Crack!" which is a typical thing the defender's teammates yell when they see a crack back coming. Either way, the yell causes the defender to turn toward the blocker, which is what we want.

If the cracker cannot get the defender to turn around, he can stop and throw his hands up like a basketball defensive player trying to draw a charging call against a dribbling offensive player. Your ball carrier must be taught to look for the crack-back block and use it.

This is a great block. We have been amazed every year at our weakest players knocking stud defenders head over heels. It just happened in our jamboree the week before I'm writing this. Our quarterback said, "I thought I was about to get killed by the defensive end when he suddenly disappeared—knocked silly by our split end." It's a fun block to throw. And it is a way for slow teams to get outside.

Above, I described the quads formation I used at Granada High School in 1996. Our best play from that formation had the inside slotback protecting the rolling-out quarterback, the other two slotbacks running pass routes and the split end cracking back.

As the contain man homed in on the quarterback, things looked dire. Then, at the last moment, kaboom! and the quarterback was again running free up the sideline.

On my 1996 youth team, we tried the lonesome polecat offense for two weeks. Nothing else was working with that group of kids. And that didn't work either. But we briefly became the crack-back block capital of the world. We had two or three crack backs on every play. Defenders were flying around like bowling pins. It got comical. They would pursue the ball carrier while constantly snapping their head back over their shoulder to see if a crack-back blocker was coming (he was).

That helped the block stay legal and it does not reduce the effectiveness at all. When they see it coming, they tend not to go flying, but they aren't making the tackle either, which is the object.

Option pitch

I like the option but I have never coached the **triple** option. On my 1996 youth and freshman team sand again on my 1997 youth team, I have run an option where we faked a fullback dive then ran a true option at the contain man. That is, our quarterback pitches to the pitch man if the contain man comes at him and keeps the ball if he does not.

None of my three option teams has ever put the pitch on the ground, which I am proud of. But the 1996 teams did not gain many yards with it either. The 1997 team ran an option pitch for a 10-yard touchdown in the pre-season jamboree.

Every coach probably ought to have the option. That seems to be pretty common at the high school and college levels these days.

The ideal youth play?

Given what I just said, maybe the ideal youth football play is the counter option. Here's one from the book *Option Football.*

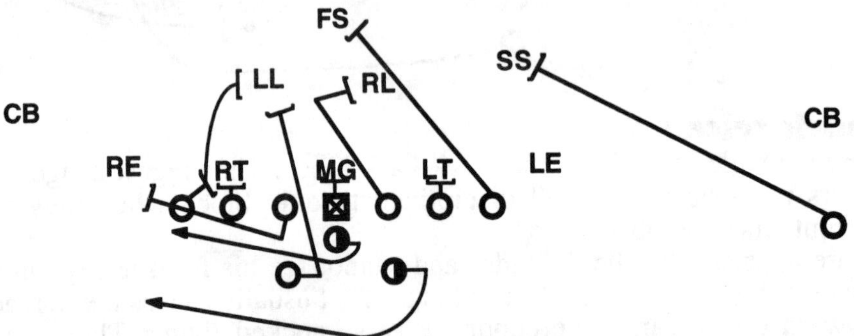

Remember the right defensive end would typically penetrate so far that the quarterback could easily run inside the trap block of the left guard. The quarterback would then option the cornerback. The right defensive tackle and middle guard would likely stand up, facilitating the block on them. And the inside linebackers would likely step one or two steps to their left in response to the initial flow of the offensive backfield. That, in turn, would facilitate the blocks of the dive back, left end, and right guard.

Pass defense

I am not aware of any pass that youth football defenses are weak on except the delayed pass like a tailback pass. In other words, youth football defenses tend to conclude the play is not a pass after a second or two of no indication of a pass. Actually, all defenses up to the NFL do that.

I have seen a pass that works extremely well at the high school freshman level. At Miramonte High School, where I coached and my oldest son now plays, we called it 26 power pass. It looks like this.

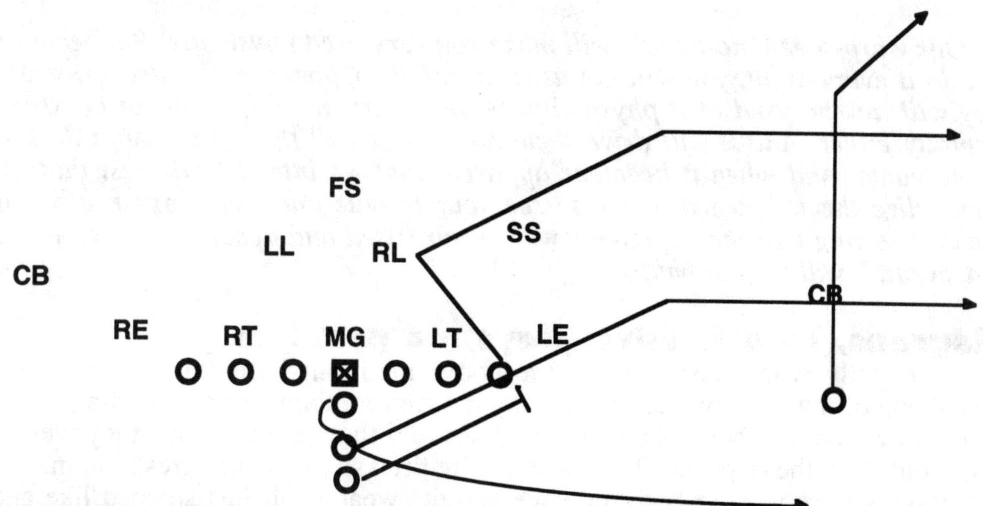

In youth football, I would not put three receivers out. Two should be enough. I would crack the flanker to give additional protection to the quarterback. I would also tell the quarterback that he was to **run** with the ball if he could, that he was only to pass if he could not run and if the receiver was **wide** open. My 1997 youth team (13-14-year olds) has been running the play with great success in practice and our pre-season jamboree.

This is a good pass because it puts all the receivers right in one line of sight for the quarterback. It enables either the quarterback or the fullback or the tight end or the split end to get out of bounds if the game situation so dictates. The pass to the fullback is easy to complete and has a very high completion rate because the passer and receiver are running the same direction and close to each other.

But forget theory. When my son was on the Miramonte freshman team, they ran this all season with great effect. I watched video of the freshman team from two years before when I coached that class their J.V. year. They were extremely successful with the pass that year as well.

In 1996, my Granada freshman team played Miramonte. I warned our defensive coordinator and our defensive players about this play. I ran it as coach of the offensive scout team. To no avail. In the game, which ended in a 20-20 tie, Miramonte completed the pass to their fullback. The pass traveled about four yards in the air, then the receiver ran about 60 yards for a touchdown.

'Used to it'

I do not like conditioning *per se*. Football players hate it. Conditioning drills are generally ugly, with much loafing, which I also hate. But I recognize that football players must be conditioned to perform at their peak during the time frame of a game. So I try to **sneak** conditioning into other stuff. Our warp-speed, no-huddle practices were an example.

Our players ran play after play for as much as forty minutes with no break and none of the usual between-plays discussions. The play was run, the dead ball whistle was blown. The ready-to-play whistle was blown within ten or fifteen seconds of the dead ball whistle, and the next snap occurred within three seconds of that ready-to-play whistle. At that rate, we ran about three plays a minute for twenty to forty minutes every night.

Your old friend, fatigue

These were run **full speed** against a scout team, although in 1993 our scout team usually only had about six players on it. (There were only 20 players on the team. With absences and injuries, only about 17 were 100% at any given moment in practice.)

I told our players at the beginning of the season,

Our warp-speed, no-huddle will make you very tired physically. But because you will do it every night, you will get ***used to it.*** *Our opponents will also get tired. But they will* ***not*** *be used to it physically. More important, they will not be used to it* ***mentally*** *either. And it will drive them nuts. They will think we cannot do this the whole game. And when it becomes apparent that we intend to do just that, it will demoralize them. You will come to see your fatigue and sweat as an ally, an old friend, knowing that the opponents will be surprised and upset by that same fatigue and sweat. It will help us win.*

97 degrees, 75 offensive plays, no problem

That's exactly what happened. In the above-mentioned Benicia game, it was 97 degrees. None of my kids ever expressed any discomfort about the no-huddle pace or the weather. They were not being stoic. We had not told them never to say they were tired. Indeed, I told them the opposite. Tell me if you're tired so I can get a fresh kid in.

My players were used to both the pace and the weather. It just seemed like another day at the office to them. Actually, games were **easier** than our practices. We had no time outs or kicks or quarter changes or half-times in the offensive team portion of our practices.

While my players were going about their usual business with nary a complaint or discouraging word, Benicia's first-string defensive players were begging to be taken out of the game.

Well-conditioned and having fun, too

I hate conditioning drills. I don't run them. No gassers or wind sprints. But I suspect my 1993 team was the best conditioned in the league by far. Yet they enjoyed a higher percentage of practice time than their less conditioned opponents, who probably all ran gassers and did pushups and so forth. Our players seemed to **enjoy** the fast-paced, nightly, no-huddle offensive practice periods. Running plays was what they came out for football to do. The fact that it improved their cardiovascular fitness and mental toughness dramatically was unnoticed by them.

Unusual offenses

Here are some unusual offenses along with books written about them.:

Offense	Title and author
Single-wing (power)	*Simplified Single-wing Football* by Kenneth Keuffel, Ph.D.
Single-wing (spinner)	*Single-wing with the Spinning Fullback* by John Aldrich
Single-wing (buck lateral)	*Modern Single-wing Football* by Charles Caldwell
Double wing (direct snap)	*The New Double Wing Attack* by Tierney and Gray
Double Wing (indirect snap)	*Dynamics of the Double Wing* by Hugh Wyatt
Short punt	*The Smorgasbord Offense for Winning High School Football* by Joe Blount
Spread formation	*Spread Formation Football* by L.R. "Dutch" Meyer
Split T	*Football: Secrets of the Split T Formation* by Don Faurot
Triple option	*Option Football Concepts and Techniques for Winning* by Scarborough and Warren
	Winning Football with the Option Package Offense by Bob Petrino with Marty Mouat
Lonesome polecat	*Run and Shoot Football* by Glenn "Tiger" Ellison

Most of these books are out of print. I have copies of all of them and have studied them all. To get them, ask your local reference librarian to do an interlibrary search or check with the out-of-print booksellers I mentioned earlier in the book.

You should note that many older football books like some of these advocate **blocking techniques** that are now **illegal**. But the illegal techniques are not crucial to any offense.

Deeper bench

If you have a deeper bench than your opponents, or some of them, you can use that to your advantage. For one thing, the warp-speed no-huddle will enable you to tire out the other team as rapidly as possible.

If you have the maximum number of players, and you come up against a team that has the minimum or just fewer than you, a warp-speed no-huddle with a fresh team going in every time the chains move could run the opponent into the ground, especially on a hot day.

Outnumbered two to one

I was on the **receiving** end of the maximum team-size mismatch allowed in our league. On the first day of the 1992 season, we played Elk Grove. They had the league **maximum** 35 players. We had the league **minimum** 18. The temperature was in the high 90s.

They were known as a very high-powered bunch of coaches. For example, they were the only youth football coaches I ever saw who used head sets to communicate with assistant coaches in the press box. I was not the offensive coach. We did not use a no-huddle that year except for an occasional three-play series later in the season.

Elk Grove did **not** use a no-huddle. But they did send in wave after wave of fresh troops while our kids were dying out there. Our boys would be down on one knee trying to catch their breath after a play when the entire Elk Grove team would trot off the field to be replaced by another string. We won the game 25-8. They scored the 8 in the last twenty seconds of the game. By then, three of our players had left the game with heat prostration. Had Elk Grove used a no-huddle, they might have beaten us.

To win, not run up the score

I am not advocating using a deeper bench to run up the score on a weaker opponent. In our league, if you get more than a 28-point margin in the second half, the game reverts to a controlled scrimmage. Rather I am telling you how you might win a game where the opposing team is stronger talent wise, but less numerous than yours.

I have seen some teams, especially in the playoffs, that suddenly have far fewer players than before. And guess who is missing? The minimum-play players. Last year in our league, the league officials called the missing players at home before playoff games to ask why they were not at the game. In some cases, they said the coach told them not to come.

If you encounter that, you should have no qualms about running the other team's "chosen few" into the ground.

Here are diagrams of each of the unusual offensive formations and some comments about them.

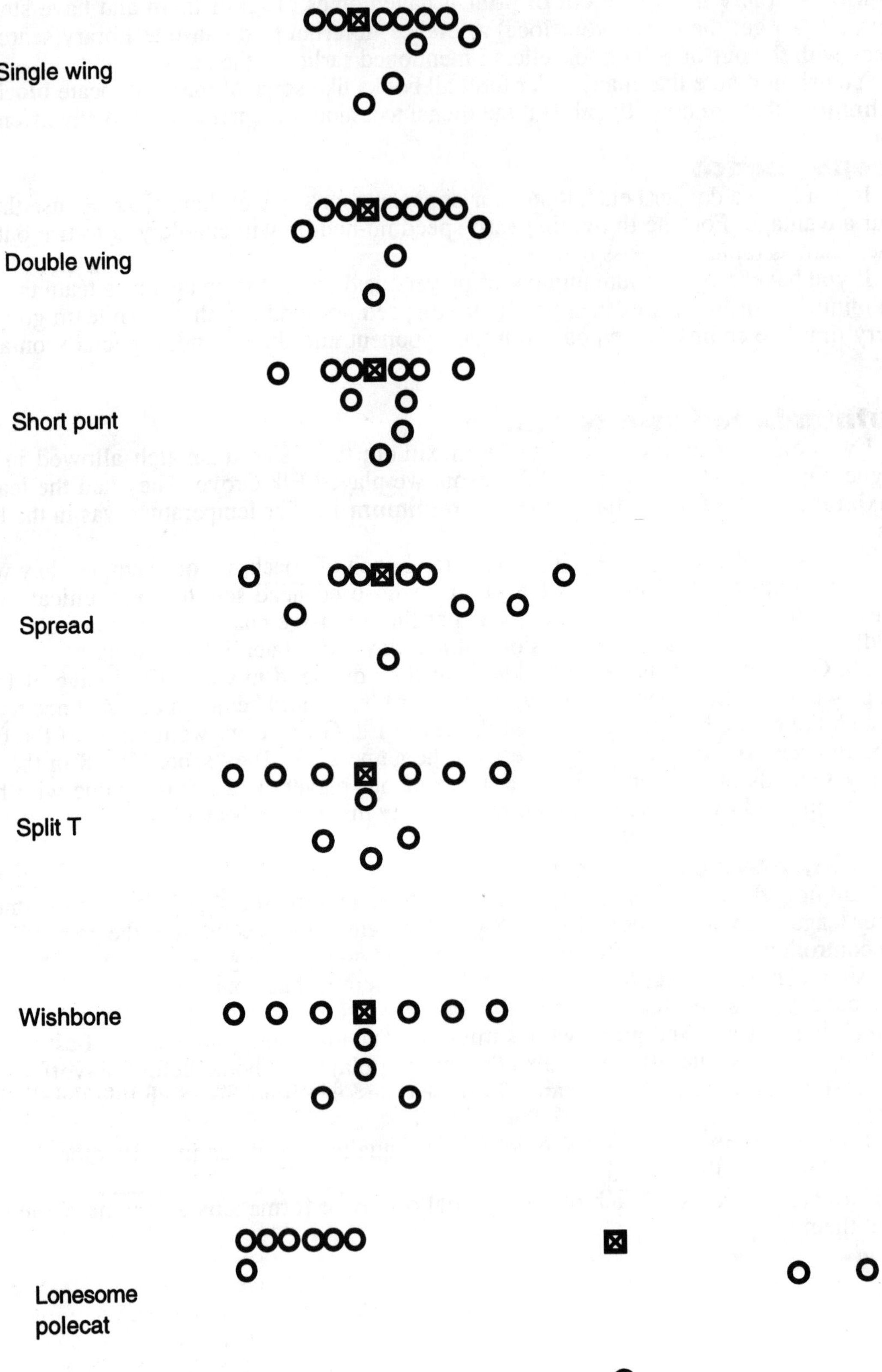
Single wing
Double wing
Short punt
Spread
Split T
Wishbone
Lonesome
polecat

OOO⊠OOO
O O O
O

Double wing
(indirect
snap)

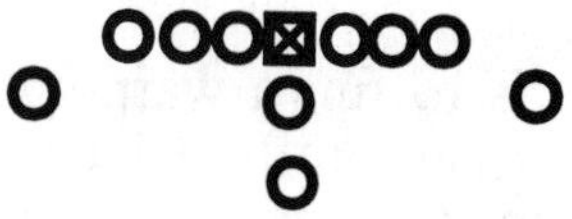

Of course, there are many variations of these formations. I have just diagrammed one of each. The unbalanced ones can be done to the left or right. The unbalanced lines can be balanced. All but the Split T, Wishbone and the second Double-Wing feature direct snaps. That is, the center snaps the ball directly to the tailback or other running back rather than to a quarterback who hands it off. In the Split T, Wishbone, and indirect-snap Double-Wing, the quarterback puts his hands under the center. The triple option can be run from not only the Wishbone, but also the split-back (veer) and I formations.

Sound offenses from successful coaches

Understand that each of these formations is proven **sound**. They are not nutcake ideas somebody threw into a book. The books named above were all written by established, successful coaches. Believe it or not, the college football national championship was, one year or another, won by teams using most of these formations (except the lonesome polecat).

According to his biography by Mike Bynum,

> *[Pop] Warner's genius also unleashed the powerfully explosive single-wing formation offense against Army in 1912 and almost overnight the game of college football would never be the same. His installation of a wingback, an unbalanced line, and an unbalanced backfield quickly became the vogue of the entire country. He would later unhatch the double-wing formation which was a highly successful passing attack.*

Short punt is a whole offense

Note that the **short punt** formation is not just for punts. It is an entire offense. It originated back in the days when quick kicks were an extremely popular tactic. It is a good quick-kick formation. But it is also a perfectly adequate single-wing type formation as well. With the short punt, the first task of the defense is to figure out to whom the center snapped the ball. There are four guys within range.

Polecat wins 98-0

Tiger Ellison invented the Lonesome Polecat in midseason when he was coach of an 0-5-1 team at a school that had never had a losing season. They won the rest of their games that season. In one, they won 98-0 in spite of trying not to run up the score. That week, their third-string quarterback was the leading scorer in Ohio. (Ellison ran the Lonesome Polecat as a no-huddle offense.) I tried the lonesome polecat in 1996 to try to make an extremely weak team competitive. It only made things worse. It requires a passer, some receivers, and at least three or four blockers. I did not have that combination. Also, I may have coached it wrong.

By getting one of these books and adopting a stripped-down version of its offense, you guarantee that your kids will have an advantage over their opponents. With each passing day, your players will get **better** at the offense in question. They will move down the learning curve in computer talk. Then on game day, they will totally surprise the teams that did not scout you and will likely be disproportionately successful against those who did.

Endless streaks

An idea I have had but did not try is to run a warp-speed no-huddle and have a succession of flankers run streak after streak on the friendly side (next to our bench) only. That is, my friendly-side flanker runs a streak route (full-speed, straight ahead, all the way to the end zone). Then he steps **off** the field in the end zone while a new flanker steps **on**to the field back at the line of scrimmage.

The rules say he must be within 15 yards of the ball momentarily after the ready-to-play whistle so watch that if the ball is not on the near hash. The new flanker runs **another** streak and steps off the field in the end zone while a **third** flanker steps onto the field back at the line of scrimmage and runs yet another streak. Combine this with the warp-speed no-huddle and you'll have the defensive cornerback on the friendly side tripping over his tongue after about three plays.

Since this is all happening within a few yards of **our** bench, the opposing coaches are unlikely to see it. When they finally figure it out, they will have a hard time matching our substitutions because their guys have to run 50 yards **across** the field each time in addition to running 50 yards **down** the field after we snap the ball. When the cornerback loses the ability to cover the receiver, throw to him.

Using your high school's system

I have made a big push for the contrarian approach in this chapter. But I know that most of you will probably **not** do that. In many cases, you may feel you **have to** adopt the system of the high school to which your players will eventually go.

I am somewhat leery of that. The head coach of the high school where I coached youth football was 0-8-2 in 1992 and made some noises about our teaching his system. My response was that we were 9-2 and that it might be more appropriate for **him** to adopt **our** system. That comment was not appreciated. But it didn't matter much because he was replaced the following season.

Will he still be there?

That's another reason to be leery about using your local high school's system. The high school coach may leave, for whatever reason, before your players play varsity football, in which case their having learned his system was a waste of time.

As I've explained repeatedly in this book, youth football ain't high school football. I have no qualms against using the local high school's hole- and back-numbering system if it's workable—although it usually . I wouldn't even mind using those plays in their play book which were well suited to youth football and the personnel I had that season.

Charge of the Light Brigade

But I would not want to coach where I had to lead a football Charge of the Light Brigade to an 0-8 season so that my players would know the local high school coach's current system for future reference. The success of the youth football team is a higher priority than the youth players learning the current high school coach's current terminology and system.

Another issue is that even if the high school coach stays, he often changes systems himself before your players join his varsity. The mimic-the-high school policy works best at the highest levels of youth football where the kids are similar in size to high school and will soon be in high school. At the lowest levels, the high school system is less likely to either **succeed** or **last** until the kids reach high school.

In 1996, I was a freshman football coach. In fact, I was the acting head coach until they hired a teacher to become the head coach. About six of my players were former Pop Warner players. What did that mean to me? Not much. I expected them to be leaders and to be over the fear of hitting. I taught **everybody** our terminology, not just the non-Pop Warner guys. I did not trust their previous youth coaches to have done that job. I did not even know what their previous coaches taught them. So if the coaches in that town's youth football had taught their players our high school system, it was lost on me. We proceeded as if the local Pop Warner team did not exist. I'm sure there are some exceptions, but my general impression is that high school coaches have no respect whatsoever for their local youth coaches. If you ask, they'll tell you they'd like you to run their system. But they really don't much care. In short, the notion that high school coaches are eager to have local youth coaches teach their system is generally a figment of the youth coaches imaginations.

Conventional offensive books

Earlier, I told you of a number of books on **unusual** offenses. Since most of you will probably go conventional, here are some references for conventional offenses. I have copies of each and have studied them all.

Offense	Title and author
Wing-T	*The Delaware Wing-T* by Raymond & Kempski
	Coaching Football Successfully by Bob Reade
	Scoring Power with the Winged T Offense by Evashevski & Nelson
Full-house T	*Missouri Power Football* by Devine & Onofrio
I formation	*The Complete Book of the I Formation* by Roy F. Kramer
Power I	*Football Coaching* by John McKay
Belly T	*Modern Belly T Football* by A. Allen Black
Power formation	*Mesa' Power Attack: Football's Winningest Offense* by Roger Worsley
Double slot	*The Explosive Double Slot Offense* by Tom Smythe

There are many other books about conventional offenses written by Bear Bryant, Vince Lombardi, Woody Hayes, and so forth. Those offenses are generally **multiple**, that is, they are combinations of the above. Multiple offenses are common in youth football. I think they are too complicated for that level.

Just use ONE BOOK

Again, I urge you to pick an offense then get a book on that offense and use **only** plays from that book. That will give you a unified, proven, field-tested, integrated system. Do **not** use **all** the plays in the book; just four to eight running plays and two or three passing plays of the nature described below.

Your high school's play book may be OK if your high school is successful and your personnel fit the high school's system. But if your high school is famous for passing, and you have no quarterback who can execute their plays, it would be suicidal to stick with the high school system. You need to identify what special talent you have on this year's team and pick the system that makes optimal use of that talent. And remember that you must **believe in** your system so that you can sell your coaches, parents, and players on it.

Number of plays

At the lowest level of youth football, 9-year olds, you should have **three**, maybe **four**, running plays and **one** or **two** passing plays. At the highest level, 14-year olds, maybe eight to ten running plays and four passing plays. Having far too many plays is probably the most common mistake made in youth football. Most youth coaches I have known put in 30 or more offensive plays. That's ridiculous.

Diagram the blocking

Coaches can diagram the backfield and receiver aspects of a play all day long. Kids can execute the backfield and receiver portion of dozens of plays. But what about the line? The main reason coaches come up with so many plays is that they leave the line blocking assignments off their diagrams.

In 1997, my play sheet handouts consist of the following for each play:

- diagram of the play against the 5-3, 4-4, and 6-2 defenses
- written description of the assignment, type of block, and first step of each player against the 5-3 and 4-4 defenses.

I can make a strong argument that even those three sheets of paper per play are inadequate. The linemen need to know how to deal with stunts by the defense. They may need to block against a defense other than these three. The guy they are supposed to block may be shaded on the wrong side so they have to make a line call asking their neighbor to switch blocking assignments.

For the offensive line, each play is really four or more plays because of all the different blocking assignments they have to execute versus different defensive alignments and stunts. So if you put in 30 plays, you're actually putting 30 x 4 = 120 plays in for the line. They cannot learn that many plays.

Practice time

At the beginning of the book, I said you should devote 30 minutes per night to offense. In our league, we are only allowed to practice three nights per week for the vast majority of weeks of the season.

That 30 minutes should generally be broken down into individual, small group and team time. For example, tight ends might practice their blocks or pass routes for ten minutes. Then they would team up with the offensive line and some offensive backs and run plays that did not involve wide receivers. Then they might do an 11-on-11 scrimmage where they execute all their plays.

Let's say they execute plays for twenty of the thirty minutes. If you run a very efficient, coach-on-the-run practice like I described above in the warp-speed, no-huddle section, you can run **three plays per minute**. That gives you 60 repetitions in twenty minutes or 3 x 60 = 180 repetitions per week.

It should be noted that the vast majority of practices are far less efficient, running maybe one play every three minutes because of lengthy discussions after each one. In that case, you get **six** plays per night, not sixty.

One play

I am intrigued by the notion of having just one play. That would give you 180 reps per week. You ought to get real good at that play.

Could you get so good at one play, say the off-tackle power play, that you could run just that play and win? No. You might be able to do it with a **triple-option** play, which is really three plays in one. You might even be able to do it with a **double**-option play like the speed option or the run-pass option. I'd like to try it some day.

You could **not** do it with one conventional play like an off-tackle because the other team would adjust. Even if their coaches did not, the kids would figure it out. They would gradually align closer to that point of attack and they would react faster and faster. That happened with the 1992 San Ramon versus Napa pee wee blast series I described in detail earlier in the book.

Three plays

How about **three** plays? That's how many the 1992 California Youth Football champion Suisun Indians told me they had. In my first two 1993 games, we were shut out. Then I said we were going back to just three plays for the third game. We won 33-6. The opponent, Delta Rebels, was weak. But getting our act together was part of the equation.

For the 1993 season, when we had our best ever offense, I mainly went with **four** running plays and two passing plays. And looking back on it, we got almost all our yardage and scoring out of **three** running plays. The two passing plays and the other running plays were a waste of time or may have even lost yards.

If you look back on your experience, I'll bet you find the same thing.

With three plays, you get 60 repetitions per play per week, if you distribute them evenly. With the usual 30-play play book, you only get six reps per play with very efficient practices. With the typical **in**efficient six-plays per night practice, you only get $18 \div 30 = .6$ reps per play per week. Is it any wonder the plays don't work on Saturday?

Which six?

Your six plays should be:

- an inside running play like a blast, wedge, or trap
- a corner running play with a double-team at the inside of the hole and a cross, trap, or kick-out at the outside
- an outside running play
- a counter or reverse
- a slant or look-in pass
- a roll-out or halfback run-pass option.

Perfect-play drill will set the number of plays

Another way to decide how many plays to run is the perfect-play drill. You simply run your various plays against a strong scout defense. Start with your most successful plays. If the play does not work, run it again looking for the problem. Then fix the problem and run it again to see if it's taken care of. Run each until all eleven offensive players do it correctly, then move on to the next play. In 1997, I found I could only get through about half of our fifteen plays in a 30-minute practice early in the season.

Inside running play

The most common inside running play in youth football is the **dive**. The dive is not a good enough play.

You should run a **blast** or **wedge** play instead. The blast is essentially a dive with one or two lead blockers. I recommend two. It's also called an **isolation** play. The basic design is that you need four backs somewhere in the backfield in the vicinity of the hole. It doesn't matter whether they are in the I or power I or wishbone or full-house T or whatever—only that they can get through the hole ahead of the ball carrier. I had much success with the inside trap play at the freshman level, which is the same age as the highest youth level.

Find it, don't design it

Don't design such a play. Get a book on an offensive system that you believe in and find their blast or isolation play and use that one. Here's a power I isolation play Ara Parseghian used when he coached at Northwestern to compensate for the fact that he had little 160-pound running backs. This is from the book, *Ara Parseghian and Notre Dame Football.*

SS FS

CB CB

IL IL

OL RT MG LT OL

Student body forward

We used the **wedge** in 1993 as our inside running play. It was our best play. I called it "Student Body Forward," which is pretty descriptive. Wedge blocking is apparently a difficult-to-learn skill. Since I never learned it, I could not teach it to our players. So we probably blocked it poorly.

But there were **so many** blockers that the defense seemed to have a hard time just **finding** the ball carrier, let alone tackling him. They knew who it was. Tailback Will Sykes wore number 22 and was the only guy in the backfield. They saw him catch the long snap and plunge into the mob. But then they lost sight of him. By the time they worked their way into him he had gained six to eight yards. Often he would go for 43 yards or so on that play, dragging tacklers with him.

Here's a diagram of the wedge play from Kenneth Keuffel's book, *Simplified Single-wing Football*.

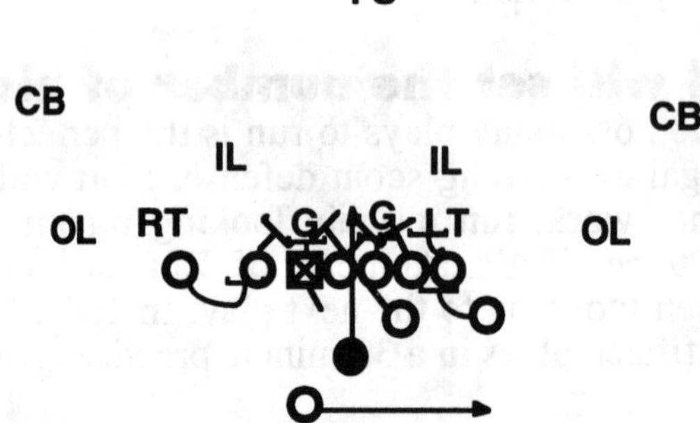

In the single-wing, you have to have the blocking back fill the gap between the center and guard because the center has his head down looking though his legs. As a result, he is slow to join the wedge. If you do not have the blocking back fill that gap, a defender will come through it.

31 Trap

There is one play I've become fond of from my high school coaching experience. Here is the I right 31 trap play used by Miramonte High School's J.V. team in 1994.

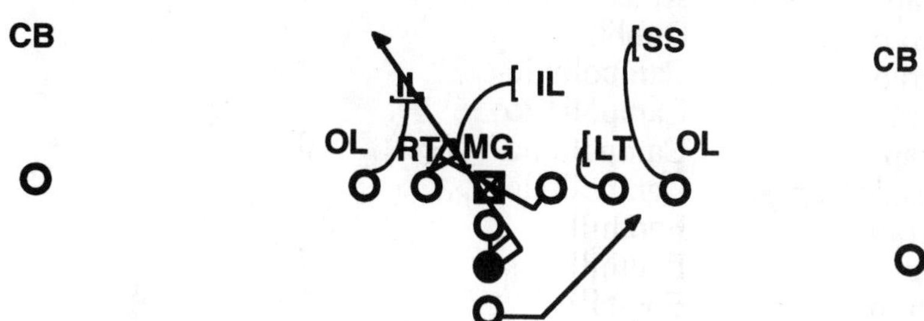

I'm covering this in the inside-running-play section. But it also could be considered a **counter**. The initial flow is to the right. Then the ball carrier cuts back to his left. The key block is the trap by the strong side guard on the right defensive tackle.

This was amazingly effective. Our J.V. team went to a week-long football camp at the University of Nevada at Las Vegas in the summer of 1994. We had to play against **varsity** teams from other schools because no one else brought their J.V.s. We generally did not do well, except when we ran this play. It went for big yards again and again in spite of the fact that it was being executed by our J.V.s against other schools' varsities, even when our weaker running backs carried the ball.

Here are some other variations we used at Granada High School in 1996.

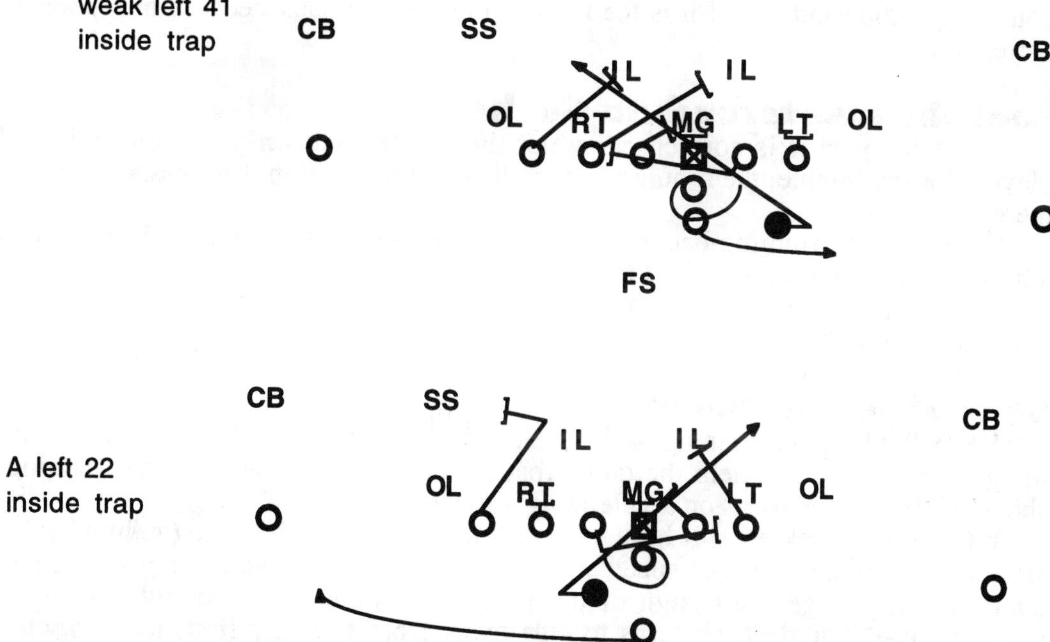

You get the idea. In all, by the end of the season, we had twelve different inside trap plays that went through the one or two holes (center-guard gaps). Look at the success we had with them:

play	opponent	average yards per play
SR DTU 41 inside trap	Miramonte	7.5
WL 41 inside trap	Las Lomas	15.5
IR 31 inside trap	Alhambra	4.5
BR 41 inside trap	Dublin	5.0
BR 41 inside trap	Campolindo	13.3
AL 22 inside trap	Campolindo	9.5
IR 31 inside trap	Campolindo	10.0
SR DTU 41 inside trap	Campolindo	6.0
BR 41 inside trap	Foothill	15.5
IL 32 inside trap	Foothill	7.0
AL 22 inside trap	Foothill	6.0
IR 31 inside trap	Foothill	4.0

I said you should only have four running plays and I've just given you three to attack one hole. At that rate, I'll be giving you fifteen. It's fun to draw plays. But don't get the impression that you should use all three of the ones I just gave you. Pick **one** only.

Tendency to slow up or stop

A common problem I see in youth football on hand-offs is the running back comes to a **full stop** to receive the hand-off. The problem there is **both** the quarterback and the running back are taking responsibility for the hand-off being made safely. The coach must teach the running back that his only responsibility is to accelerate into the hole with a proper pocket and to tuck the ball away after he receives it. It is **solely** the responsibility of the **quarterback** to make the **hand-off**. The running back must focus his eyes on the **hole**, not the ball. And he must not reach for the ball.

If you are having trouble with hand-off fumbles in practice, station yourself where you can see the hand-off. If it is the fault of the running back because of a poor pocket, correct him.

Beat the quarterback to the hole

But if his pocket is correct, chew out the quarterback **only**. If you criticize **both** players for the fumble, the running back will slow up to a stop if necessary to make sure there is no fumble.

I was the J.V. running-backs coach at Miramonte High School in 1994 and I often admonished the running backs to, "Beat the quarterback to the hole!" on quick-hitting plays. It is a cardinal sin to let the running back slow down to accommodate the quarterback.

Don't slow the runner

You must keep the running back accelerating into the hole. You must **not** let him try to use slower speed to help the quarterback. Putting a stopwatch on the running back should help keep his focus on accelerating into the hole.

If the quarterback doesn't have enough time to get the ball to the running back, don't slow up the running back, speed up the quarterback. If you cannot speed up the quarterback, change the design of the play. For example, you could change from a **reverse pivot** (quarterback turns to side away from the play first) to an **open pivot** (quarterback turns to the play side first). Or you could have the running back line up a step or two **farther back**.

But do **not** allow the running back to slow up or stop as a way of correcting hand-off fumbles. (In some plays, the running back delays leaving because some other business, like a fake hand-off, must be completed first.)

Integrated system

Now I want to give you some corner running plays, that is, off-tackle plays. But you should try to have an overall integrated offensive system. By that I mean that you should have a series of plays which **look like each other**, at least in their initial stages. If each play has a totally different look, the defense can tell which one you're running as soon as your players take their first step. That's why you should get your whole offense out of **one book**.

Here's how Roger Worsley, author of *Mesa's Power Attack: Football's Winningest Offense,* introduces their off-tackle play:

> *In the Power Offense we feel we have the best off-tackle play in high school football. Over the 25-year history of the Power Offense this play has been our most consistent ground gainer. Everyone we play has a defensive alignment just to stop this play. Not many have ever succeeded in doing so. If the defense does not overshift into the off-tackle hole, we feel we can run any basic defensive alignment off the field with just this one play.*
>
> *With this introduction to what we in Mesa feel is the best play in high school football today, we give you the off-tackle play of the Power Offense.*

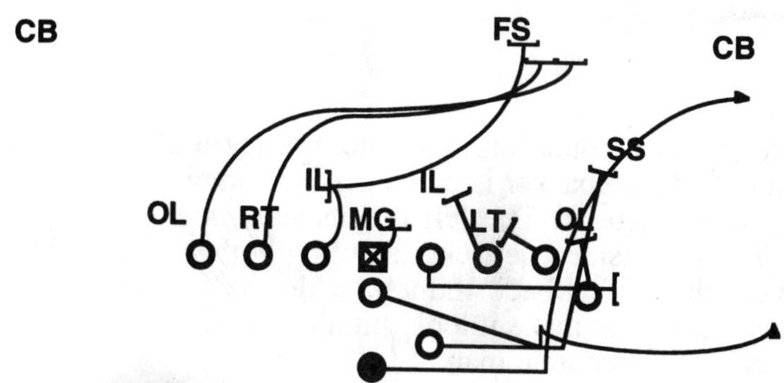

Single-wing type backfield except for quarterback

Although Mesa has a conventional quarterback under center, their backfield is otherwise lined up in single-wing fashion. Their pulling guard's trap block is also a classic single-wing maneuver.

Mesa has a "strong" backfield. That is, they are all on one side. As I said earlier in the book, I think youth football offenses are pretty good about adjusting their alignment to **wideouts**. But they generally **ignore** unbalanced **backfield** alignments as long as the backs are inside the tight ends. So you might want to take advantage of that by using a strong backfield. Note also that the defense in Mesa's diagram has shifted to reflect the strength of the Mesa backfield. In youth football, you would probably not see this.

Four double-teams

The most powerful off-tackle play I ever saw in a book is Play 36 from Joe Blount's *Smorgasbord Offense for Winning High School Football*. That, you'll recall, is a form of the single-wing known as the short-punt offense. Here's how he describes it.

> *Play 36, the tailback off-tackle to the strong side, has gained more yardage and scored more touchdowns than any other single play in our attack. There is an old saying among our quarterbacks, "When in doubt, call play 36."*

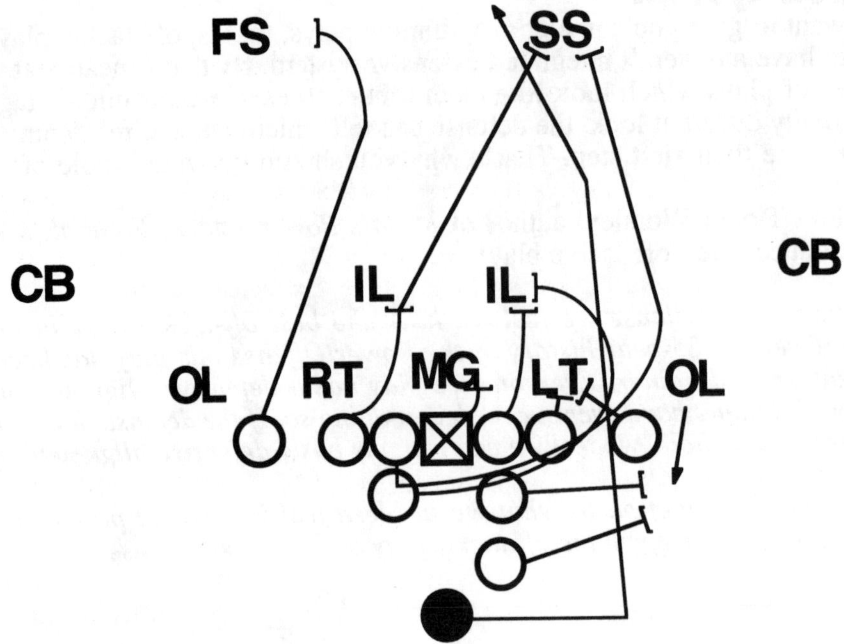

Note that there are **four**, count 'em, four, **double-team blocks** in the running lane on this play. The left outside linebacker is crunched by a running double-team trap block by the fullback and right halfback. The left defensive tackle is hit by the right end and offensive tackle. The left inside linebacker is hit by both guards and the strong safety is sandwiched between the left halfback and left tackle. As with Mesa's off-tackle play, the ball carrier and his teammates make it look initially like a **sweep** before the tailback cuts behind the trap block on the contain man.

Outside running play

The main outside running play is the **sweep**. For teams with a fast back, it is probably the main play in youth football. (In high school, the main play is the power off tackle.) If you do not have speed, you still need a way to attack the outside, if only to force the defense to station guys out there. Here's the great Green Bay Packers power sweep made famous by Vince Lombardi. There's a 47-page chapter on just this play in his book, *Vince Lombardi on Football.*

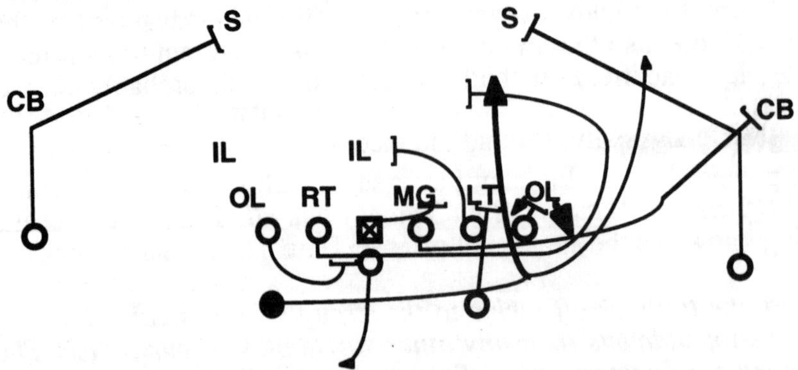

The key block in the Lombardi sweep is thrown by the tight end. He blocks the outside linebacker "whichever way he wants to go." The ball carrier reads that block and "runs to daylight." That is, if the outside linebacker goes outside, the ball carrier goes inside, and vice versa.

My play book

I'll give you my whole 1993 playbook later in this chapter. It shows our single-wing sweep. The key feature of our sweep was that it began like our off-tackle play and reverse. We also had the flanker crack back on the contain man and the upback block out of the cornerback, thereby creating a sort of long-range cross block. But the key to the success of our 1993 sweep was generally not blocking, it was Will Sykes' speed and his little inside shoulder dip fake as he reached the critical turning-the-corner point.

What if you don't have that speed? Our 1992 team got a lot of mileage out of a fake pitch right, hitch pass left. A hitch pass is a pass to a player who stands still. In fact, we got one of our two touchdowns against Vallejo with it. We beat that previously undefeated team 13-6.

Not against my defense

But I always told the offensive coordinator who ran that play that he should be glad he was not playing against **my** defense. I would have seen that play in scouting, licked my chops, and had my scout team run it over and over. We almost certainly would have intercepted that pass and ran it back for a big gain, if not a touchdown.

In fact, the fake pitch was a nice early warning of the hitch pass because we had no pitch play at all. The **only** play with pitch action was the fake pitch right, hitch pass left play.

I would have trained my cornerback to react to the pitch action by running up to intercept the pass. The pass did not cross the line of scrimmage so the defender could shove the flanker out of the way to grab it. There is no pass interference on passes that do not cross the line of scrimmage. He could also just bat it down then run over and pick it up because it usually was a backward pass. So with that warning, I will nevertheless note that our offense never got burned and often gained big yards with that play.

Artificial speed

You can artificially create speed by having the sweeping back go in **extended motion** before the snap. You need many repetitions to get the timing down. You would snap the ball so that you could pitch or hand the ball off to a back who was running sideways at full speed. Such a head start may be enough to get your slow running back around the corner. We sometimes have our scout offense team use that technique to simulate speed in an upcoming opponent.

Deep wing

Here I'm violating my advice to stick with established proven plays. But I've had this notion for years and still suspect it might work. Wingbacks who are a yard outside and a yard back from the tight end or tackle, always bothered me as a defensive coordinator. I told my youth defensive ends to line up **one** yard outside a **tight end**, but **two** yards outside a **wingback**. Basically, I found that necessary to get the end into the backfield to the sweep spot untouched.

Caused us trouble in high school, too

Even in high school, we had to do extra practice the week we were going up against a Wing-T team to figure out how to handle the wingback.

Our J.V. head coach insisted on the outside linebacker being aligned on the outside shoulder of the tight end even when there was a wingback. We found we had to put the outside linebacker in a **three-point** stance to deal with the double-team block by the tight end and wing. Normally, the outside linebacker was in a **two**-point stance. We also had to tell the strong safety or corner that if he saw the wing block down on the outside linebacker, the strong safety or corner immediately had to take over the outside linebacker's **containment** responsibilities. That's because it took all the outside backer's strength just to hold his position against the wing-tight-end double team.

Two yards

But what if the wing is one yard outside the tight end and **two** yards off the line of scrimmage? Logically, my youth defensive end would have to move even farther outside than two yards to make sure he could get to the sweep spot untouched. It seems to me that a **deep** wing can control a lot of ground at the corner. In sweeps, the contain man need only be stopped momentarily for the play to work.

Motion to wing

You could station a man outside the end as a wing. But most youth teams adjust their alignment pretty well to players lined up outside the tight ends. Or you could **motion** him to that spot where he suddenly turns upfield and blocks the contain man in. Youth teams often do **not** adjust properly to **motion.**

Vacaville once put a deep flanker out wide of my defensive end when he would not let the offensive end get outside position on him. The flanker went in motion then cracked back on my end. The sweep gained big yards but was called back because the man in motion went **towards the line** before the snap. That's illegal motion.

Other tricks for getting outside when you are slow

You could use the **speed option**. In that play, the contain man is not blocked, he is optioned. That is, the quarterback runs along the line of scrimmage **at** the contain man. If the contain man comes at **him**, he **pitches** to a back who is four yards deeper and four yards outside him. If the contain man goes for the **back**, the quarterback **keeps** the ball and cuts up inside the contain man. Whatever the contain man does is wrong.

Napa ran this play against us for a touchdown in 1994. My 1997 team ran it for a touchdown in our pre-season jamboree. I had no confidence in the play at that stage of the season. I only ran it to scare the opponents who were scouting. I laughed when it worked. It takes a lot of practice to avoid making bad pitches or bad reads.

Run-pass option

Another option-type play is the sprint-out, run-pass option. In this, your quarterback sprints out to one side and looks for a guy to pass to. If the quarterback has a running lane open, he tucks the ball away and runs. If not, he looks for an open receiver. If he finds one, he passes to him.

The threat of the pass tends to make the defenders hang back, which enables the quarterback to gain yards by running. Most youth quarterbacks have trouble throwing on the run. They usually have to pull up and stop to throw. You have to teach them how to throw on the run and drill them on it a bit. It's relatively easy to learn. Some kids figure I out instinctively. Every player can do it if they know the correct technique and drill it until it becomes instinctive.

Throwing-on-the-run technique

The quarterback must run while holding the ball with two hands in front of his chest. The throw comes between the throwing-arm-side foot hitting the ground and the other foot hitting the ground. Let's say the quarterback in question is right-handed. As he steps with his right foot, the quarterback must cock his upper body. That is, he turns his upper body so his left shoulder points at the target and his right shoulder points away from the target. The ball moves back to his right shoulder. As he takes the next step with his left foot, he throws the ball.

The path on which he is running should be **at** the receiver. He should **not** throw across his body (to the left of the path on which he is running) or throw away from his body (to the right of the path on which he is running). Actually, if the receiver is close, you can violate those rules. But if the ball needs any velocity because of distance or the need to zip the ball near defenders, the technique must be correct.

After the throw, the passer must continue running at the target. He must not come to a stop like a baseball pitcher.

To teach this technique, go step by step. Start the quarterback with his non-throwing side foot forward. For a right-handed quarterback, that is his left foot. Say, "Step and cock." On that command, the quarterback steps with his right foot and simultaneously cocks his upper body and the ball. He freezes there awaiting the next command. You check his position then say, "Step and throw." He steps forward toward the target (coach, receiver, or another quarterback) and throws doing his normal follow-through (should end up with thumb near crotch and palm facing outward). Again he freezes while you check his position. Then you say, "Step. Step. Step" The passer then walks three steps toward the target.

Do this over and over, gradually speeding it up until the passer can do it at a walk then at a jog then at a run. It will become second nature if you give him four or five reps a night in a drill then also do it is scrimmage or some such.

Wide slot

You could try to overcome your speed handicap by using the best formation for the sweep. That's probably the wide slot. In fact, in preseason jamborees, I can usually tell that the opponent, whom I have **not** scouted, plans to run a sweep, whenever they come out in a slot. Using a slot formation **only** when you plan to sweep is dumb. But if you **always** use a wide slot, you put yourself in the best possible position to run the sweep without giving the play away.

Best blocker

The key block in the sweep is the **reach or hook block** on the contain man. If you lack speed, that block becomes even more important. You could assign your **best blocker** to the position that makes that hook block to help your slow running back turn the corner.

The standard sweep is the **quick pitch**. Some youth teams try to use a hand-off to start a sweep. If you lack speed, you'd better use the quick pitch. It takes a lot more practice than a hand-off but can be mastered by youth football players.

In 1994, our wide-side defensive end **intercepted** a Berkeley pitch and ran it in for a touchdown.

Delayed plays

Delayed plays like the **end around** might work by waiting until the contain men have begun to converge. The same is true of a **delayed swing pass to a back coming out of the backfield**. Youth football teams rarely cover backs coming out of the backfield. Heck, high school teams have trouble with that, especially if the back delays. Once the play gets started, the defenders tend to focus on the ball carrier and jump to conclusions about what he is going to do.

Fake reverse

In 1994, when I was special teams coach, we got ahead of the Oakland Saints 14-0 at halftime. But in the second half they scored a couple of touchdowns. They ran two reverses which were not very successful. Then they ran a fake reverse which went about 30 yards for the winning touchdown.

In 1996, I put a reverse into our freshman offense. But the reverse scared me so much that I never ran it. However, when we played Miramonte, I put in a fake reverse. I figured you could not run a fake reverse unless you set it up with a real reverse, the way the Oakland Saints had done to us. But in the case of Miramonte, I decided setting it up was not necessary because they had set themselves up. The previous year, my son was the tailback who ran the reverse on the Miramonte freshman team. In fact, it was almost their only PAT play.

So when we scored against them in 1996, I called a fake reverse for the PAT. It worked perfectly. Their contain man chased our faking wideout halfway across the field.

I concluded that it was not necessary to set up the fake reverse with a real reverse. Most teams had run the reverse themselves or seen it enough times that they were sufficiently set up. So we ran the fake reverse but not the reverse.

Alhambra beat us 30-0 and held us to an average 1 yard per carry. But our fake reverse went for eight yards against them. It went four yards against Acalanes, three yards against Dublin, 21 yards against Campolindo, and two yards against Foothill. Never lost.

We tried to help it with some sideline sound effects. Just before the snap, I would gather a group of sideline players and tell them to yell "Reverse!" on a count of three. I would then count so that the word "reverse" would be yelled just as the ball carrier started to sweep. I don't know if it did any good, but we had fun doing it.

On opening day of the 1997 NFL season, Mike Ditka's New Orleans Saints ran a fake reverse on a kick return. It went all the way for a touchdown.

The bottom line is that all teams need a way to attack the hole outside their linemen. If you cannot force the defense to defend the width of the field, they will concentrate their forces between the tackles and shut you down. If you don't have the **speed** to get outside, you'd better find a **finesse** way to get out there.

Counter

If the initial flow of your backs always indicates the direction the play is going, the defense can react quicker and more decisively to your plays. So you should have some play that starts to go one way, then goes back the other, to keep the defense honest. Counters and reverses are the plays that do this.

I've already given you Miramonte's 31 trap, which is a sort of counter. The offense that is best known for counters is the wing-T. The dean of Wing-T football is University of Delaware coach Tubby Raymond. Here's his "134 counter trap" from his book, *The Delaware Wing T: An Order of Football.*

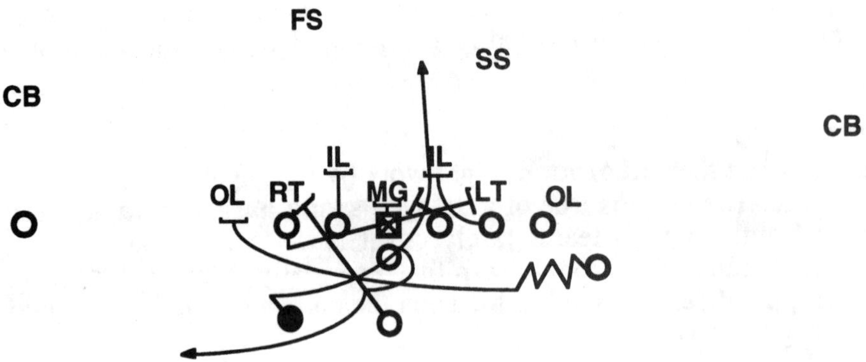

Raymond says,

> *The addition of the tackle trap, which was introduced in 1955 and consummated in 1957 as 134 counter trap tackle pull, resulted in the development of the most classic of all Wing-T running plays. This play is the foundation of the attack and is used by virtually every NFL team.*

Note that counters are generally characterized by **initial** movement **away from** the real direction of the play, along with a trap block. In this case, the fullback and halfback initially move to their left. The wingback was also in motion that direction before the snap. The quarterback reverse pivots (turns to his right to make a hand-off to the left of his original position) then goes to the left as well. The ball carrier, the left halfback, takes one step on his left foot then attacks the right side A gap. (Raymond's exact words are, "Rock weight on left foot") He receives an inside hand-off, that is, the ball is handed by the quarterback **toward** the line of scrimmage. The left offensive tackle trap blocks the left defensive tackle.

Reverses

Reverses go for big gains in youth football, often long touchdowns. But I have trouble getting excited about the reverse because my defenses have usually turned them into big losses for the offense. If the defense you oppose does not have disciplined trailmen, players who trail sweeps away from them through the offensive backfield, and your reverse ball carrier has a modicum of speed, the reverse should work.

Our 1993 reverse

The play we used as our counter in 1993 was a wing reverse with an inside hand-off. Most reverses feature **outside** hand-offs That is, the hand-off direction is **away** from the line of scrimmage.

Our single-wing reverse also occurred right behind the line of scrimmage. Most reverse are **deep**.

Our reverse hand-off occurred very late in the play. That's true of most reverses. But in our case the ball carrier was about to cross the line of scrimmage when he gave the ball away. That's unusual.

Finally, our reverse was an **off-tackle play**. Most reverses go wider. In all, it was a play the likes of which our opponents had never seen.

Our 1997 reverse

I used a similar play in 1997 on my 12-14-year old team. It worked big time in our first game of the 1997 season. Basically, we faked a dive right, then gave an inside handoff to the right wing going back across to the left. On the first play of the game, it went 25 yards. It was stopped for a two-yard loss when a safety made a lucky blitz right through the pulling guard hole. Then it went 60 yards for a touchdown. I immediately put in a mirror-image version going to the other side. It averaged 17.8 yards that day.

Funny to watch

When it worked well, our 1993 reverse was comical to watch. Opposing players would run right past the ball carrier and do a double take.

There is a rhythm to the usual conventional football play. The ball is snapped to the quarterback and he immediately hands it off or pitches it or throws a pass. With our reverse, that rhythm was broken.

Very late exchange

Our 1993 snap went back five yards to a tailback. That took more time than usual. He then ran to one side. Then he cut toward the line of scrimmage. By this time, the defense feels certain they recognize the play: off-tackle to the strong side. Just at that moment, another player streaks in front of the ball carrier heading for the other side.

Third-string

But this play often failed for us in 1993. For one thing, we frequently had to run it with a third- or fourth-string wingback who kept turning it into a sweep rather than an off-tackle play. Also, one of the linemen on the play side admitted to me after the season that his teammate who was playing next to him never blocked on that play—or any other.

Shame on me for not seeing that. But, on the other hand, there was probably no one on the bench that season who could have done better. In short, I probably did not have enough reasonably good players to run at four different points of attack that season.

Passes

Passes are close to a nonentity at the jr. pee wee level (lowest). They can be important at the midget level (highest). The only jr. pee wee game we ever lost because of the pass was to the Tri-City Cowboys in 1990. Then we played them again in a post-season game and shut down their passing game totally except for one short gain. Other teams beats us by a couple of touchdowns, one of which came on a pass play. So if those games had been closer, we could have lost by the margin of the pass.

At higher levels, like midget, I have seen far more games decided by passes.

The greater the distance, the more practice

The greater the distance between the guy with the ball and the guy who is supposed to end up with the ball, the more practice is required. That is, it takes more practice to execute a hand-off play than it does to execute a keeper play. And it takes more practice to execute a pitch than a hand-off. And it takes more practice to execute a look-in pass than a pitch. And so on.

Furthermore, the number of reps required rises exponentially. Here's my estimate of the number of weekly reps required to master each of the following plays:

Play	Repetitions per week
keeper play	0
hand-off	30
pitch	60
look-in pass	150
deep spot pass	200

Look-in pass

You ought to have a look-in pass. It has been very successful in my experience in youth football. It hardly merits a play diagram. A tight end or wide receiver simply takes off on an inside route at a 25- to 45-degree angle to the line of scrimmage. You might want to have him go straight ahead for two steps or so to make the cornerback start his backpedal. The quarterback or tailback or whomever gets the snap immediately throws him the ball.

The trajectory of the throw is **line drive**. The aiming point is **low**, around the inside hip of the receiver, to make the pass hard to intercept in that crowded area of the field. Since the pass is being thrown from close to the line of scrimmage, the offensive line must hit the man in front of them hard in the **stomach** to force him to keep his hands down.

Precise routes?

In the spring of 1995, I was the wide receivers coach of the Miramonte High School varsity for the first week of spring practice and the tight ends coach for the second week. Wide receivers, who operate in the wide-open spaces, must run very precise routes. To make the connection as far apart as the wide receiver and quarterback are requires accuracy in both the route and the delivery of the pass as well as correct timing in both. Passes to wide receivers require different varieties of touch. The fade is a high rainbow to the corner of the end zone. The out is drilled low. Deep passes are thrown so that the receiver can run under them.

Tight ends, on the other hand, often do not run precise routes. Rather they run into a crowd of inside linebackers and maneuver around for an open lane between them and the quarterback. All passes to tight ends over the middle are thrown hard and low to prevent interceptions. The tight ends expect to fight for the ball and to be hit immediately after touching the pass. Timing and precision are both less necessary and less possible because of the short flight of the ball and the congestion in the impact area.

50 reps a night

You need 50 reps a night per quarterback and receiver of your look-in pass. At Miramonte we got reps for the center, quarterback, and receivers in the initial warm-up and during sled work among other times.

Just have a center snap the ball to a quarterback who throws a look-in to a receiver. Make sure you go **both sides** and that each center, quarterback, and receiver gets his reps. I recommend that you carry a countdown **kitchen timer**. Set it for the duration of the drill. For example, I would set 5 minutes for this drill.

Non-stop

The drill should be non-stop. You need two balls per station to achieve maximum efficiency—maybe three if you have a lot of misses. After a receiver catches a pass, or picks it up off the ground, he carries it back and **hands it** to the next center. He does **not** toss it to the center. Tosses result in misses, which result in wasted time.

You should have two centers and two quarterbacks so run this as a **two-station** drill. After each receiver runs his route and catches a pass, he goes to the center and hands him the ball as soon as he is ready for it. Then the receiver gets in the other line to receive a pass on his other side. Halfway through the drill, the quarterbacks change centers so that they throw an equal number to each side. Here's a diagram:

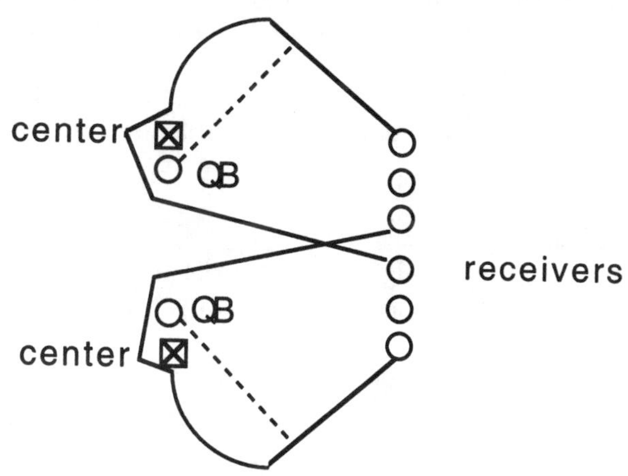

If your organization does not provide you with enough balls, complain to them. Show how much time you are wasting waiting for balls to get back to the center. If they **still** don't provide enough balls, bring some from home and ask your players to do the same. Ideally, you should be using all game-type balls. But it's more important to get the 50 reps than to do fewer in order to only use game balls.

One rep every five seconds

If you get this drill moving and you have enough balls, you should be able to get one rep per quarterback every five seconds. That's 60 reps per quarterback per night in a five-minute drill period. The receivers, being more numerous, will get fewer reps. You may not get a rep every five seconds the first night. But if you do this drill daily, your kids should become very efficient at it.

After the first couple of nights, do not tolerate dropped passes. Give any receiver who drops a pass five quick reps of remedial look-in and tuck (see below).

Third-string quarterback

Have your **third**-string quarterback replace each of the two top quarterbacks once a week. That way each quarterback gets 120 reps per week of this drill.

Reps of the center-quarterback exchange

This also gives your centers and quarterbacks reps at taking snaps. If you don't get those reps, you will have fumbled snaps. The quarterback should call cadence if that's the way you run your offense. In mine, the tailback would flick his thumb and the receiver would go on ball movement. If you vary the snap count, your quarterback should vary the snap count in this drill.

Catching technique

Your players should catch the ball with their **hands**, not their bodies. After each catch, they should look the ball all the way into their carrying position—the "look-in and tuck" drill.

Look in means to focus your eyes on the ball from the time it is thrown until after you have caught it and tucked it safely away in the carrying position of one point in your arm pit and the other in your hand.

Look-in-and-tuck drill

I do a look-in-and-tuck drill at the start of every practice and a remedial drill whenever a player drops a pass with that player only. I form the players in a circle around me for this drill. I go around the circle once for their right hand and once for their left.

Anyone who does it less than perfectly, must do it over. The players tend to not look the ball all the way in and to be sloppy about their eagle claw. I had one high school freshman who kept putting the ball in the armpit on one side and holding the point of the ball with the other arm.

High and low balls

When the ball is thrown **number high** or above, the thumbs and index fingers should touch as the ball is caught. When it is **lower**, or coming from over the shoulder the little fingers should touch. When the ball is shoe-string high, the little fingers **and elbows** should be together, to make the catch look clean to the ref

Receiver drills

There is a short list of standard receiver drills you should do. One is the **bad-ball** drill. Players run sideways in front of you and you throw them off-target but catchable balls. Do it both directions. Or they come directly at you and you do the same.

Distraction drill

Another drill which is excellent and very much needed by your receivers we call the **distraction** drill. In that one, you have a line of receivers on one side and a line of distracters on the other. They run at each other slightly off line so they don't collide.

The coach throws a ball perpendicular to their path. The distracter almost touches the ball. The receiver catches it. He then runs around and hands it to the coach before getting into the distracter line. He does **not** toss the ball because tosses mean misses which waste time. The purpose of the drill is to give the receiver practice at maintaining his concentration in spite of the distraction. Reverse direction halfway through the drill period. Here's a diagram:

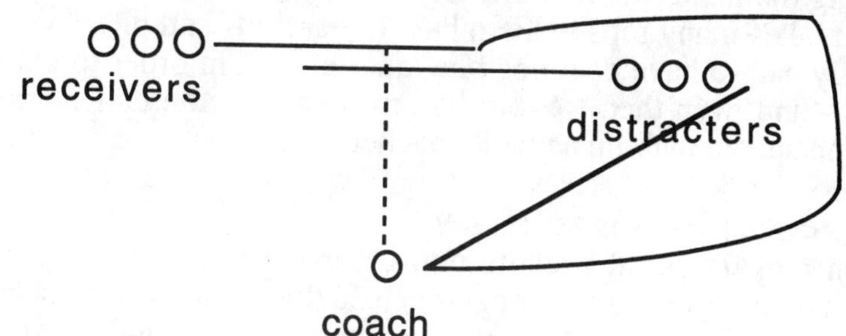

When the third string has to take over

One of the biggest benefits we got from our lack of quarterback-under-center snaps and hand-offs came when our first- and second-string tailbacks were out of the game because of injuries. That happened in the 1993 Oakland Saints game. I yelled out to our blocking back, "Hey, Paul. Play tailback."

His response was a vehement, "What!?" He heard me. He just couldn't believe what I had said. Paul Doerner had never taken a single snap at tailback (our equivalent of a quarterback) in either a game or in practice. But he did as told, ran the play perfectly, and gained four yards. Had we been a normal quarterback-under-center team with hand-offs, I can almost guarantee you that a player who had never taken a snap would have **fumbled either the snap or the hand-off.**

Put the end at tailback

Later in that game, we also had the long side tight end play tailback. He, too, had never taken a snap at tailback in practice or in a game. He carried eight times for sixteen yards. Then the upback went to tailback again and carried four times for nine yards. None of the plays that they ran were fouled up in terms of not being executed properly. The problem was lack of first-string blockers in front of them.

Linemen at tailback

In the Walnut Creek game, where we were ahead 25-0 at the end of the first quarter, we let linemen play tailback. Again, there were no fumbled snaps and the plays were executed correctly by the linemen who had never taken a snap before. Inside guard Kyle DeYoung gained two yards on a seam buck. Outside guard Josh Brown lost seven yards on his first two carries. Then he ripped off a 45-yard run that would have been longer and a TD had he not slowed down to avoid our margin going over 28 points. The tight end even completed a pass in that game.

Scout team T-formation execution

Conversely, we had the **opposite** experience on our **scout** team which was usually running indirect-snap, T-formation plays. The scout team is the players who pretend to be the upcoming opponent so our team can practice against their alignments and plays.

We had a terrible time training the center to get the snap to the scout-team quarterback. The players—most of them from our first-string offense—fumbled the quarterback-under-center snap so often we frequently said the heck with it and had a coach snap. Or we used two balls: one for the center to raise up as if he were snapping it to the quarterback and another for the quarterback to hold and hand-off or pitch or pass.

Trouble with the hand-offs

Even after thus eliminating the center-quarterback exchange fumble, we still had great difficulty making the hand-offs and pitches. This was because we only had a couple days to learn it and it takes many reps to learn how to hand-off and pitch without fumbles.

We generally had to have **coaches** play quarterback in order to get the hand-offs and pitches correct—and even then we still had trouble with the ball carrier taking the right path, running full speed, making a proper pocket, etc.

Keepers great the first time

So our own players could execute our super-simple, long-snap, no-hand-off plays perfectly the **first** time they ran them—even if that first time was in an actual **game**. Meanwhile, our scout team and our game opponents were fumbling the ball right and left when they tried to execute the quarterback-under-center-hand-off offense. Even by the **end of the season,** our opponents and our scout team were still fouling up the center-quarterback and hand-off exchanges.

Hand-offs require practice to avoid fumbles. The same is true of the center-quarterback exchange, which is a form of hand-off. If you have any fumbled snaps or hand-offs, you did not practice enough. We had no fumbled hand-offs in 1993. We fumbled two long snaps. Although I have no idea why. They both hit the tailback in the hands.

Faking

Virtually every football team uses fakes. But virtually all the fakes **stink**. The quality of the fakes at all levels of football is a **joke**.

If you're going to put a fake in your playbook, the execution of it must meet certain standards. That takes practice. It also delays the arrival of the ball carrier at the line of scrimmage. If it **works**, the delay will be worth it. If it does **not** work, you are **worse** off because of the extra practice time you wasted and because of the extra time you gave the defense to get to the ball carrier.

Dan Devine was the very successful coach at Michigan State, Missouri, and Notre Dame. He was famous for the power sweep at Missouri. He said his high school football coach told him, "Any team you can beat by fooling, you can beat without fooling."

Fake whom?

The first thing you must do when putting a fake into a play is to ask whom are we trying to fake? The answer is one or more defenders who are lined up at or near the play's true point of attack.

Faking is making the defender think a player who does **not** have the ball **does** have the ball. In order to do that, the faking player must hold his hands against a part of his body that **could** conceal the ball and the actual ball carrier must do the same.

Behind trunk or hips

In general, only the trunk is big enough to conceal a football. That means the faking and actual ball carrier must hold at least one hand against their belly or chest or hip and turn their back to the defenders they hope to fool. Or they must hold at least one hand against their watch pocket or hip pocket area on the opposite side of their body from the defenders they hope to fool. You can also use another teammate's body to conceal the location of the ball.

Faking is rarely discussed in such detailed terms by coaches or even books on football. But fundamentally, that's the deal. The **faker** must conceal the fact that he does **not** have the ball and the **ball carrier** must conceal the fact that he **does** have the ball.

Faking well works

I will be the first to acknowledge that faking well works. It is possible to fake an entire team, the referees, the crowd, and the cameramen. We've all seen it at live games and on TV. But if you think about it, you will agree that you have also seen a zillion fakes that fooled no one.

The test of a fake is that a defender who was key to stopping that play **tackled the wrong player or stepped in the wrong direction or simply froze** when he should have been moving toward the point of attack.

In 1992, my alma mater, Army, won the Army-Navy Game largely on two extremely well-executed bootleg fakes (keepers) by the quarterback. Our 1993 single-wing reverse play sometimes fooled opposing players thoroughly.

Lost touchdowns

Spinning fullback (a highly deceptive form of the single-wing) single-wing coaches report that they lose a touchdown every now and then because their faker fooled the defense into tackling him and the referees blew the play dead. Meanwhile, the **real** ball carrier was running down the sideline in the clear.

In the **single-wing spinning fullback** series, the ball is snapped to the fullback. He spins around so that his **back is to the defense**. While he is in that position, the tailback and wingback cross sequentially right past his hands.

Each approaches with his hands openly in a hand-off pocket. But as each passes the fullback in sequence, he closes his pocket **and twists at the waist** so that he is running toward the sideline with his **back to the defense**. The fullback comes out of the spin running toward the line of scrimmage **bent over at the waist** so that defenders cannot see whether he has a ball because his shoulders overhang the ball-carrying pocket.

Running bent over or twisted at the waist is a bit awkward. But it **does** conceal the ball. Unless the fake does that, why bother with it?

Elements of a good fake

Most fakes fail because the players are not disciplined enough regarding the following points:

- Real ball carriers run at **top speed**; fake ball carriers tend to **jog**
- Real ball carriers **focus their eyes intently** on possible tacklers; fake ball carriers tend to **stare off in the general direction they are running, or even worse, watch the real ball carrier**
- Real ball carriers hold a ball with one hand except in traffic; fake ball carriers tend to **hold the ball with two hands even though they are not near possible tacklers**
- Real ball carriers **fight** to avoid tacklers; fake ball carriers tend to **allow themselves to be tackled easily**
- Real ball carriers run are **watched by their teammates** who have hit and quit; fake ball carriers are **ignored** by their teammates.

Broken plays are great fakes

Note that all eleven players are involved in the fake, not just the ball handlers and fake ball handlers. That's why **broken plays** work so well. Ten guys think the ball carrier went one way and because of that belief, they give the defense a false picture. When they know about a fake, they show it to the defense in a bunch of subtle ways, the cumulative effect of which is not subtle at all.

If you tolerate these lapses, all the time you are spending practicing fakes is **worse than wasted**. In fact, your fakes are helping your opponents because they are delaying the ball carrier's arrival at the point of attack and fooling no one. **When it comes to fakes, do them right—or don't do them at all**!

Sloppy fakers

Note also that your team can enhance their fake by behaving as though they were poorly disciplined fakers. For example, the quarterback bootleg after a fake hand-off often works because the quarterback jogs and turns his head to watch the faker. I prefer that your players behave like a disciplined team all the time. That means both the fakers and the real ball carriers run like they have the ball. But it is true that acting like the ball carrier does **not** have the ball can work as well.

Remember, the efficacy of your fakes should be apparent in the videos of your practices and games. If you cannot see defenders falling for the fakes to the extent that the ball carrier is helped, either get rid of the plays or practice them better so they become effective. Do not continue to fake when it's clearly not working.

Pitches

Pitches are dangerous. They are not hard to catch if they are in the right general area. But if they are way off target, they will probably end up on the ground bouncing toward the wrong goal with few, if any, of the offensive team in the vicinity. Practice, practice, practice until you are virtually certain none will be incomplete.

Passes

Passes are a whole new ball game. Your quarterbacks and receivers must rep passes by the **hundreds**. If I had 1993 to do over again, one of the things I would do is all but eliminate practice of keeper plays. I would do more reps of the reverse. And I would rep the heck out of the passes.

Almost any practice you do of keeper plays is a waste of time. With hand-offs, you can very quickly reach the point of diminishing returns. But you probably cannot throw too many passes in practice. (Although you can easily throw too many long passes early in the season and wear out your quarterbacks' arms. Build up gradually.)

Flip-flopping

If you run the triple option, you may want to go **right** only. That's because Bob LaDouceur, head coach of the nationally ranked De La Salle High School team (Concord, CA), told me his week-long youth football camp was able to teach the veer option to the **right** to kids, **but** not to the **left**. Actually, a **left-handed quarterback** would be able to do it to the **left**, but not the right.

Most coaches would protest that if you always ran to your right, the other team would put everybody over there and stop you. I doubt they'd have the guts.

Those coaches say you need to be able to go to both sides. One way to do that is to have your players flip-flop or line up on different sides of the ball depending on what play is called.

The threat of the counter...

Woody Hayes said the **threat** of the pass is more important than the **pass** itself. The same may be true of the **counter** (a running play that starts out to one side then suddenly goes back to the other side). The other team knows that if they leave your left side unprotected, you will attack it. Heck, even if you had no such play, you could make one up during a time out and run it effectively as long as no hand-offs were involved.

My experience with flip-flopping

My 1993 team ran an unbalanced-line single-wing. We flip-flopped. That is, we had a short side end and a long side end rather than right and left ends. Our three guards, wingback, and blocking back were always on the long side. Our one tackle was always on the short side.

Did that have advantages? Yes. Most defenses assign their players to the left or right side, that is they have a left defensive end and a right defensive end and so forth. Furthermore, most assign their **best** players to the offense's **right** side on the assumption that 90% of the players are right-handed so the offenses will run to their right most of the time. (Actually, in my defensive scouting over the years I've found that nearly all teams run 50% right side and 50% left.)

Scored more points against Berkeley than anyone running right only

For example, in our 1993 Berkeley game, we were down 21-0 at the half. But I noticed in my game chart that we were generally successful when operating out of **right** formation, but unsuccessful when operating out of **left**. So for the second half, I told my kids to stay in right formation until further notice. We scored 19 quick unanswered points. (We lost the game 27-19 when Berkeley knocked a fumble loose and ran it in for a TD. The tailback was trying a last-minute desperation pass when the ball was hit out of his hand.)

I like having the ability to go both right and left so that we can attack the weakest side of defenses that have a weaker side.

Flip-flopped defenses

However, many of our opponents flip-flopped their defenses. That is, they had **strong-side** and **weak-side** linebackers and safeties. My own 1993 defense flip-flopped the ends, cornerbacks, and linebackers—although we flip-flopped according to **hash** position. That is, we had a wide-side end and a short-side end and so forth. Against flip-flopping defenses, we were going up against the same defensive kids when we flip-flopped as when we stayed in right formation.

I suspect some of our opponents never flip-flopped until they played **us**. But when you are up against a flip-flopping, unbalanced-line single-wing, you'd better be equally strong on both sides of your non-flip-flopping defense or you're going to have your head handed to you.

Slows up the hurry-up

Flip-flopping caused a couple of problems for us. We ran a **hurry-up offense** almost the entire season. The effectiveness of the hurry-up is inversely proportional to the number of seconds that elapse between the referee's ready-to-play whistle and the snap. That is, you want to snap the ball within two or three seconds of that ready-to-play whistle to get full benefit of the hurry-up. Flip-flopping takes time. That gives the defense time to get ready. With a "full-court press" hurry-up, they are often not lined up yet when the ball is snapped.

Wrong side

Another problem with flip-flopping is the same problem that occurs whenever you inject a **second anything** into your playbook. There's always 10% that don't get the word and line up on the wrong side.

If you **always** line up in **right** formation, your players will never line up on the wrong side. But once you create a two-sided offense, you create the possibility of a **wrong** side.

Got it wrong if we did not change often

Our kids frequently lined up on the wrong side, especially when we had been staying on one side for an extended period. At the beginning of the season, we told the tailback to signal for everyone to line up with the **long** side of the formation to the **wide** side of the field. He would hold his arm out to the side he wanted to be long. Because they knew we were always long to the side, the players could line up correctly without even looking at the tailback except when the ball was in the middle of the field.

But later in the season, we would stay in the same formation, right or left, for most of a quarter, occasionally testing the other side. In those cases, the players often had stopped looking back to see which side they were supposed to be on.

Illegal procedure

Since we had our players go down into a set position on the ref's ready-to-play whistle, once they got down on the wrong side, they could not move without triggering an illegal procedure penalty. In fact, we did draw a couple illegal procedure calls when players discovered they were in a set position on the wrong side and suddenly bolted to the other side.

If they stay in position, they do not draw an illegal procedure penalty, but we may no longer have our unbalanced line. If they are still unbalanced, we can move the backs to the side the linemen have mistakenly chosen to be long and we are OK.

If only one way they can't do it the wrong way

In short, having two of something in your playbook invariably creates situations where somebody is in the wrong one. So I am biased in favor of doing things only **one way.** I will add a second way if I can be convinced that the advantages outweigh the disadvantages. But I am hard to convince. And I hate confusion among my players.

Bill Cosby says parents of **only** children are not real parents because they always know which kid caused problems and because their kid never fights with his siblings. There is a similar night-and-day change in your football team's performance when you go from an "only-child" way of doing things to having **multiple** ways of doing things. Be extremely reluctant to add that second way.

Same formation, play goes other way

Flip-flopping isn't the only way—or even the most common way— to attack the other side of the defense. You can simply run the same play to the left out of the same formation. For example, you can easily run the wishbone triple option to the right or left without moving any players before the snap.

But once again, you have two of something—two directions. And that will inevitably result in one or more of your players going the wrong direction on some plays. In the wishbone or veer triple option, if one of your halfbacks goes the wrong way, he will either run smack **into** the other halfback or run **away from** the correct direction of the play. If you run the same direction all season, that will never happen.

Look at the numbers

The question is, who is hurt more by flip-flopping or bi-directional plays: **your** team or the **defense**? Most coaches would say the opponent. I say look at the numbers, That is, try it both ways and see if your average yards per carry is higher when you flip-flop or run bi-directional plays than it is when you stick with one side. Make sure you include the penalties and broken plays from confusion in your flip-flop or bi-directional numbers.

Stick to one side except for the sweep

I recommend you stick to one side. I suspect the benefits of doing so in lack of confusion and increased expertise (e.g., always blocking the play with the same shoulder) outweigh the advantages of an attempt to play ambidextrously). Although, if you have a running back fast enough to run the sweep, you probably need to run that play to the **wide** side of the field when the ball is on a hash mark and that requires flip-flopping or bi-directional play execution.

Line splits

Line splits are the widths of the gaps between the offensive linemen. We used **zero** in 1993. I was pleased with the result. For one thing, the shorter the line splits, the easier it is to line up in a **straight** line.

Tight line splits also **prevent penetration**. With a single-wing, penetration is a more of a danger because it takes longer for the ball carrier to get to the line of scrimmage. Penetration generally was not a problem for us in 1993.

Even the high school and college books on the single-wing call for zero line splits. The single-wing is characterized by massed, concentrated power at the point of attack. Zero line splits are part of that concentration of power. In my 1997 double wing, we started with zero splits then switched to six-inch splits, then varied between the two.

Nowhere to blitz

Zero line splits also seemed to nullify **blitzing**. We had scout team players blitzing in practice the week before we faced a blitzing team. But we never noticed a blitzer during the season. They just seemed to get lost in the crowd at the line of scrimmage. In 1990, we got killed by blitzing teams. I do not know what our line splits were that year but I suspect they were wide.

I have not read every book ever written on football—but almost. Those books are generally aimed at high school, college, or pro players and coaches. They generally prescribe extremely wide line splits by youth standards. In his book, *Football: Secrets of the Split-T Formation*, Missouri head coach Don Faurot calls for the following splits against a five-man-line defense:

A gap	one foot
B gap	three feet
C gap	three to four feet.

Three feet

In their book, *Winning Football With the Air Option Passing Game*, Homer Rice and Steve Moore call for three-foot splits in all gaps. And their quarterback is under center. I don't know how he would ever get away from the center. But Rice and Moore both have impressive credentials.

I suspect many youth coaches learned these wide splits when they played and that's why they have their youth teams split wide.

Zero to eight inches

My experience coaching youth football defense for four years is that the splits at the lowest level range from zero to eight inches. Twelve inches strikes me as suicidal. With older boys, you can probably widen them toward high school width.

We use eight-inch splits in a two-on-one defensive gap-charge drill to make it easy on weaker players. The offensive blockers complain that they have no chance to stop the defender with such big splits.

If wide splits are important to your offense, I suggest you try them but carefully monitor whether your linemen are achieving the desired result. If not, you'd better tighten up.

The wider, the farther back they should be

In general, the wider the line split, the farther **back** the offensive lineman better be. Part of each lineman's body must cross the center's belt. None may be beyond the nearest tip of the ball. That creates about a six-inch to 18-inch wide room to maneuver for your line. With wide splits, set them as far back away from the ball as you can.

Also, a **shotgun** snap will enable you to widen. The quarterback or other recipient of the snap will have more time to throw a pass or elude tacklers when he's that far back. Although the usual purpose of widening splits is to run inside the tackles and the shotgun is not designed to do that.

Wider to the outside

The farther the lineman is from the center, the wider his split can be. In his book, *Single-wing Football with the Spinning Fullback,* coach John Aldrich tells his ends to split up to three yards. Some coaches call that the **"nasty" split.** If the defensive tackle or end maintains an **outside** position after a three-yard split, Aldrich says to stop there and just run **inside** him all day. If the defensive tackle or end lets the offensive end get **outside** him, run **around** the defender with the offensive end blocking down on him.

Carrying the ball

The defenses in pro and college games increasingly work hard to **strip** the ball. That lesson has not been lost on youth coaches who are increasingly coaching their players to do the same. So protecting the ball is more important than ever.

Your ball carriers need to carry the ball **against their body** with pressure from the **bicep**, **forearm** and **hand**. One **point** of the ball is in the **armpit**, the other is in the **hand**. The hand covers the point of the ball in eagle claw fashion with the point of the ball showing between the longest fingers. The ball should be in the hand **away** from the likely tacklers. When a tackle is imminent, the ball should be protected by **covering** it with he free hand and arm and by curling the trunk over the ball.

Common mistakes are:

- holding the ball away from the body
- holding both points of the ball with the hands rather than putting one point in the armpit
- holding the fat part of the ball with the hand instead of the point.

Bo taught me

In 1990, our local paper ran an action photo of each local football team. In each case, they showed a ball carrier. Our player, Chris Noon, whose father was a college running back, was the only one who carried it correctly. I had also been teaching the correct way to our kids because I learned it just a few weeks before from Bo Schembechler's video, *Teaching Kids Football.*

All the other teams' running backs carried the ball with their hand around the fat part of the ball. We taught the correct way by demonstrating it, then having each kid do it correctly. We also had kids carrying the ball in tackling drills and we would always correct them if they carried the ball incorrectly. Even in games, we would immediately yell out to a player between plays if we saw him carry the ball without his hand over the point on the previous play.

No fumbling problem

We never had a fumbling problem. In 1993, the only fumbles I remember were a ball knocked out of a passer's hand when he had it cocked for a pass, two good snaps that were inexplicably muffed, and a post-whistle "fumble" that the ref told me they let the other team have because we were ahead by a huge margin.

One team we played—Berkeley—tried hard to make us fumble. At one point, their coach yelled out something to the effect of, "Why aren't you guys knocking the ball loose like we worked on in practice?"

They are the team that got the cocked-arm passing fumble—and ran it in for a touchdown. But they never got a fumble on any other plays. Although once I remember our tailback having the ball go around his back while he was being gang tackled. He maintained continuous contact with the ball and resecured it. But it looked like a Harlem Globetrotters ball-handling routine there for an instant.

If you have a **chronic fumbling problem**, you need to either replace the ball carrier in question or straighten him out with gauntlet drills.

Motion

There are seven reasons to use motion:

- To change the strength of the formation at high speed
- To help a receiver release on his route faster
- To force the defense to reveal before the snap how they are covering pass receivers
- To give the man in motion momentum
- To remove possible blitzers
- To discourage the defense from varying their defenses
- To confuse the defense generally.

Motion has these **disadvantages**:

- Delays snap and may thereby cause delay-of-game penalty in some situations
- Takes extra practice time
- Creates the possibility of penalties for:
    - false start
    - illegal motion
    - illegal procedure
- The adjustment the defense makes may confuse your blockers
- Quarterback must learn when to start motion and at what stage of motion to call for snap.

Motion is a complication

Motion is a complication. I don't like complications. On the other hand, if the value of it exceeds the problems caused by the complications, it should be used. With motion, I think it might be worth it.

Change strength of formation

Defenses have been trained to line up in a certain way for each formation that they expect to see. Also, defensive players sometimes have different job descriptions for different offensive formations and motions. If you line up in static fashion, the defense has a lot of time to figure out what each player is supposed to do. That's especially true if you stay in the same formation for the entire game or entire season.

When a man goes in motion, he changes the nature and strength of the formation with every step he takes. Let's say he starts at right flanker and goes in motion toward the ball.

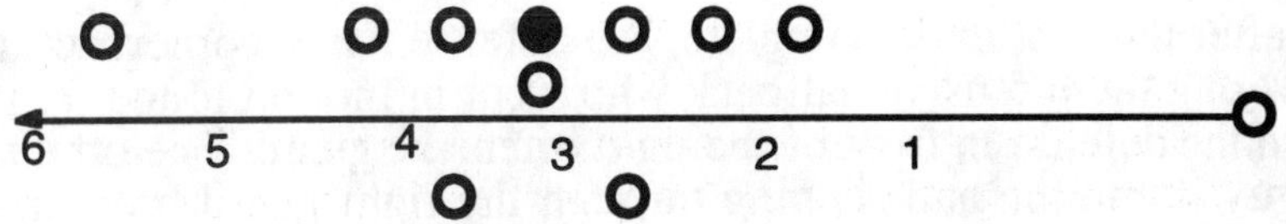

When he gets to point #1, your formation changes from flanker right to wing right; 2, upback right; 3, wishbone; 4, upback left; 5, slot left; 6, twins left. Each of those formations represents a different threat to the defense.

Each should be defended differently. But it's hard for the defense to be in the right alignment and frame of mind when they have to adjust to a guy who is literally on the run. If their defense for each of these formations require **multiple changes** in the defensive alignment, they have no hope of responding correctly. Try putting a man in motion and see how the defense responds. If the motion seems to help your play succeed against that particular opponent, keep using it.

You can, therefore you should

When your offense lines up in a formation, the defense sees it and mentally figures out where they should line up and what they should do when the ball is snapped. In many cases, their captain yells out instructions based on the formation you show. Obviously, it would be nice if you could run the play without them seeing your formation or with them seeing for the least amount of time. Motion and shifting allow you to reduce the amount of time the defense has to one second.

See how the defense responds

Most youth defenses line up in a way that is sound, if you show them a common offensive formation. If you line up in an **unusual** formation—like trips (three wideouts on one side) or an unbalanced line or a lonesome polecat—they may **not** line up in a sound defense.

Some youth defenses also do not respond correctly to motion. They may ignore it—which is a no-no from the defense's perspective. The offensive should throw a pass to a man who goes in motion out wide and is not covered by a defender. If the motion man lines up wide, has a defender on him, goes in motion and the defender does not go with him, the offense should run to the hole the motion man is at when he ball is snapped. The defender who was lined up on the motion man before he went in motion has taken himself out of the play.

May go from sound to unsound

Or they may change their defensive alignment to one which is unsound. For example, they might have an inside linebacker go in motion with a motion man who is going out when they already have another defender out wide and you have no one but the motion man out wide to that side. This will result in their **double covering** the motion man and leaving a weakness where the inside linebacker came from. Here's a diagram:

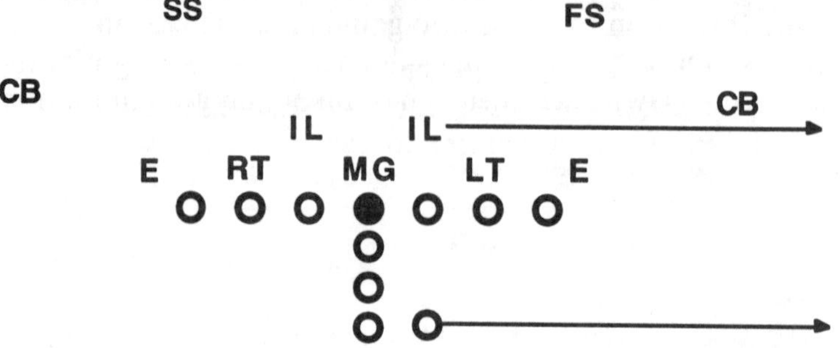

Note that after the motion is complete, the defense has a cornerback **and** an inside linebacker covering the offensive halfback who went in motion to the far right flat. That leaves a hole in the defense in front of the right offensive guard. The offense should keep sending that guy in motion and running through the right guard hole until the defense wises up.

Must be practiced

You have to practice motion before you can put it in a game. The quarterback and motion man must know the pertinent rules and learn to comply with them. That is, the motion must be parallel to or away from the line of scrimmage and everyone must be set for at least one second before the man can go in motion.

The usual signal to start is for the signal caller to pick his heel up and put it back down. If you plan to run to the motion man's location at the snap to take advantage of the extra blocker at that hole, you should probably just tell your players to follow the motion man. That way you don't have to get precise timing down as you would if you called a play in advance to a hole then tried to call for the snap when the motion man was at just the right spot.

The motion man would watch the ball throughout his motion then cut upfield or crack back on the end when it was snapped.

Wide guys attract attention

I get the impression that defenses pay a lot of attention to eligible receivers who are **outside** tight ends but that they tend to ignore those **behind the offensive line**. You may find that you can run a back from end to end without the defense adjusting. If so, you probably should line him up on one side, motion him to the other, and run a play at that off tackle hole when he arrives at the other side. If the defense respects his original position but does not go with him when he goes in motion, you should have them outnumbered at the point of attack. If they do not respect his **original** position, forget motion and run there.

Type of pass coverage

At higher levels, offenses try to find out what pass coverage the defense is planning to use on the play. Motion that takes a long enough time to let the defense respond should reveal the type of pass defense.

If one defender locks onto the motion man, they are apparently in **man-to-man** coverage. Man-to-man coverage is vulnerable to personnel mismatches (your receiver is better than the defender who is covering him) and to two-receiver crossing patterns that act like picks. Picks, *per se* are illegal.

Receivers out of the backfield

I suspect man-to-man is also vulnerable to passes to receivers coming out of the backfield—especially out of an I-Formation—because they are not seen as receivers before the snap. When the offense is in an I, the defense needs a special rules to determine who covers which back in the I. Normally, defenders cover the guy on their side. But with an I, the offensive backs are on **neither** side, they are right in the middle.

If the entire defensive secondary shifts in response to motion, they are apparently in a **zone** defense. Zone defenses are vulnerable to passes to receivers in the seams between zones and to flooding (sending two or more receivers into a zone covered by one defender).

Momentum

It takes a person a second or two to get up to full speed from a standing start. That's the physics principle of inertia. It would be nice to have at least one of your guys at or near full speed when the ball is snapped. For example, if you were running off tackle and snapped the ball when the motion man was behind the guard on the play side, the motion man could adjust course about 45 degrees at the snap and head for the defensive end with a full head of steam.

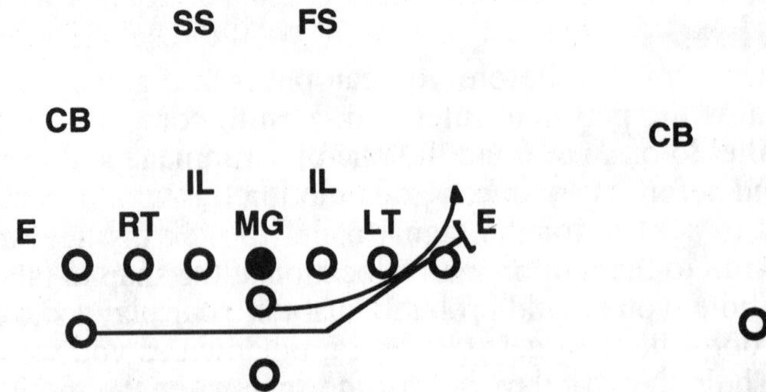

That extra oomph might be just what you need to spring your ball carrier for a big gain. The same principle could apply to a wide-out going in motion inward. He could crack back on an end for an end sweep or a linebacker on an off tackle play.

It can also get a receiver upfield quicker on a pass pattern.

It's crucial that the motion man not change direction until **after** the snap. You must watch that in practice.

Fewer blitzers

If you put a guy in motion, the defense will generally send somebody with him. That somebody will usually be a linebacker, safety, or halfback. Linebackers, safeties, and halfbacks are the guys who blitz. One less of them in the vicinity of the ball means one less guy who can blitz.

Shifts

I love the idea of the offense shifting. I didn't do any of it in 1993 because I only had three offensive veterans, my kids were at the youngest level of all tackle football, and I was a rookie offensive coach. But I saw opposing teams and teams in scout games use the shift to great advantage, so I know it can be successful. In fact, I saw the most shifting at the various youth football championships I have attended. Shifting appears to be most common among the best teams. Maybe there's a correlation there.

Rules

Shifting is another complication. In order to do it, you must teach the following to your kids:

- Do not place hand on or near the ground until **after** shift. Rule 7-1-6
- Pre-shift formation and stances
- Paths to take when shifting (to avoid collisions and stepping into neutral zone—a shift is almost like a play)
- Need to be set for at least one second after the shift before snap. Rule 7-2-6
- How to tell what pre-shift and post-shift formations the coach wants
- If you use both motion and a shift on the same play, the motion may not begin until one second after all eleven players have been set. Rule 7-2-6
- The shift may not simulate a snap or clearly be intended to cause the defense to encroach. If the **quarterback** is going to shift, he must not put his hands under center before he shifts because it would simulate a snap if he then pulled out. Rule 7-1-6

Movement tends to freeze the defensive alignment

Defensive coaches run scared. On offense, you've got eleven guys who know where the play is going. If the defense leaves an uncovered gap somewhere, and the offense finds it, good-bye.

When you start doing last-second things like motion and shifting, the defensive coach generally gets scared that his guys will get out of position and tells them to forget about defensive trickery.

If offense moves, defense cannot

To put it another way, the **defense** can only play games like stemming, looping, blitzing, and slanting if the **offense** holds still. If the offense is shifting or going in motion, the defense has to reevaluate the offensive alignment at the **end** of the offensive movement before they decide to go ahead with a stunt. And they don't get enough time to both adjust to your movement **and** call a subsequent stunt. Stunting into an offense that moved **after** the defense called the stunt can be **disastrous** for the defense.

The rules say both teams can move just before the snap. But as a practical matter, only one team can do so—and the offense has first dibs.

Potential of the shift

Shifting changes the strength of your formation. Motion does that, too. But shifting can change it massively. Motion only changes one player's position. All eleven men can shift—although I recommend that you have the center place his hands on the ball and be ready to snap without shifting. In that case, only ten players can shift.

The shift with the most leverage is moving a man onto or off of the line of scrimmage. You can do this by moving just one player. But that requires you to be in an illegal (for snapping) formation before the shift. Here's an example of a shift from an illegal (eight men on the line) formation to a legal formation.

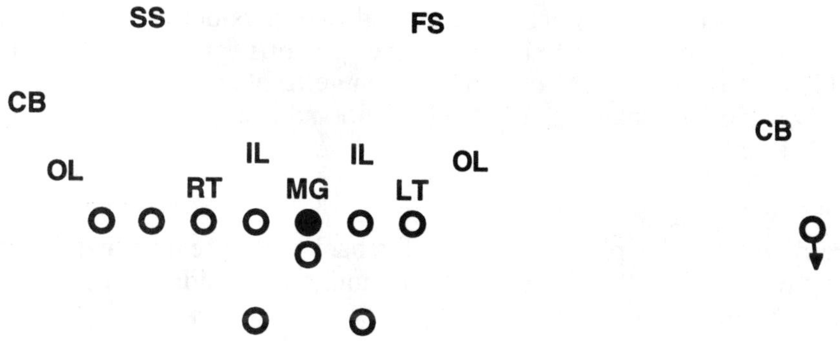

SS FS

CB CB

OL IL IL OL

RT MG LT

In this case, the **pre-shift** formation has **eight men on the line**. But the right split end shifts back off the line to a flanker position, thereby making the right tackle suddenly an **eligible receiver**. He must have an eligible jersey number. A sharp-eyed defender will spot the jersey number. But few defenders are that sharp-eyed.

Ineligible suddenly eligible

This shift forces the defenders in the vicinity of the right offensive tackle to suddenly regard a previously ineligible receiver as eligible. And they only have one second to recognize what has happened and reorient their thinking. The defenders in that area may not even notice that the split end has stepped back to become a flanker.

As an **in**eligible player, the right offensive tackle crossing the line of scrimmage means the play is a **run**—because ineligible receivers can only go downfield on a running play. Many defensive backs **key** on ineligible receivers and charge forward if the offensive lineman crosses the line of scrimmage. Suddenly, after this shift, the **opposite** is true. Once the right offensive tackle changes into an eligible receiver, his going downfield is likely to be a **pass pattern**. If the defensive back charges forward in response, he is doing the exact opposite of what he should be doing.

Becoming ineligible

You can also do the reverse—start with an illegal formation because there are too few men on the line. Then shift to a legal formation by rendering a seemingly eligible receiver ineligible. Here's how that would look:

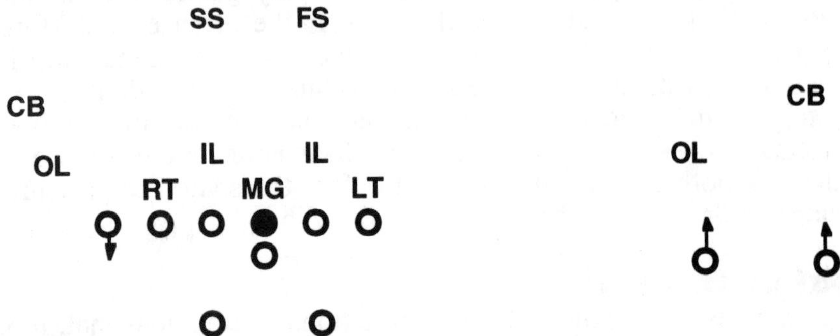

In this case, you appear to be in a twins right formation before the shift. This formation is **illegal** because you **only have six men on the line**. Furthermore, the inside twin is wearing a jersey numbered 50 to 79. When the twins shift forward one step to the line of scrimmage, the inside twin becomes an ineligible receiver because only ends are eligible on the line.

Three on one

If the defense was in man coverage, they had two guys out on the twins and another on the right tackle who appeared eligible in the pre-shift formation. After the shift, the defense suddenly has three guys covering just one eligible receiver—the right end. And the guy who was the left tackle, is now the left end and is eligible. (He should be wearing a jersey number other than 50-79.)

Can catch a backward pass

If you're running a pass play, the outside linebacker may realize that the inside twin is ineligible and rush back to the ball area. But although the inside twin is not eligible for a **forward** pass, he is eligible—as is **every** player—for a **backward** pass. So the inside twin could trot back until he is deeper than the passer and thereby receive a backward pass. He could then run or himself throw another pass.

Since five receivers must always be ineligible, that leaves six eligible receivers. In effect, this shift and the post-snap running to a depth behind the passer suddenly creates a **seventh** "eligible" receiver. You could do it on **both sides** and create an eighth "eligible" receiver. I'd like to see how defenses cover that. Note that there are also no incomplete backward passes. They are live balls if dropped or missed.

Snap on "Shift"

I think you are better off with both your pre-shift and post-shift alignment being legal. That enables you to snap the ball on the command "Shift."

You line up in a pre-shift alignment. All players freeze for one second in a legal formation, that is, seven men on the line, five of which are interior linemen and are wearing jersey numbers 50 to 79. Nobody's hand is on or near the ground except the center's. He is ready to snap. The other players could get low by putting their forearms on their knees.

The offensive captain yells, "Shift" and those who need to, shift to the post-shift alignment. After waiting until all players are set for at least one more second, you either snap the ball or put a player in motion then snap the ball.

As a change-up, you can also snap the ball on the command, "Shift." That is you can snap on "Shift" if your formation was legal. After you have shifted several times before snapping, the snap on "Shift" should take the defense by surprise. Once you show that you can snap on "Shift" or after you shift, the defense will get paranoid and tense up every time you line up. Meantime, your guys can relax because they know the snap on "Shift" is not on for this play.

Snapping on "Shift" requires that all your players fire out from the upright two-point stance. That's not the ideal fire-out stance for interior linemen. But the element of surprise should more than compensate for the lost power.

Snap and shift on "Shift"

If you **really** want to confuse the defense, do **both**. Line up in a legal formation. Then the offensive captain yells, "Shift." Whereupon the center snaps the ball and the quarterback or whomever he snapped it to takes off running.

Meanwhile, the rest of the offense including the center acts as if the ball has not yet been snapped. That is, the center stays in his snapping stance and the rest of the non-ball carrier players shift as if the snap has not yet occurred. The play ends with the entire offense in a set position except for the ball carrier who is hopefully running full speed down the field toward the end zone.

Tell the refs

It would be wise to tell the refs about this play before the game. It looks like a false start. In fact, it is not. But the defense has a tendency to just stand there waiting for the whistle that never comes.

One way to run this play might be for the center and player who receives the snap to agree between themselves to run this—without telling the other offensive players. That will ensure good "acting" by the non-ball carrying players. They, too, will look around for the dead ball false start whistle thereby adding to the general false start look of the play in the eyes of the defense.

The freeze play

In 1989, my son was an eight-year old rookie on the Bears junior pee wee team. I was not a coach that year. They went 1 and 7. The one victory came on a freeze play in which they ran a quarterback sneak. The entire team except the quarterback stayed in a set position even after the snap. The quarterback ran right up the middle for 70 yards and a touchdown. When I complimented the coach on his quarterback's making the most of a busted play, he said, "That was no busted play. It was designed. That's our freeze play. Everyone freezes except the ball carrier."

The defense simply stood and looked around at the refs for a whistle. They finally blew it while simultaneously raising both hands over their heads signaling touchdown.

I do not like the usual trick plays because they involve lots of fancy ball handling and that takes more practice than you can afford to devote to a trick play. **This** trick play is just the opposite. It's simpler than simple. Not only is there no ball handling beyond the minimum required by the rules, no one else even moves.

Two-center shift

This shift does **not** allow you to snap on the command "Shift" because no one has their hands on the ball to center it when the command is given. But it does create the fastest unbalanced line in football. You line up in a balanced line. You have two centers who are positioned where the guards normally are. On the command, "Shift," the entire line shifts one man to the right or left thereby creating an unbalanced line. The shift is done in step so that the snap can be made as soon as possible after the shift. Here's the pre-snap alignment. The middle lineman is on the ball but does not bend down to touch it or get his hands near it.

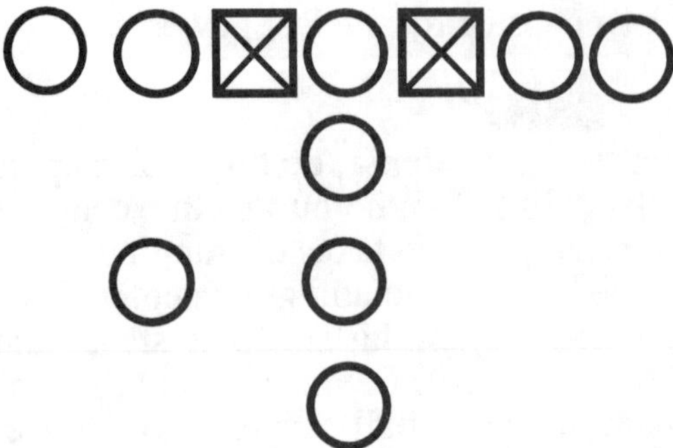

Here's the after alignment. The line has shifted one man to the left thereby unbalancing the line to that side. Now the center who was at right guard is over the ball and he gets down to snap it.

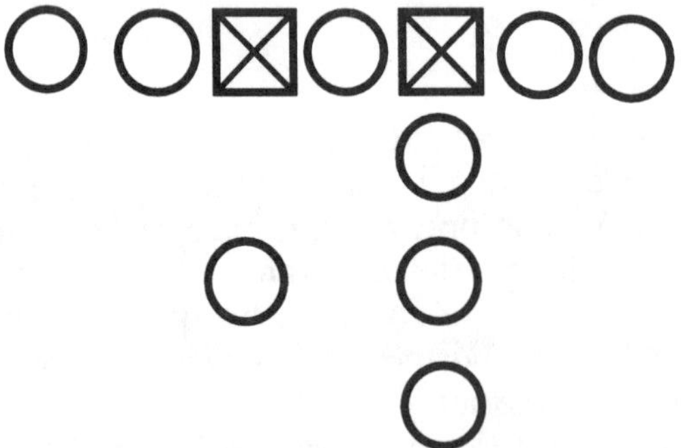

Note that the backfield has not moved. They could. But in this example, they didn't. The formation is now heavily unbalanced in both the line and halfback to the left. The defense needs to overshift to that side. But they must be careful not to overdo it or the offense could run plays back to the right. With all that power in the I, which is now on the right side of the backfield, the offense could hit the short side with three blocking backs, a ball carrier, and any linemen they wanted to pull.

The defense has to figure out what they are facing **after** the shift and adjust to it—all within about two seconds—one to get set and one to comply with the rules.

Friendly side

We did something in 1993 that we found very useful. But I have never seen it in any football book or video or heard it at any football clinic I've attended. We favored the

friendly side of the field. That is, the side where our bench was located. We called the other side the enemy side. That's a sort of quasi-one-way of doing things.

Better the second time around

If our friendly-side flanker was not covered, we automatically threw the ball to him. He just stood still until he caught it. No audible was used. The other players did not need to know that the original play was called off.

Oddly, we frequently found we could throw this pass on **two** successive plays and we would get **more** yards on the **second** one. I always ordered the tailback **not** to throw it a **third** time for fear it would be intercepted.

58-yard touchdown

On one occasion, just before the half in the 1993 Pittsburgh game, we put a rookie with a strong arm at tailback and our best runner at flanker. The rookie's first ever game pass went for 58 yards and a touchdown. So defenses absolutely had to honor our flanker even though half the time he was just a decoy. Telling which were the decoys was too tough for the defense to do play after play.

Our flankers also often made key **crack back** blocks on our **sweep**. Because that block is relatively easy and requires no contact, even our weaker players could do it effectively. All they had to do was get in the way of the defensive contain man and our tailback would break loose around end.

Easier to sub and coach

By keeping them on the friendly side, we made it **easier to substitute** them and we could **coach** them from the sidelines. I spent half the 1993 season saying, "Hold still!" to flankers who were fidgeting around or still moving as the tailback was getting ready to call for the snap. We still got hit with several illegal procedure or illegal motion calls as these flankers wandered lost while the snap was made.

In the latter part of the season, we had the offense start out long to the friendly side of the field so we coaches could yell out blocking instructions. When the offense is moving to your right, and they go in right formation and run virtually all plays to their right, they will put the ball on the right or friendly-side **hash mark** and keep it there. That puts most of the blocking a mere twelve yards from the sideline. If the ball was between the 30-yard lines—which is the limit of how far coaches can go down the sideline—we had a cat-bird seat.

Conferring without calling a time out

We would run a play and my assistants and I would study the defensive reaction. Then we would yell out to the offense stuff like, "Art, you need to get number 43 on that play. He made the tackle. Paul can handle number 32 by himself."

In that manner, we could study what was going on and fine tune our approach to that particular team and defensive alignment without calling a time out. At the same time, the **opposing** coaches needed binoculars and press-box altitude to figure out what was going on forty yards across the field. And they found it next to impossible to communicate with their players while we were conversing with ours and hardly raising our voices.

Decoys and stalk blockers

In youth football, all players must play. But some can't block or tackle effectively. You may be in a program where such players are cut. We never had enough try out for the team to do that. We've always had to play them.

If a boy cannot block, it is inappropriate to put him in a position where he must block during a game. You should **teach** him how to block in practice **all season long**. You should give him **daily** opportunities to show that, at long last, he has learned how to block. But you should not doom him to failure and nullify his teammates' efforts by putting him in a position where the team depends upon him to do that which he cannot do.

Guaranteed to fail

I have seen coaches put boys who could not block in the interior line during games. In one semi-final playoff game, we were driving down the field. But a six-play player had not yet gotten his playing time. He had to go in. He went in at tackle with first and ten. For the next four plays, the player he was supposed to block blew through the line and sacked our ball carrier. That was the end of our drive. The efforts of the other players in that series were made irrelevant because a chain is only as strong as its weakest link.

I do not know if the boy was doing his best. I coached defense that year. If he was doing his best, the fault lies with the offensive coach for asking the boy to do that which he had amply demonstrated he could not do. Given what had transpired in practice and previous games, the boy was almost guaranteed to fail.

If the boy cannot carry the ball, you should not make him a ball carrier. That's usually not a problem. Although I did have one father complain that his boy did not get a fair chance to be a running back. In fact, his son showed no aptitude or interest whatsoever in carrying the ball. We give all players a chance to carry the ball in practice as members of the scout kick return team.

If he cannot catch, don't pass to him

If a boy cannot catch passes reliably, do not pass to him in games. To pass to such a boy will demoralize your team and embarrass and humiliate the boy. Give him a chance to catch passes every day in practice. Many boys who at first cannot catch later learn how. We had a boy one year who I put at flanker because he could not perform any football skills. But after just one week, he suddenly learned how to catch. So I immediately took him off the no-pass list and told the tailbacks to pass to him if he was open.

Explain to the parents

I explained to the parents and players at the post-season awards banquet about our use of the flanker position. I told them it was normal for our youngest, smallest players to ride the bench their first year. My sons did.

I explained that their size and inexperience made it hard for them to block bigger boys on the line. I said they were best able to contribute to the team effort at flanker where they typically drew a top defensive player out away from our point of attack.

Multi-year process

And I urged them to come back next year if they liked football. Then, I said, you will be older, bigger, faster, and stronger and the new, younger boys will play flanker while you play line and end and running back. I assured them that the vast majority of boys who stick with football for the first three years will find that they get overall equal playing time by the end of the three years.

Invite them to practice

One effective thing we've found over the years regarding playing time or position complaints from parents is to invite them to observe practice. One extremely heated father calmed right down after watching one practice. He agreed his son was not ready.

I have never understood why parents think we coaches want to keep their son on the bench in spite of his talents. Frequently these are the same parents who accuse us of being overly interested in winning.

No coach who wins can ever fully escape the overly-interested-in-winning rap. But you'd think we could at least avoid being accused of both wanting to win too much and deliberately benching a superior player. It's hard enough to win games with your best players in the right positions.

Right side of the ball

My first son has generally been a star since his second year. But my second son was not the hard-hitting type and quit football after his first game. Because I was the defensive coach, they assigned that second son to the defense.

When it became apparent to me that he was not the type, I asked that he be switched to offense. They refused to put anybody but stars at flanker. I thought my son could survive and have a more enjoyable experience at weak-side tight end. The offensive coach wouldn't hear of it and my son quit. There's a good chance he would have quit no matter what position we put him at. But the pressure would have been far less at flanker. I am sure that some first-year players who would have continued with football and excelled at it, quit because they were forced to spend their first year getting beat up by much bigger boys in the interior line.

'Don't depend on the undependable'

Offensive players do four things:

- carry the ball
- block
- catch passes
- decoy defenders.

In the book, *Saint Bobby and the Barbarians*, Florida State University football coach Bobby Bowden is quoted as saying, "Don't depend on the undependable." You must keep that in mind when you assign positions and job descriptions to your weakest players.

The pitch

I prefer keeper plays. I am willing to use hand-offs and did. But I don't like the dramatically increased practice time they take above and beyond what keepers take. And I don't like the increased incidence of fumbles that hand-offs cause.

You probably think that if I don't like hand-offs, I must really hate pitches.

Actually, the pitch is sort of half way between a hand-off and a pass regarding its potential **reward**. Unfortunately, it's sort of half way between a fumbled hand-off and a blocked punt in terms of **risks**.

Two kinds of pitches

There are two kinds of pitches:

- called pitch—usually an underhanded no-spiral pitch
- option pitch—usually an end-over-end one-handed flip.

Both pitches require much practice. But the option requires much more practice than the called pitch.

Pass

The pass makes more sense than many hand-offs because it at least offers a reward to match its risk. But most youth coaches grossly underestimate the difficulty of installing a legitimate passing game.

Pro football is predominantly a passing game. Many colleges feature an offensive attack that is heavy on passing. Many high schools throw a lot of passes. But much of the literature I read about high school varsity coaching acknowledges the difficulty of installing a viable passing attack even at that level.

The vast majority of youth football teams would see about a 40% improvement in their offense if they followed just one rule: Don't pass.

'Real' men pass

I sense that many youth football coaches regard installation of a passing game as a test of their manhood. As in "**Real** football coaches have a passing game."

Any coach can tell his quarterback to run a pass play. And coaches can blame the kids if the pass is intercepted or falls incomplete.

But the test of whether you have a passing attack is not whether you can put passes in your play book, not whether you can run passes in practice, or whether you can call a pass in a game and have your quarterback throw it. The test is whether the average yards you gain per pass is high enough to warrant throwing them. By that standard, a lot of youth coaches who think they have a passing game do not have a passing game.

Passer rating

You might calculate your team's quarterback passer rating. That's an NFL stat which is calculated as follows. I'll do as they do and use Steve Young's record 1994 stats to illustrate the calculation:

1. Subtract 30% from the completion percentage and multiply the answer by 5. If the result is less than zero, use zero. If it is greater than 2.375, use 2.375.
2. Divide the yards gained passing by the number of passing attempts then subtract three yard from the average. Multiply by .25. If the result is less than zero, use zero. If it is greater than 2.375, use 2.375.
3. Multiply the percentage of touchdown passes by .2. If it is greater than 2.375, use 2.375.
4. Multiply the interception percentage (per attempt) by .25 and subtract the answer from 2.375. If the result is less than zero, use zero.
5. Add the four results together, then multiply by 100 and divide by 6.

Don't ask me why regarding any of that. The NFL came up with it and I'm sure they had a bunch of PhDs do the underlying analysis. The all-time NFL single-season record is Steve Young's 112.8 in 1994. Only 21 quarterbacks have ever had season ratings over 100. At present, two weeks into the 1997 season, my youth quarterback, Sam Keller, has a passer rating of 143.75. That's because he and my receivers are very good and I have been overly conservative about calling pass plays. The lowest team passer rating in the NFL in 1996 was the Giants' 60.6. My local high school leagues ranged from 75.8 to 216.8 for the 1996 season.

A typical youth team probably has a completion rate of 15%, an average yards per attempt of 1.5 yards, a touchdown pass percentage of 10%, and an interception rate of 15%. That gives a passer rating of .33. That's not 33, it's **point** 33. Who are they kidding?

Let's back off and discuss it in simpler terms. If your completion rate is 0%, you obviously do not have a passing game and should not call pass plays. If your completion rate is 100%, you obviously have a great passing game and should call more pass plays. Equally obviously, somewhere between 0% and 100% there is a line that you cross between where you have a passing game and where you do not.

Pass Efficiency Rating

The *Wall Street Journal* says the best way to evaluate a passing game is their Pass Efficiency Rating or PER. The formula for PER is

[yards gained passing - (50 x number of interceptions)] /number of pass attempts

The reason you multiply interceptions by 50 is the average interception in the NFL costs the team that threw it 50 yards. In other words, they would have gained 50 more yards had they not thrown the interception.

Basically, the *Wall Street Journal* formula is calculating the average yards gain per pass attempt. They say that their computer has determined that the PER is more closely correlated with winning in the NFL than any other quarterback stat. I believe them. Completion percentage is really not meaningful, only yards gained are. And the percentage completion percentage is contained within the yards per pass because every incomplete is a zero yards for that pass.

The 9/19/97 *Journal* said the best quarterback in the NFL according to PER was Jeff George of the Raiders. His PER then was 8.97 yards per pass attempt. The career leader is San Francisco's Steve Young at 6.77 at the beginning of the 1997 season.

What is the PER of my typical youth team described above? Assume 20 passes for 30 yards and three interceptions. The PER would be [30 - (50 x 3)]/20 = [30 -150]/20 = -6 yards per attempt. That's **minus** six yards per attempt. And the coach of that team is still calling passes!? The PER of my 1997 youth quarterback, Sam Keller, has a PER of [45 - (50 x 0)]/5 = [45 -0]/5 = 9 yards per attempt. Jeff George, eat your heart out.

I'd guess that the line between having a passing game and not having one is a PER of around 3. If your PER is 3 or lower, you do not have a passing game and you are committing coaching malpractice if you pass. Rather you should go back to the drawing board and select higher percentage routes, give more protection, work on mechanics, get a better quarterback, or something.

The vast majority of youth coaches are on the wrong side of the line and should not be calling passes until they straighten out their problems. In fact, those coaches are blind to the fact that they do not have a passing game and they kill their own drives by throwing incomplete passes and interceptions.

Passes called but not thrown

I would argue that the efficiency of one's passing game should not be determined only by what happens after the ball leaves the quarterback's hand. Rather it should be judged by what happens after the coach calls for a pass play. That would add sacks, quarterback fumbles, quarterback scrambles for a gain, and so forth to the mix. And those things should be included. Getting the pass off means the play was a relatively successful pass play. It is misleading to judge pass plays only by the relatively successful ones.

In my own team stats, I keep track of the yards gained by each play. For passes, I include not only the passes that were **thrown** but all the pass plays that I **called**, including those that ended in sacks and such. I have only called two types of pass plays this season. One has an average yards per time called of 11.00 yards and the other is at 3.60. The latter play once resulted in a sack for a seven-yard loss.

Play-by-play decision

The better way to look at calling passes is the way it's done in a game, on a play-by-play basis. Let's say you face a so-called passing situation: third and six.

The real question is not, "Is this a passing situation?" It is, "What play in our repertoire is most likely to gain six yards?" That can be determined from two things:

• the statistical history of each of your plays over the season

• whether you have run that play so much in the current game that it's effectiveness has diminished.

During my 1996 season as a freshman coach at Granada High School in Livermore, we played Campolindo in the next-to-last game of the season. We threw ten passes in that game, which we won by one point on a field goal that was snapped with one second left on the clock. Seven of the passes were incomplete. The three completions gained 8, 3 and 7 yards. There were no interceptions or sacks.

So for starters, it would appear that a pass play would have a 70% probability of zero gain. One of the completions was for less than six yards so the failure probability for a pass play gaining a first down in a third-and-six situation is 80%. Is that better than my worst running play? Actually, no. In that game I had eleven different running plays that averaged six yards or more. We had run those eleven plays a total of 28 times during the game. Obviously, to me anyway, I should call one of those running plays. But no doubt the parents of the wide receivers will criticize me for not passing in an "obvious passing situation."

Folks, it may be a passing situation in the NFL and in some college games. But it is most definitely not a passing situation in a game where your passes have gained less than six yards 80% of the time and eleven of your running plays have gained an average of six yards or more per play. You're an idiot if you call a pass in that situation. But a high percentage of youth—and high school—coaches would do just that—responding to the echoes of Al and Frank and Dan and all their rowdy friends in their heads as they did.

If you pass, you punt

For most youth teams, if they pass, they punt. The typical youth pass is an incompletion. An incomplete pass wastes a down. With three downs, you have to gain 3.33 yards per play to get a first down. But when you waste a down with an incomplete pass, you only have two downs to gain the ten yards.

That means you have to gain **five yards per play**. It is usually a lot easier to gain three-and-a-third yards than five yards. If you are averaging **four yards per play** in a particular game, you are doing quite well and you will probably win the game—unless you do something stupid like throw a bunch of incomplete passes. One incomplete pass per series (four downs) means that you have to average five yards per play (in three-down territory). Since you are, in fact, averaging only four, you will end up with fourth and two.

If you pass, twelve things can happen...

Coach Bob Neyland of Tennessee uttered the famous words, "If you pass, three things can happen and two of them are bad."

In fact, twelve things can happen and nine of them are bad:

1. completion
2. incompletion
3. interception
4. sack
5. quarterback fumble
6. receiver fumble
7. pass interference on the defense
8. pass interference on the offense
9. ineligible receiver downfield
10. roughing the passer
11. illegal forward pass
12. intentional grounding

Observations on youth football passing

I spent eight years in youth football. I've watched my own team pass and I've watched many opponents and other teams throw passes in games I scouted and games I watched just for the heck of it. I made a video tape containing mainly pass plays by the Bears jr. pee wees and their opponents from 1991 and 1992 games. The plays include both complete and incomplete passes as well as sacks.

Nine zones

It is useful to divide the field into nine zones to discuss passing.

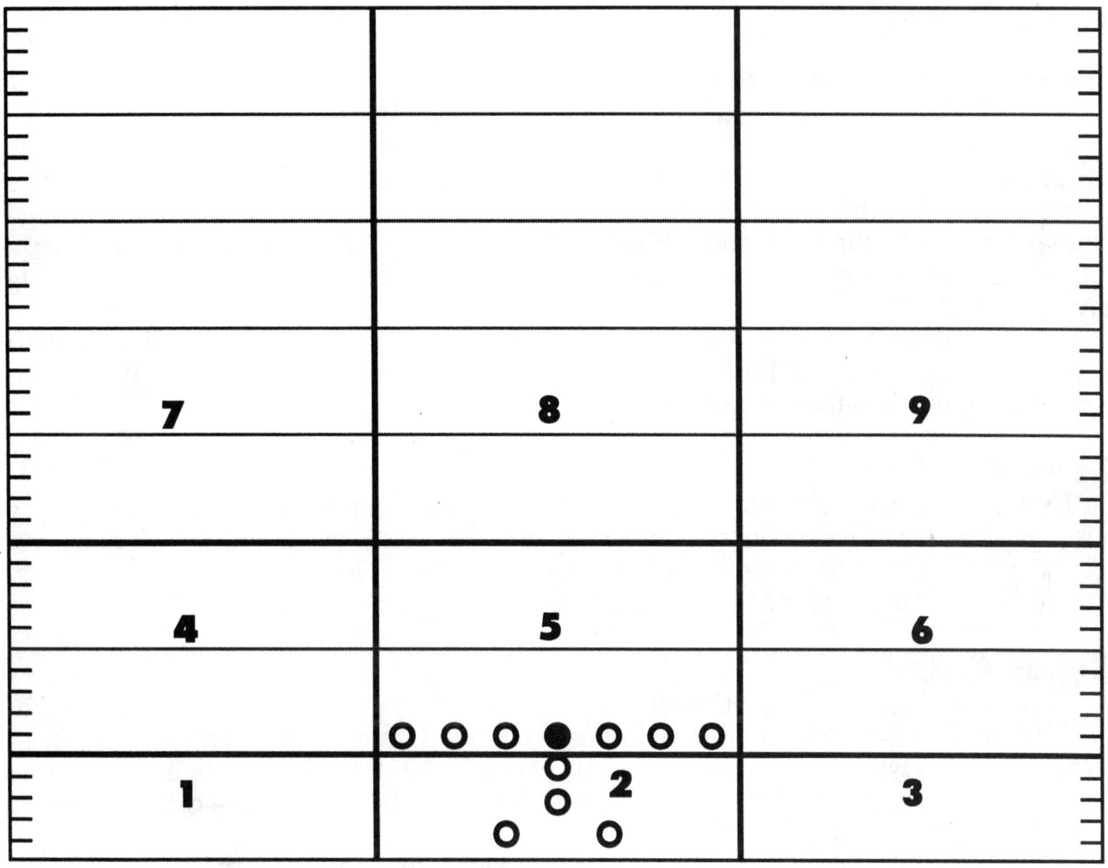

Zones 1 and 3 are for hitch and swing passes. Our team was quite successful throwing **hitch** passes to wideouts in those zones in 1992. However, that success was due in part to **inadequate scouting** by opponents.

Our only opponents who ever tried hitch passes to zone 3 were Napa and Manteca in 1991. We saw the passes in scouting, put them in our scouting report, and practiced intercepting them. We **did** intercept the Napa pass and ran it in for a touchdown. The Manteca lateral pass was muffed and almost recovered by our team

Our 1992 offense, which I did **not** coach, would always throw a hitch pass to the wideout whenever there was a wideout. That would have been suicidal against our defense because our scouting would have seen that. In the event, our 1992 offensive coach got away with it. We only had one tipped and that was in the semi-final league playoff game. Actually it should have been intercepted and run in for a touchdown, but the defender bobbled it.

Eating the ball

I made a highlight and lowlight video of most of the passes thrown by either team in our game videos. I noticed that when a passer was unable to throw on schedule, he almost always ran **backwards** and got sacked. The passer must be drilled to either throw an incomplete pass, hit an outlet receiver, or charge **toward** the line of scrimmage. The habit of running **away** from rushers cost us and our opponents an average of five or ten yards **more** than the offense would have lost if he had just dropped to one knee upon seeing that his receiver was covered.

Eating the ball must be practiced. Otherwise, the youth quarterback will either throw the ball when he shouldn't or he will act as if there's a prize for avoiding being tackled for the longest period of time. He will then pursue that prize by running **away** from the line of scrimmage.

Practice taking a sack

You should first tell the quarterback to eat the ball without losing any more yardage no matter what in a practice drill. Then, once he is comfortable with taking the sack, introduce throwing the ball away. That is, have a receiver go against a defender. The quarterback must throw an incomplete pass, but not an interception or intentional grounding, within three seconds. Finally, have him read a receiver going against a defender and throw a completed pass, incompletion, or eat the ball—again, without losing any more yards.

If they have trouble not running away from the line of scrimmage. Have them do this drill in front of a **wall or fence** so they absolutely can**not** run away from the line of scrimmage more than their drop-back depth.

Zone 2

Neither the Bears nor their opponents threw to zone 2 in my video. That's probably a mistake. Most teams have poor pass blocking and strong pass rushes. And most defensive secondaries are trained to backpedal during pass plays. That leaves Zone 2 open for shovel or screen plays. Our Junior Midgets had a strong screen pass in 1992.

Zones 4 and 6

Zones 4 and 6 are either not covered or are covered by defenders who responsible for covering **both** passes to their zone and runs through it. Offenses should attack such dual-responsibility players with **run-pass option plays**. If the defender comes up to stop the run, the runner passes over his head to the zone he vacated. If the defender stays back, the runner fakes a pass and keeps the ball.

We had this play in 1993, but our tailback **always** threw the ball in games. That's my fault. I should have had them run it more often in practice. This is a great play but the passer must learn to read the defense and make the right decision. Our tailbacks thought of this as strictly a pass play.

Key on the cornerback

One defender should be designated as the key—generally the cornerback. If he comes toward the passer and a receiver is open, he passes. If the cornerback chases the receiver, the passer runs with the ball.

At the high school and higher levels, Zones 4 and 6 can be attacked by superfast **out**, **fade**, or **hook** patterns, or a **look-in** by a wide receiver. As a practical matter, you can probably only do the hook and look-in at the youth level. Outs and fades are difficult for **high school** players to complete, let alone youth players.

Favorite high school pass plays

I learned a lot about the pass when I coached high school football for three years. The high school coaches, who typically have been doing this for decades, have all acquired favorite pass patterns which they had success with. I've already told you about the 26 power pass Miramonte uses. That pass is the main one my youth quarterback's has used to achieve his 143 pass rating.

At Granada High School they like 229 bench. The three numbers represent the routes each receiver takes from left to right. Two is a slant in. Nine is a streak. Bench is a running back route which is a sort of shallow out pattern. The theory is that the twos and nine clear out the defensive backs who are covering those zones then the fullback comes out late running through the area cleared by the earlier receivers. I looks like this:

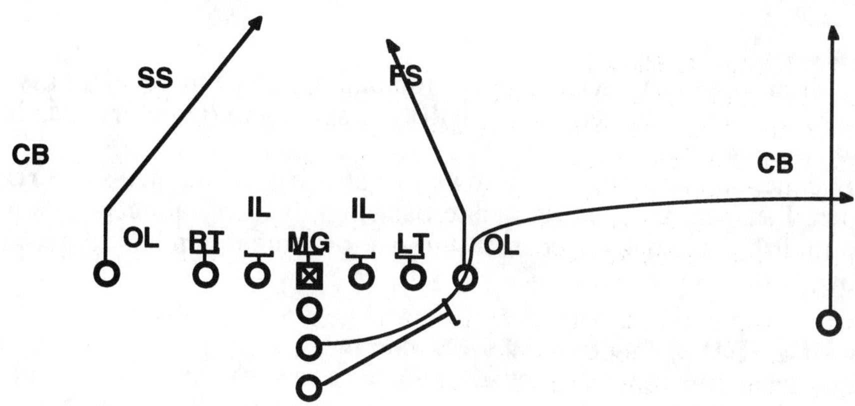

X twirl

A pass route that impressed the heck out of me was what we called X twirl at Miramonte and Q out at Granada. I ran the varsity offensive scout team at Miramonte in 1995. The varsity defense never stopped this route even though I was running it with second-stringers. It looks like this:

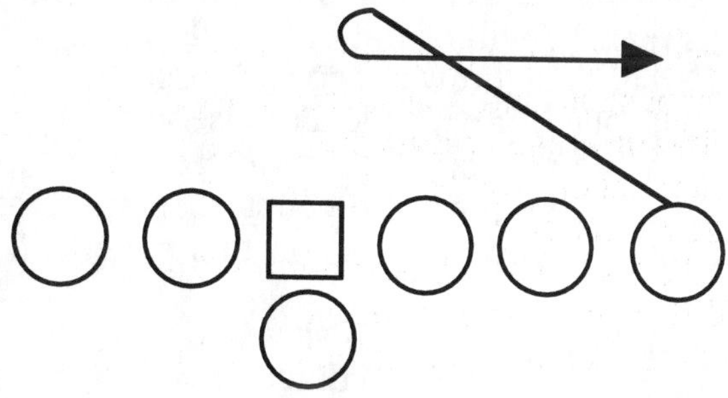

The receiver runs a quick slant then turns toward the quarterback continuing to pivot until he is running straight at the sideline. It is about a 200-degree turn. The optimum time to throw the ball is when the receiver has just completed the turn. It is next to impossible to cover this cut.

The pass is easy to complete because the receiver is right in front of the quarterback. However, there is one proviso, you must either throw through a lane which is not occupied by linemen or get the linemen of both teams to stay real low and throw over them.

You get them to stay low by running this play as a play-action pass. That is, you should fake a dive handoff or similar inside running play to get the linebackers to react toward the line of scrimmage. Then you throw the pass.

Your linemen block it the same way they block the run it's supposed to look like, except that no one goes downfield. By driving out hard and low as they do in a run block they will force the defensive linemen to stay low to meet shoulder with shoulder. Even if the defensive linemen stand up, they will quickly bend back down as they instinctively use their hands to protect their legs from the block.

You hear people say coaches want tall quarterbacks so they can see over the linemen. Nonsense. Simple arithmetic tells you even a 6' 3" quarterback cannot see over 6' 5" linemen. Taller quarterbacks can see better than shorter ones. But they need a lane to look through. NFL linemen generally try to push pass rushers outside. That is partly to keep them from sacking the quarterback and partly to keep them from blocking the vision of the quarterback. In youth football, you will probably have more success forcing the defensive line to get low than moving them out of your quarterback's line of sight.

Spot pass

The only deep passes I've seen in youth football appeared to be spot passes. That is, the quarterback immediately heaved the ball to a spot. The trajectory was high so the receiver could run under it.

Correctly done, the pass would be thrown to a spot based on a **pre-snap read** that the spot was open. I suspect most youth quarterbacks don't worry about who's at the spot. You'll have to drill them with a receiver and one or more defenders to get them in the habit of throwing to an open spot.

Outrunning the quarterback's arm

The typical deep pass in youth football involves a receiver running straight downfield then coming back to the pass because he outran his quarterback's range. Passes like that are highly interceptible. This problem can be fixed by several methods:

- throw sooner
- delay release
- shorten the drop.

Waiting too long to release a pass is a perennial problem with young quarterbacks. If the receiver is running a streak, he will be out of the QB's range in two or three seconds. You must drill your quarterbacks to throw as soon as possible.

If you cannot throw that soon, for example, because you are doing a play-action fake, you should delay the receiver's release. A pass we are using this season on my youth team has the left tight end blocking for a two-count, then releasing on a flat out pattern. We threw the game-winning touchdown pass on this pattern in our first game of the season.

Your quarterback's drop in youth football should be one step, two steps (in the case of a pop pass), or three steps. A pop pass is a quick pass thrown immediately after a fake dive handoff. After the fake, a right-handed quarterback would cross his left foot back over his right then bring his right back and throw. High school and higher levels also use five- and seven-step drops. But there is no way your quarterback can throw as far as his receivers can run during a five- or seven-step drop. When I coached Granada's freshmen in 1996, all of our deep passes resulted in the receiver having to come back to the ball. Our deepest drop was five steps. But even five steps was too many if the receiver went straight downfield from the snap.

We asked the varsity head coach if we could shorten the stems of the deep routes, that is, have the receiver make his cut sooner, say at eight yards rather than twelve. The varsity head coach refused our request. He insisted that we work with on the quarterbacks' mechanics to enable them to throw farther. We tried but were not successful.

Trap left boot pass

The quarterback fakes an inside trap to the fullback then boots out to his left. The right wing is in motion and makes a key right-shoulder block on the defensive contain man (marked OL in the diagram). The play is a run-pass option. So this is not only a pass play for us, it is also the closest thing we have to a sweep left.

Coaching points on this play: the left end has a tendency to cut his block short of two seconds, which enables the man he's blocking to sack the quarterback. He also has a tendency to run a **flag** route (toward the corner of the end zone) rather than run parallel to the line of scrimmage.

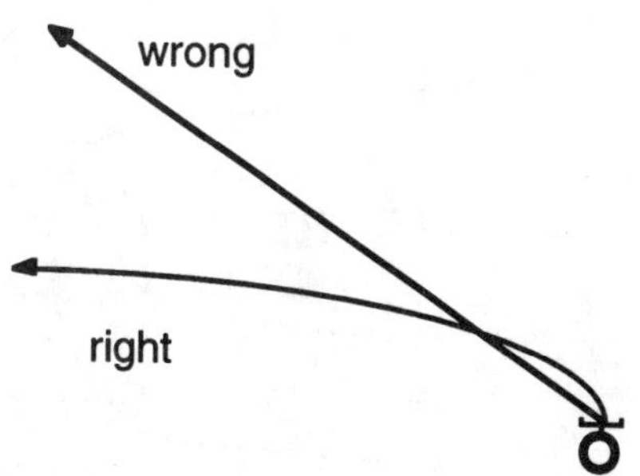

Our only incomplete pass of the year came when he ran the incorrect flag route. He was wide open, but the quarterback overthrew him. I gave the left end at least half the blame, however, because the route **as designed** is easy to complete.

Since both the QB and the receiver are running parallel to the line of scrimmage in the same direction, the QB does **not have to lead** the receiver. The QB's own movement takes care of that. But if the receiver is moving **away** from the line of scrimmage, his sideways-only speed is **less** than that of the quarterback so the quarterback has to throw **behind** the receiver. Furthermore, because the receiver is now moving away from the QB in the **vertical** direction, the QB has to lead the receiver toward the goal line. In other words, when the receiver runs the wrong route, the quarterback has to throw **behind and beyond** where the receiver is at the moment of the throw. That's rather complicated geometry. With the correct route, he simply throws directly at the receiver.

Here's a diagram of the correct pattern:

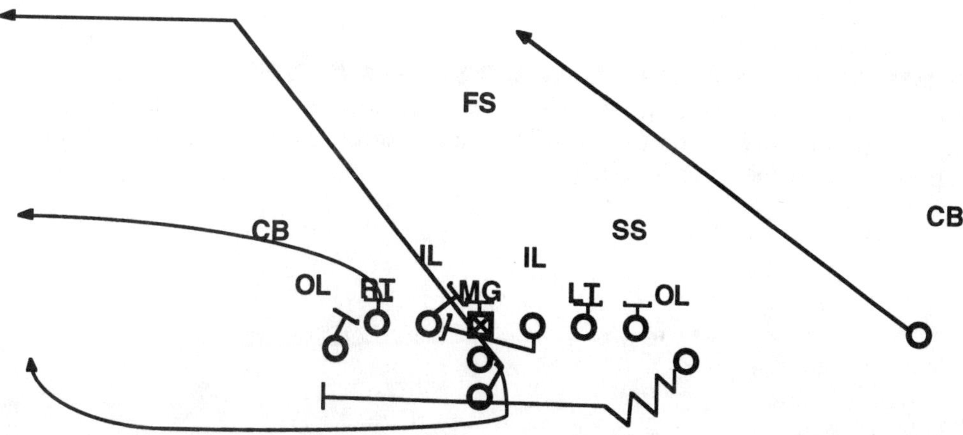

Waggle

The wing-T offense is famous for the waggle pass, among other things. It is a fake sweep to one side and a bootleg to the other. One or two guards pull toward the bootleg to protect the quarterback. The sweep fake gets the defense going away from the real point of attack. Here's 80 waggle from the book, *The Delaware Wing-T*:

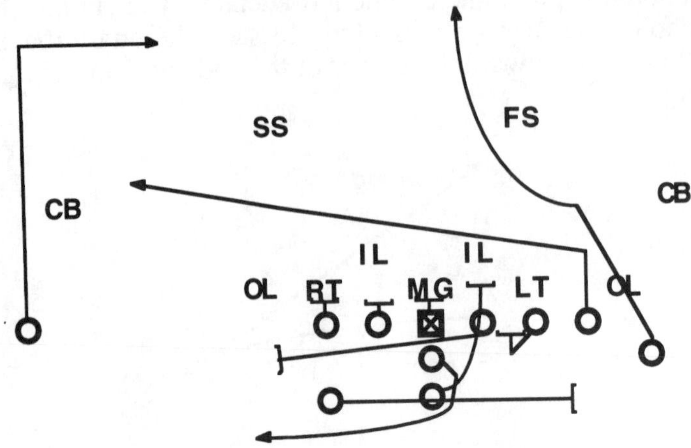

Zone 5

Zone 5 can be attacked successfully with quick slant or look-in passes. Virtually every team on my video was able to complete this pass when they tried. The pass to the tight end can be stopped easily by blocking the tight ends on the line of scrimmage. But few, if any, teams do that. It's harder to stop when a wideout is the intended receiver.

De La Salle High School, which is near where I live, has a 65-game win streak, the longest in the U.S. at the moment. The national record is 72. I taped their first game of the 1997 season which was broadcast on local TV.

The first play of that game was a 75-yard slant pass for a touchdown against perennial power Nevada Union. The left wideout, who was untouched, ran a few steps straight downfield then slanted in at a 45-degree angle. The De La Salle quarterback ran a fake option left then simply threw the ball before he got to the end.

Deeper or slower patterns like crossing routes, curls, and hooks are generally **doomed** in this very congested area. Although I did see a junior midget team pick my son's team apart with **crossing routes** in one game in 1993. The crossing route is very similar to the slant.

Fake one way, roll out and pass the other

I have long been amazed at how open some of Miramonte's receivers get. Usually it's on a play where they fake a run to one side then roll out the other. Miramonte's gray right counter boot looks something like this.

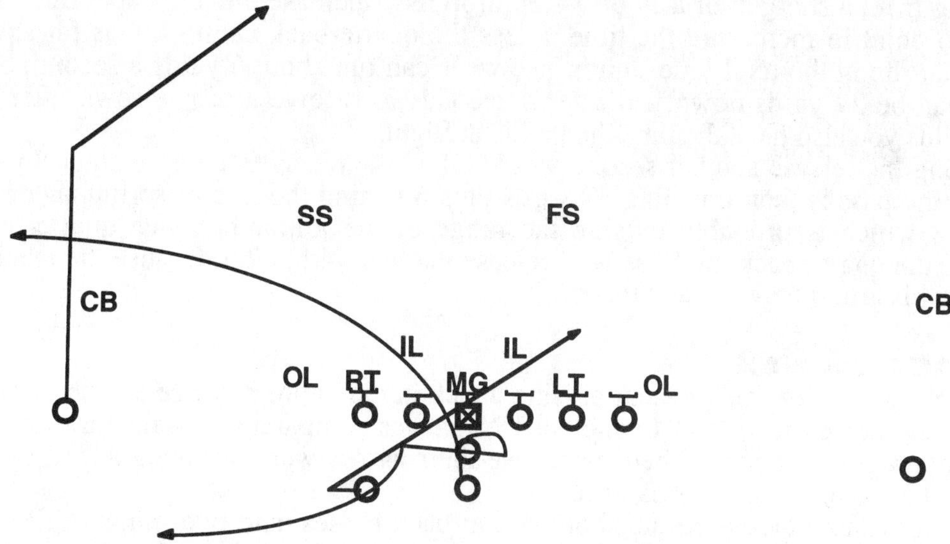

Zones 7 and 9

Like zones 4 and 6, **zones 7 and 9** can be attacked with quickly-released, high-arc passes thrown to a spot. Flag patterns would work, as would streaks against shallow-playing defenders, if your quarterback can throw that far.

Zone 8

Zone 8 is the **interception capital of youth football**. Passes thrown to this area were generally covered by no less than three or four defenders. This area can only be attacked by well-executed **play action** that draws the deep defenders to the line of scrimmage

Zones 7, 8, and 9 can all be attacked successfully with such play action passes as **halfback passes** and **double passes**.

The one-exchange assumption

Defenders almost invariably operate on the **one-exchange assumption**. That is, once the ball has been exchanged from the quarterback to another player, they assume no further hand-offs or passes will occur and they all run to the ball carrier. Oakland threw a successful halfback touchdown pass against us in a 1991 game. Napa almost completed one against us in 1992. A flea flicker we tried against Manteca was thrown too quickly. The defensive secondary did not have time to read our fake. It fell incomplete.

Passes that do not cross the line of scrimmage

Most coaches and players do not understand **three important passing rules**: There is no prohibition against pass interference, blocking while the ball is in the air, or ineligible receiver downfield **when the pass does not cross the line of scrimmage**. In other words, while the pass is in the air, a blocker can total a defender who is going for it. A receiver of such a pass could be assigned an escort who does just that. This would be a blocker's dream situation.

Three seconds tops

A slant or look-in pass only takes 1.00 to 1.70 seconds to release and can be stopped by delaying tight ends that long.

When the clock strikes 3.00 and the quarterback still has the ball, bad things are almost certain to happen. Quarterbacks must be drilled to get rid of the ball by about 2.80 seconds.

Passing from a shotgun or a 5- or 7-step drop may increase the allowable time. But there is no point in increasing the time unless the quarterback can throw as far as the receiver can run in the total time. Junior pee wees can run about 6 yards a second. So a receiver can be 24 yards downfield after 4 seconds to receive a pass thrown after 2.5 seconds. Plus you also have the time the ball is in flight.

Delaying the release another second would allow the receiver to get another 8 yards or so, but the pass is then traveling 32 yards plus 6 behind the line of scrimmage for a total of 38 which is probably outside the range of the junior pee wee quarterback. Therefore, the quarterback might as well release the ball within 2.5 because the receiver will outrun his arm if he waits any longer.

Napa passed well

I thought we had the only decent passing attack in the junior pee wee league in 1992. But upon reviewing the videos, I concluded Napa was comparable. Against a team that scouted thoroughly, Napa was better because their passes were not telegraphed by the formation the way our hitch passes were.

Napa's passing attack used the shotgun, halfback passes, and two-minute-drill-type out passes. Napa seemed to have figured out much of what I've written above

Don't throw same route repeatedly

It is not good to throw to a receiver running the same route more than **twice** a game. In the typical series of repeating a pass route in a game, the first pass is complete, the second is tipped, and the third is intercepted.

Most teams learn very fast how to read a particular pass pattern that you show them in a game.

Look-in is exception

Tri-Cities threw look-ins for three touchdowns against us in 1990. I saw the Oakland Dynamites go ahead then win a 1994 playoff game that was stalemated by suddenly starting to throw look-in passes. The Vallejo Generals couldn't stop them. I think they threw it four or five times successfully in the fourth quarter. (It should be easy to stop. Block the ends on the line and station a linebacker at ground zero.)

It is very dangerous to throw the same pattern **three** times in one game. I saw our 1991 pee wees do it in a short span in one home game. The first two were complete, the third was tipped, and the fourth was intercepted. They were following the approach of if-it-worked-run-it-again. That applies to the **running** game, **not** passing.

Look-in

You should definitely install the look-in as one of your passes. Throw it not only to the tight ends, but also to split ends and flankers. Wideouts, especially flankers, who are back off the line of scrimmage, have an easier time releasing into their route than tight ends. Don't have a set place for the intended receiver to line up. Just put him wherever the defensive alignment and execution dictates.

Releasing receivers

One of the things that surprised me at the high school level is how much time we spend teaching and practicing receiver release techniques. Release means getting off the line of scrimmage and into the pass route.

Defenders often play tight bump and run. That is, they block the receiver so he cannot leave. As I said in the defensive section, that is exactly what my 8-2-1 and 10-1 linebackers were coached to do. Defenders who practice this can get quite good at it and can wipe out your passing game. So you must teach release techniques and practice them in game conditions.

Swim, rip, and hitch

The main release techniques are the swim, rip, and hitch. In the swim, the receiver steps about six inches to the side of the defender he wants to go around, slams the heel of the hand on that side into the side of the defender, then throws his inside arm over and steps through with his inside leg.

In the rip, the receiver steps about six inches to the side of the defender he wants to go around, then simultaneously throws his inside leg through and his inside arm rips up violently to knock the defenders hands off the receiver.

In the hitch, the receiver fakes one way then releases the other. You can fake with your head or shoulders or whatever works.

Except for my teams, I have seen virtually no bump and run in youth football. But if you have it in your league, you must teach and practice release techniques. Otherwise you'll have receivers whining about the defender not letting them off the line.

Quarterback's eyes

When the quarterback shows pass, the defenders look for the receiver the quarterback is looking at and run to him. The youth quarterback's range is so short, as little as 15 yards beyond the line of scrimmage, that the typical fast defenders can get to any receiver within two seconds. Since the flight time is 1 to 1.5 seconds, the passer had better not look at the intended receiver for more than about .2 seconds.

If the quarterback looks at the receiver he throws to for one second or more before throwing, there will be a convention of defenders at ground zero by the time the ball arrives. Teach your quarterbacks to point their **head** off line while still focusing their **eyes** on whether the receiver is covered.

Tinted eye shields are now available. The dark sun glasses color made famous by Jim McMahon will hide your quarterback's eyes.

Backward pass

The backward pass has few advantages and a huge risk. We lost possession of one against Vallejo. The defense would probably turn some dropped backward passes into defensive touchdowns if they were coached to pick up the ball rather than fall on it. The same play can be run with little change as a forward, behind-the-line-of-scrimmage pass thereby preserving the right to have ineligible receivers downfield, block while the pass is in air, and be immune from interference calls while avoiding the hazards of a dropped lateral.

On the other hand, in 1992 we **did** make a big gain against Manteca and a touchdown against Richmond by picking up dropped backward passes and running with them. As a **designed** play, dropping a backward pass may be a worthwhile tactic, especially if the receiver has an escort blocker.

Tell the refs before the game

Although the referees mistakenly whistle dropped backward passes dead almost as often as not. (They did that in our games against the Falcons and Napa in 1992.) That might be prevented by telling the refs about the play before the game and running the play early in the game.

Sprint-out passes

Junior pee wees generally cannot throw overhand on the run unless you teach them the technique. Virtually all shallow roll-out passes end in disaster at that level. One common mistake is to have the quarterback throw while running to his running-hand side. That causes coaches to think it can only be done to the dominant hand side. You often hear TV football announcers express amazement that a right-handed quarterback threw a sprint-out pass to his left.

It is ridiculous to see anything amazing about that. The correct technique calls for the passer to loop deep so that he is running **directly at** the receiver when he throws. In other words, sprinting out quarterbacks do not throw to their right or left at all. They throw only to their **front**, so it makes no difference whether they ran to the right or left to get to the spot from which they threw.

Many defensive backs give the receivers an **enormous cushion**. They should be attacked with short passes and double passes (receiver catches ball then throws to another receiver who has sneaked behind defender).

Halfback pass

The halfback pass is a mighty play in youth football. What's more important is that its power is generally overlooked.

I recommend that you do a halfback run-pass option. That is, the halfback can show pass and throw or show pass and then pull it down and run. If you only do the halfback pass, you'll be limited to one or two plays per game.

Must have one exchange before the pass

The ball should be transferred from the original recipient of the snap to someone else. That transfer triggers the one-exchange mentality of the defensive backs. That is, they figure the ball is only exchanged one time after the snap. Once there is a pitch or hand-off, they figure the play is surely a run and abandon their pass defense responsibilities.

Your receiver should delay his route for one second or so. Fiddle with the timing to see what works best for you.

The pass should probably be a **spot pass** with a **high trajectory**. It should be deep.

Not in all books

I told you to get a book on an offensive system that you believe in and get all your plays out of that book. That should work on all the **other** plays you need. But many books do not have a halfback pass. So you may need to design your own.

It is a **play-action** pass so it must start out looking like one of your **running** plays. Generally, a halfback pass is designed to look like a **power sweep** initially. Power sweeps have the blockers you need to protect the passer. They also take long enough to let the defensive backs decide the play is a run and abandon their pass defense territory.

Here is a professionally designed halfback sweep pass from the book, *Directory of Surprise Plays for Winning Football* by Tom Simonton.

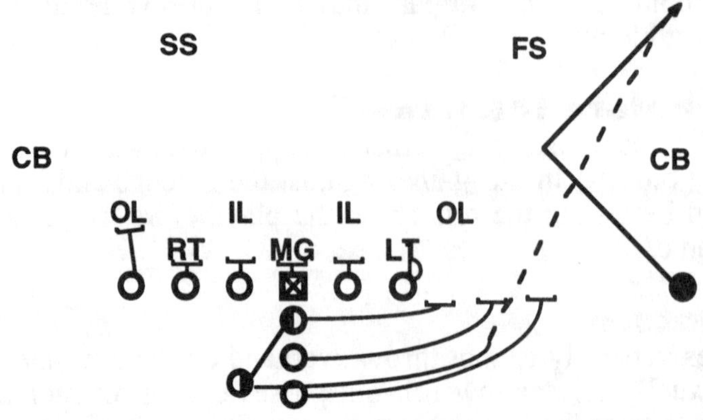

Make it look like a sweep

The key to this play is to make it look convincingly like a sweep. To do that, everyone must behave as they do on the sweep for the first two seconds or so. I recommend that you design this play to look just like your sweep. Then video your sweep and your sweep halfback pass from the perspective of the safety or corner back who is the biggest threat to the completion of the pass. See if you can spot any tip-offs in the pass play.

If and when the halfback decides to run with the ball, he should yell, "Go!" to his blockers as is often done in screen plays and wedge kick off returns. You must practice this.

I had enormous trouble getting my halfbacks to fake the sweep so in frustration, I reversed the concept. At the end of the 1996 freshman season, my Granada team was running what I called the fake tailback pass. That is, we had the tailback receive the pitch then run holding the ball in two hands in front of his breast bone as if he were going to pass. In fact, we wanted him to sweep. The fake pass look was to get the defensive backs to stay back too long. We even had him continue to hold the ball that way until he got five yards beyond the line of scrimmage because the defensive backs cannot tell that he is past the line of scrimmage.

Single-wing halfback passes

If you use a **single-wing** offense, you cannot just modify your sweep because it's probably a direct snap to the tailback. You need a hand-off or pitch to trigger the one-exchange mentality of the defensive backs. The single-wing halfback pass play I recommend is the **buck lateral** pass. Here is a single-wing buck lateral sweep from John Aldrich's book, *Single-wing Offense With the Spinning Fullback*. I have added the run-pass option.

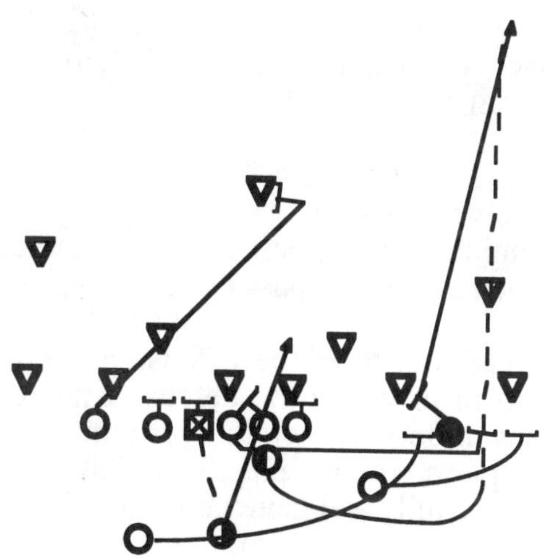

The ball is long snapped to the tailback which is the player with his right half darkened. He runs into the line handing off at the last second to the upback or blocking back which is the player whose left half is darkened. The upback spins around with his back to the defense and forms a hand-off pocket when the ball is snapped. He does not take any other steps until after he gets the ball. Then he sprints out to the right and throws or runs according to whether the receiver is open.

Dr. Keuffel's halfback pass

Dr. Kenneth Keuffel's book, *Simplified Single-wing Football* **does** have some halfback passes. Here's his favorite.

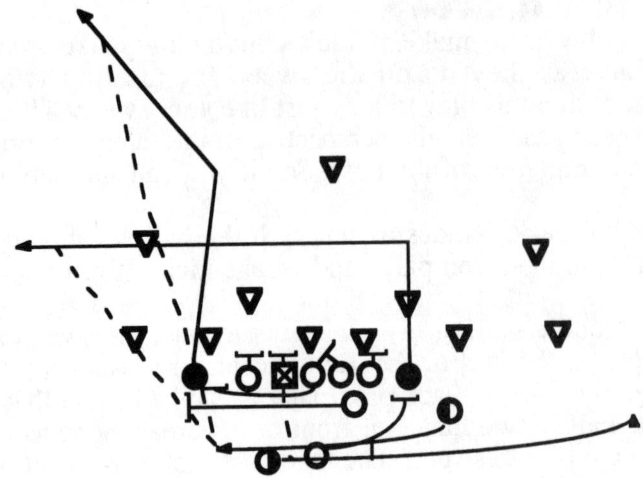

This is a play-action version of Dr. Keuffel's reverse. It not only tries to fool the defense by passing after the ball has been exchanged, it also sends everybody in the wrong direction with its initial flow. He puts two receivers downfield.

Four plays in one

This is really four plays in one and you must practice each.

- completed pass option
- run option
- incomplete pass that does not draw intentional grounding penalty
- take a sack.

As with the look-in pass, you should practice all four without the complication of reading the defense. That is, tell the halfback to

- pass no matter what,
- run no matter if the receiver is open
- throw an incomplete, uninterceptible pass near the receiver no matter what
- hold the ball until tackled even if the pass or run are open.

Then progress to the read and have the offense attempt to make the best of the situation in a competitive drill in which the defense tries to beat the offense. This is probably best done in a seven-on-seven or full scrimmage where the offense has the option to do any of the four plays within a play. Hopefully, the offense will get to where they can read the defense masterfully and gain yards either by throwing or passing.

Stop-the-clock play

When you are trying to conserve the clock, the no-huddle is good but it's also nice to be able to stop the clock. You do that by running **out of bounds**. You can also do it by throwing an incomplete pass, but that's undesirable because you have to waste a down.

If you only had a look-in pass, you would have no pass that would lend itself to getting out of bounds after the pass is caught. The halfback pass, on the other hand, does take place near the sideline so the receiver could get out of bounds after catching the ball. The play also allows the halfback to keep the ball and run out of bounds. Of course they should not run out of bounds until they are confronted by a tackler. Running into the end zone stops the clock, too.

Passes like the 26 power pass are also good for getting out of bounds.

Blocking

It is crucial that two things happen with regard to blocking in pass plays:

- no ineligible receivers downfield
- good protection for the passer.

The center and other linemen who are not ends must not go more than one yard downfield on this play or the pass option will become illegal. You should use **even** numbers for **passes** and **odd** for **runs** to help clarify this. And you must run every drill you can think of to make sure the ineligible receivers concentrate on not breaking this rule. Note that the guards in the diagram do not go downfield to block the linebackers the way they normally would on a sweep. That's why some linebackers are taught to key on uncovered ineligible linemen.

Protect a spot

The blockers have their backs to the passer, so he must go to a prearranged location. They will protect that spot. If he wanders, the protection will be useless. You should probably use **area blocking**. That is, each blocker takes an area and blocks whomever comes through it. If no one comes there, he helps his neighbor. But he does not run off chasing a defender, thereby leaving his area unprotected. Defenders trying to run around the entire blocking echelon are probably not going to arrive at the passer in time.

You must get many eleven-on-eleven reps of this play live to make sure the blocking is squared away. The backs can count their steps starting at the snap or line up around the fullback or whatever it takes to get to the right spot. The passer must learn where to go as well.

These eleven-on-eleven reps will also enable you to get the timing down. You must find out the best time to form the protective wall and the best time for the passer to bring the ball up to pass it.

Run the sweep first

You probably need to run your sweep before you run the halfback sweep pass to set the defenders up for the play. But on the other hand, your sweep probably looks like everybody else's so they may already be set up before kickoff.

Be patient, passer

The main mistake made on this play is that the halfback is too anxious and starts showing pass immediately after he gets the ball. He must be disciplined to tuck the ball away just as he does on a real sweep for several steps. Only then can he bow back away from the line of scrimmage and throw his pass.

I recommend that you give him a sequence to memorize and say in his head. Initially, in practice, you could have him say it out loud—something like, "Catch, tuck, step, step, step, bow back and throw." Walk him through it until he gets the rhythm down so well he can do it in his sleep. Keep in mind that people says things silently a lot faster than they do out loud. You may find that when the back switches to the silent mode he needs in games, that he does not take enough time.

Reps

I have recommended six plays in this book. Of the six, the halfback pass should get the most reps. This is one of the biggest examples of oomph in the book. On a number of occasions in both high school and youth football, I have seen this play work beautifully—except for one thing. Last year on our J.V. high school team, the receiver was wide open, but the halfback did not put a high enough trajectory on the ball and threw a less than perfect pass. Why? Not enough reps.

Earlier in this book, I said you need 200 reps a week to have a deep spot pass. The halfback pass is a deep spot pass. I recommend that you practice offense and this play every day. So you need 67 reps a day in a three-day practice week. If you reject my recommendation, and only practice offense one day a week, as many coaches do, you need all 200 reps that day. The problem with that is boredom and overuse of the arms of your passers.

You can practice look-in passes in your pre-game warm-up. And you should. But you probably should not practice the whole halfback pass in the pre-game warm-up except to have your wide receivers going out for a **generic** deep spot pass thrown by **all** your backs.

Be patient, coach

The halfback pass works, but **not** the **first time** you practice it. You must keep the faith and keep on practicing even though you will be discouraged in the early weeks. This is the most complicated play I have advocated in this book. Accordingly, it will take a lot of reps to get it right.

Don't get discouraged. Don't let your fellow coaches or players or parents get discouraged about this play. Keep fiddling with it until you iron out all the kinks. You'll have problems making the connections: snap, pitch, or hand-off. You'll have trouble completing the pass—even against air (no defense). Don't get discouraged. You'll have problems with the protection. You'll have problems with the halfback making the right run-pass read. Don't get discouraged.

Teach it step-by-step

Coach the play progressively. That is, teach it in simple steps. Don't try to put it all together too soon. Learn the pitch or hand-off first. Work on the pass and catch at the same practice but not in the same drill. Work on the fake to make it look just like your similar running play until the last second.

You will have problems putting this play in. The solutions to those problems will involve changing the play slightly—new routes, a delay here, a higher trajectory there. You may find that you have the **wrong player** in a key position and that you have to replace him. In fact, you will **probably** find that.

Catching passes can be learned by anyone willing to work hard. But it's also true that most people do **not** work hard and that some people can catch better than others. You need your **best** deep pass receiver to be the primary receiver on this play.

Alternate play and play action pass in practice

When I practice play-action passes, I like to alternate back and forth between the play and the play-action pass based on it.

At Miramonte High School in 1994, we had a play called 26 Power and another called 26 Power Pass. 26 Power was the typical off-tackle play with a lead block by the fullback and the tailback carrying the ball. 26 Power Pass was designed to look the same only the fullback deliberately missed his block and ran a pass route into the flat. The tight end did the same only deeper. The quarterback sprinted out on the run and sprinted out and threw on the pass.

Poor fakes

By running 26 Power then 26 Power Pass with each set of backs, differences between the plays became apparent. The quarterbacks tended **not** to get close to the tailback for the hand-off fake but they **did** get close on the actual hand-off. I made them get close for

both. They also tended to do the sprint-out half-heartedly on the run but at full speed on the pass. I made them run it at full speed on both.

Alternating the run with its companion play-action pass every other play helped me as a coach spot the flaws in the fakes. It also helped the players see and understand the ingredients of and importance of a good fake. A **good** fake **aids** the running back by sending defenders off in the wrong direction. **Bad** fakes, on the other hand, **hurt** the ball carrier because they delay his getting to where he wants to go. You are far better off not faking at all than making a poor fake.

Our 1993 playbook

Here is our 1993 playbook. Actually, it was more of a play **sheet**. You don't give a book to youth football players.

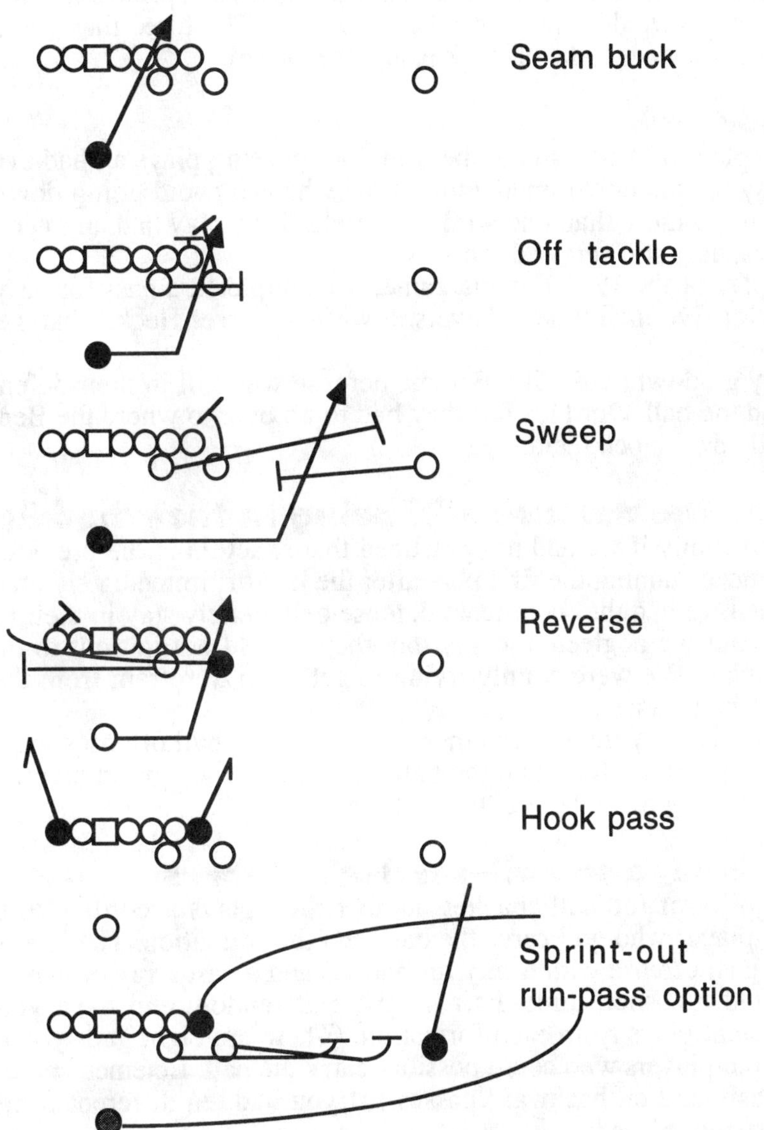

The numbering system for the warp-speed, no-huddle, white-board code was:

Play #	Play
1	Off tackle
2	Sprint-out run-pass option
3	Sweep
4	not used
5	Reverse
6	Hook pass
7	Seam Buck (Wedge)
8	not used
9	Punt
0	not used

In retrospect, we could have forgotten about the reverse, sprint-out run pass option, and hook pass and we would have had a better season. The three that got the job done were the seam buck or wedge, the off tackle, and the sweep.

Even and odd

Our **running** plays all had **odd** numbers and our **passing** plays all had **even** numbers. That made it easy for the down linemen to know when to avoid going downfield. They simply were not to go more than one yard downfield if the play had an **even** number. As simple as that was, they still screwed it up.

On the first play of the 1993 Benicia game, we completed a pass for 43 yards. But it was called back for five ineligible receivers downfield. **Five**! Heck. That's every single one of them.

Why did they go downfield? The Benicia defense was still in their defensive huddle when we snapped the ball. Our kids felt they had to go over to where the Benicia players were so they could pass block them.

We practiced the defense still being in their huddle!

That would be funny if we had not practiced that exact thing the previous Thursday. We literally practiced running the first play after the kickoff immediately after the ready-to-play whistle and we had the scout team defense deliberately stay in their huddle while we ran the play. But we neglected to say that they should not got out to the huddle to block on a **pass** play. We were mainly trying to get them to refrain from the **politeness** we had seen over the years.

Unless you consciously train them otherwise, youth football offenses will wait for the defense to get ready before they snap the ball. It's a habit they get in practice where the coaches want everybody ready before they run a play.

Formation, hole, and ball-carrier numbers

The vast majority of football coaches number their plays according to the hole the play goes to, the player who will carry the ball, and the formation. That's a brilliant way to communicating an offense with **many** formations and a vast array of plays. In fact, it's so great you could just pick three-digit numbers at random and have your team run eighty-eight different plays from each formation. (There are eight gaps you could run to and there are eleven players who could possibly carry the ball. Linemen can carry the ball on the fumblerooski and on backward passes.) If you had ten different formations, you could run 880 different plays.

The players may never even have heard of the play before. But those wonderful three-digit numbers tell them which formation to line up in, who gets the ball, and which hole he runs through. Intelligent players could interpolate their ball-exchange and blocking assignments from the hole, ball carrier, and formation numbers.

Too complex

Now forget about that. This book is about the **simple** approach, remember? I tip my hat to the inventor of the hole-ball-carrier-formation numbering system. But I just as quickly denounce it as one of the chief causes of teams having too much offense.

My code system forces you to have no more than **ten** plays. That ten-play limit may be more important than its ability to let you send in plays quickly and without misunderstandings. Even ten is arguably too many plays. Forget 880.

Line and back blocking

I deliberately made special teams the first chapter of this book. The reason is I know you're excited about offense, but it's important that you also get excited about special teams and defense. So I put offense last.

By that same logic, I should have put blocking first in this offensive chapter. Like special teams, blocking gets a lot of lip service from coaches. Like special teams, blocking is extremely important to the success of your team.

What position does the offensive coordinator coach?

Offensive coordinators generally coach a position and the position they choose most often is quarterbacks. Miramonte head coach Floyd Burnsed coaches quarterbacks. So did Roger Theder when he was offensive coordinator of San Jose State.

At the high school and higher levels, that's probably appropriate because the quarterback is the most important member of the team. But at the youth level, where passing is less important, the quarterback is not the most important member. Running backs are probably the most important players in youth football. So offensive coordinators should make themselves running backs coaches? No. Running backs are important. But it is not a very coachable position. Running backs are more born than made. The coach's job is to find them more than it is to create them.

When I did my one year as head coach, I assigned myself the running back's coach job on offense. If I had it to do over, I would have take the line coach's job. Running backs are important but relatively uncoachable. The line is also important and it is one of the most coachable positions on the field. De LaSalle head coach Bob LaDouceur coaches his line in recent years.

I want the offensive line coach's job

In 1994, I was special teams coach of a pee wee team. But I became a sort of occasional offensive coordinator of the second-string offense because I was the only experienced coach to work with that group. I coached the whole team but spent most of my time working on blocking because, as I said, the ball handlers' jobs were simple.

By the end of the season, our second-string offense often surpassed or equaled the first- in spite of greatly weaker personnel. The reason was that the offensive coordinator taught the first-string what I thought was a poor blocking scheme (a sort of man-to-man drive block for everybody).

I taught classic single-wing blocking from my reading and consultations with experienced single-wing coaches. The play where this mattered the most was the off-tackle. I thought our second-string ran the play much better than the first- because of the superior blocking. Here are diagrams of what the first and second string did.

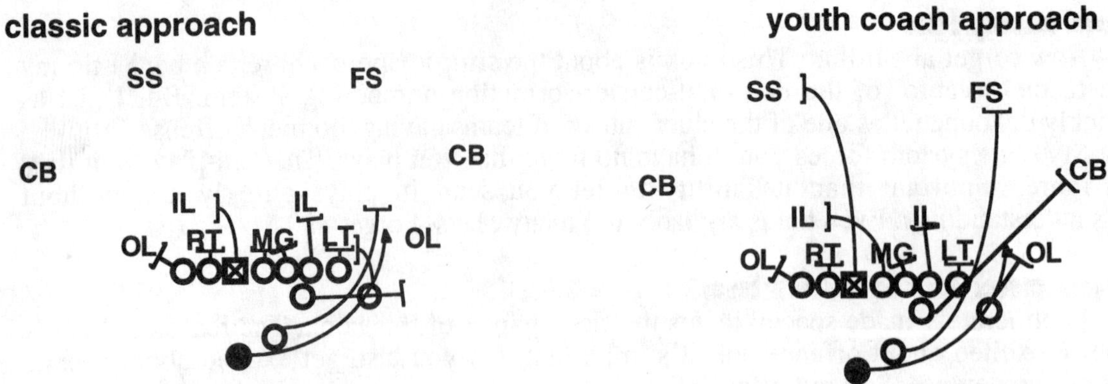

The second-string approach that I used has classic off-tackle blocking, that is, a **double-team** to the **inside** of the hole and a **trap** block on the **outside** of the hole. The fullback leads up through the hole and gets the most dangerous defender. The other blocks mainly serve the purpose of making sure the play is not disrupted before it gets going.

Block everybody?

The youth coach approach may not be exactly what the offensive coordinator did. But it is my best recollection. Basically, his theory was that every member of the defense except one must be blocked one-on-one by the offense. One is left unblocked because one offensive player is carrying the ball and therefore cannot block.

I think the reason this play is blocked the classic way and not the youth coach way is as follows. This play is designed to gain about four or five yards. Only certain defenders have a chance to stop a four- or five-yard gain at the off-tackle hole. They are the defensive tackle, the outside linebacker and the cornerback and inside linebacker.

We are going to stop the defensive tackle with a double-team. If that block is competently executed, the defensive tackle will have no chance to stop the play. The same is true of the trap block on the outside linebacker by the upback. The first defender to threaten will be hit by the fullback and the tailback, who is carrying the ball, will have to deal with the remaining defender using jukes, stiff arms, speed, etc.

Block the point of attack, not the whole field

We do **not** have to block the other defenders because they have lined up so far from the play that they generally would not be able to stop it short of a four- or five-yard gain even if the entire offense, except for the ball carrier, went down on one knee.

The flaw in the youth coach approach is that he is robbing blocks on **dangerous** defenders to make blocks on **irrelevant** defenders. He is trying to design every play to be a touchdown.

Most plays are NOT designed to go all the way

You often hear that all plays go for touchdowns in the play book. I don't know why people say that. Most plays are **not** designed to go for touchdowns. True, you want your players to get into the habit of blocking downfield. But first things first. The job of the off-tackle play is to get four or five yards. You must design your blocking to achieve that end first, then do the best you can with what's left.

One of the main reasons to seek out a book written by an experienced, successful coach is to get proven blocking schemes. Do **not** design your own plays or your own blocking schemes.

Body position not body composition

One of the most important and encouraging discoveries I have made in my football coaching career is that most failures come **not** from the other players **beating** your guy, but from your guy being in the **wrong place** or doing the **wrong thing**. People talk as if football games are won and lost on conditioning or athletic ability alone. But when I've studied game videos, I found that is rarely the case.

Rather the little play-by-play failures that cumulatively add up to a lost game are generally **mechanical** rather than fitness or athletic ability. By mechanical I mean the player who failed did so because of the **position** of his body, not because of the **composition** of his body. That's encouraging because the position of the body is usually easy to fix. Composition is much harder.

Still need the best kid

Now I'm not contradicting my earlier emphasis on picking the right kid for each position. Rather I am saying that once you have your best kid in the position, you generally do not have to worry that the other team's best kid will beat your guy because he is a better athlete or is better conditioned. I still say that putting your weak kid against the other team's strong kid will get you into trouble.

Examples of body positions that get you beat include:

- lining up at the wrong place
- standing up too high when you are about to make contact
- stepping the wrong direction after the snap.

'Mistakes got us beat'

You hear coaches frequently say, "Mistakes got us beat." That's is a variation on what I'm saying. Players doing the wrong thing is far more likely to get you beat than players trying to do the right thing, but failing. In fact, I have rarely seen even a single play where a player tried to do the right thing but got beat.

I've seen ball carriers try futiley to gain yards. But when I've analyzed the play, I found that a key blocker blocked the wrong guy or got too high or put his head on the wrong side or some similar mistake. This might be a good time for you to put down this book and get out a video of one of your past games. Analyze why a particular play failed. I'll bet you'll find it was because someone was trying to do the wrong thing.

Whom to block

Lining up at the right place should not be a problem for you on offense if you follow my recommendation to use only one offensive formation. To the extent that you use multiple formations or flip-flop, you must give your team many repetitions of just lining up to make sure they line up in the right place. The good news is that you can get a lot of reps of just lining up if you do not waste time by running plays in between. In high school football we have a lot of line-up or one-step drills. Youth coaches tend to run entire plays whenever their team is in formation.

So once you teach your players to line up correctly **every time**, you are ready to teach them **whom** to block. When you think about it, this is crucial. Many youth coaches spend a lot of time practicing blocking because they think, correctly, that it is important. But they are practicing blocking **technique**. That's putting the cart before the horse. Before you teach **how** to block, you must first make sure the players all are absolutely sure **whom** to block.

Many combinations

When you think about it, whom to block can get highly complex. Question one is how many plays do you have? If you have six, there are at least **six** blocking assignments for every non-ball carrier. But that's only if every defense in the league always lines up exactly the same way, that there is just one defense in the league and no player or coach ever makes an adjustment. If there are two different defenses used in your league, each player has to learn **twelve** blocking assignments.

But are there just two different alignments for each of the players your blockers face? Of course, not. Each player can face a defender who is nose-to-nose, on his inside shoulder, on his outside shoulder, back off the line, in the gap to his inside, in the gap to his outside, a yard outside him, etc., etc.

Let's say each player may find the guy he is supposed to block in any of eight positions. That means he has to learn **48** blocking assignments if you have just six plays. I have strongly urged you to limit the number of plays you have to three to six. I have given you many reasons. But this is the biggest. The more plays you have, the quicker your blockers are overwhelmed by the complexity of figuring out whom to block.

Rules, calls, zones, defensive recognition, and numbering systems

Generations of coaches have tried to simplify the question of whom to block by using various systems. Many youth coaches remember their high school or college coach's approach and use it on their youth team. The best book I have ever seen on blocking is *Attacking Football Defenses With Radar Blocking* by Leo Hand. In fact, it's just about the **only** book strictly on blocking I have ever seen.

Here is a discussion of the various approaches to deciding whom to block based on Hand's book.

Defensive recognition

In defensive recognition, the blockers are taught, "If they are in Defense A, you block this guy on this play. If they are in Defense B, you block this guy on this play." This is good when you scout and you know that the upcoming opponent has only two or three defenses. You can teach defense recognition the week before playing that opponent.

The trouble with defense recognition is that you cannot assume that any defense will limit itself to the defenses you teach. You really have to teach whom to block in **every conceivable defense**. Furthermore, three is no law that says every player has to line up exactly the same way in, say, a five-man defensive line.

For example, when I was defensive coordinator for the Miramonte High School Junior Varsity in 1994, I could use a knocked-down 50 with the nose shaded to the strong side of the center, nose in the gap, the nose shaded to the weak side of the strong guard. I could also stunt either or both inside linebackers and I could stunt them in different ways. In another five-man defensive line which we called "Okie," I could hit and read, slant left, slant right, pinch (slant in on both sides), and blitz both inside linebackers.

So you can see that the permutations quickly become overwhelming when you try to use defensive recognition as your way of teaching whom to block.

Numbering systems

Numbering systems are common with offenses that spread the defense like the Split T and the triple option. In a numbering system, the defender lined up over the center is 0 and the other defenders are numbered out from the center. Defensive secondary guys are generally ignored in numbering systems. Here's an example:

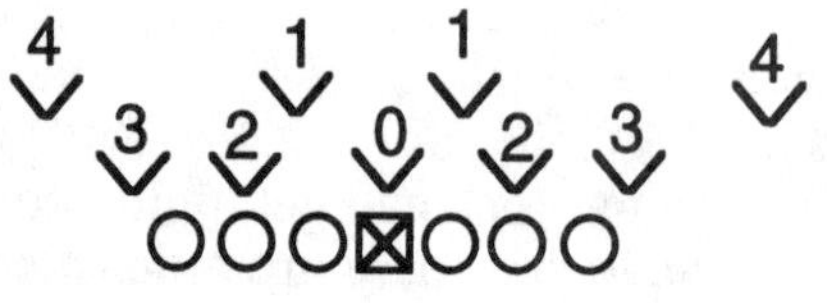

```
4      1    1       4
   3  2   0   2  3
    OOO⊠OOO
```

If the defense had an **even front** (no one on the center), you would not number any defender 0. If the defense has any **stacks** (linebackers directly behind linemen), you give the lower number to the player closest to the line of scrimmage.

'You block number 3'

Under a number blocking system, offensive players are told, "On the counter, you block number 3 on the left," or whatever. You may recall that I already recommended a blocking assignment system like this earlier in the book—the **kickoff return**. Only there I numbered from the sidelines in. As with the Split-T and triple-option offenses, the kick return is characterized by defenders that are **spread out** sideways and therefore easily numbered based on the horizontal position.

This generally only works in the Split-T and triple-option offenses because the line has **wide splits** and the defense has a hard time changing position after the offense gets set because they have so far to go. But they still can stem (suddenly change alignments while the quarterback is calling cadence). Stemming can foul up numbering systems.

Might work in youth football

Numbering systems might work better in youth football than in higher levels because the defenses do not stem much. But in youth football you have the problem of undisciplined defenders. When I scouted, I often had a heck of a time figuring out what defense a team was in because their players never settled down and came to a stop before the snap. You cannot assign numbers to them until they stop. And on defense, they do not ever have to stop moving.

If you use a numbering system, tell your players not to reveal that they are counting, like pointing their fingers at each player as they count, or counting out loud. If they know you are counting, opposing players and coaches will, even without training, probably figure out that they can mess you up by switching positions at the last second.

Rule blocking

In rule blocking, blockers have a set of rules which tell them the priority of whom to block. A typical rule would be a guard being told to block

"Gap, On, Over"

on a certain play. That means the guard must go through the following thought process when he gets set.

"If there is a defender lined up in the **gap** to my inside, I block him.

"If there is no defender in my inside gap, I block the defender who is lined up **on** me, that is, with his nose on or between my shoulders and is on the line of scrimmage.

"If there is no defender on me then I block the defender who is **over** me, that is, has his nose on or between my shoulders and is within five yards of the line of scrimmage."

Stunts are a problem for rule blocking because the blocker has to decide whom to block before the snap. Stunts change the alignment of the defenders right after the snap.

Area blocking

I have already discussed area blocking in the special-teams sections. In area blocking, each player has a territory to cover. He blocks anyone who comes into his territory. If no one comes, he blocks no one. He must maintain a seamless front in conjunction with his adjacent teammates.

Area blocking makes a lot of sense for set-piece plays like a drop-back pass, punt, or PAT kick where everybody pretty much knows where the action will be and that spot must be protected. Leo Hand says area blocking is ineffective against the stunt. I don't understand why he says that. It seems to me to be **designed** for the stunt. Stunts cause defenders to end up different places than where they start. But with area blocking, you ignore where they start.

Calls

In calls, offensive players call out code words that indicate to their teammates whom to block. The quarterback may make the call, or the center, or some other designated lineman. You might have several guys make calls like the left tackle makes the call for the left tight end and left tackle. The center makes the call for the center and guards. And the right tackle makes the call for the right tackle and right tight end.

I have an NFL video which shows a bunch of linemen on a field goal team actually pointing to the guy they're going to block. But the defense kept shifting and the offense would have to start pointing all over again. That was on a blooper tape because it looked silly.

The most common line call my kids make is for a **cross block**. In two of our plays in 1997, we base block. That is, everybody just blocks the nearest guy and puts his helmet between the bad guy and the path of the ball carrier. But sometimes, the guy you are supposed to block to the **left** is on your **right** shoulder, which makes it very hard. You have a lousy angle. In that case, we expect the lineman in question to call for a cross block. Here's a diagram:

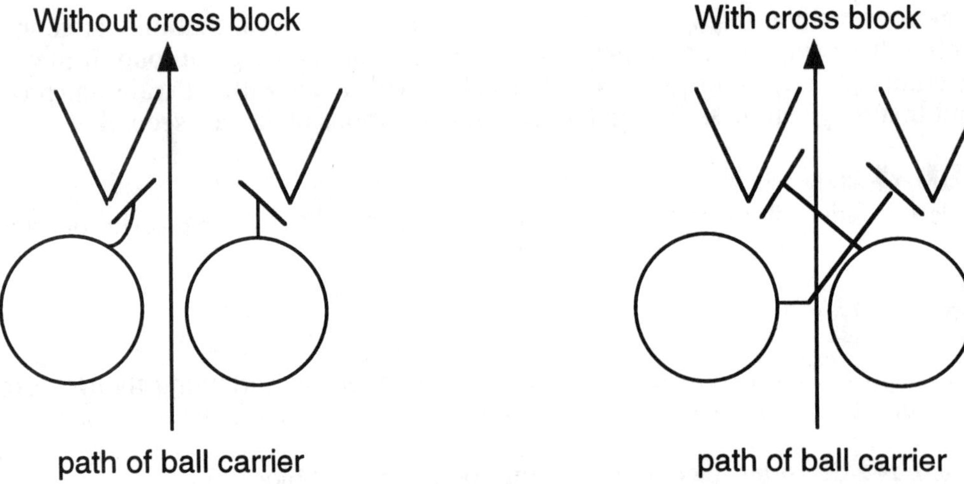

Note that the left offensive player now has a much better angle. Note also that the most dangerous defender must be blocked first. In this diagram, assume that the center is to the left of these two offensive linemen. That means the inside defender is closer to the early path of the ball and is therefore the most dangerous. So the outside cross blocker goes first.

A line call simply means the players talk to each other. At Miramonte High School, the tight end was named Joe so the tackle would call, "Joey," when he wanted a cross block.

Call out jersey number?

Some coaches think calling out the number of the guy you are going to block is best because there is less chance of confusion and it will intimidate the defender in question. I don't buy that. I would be delighted, as a defender, to know, in advance, where the guy assigned to block me is coming from. Furthermore, in time, intelligent defenders will be able to tell where the ball carrier is going from the advance notice of the blocking scheme. In general, the ball carrier will be passing where the blocker's **behind** points. If the guy assigned to block me is on my left, the ball carrier will be passing to my left.

Radar blocking

Leo Hand's Radar Blocking is basically a combination of calls and rules. He uses rules to establish a basic system for handling any defense. Then he uses calls to add flexibility for special situations where the rules seem like they will not achieve an adequate result.

I have no preference

I have no great recommendation to make to you on which system to use. That's probably because I made the mistake of not taking the line coach job. In 1995, I was a tight ends coach on the varsity so I learned a lot about blocking. After a year or two of coaching linemen, I will probably have a favorite approach.

I adopted a gap-on-area rule for the playside of my line in what I call slow-developing plays in 1997. That is, if the ball is coming to your side on a slow-developing play (e.g., off-tackle, counter), you block a guy to your inside if there is one, a guy on you if there is no one to the inside. If no one is in either spot, you stay where you are and wait in case someone tries to come through your area. I used to send uncovered guys down on a linebacker but I found the resulting hole often let somebody through. Now I let lead blockers get the linebackers.

Bird dog drill

As soon as you adopt your blocking system, you should teach it and test the players with a bird dog drill. You should do the bird dog drill weekly with your scout defense lined up in the various alignments the upcoming opponent will use.

In the bird dog drill, you line up your offense and the scout defense teams. On the snap count, the defense stands still and the offensive players all take one step and point to their target on the man they are assigned to block. In blocking technique, it is important that they step with the correct foot.

Fit and freeze

I actually prefer a drill I call fit and freeze. The problem with the bird dog drill is pointing is a bit ambiguous and does not show head position. With fit and freeze, each player walks to the defender he is going to block, fits his body against the defender and freezes while I go around and check to make sure each person is blocking the right guy and has the right body position.

If you insist that the players actually freeze and stay quiet, you can rapidly go through your whole play book and make sure everyone knows their assignments.

Blocking technique

Here's a blocking technique I saw taught at camp at San Jose State in 1995. If the blocker is a lineman who is going to block a defender near him with his **right** shoulder, he must take his **first step** about **six inche**s with his **left** foot. His **second step** is a big **long** one **between the legs** of the target defender and he hits the defender with his **right shoulder**, **forearm** and the **heel of the left hand** simultaneously. The blocker must keep his shoulder **pads lower than the pads of the defender.** At the moment of impact, the blocker must **thrust his pelvis forward violently** to achieve the desired lifting effect.

As the impact begins, the blocker's body is close to **horizontal**. As he completes the second step with his hitting and lifting action, his trunk becomes almost **vertical**. The blocker's trunk rotates almost 90 degrees during the hit. The head is up throughout the block and any other contact.

The second step is followed by another **long third step past the defender's right side with the left foot. Left** shoulder blocking is the mirror image of this block.

Hit sled from knees

One drill that's done on the blocking sled to teach the pelvic thrust and lift is to have the blockers get on their **knees** right in front of the sled pad. They dig the cleats of their toes into the ground. On command, they hit the sled pad with their forearm, same shoulder, and heel of the other hand and lift the sled as high as possible. They must thrust their pelvis forward to achieve the lift.

Sleds are a bit problematic for youth players because their weight is designed for high school and older athletes. Do the best you can with your high school's sleds. You might try putting **two kids on each pad** of a popsicle sled (one-man) or a two-man Crowther sled. Whatever you do, do **not** have a coach or player stand on the sled like my high school coach used to do.

Step and point

In the bird dog drill, you only want the lineman to take the first step, with his left foot in the example just stated, and point with either hand at the spot on the defender's body where his shoulder will hit. This is called the bird dog drill because the offensive players are pointing and freezing like a bird dog pointing at a bird in hunting.

While your players hold their step and point, the coaches check each player to make sure he has stepped with the correct foot and is pointing at the right man and target. Do it over until everybody gets it right. If you suspect any player is waiting for his neighbors to point then pointing at who's not yet taken, make him do the drill alone. That is, tell all but one player to take a knee. Then run the suspected cheater through all the plays to make sure he can do it without waiting for his neighbors.

Vary the defense

Put the defense scout team in the upcoming opponent's various alignments. Then fiddle with them slightly to see if the linemen can still figure out the correct guy to block. This drill is far more important than a blocking-technique drill where you slam into a sled or dummy with each shoulder.

Whom is more important than how

It is far more important that your players know **whom** to block than it is that they know **how** to block. Blocking technique is nice. I teach it and drill it. You should, too. But we have in our favor a basic principle of physics: **two bodies cannot occupy the same space at the same time**. If your blocker gets to the right place, even with the wrong technique, he is at least there and must be moved by the defender before he can tackle.

Of course, I want my blockers to pancake or move the defender whenever possible. And we drill for that purpose. But great technique is worthless if the player blocks the wrong man. The result of a player not blocking his man usually is an unblocked defender flying in untouched and looking like an all-pro.

The sequence of teaching an offense

Most coaches say fundamentals are important so you teach them first. Wrong. They are important, but you have to teach **plays** first because practice time is so limited.

Suppose I gave you a team for the first time and said, "You will scrimmage in an hour. Get them ready right now."

Obviously, you could not take time to teach blocking technique. Rather you would have to rush to put in about three plays focusing mainly on the quarterback's footwork and handoff technique, the path of the ball carrier, and the blocking assignments. If you started teaching fine points of blocking like hand position and so forth, you would not be able to execute any plays and you would make fools out of yourselves in the scrimmage.

In effect, a youth season presents a similar problem. The most difficult thing in my experience is to make sure every player knows exactly what he is supposed to do on every play and that he does it. If you let them, kids will be slobs about knowing their assignment and they will hit and quit and turn around to watch how the ball carrier is doing.

Once you make sure they know their assignments, then you can teach technique.

Instant replay scrimmage

My favorite technique for teaching and testing offense is to run a play against the best scout team we can put together. If it succeeds, that is gains four yards or more, we move on to the next play. But if it fails, we stop and find out why.

"Who made the tackle? Where'd you come from? Who was supposed to block him? Why didn't you?" We then rerun the play with all coaching eyes focused on the player who failed the first time we ran it.

Often, we will spot poor technique, like being too high. At that moment, we will teach correct technique to that player and that player only. Others are watching and can learn if they pay attention. But we are not forcing every player, including those who already know the technique and those whose positions do not require the technique to participate in a time-consuming drill that teaches the technique.

In other words, we use drills as a sort of spot remedial teaching device—and then as little as possible.

Double-team block

Off-tackle and trap plays typically feature a double-team block on the inside of the hole. A double-team block is not just two guys hitting one. It should be done in a prescribed manner.

The guy on the left of the defender does a right shoulder block and the guy on the right of the defender does a left shoulder block. This puts the defender in a pincer between the heads of the two blockers. They should squeeze their heads together to hold him there.

Seal the seam between the blockers

The blockers must also keep their shoulders, sides, and hips touching each other. Well-trained defenders will try to split the double-team block by stepping between the blockers. They must seal the seam between them tight throughout the block. A normal drive block is often a stalemate, which is good enough for many plays. A double-team block should not be a stalemate. The double-team blockers ought to drive the defender away from the hole.

A well-trained defender will also drop to all fours if he feels himself losing the battle against a double-team block. So it is more important on a double-team block than on others to get your shoulder pads below those of the defender.

Trap block

The outside of the hole on an off-tackle or trap play is often opened with a trap block by a pulling lineman or upback. Pulling itself must be practiced. The lineman's first step is to pick up his pull-side foot and put it back down again in the same spot only pointed 90 degrees to the pull side. He simultaneously snaps his pull side elbow back violently across his back to spin his upper body 90 degrees. He must not raise up. He should still be as low as his initial stance.

Trap under a chute

You should practice this move by putting your blocker next to a **chute** so that when he pulls he goes through the chute. Normally, a blocker faces the chute to use it. When practicing pulling, the blocker would face at a 90-degree angle to the chute so that when he pulled, he would go through the chute. (A chute is a set of bars that force linemen to charge low. You high school probably has a set around their field.)

Have your trap blockers practice their pulling and trap blocking daily if you use this type of block. Make them go both directions if they go both directions in games. Do not waste time making non-trappers practice this block. He then charges low down the line of scrimmage immediately looking for the guy he is supposed to block. He must block the defender with his helmet on the hole side. In a trap block, that's usually on the back of a penetrating defender. Putting the helmet on the wrong side is a common mistake made by trap blockers.

The farther the defender penetrates into the offensive backfield, the easier the trap block. If the penetrater goes far enough, the trap blocker can even ignore him and block someone else. He can also clip within the free blocking zone although he should not do so below the waist. The American Football Coaches Association Code of Ethics says,

> *Even though blind-side and peel-back blocks are legal near or behind the line of neutral zone in certain instances, the AFCA Ethics Committee reminds the membership that teaching players to block* **below the waist** *in those instances is ethically improper and should be avoided because of the high probability of serious injury. The Football Code states, 'Teaching or condoning intentional roughing, including blind-side blocking an opponent below the waist anywhere on the field, is indefensible.' [emphasis added]*

Root him out

If the defender is well-coached, he will stay at the line of scrimmage and the trap blocker will have to "root him out." That is, the trap blocker must be disciplined to go after his man even if he has not penetrated across the line and made the block easy for the trapper. Here's a diagram showing a trap blocker having to root out a well-coached defender on an off-tackle play.

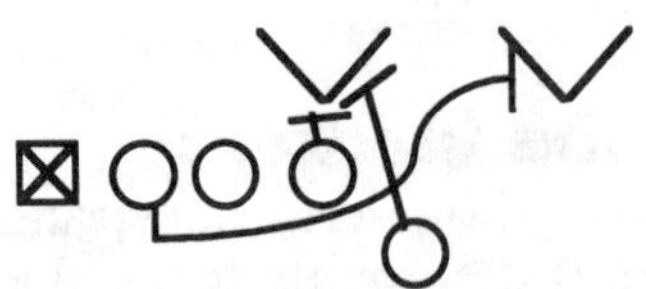

If he seals down tight, forget the trap

You should note that if the target of the trap block, seals down tight against the block on the defensive tackle, the trap blocker should forget the trap block, which would then be almost impossible, and just seal the man **in**. The ball carrier will then run farther out but that won't be a problem because the man has taken himself out of the play by sealing too tight.

The trap block was originally called the mouse trap. A defender is allowed to penetrate into the offensive backfield untouched. But it's a trap. When he's about to be a factor in the play, he gets hit from the inside by a full-speed blocker he did not see coming.

Reach block

On a sweep, the end or wing usually has to reach block the contain man. I have seen technique for this block. But I am inclined to tell the blocker to just find a legal way to get it done. He needs to get his helmet and as many other parts of his body outside the contain man as possible and block him in.

The offensive players who need to throw this block should get lots of reps against players who are lined up at various spots in relation to the blocker. The center, quarterback, and ball carrier should also be a part of these reps. They need to learn what they can do and what they cannot do. When the contain man is lined up too far out for the end or wing to reach him, you must either have a wide-out crack back on him or the end or wing should kick him out and the ball carrier must cut behind the block.

Results orientation

I am increasingly moving toward a result orientation in teaching as I mature as a coach. That is, I tell the player,

> *Preventing this defender from making the tackle is your responsibility. I don't care how you do as long as it's legal and ethical. I will suggest techniques that may help you, but basically I just want you to get the job done.*

I switched to this mode rather than the control freak's, "Put your left big toe here and your right wrist here, etc." I was at a baseball clinic where the Stanford coach was asked for a detailed description of the shortstop's footwork on a double play. The coach got exasperated and said, "We just tell 'em to catch the damned ball and throw it to second."

I also read a book called the *Inner Game of Tennis.* In it, a professional tennis instructor tells how he decided to shut up one day during lessons. He was in a bad mood. He just demonstrated the correct technique and said, "Do it like this." He found that worked far better than his previous method of verbally describing where every body part went on a backhand stroke.

Indeed, I have found that giving kids a long, detailed verbal description of technique generally makes them awkward and tentative. If coaches taught kids how to walk they would stagger self-consciously across the room like polio victims.

> *You've got to hit the ground with your forward heel then you roll from the heel to the front of the foot. Simultaneously, you are swinging your opposite arm forward and your same side arm backward. Your arms would swing six inches to the front and three inches to the rear. Etc. Etc.*

The responsibility approach also gives the kids a pride of ownership in their technique. Figuring it out for yourself is better than being dictated to. You tend to believe firmly in that which you figure out for yourself while you are skeptical about that which you were taught.

Pass block

In drop-back pass blocking, the linemen must get into a "good football position." That is, legs bent at the knee and ankle. Their backs must be straight and near vertical. Their elbows are in front of their ribs an their hands are held up in front of their chest with the thumbs touching so that their hands form a letter W.

They must attack when attacked. But they are passive until attacked. Unlike run blocking, where you fire out aggressively, in pass blocking you get up into your pass-blocking position and wait for the defender to come to you. When he does, you hit and fall back about six inches or so. The hit is done with the heels of both hands in the sternum of the pass rusher.

If rusher tries to go around

If the rusher tries to go around the blocker, he must step quickly to that side, keeping his shoulders parallel to the line of scrimmage, and shoot the heel of the hand on that side to the outside number of the rusher. When moving sideways, the blocker must be careful not to cross his legs or "click his heels" (that is, let his feet get within 12 inches of each other). He must maintain a **wide base** and shuffle sideways and he must keep his **shoulders parallel to the line of scrimmage.**

Dummy between the legs

Two ideas have occurred to me regarding that footwork and body position. One is to tie a fat **dummy between the legs** of the pass blocker and have him slide right and left to block a rusher who is trying to go around him. That would force him to shuffle his feet without crossing them or getting them close together.

Pole through the sleeves

The other idea was to put a **pole vault pole through the sleeves** of a blocker so that it was sticking way out of each sleeve. Then have him work on his pass blocking against a rusher who is trying to go around him. He must do so without swinging the ends of the poles around. You might have him practice near an obstruction, like a fence, so that every time he got out of parallel to the line of scrimmage, the pole hit the obstruction.

Competitive pass blocking drill

I had much success with a competitive drill for pass blocking. The players love competitive drills so they are very intense when they do them. Put a large stand-up dummy on a hash mark. Then put a defender and pass blocker five yards away.

On ball movement, you start a stop watch and the defender rushes and tries to touch the dummy as fast as possible. The pass blocker tries to keep the rusher from touching the dummy as long as possible. Stop the watch when the rusher touches the dummy or at five seconds, whichever comes first.

Elimination tournament

Run this drill as an **elimination tournament.** Keep track of the times on a clipboard and ascertain the champion pass blockers (longest times preventing touching the dummy as blockers) as well as the champion pass rushers (shortest times to touch as rushers).

This drill will also show the players and coaches (and disgruntled fathers) the importance of using athletes rather than left-over fat kids as blockers.

In 1994, at Miramonte H.S., I did this drill with both my running backs and the defensive line. The best pass **blockers** were also the three best running backs. They were also the best pass **rushers**. When I did this drill with my 1993 junior pee wees, the best pass blocker was the starting **wing back,** Ryan Chiarelli. Correct technique is important, but getting the best athletes in the position is far more important.

Different pass blocking for the look-in and halfback pass

The pass blocking described above is for drop-back passes. For the look-in and halfback passes, the blocking is different.

Your ineligible receivers still have to avoid going downfield. But they also have to avoid showing the defense that the play is a pass.

The look-in pass is extremely quick. Because the passer is right behind the line of scrimmage when he throws it (quarterback under center type offense), the defensive line raising their hands is a danger. Accordingly, the offensive linemen should aim at the softest spot on the defensive lineman's body, the belly button. Try to pop them hard so they keep their hands down to protect their stomach.

Halfback pass blocking

I can't get too detailed about the halfback pass blocking. I want you to work that out on your own. It's a function of your personnel and their ages and athletic ability. But the basic principle is that a halfback pass is a **play-action** pass and therefore must be blocked **like a run** to create a good fake. If an uncovered lineman pops up into a standard drop-back passing stance, the defensive backs should see that and yell, "Pass!" So much for your halfback pass. Instead, they should help block their neighbor's man. And the ineligible receivers must not go more than one yard downfield.

Downfield blocks

You generally need one block by a running back on a typical play to get a decent gain. Additional downfield blocks by running backs or receivers or backside lineman are what spring runners for **touchdowns**.

Downfield blocking is not line blocking only with the blocker running a distance before he throws the block. Several head you coaches I worked for decided blocking was important so they had a nightly drill in which each player blocked a close-up dummy, a medium distance away dummy, and a far distance away dummy. In each case they did a shoulder block.

These coaches were half right. Blocking is important and deserves a lot of practice. But they were wrong about that drill. It was largely a waste of time.

The train timetable

Downfield blocking is most important on plays that clear the initial wall of defenders. A play that goes more than a few yards, has a timetable like a train. If the ball is snapped at the defense's 45-yard line and they run a sweep, the ball will probably be at the 50-yard line after one second (because of the pitch back to the ball carrier), back to the 45 at two seconds, to the 40 at three seconds and so forth. If you think of each yard line as a stop on a train route, it should become apparent to you that the **timing** of downfield blocks in crucial.

In the **trenches**, the timing of blocks is clear—**as soon as you can**. But players too often apply that same principle to downfield blocking (and kick-return blocking which is all downfield blocking). The result is a block being thrown at the 40-yard line when the ball is at the 50. What good is that? If the blocker can sustain it for two seconds, which is very difficult, it helps. But why bother? Why not wait until the ball is approaching the 40-yard line to block the defender who is there?

You must work out the timing of downfield blocks in practice and make sure your players are not throwing them too soon. If a player who takes a **direct** route does arrive too soon, have him switch to a **circuitous** route. That will probably also give him a **better angle** in that the defender won't see him coming. These downfield blocks are often called stalk blocks because the blocker kind of sneaks up on or stalks the defender waiting for just the right time. Don't get too fine. It's better to be too early than too late.

Not so hard

The other common mistake on downfield blocking is the blocker tries to total the defender and takes the attitude that effort matters, not result. In fact, result matters. There is no place on the scoreboard to record effort.

In the open field, defenders can see you coming. If you get up to a speed where you are out of control, they can easily sidestep you. You must stay **under control**. That means you must have a wide base, approach the defender with your feet somewhat spread apart so you can change directions rapidly if necessary. Get a little bit low for the same reason.

Not a shoulder block

The open field block is **not** a shoulder block unless the defender either does not see you coming or cannot escape (because he has a hand on the ball carrier or is hemmed in by other players). Rather you "get in his face" and shove him in the sternum the way kids do when they are trying to pick a fight. "Hey, man. Stay away from my ball carrier. Understand?" Don't let your players **say** anything out loud. That's unsportsmanlike conduct. I'm just trying to depict the correct attitude and technique.

Downfield blocking actually requires little or no contact. The blocker need only **get in the way** of the would-be tackler momentarily because at that point the downfield block is thrown, the ball carrier is usually moving at top speed. Your blockers could probably even just **screen** the defender and get the job done. A little shoving is generally necessary though.

If he crosses his legs, total him

If the defender is foolish enough to cross his legs while your blocker is in the vicinity, the blocker should instantly lunge out hard into the defender. Since he has his legs crossed, he will be flattened to the ground by the lunge. In the absence of the defender crossing his legs, a lunge is bad technique.

When I played sandlot football as a kid, I remember many situations where a ball carrier was running down the sideline with an escort in just the right position in front of or beside him and a defender who was there could not even attempt a tackle because the blocker was in the way. No contact involved.

Glancing blow

I saw something similar when I coached J.V. high school running backs in 1994. When we ran 26 Power (off tackle), our fullback had to lead block the first bad guy who appeared in the hole. Through trial and error, we found that the **best** block was a glancing blow.

Essentially, the ball carrier was moving so fast at the time of the block that he only needed a momentary screening to get past the tackler. On the other hand, if the fullback tried to make the Hit of the Game, there would usually be a wrestling match in the hole. Wrestling matches take up a lot of space and make the hole smaller.

Wider obstacle

The glancing blow forced the blocker to be somewhat bent over, which made him a wider obstacle to go around. The tailback with the ball is right behind the fullback. The tailback reads the head of the fullback and follows it. That in, if the fullback puts his helmet on the right side of the linebacker, the tailback cuts to the right.

At that point, the tailback is up to full speed, which is about eight yards a second. The danger zone for being tackled by the linebacker is probably only about three yards in length. At a speed of eight yards per second, it only takes the tailback .375 seconds to pass through that three-yard danger zone.

In June 1995, we took 84 Miramonte H.S. football players to a full-contact camp at San Jose State. At that camp, we scrimmaged other high school teams. In one video of a 26 Power play, I saw a fullback whom I had trained the previous year execute the glancing blow block on a linebacker and it worked perfectly.

Teach the rules

It is easy to violate rules when blocking. And penalties are devastating. In the vast majority of cases, a penalty equals a punt. You only get the ball eight to ten times a game. You cannot afford to give up any of those possessions because of penalties. You must teach your players the rules and you must enforce the rules in practice to make sure they do not violate them in games.

The free-blocking zone

Blocking below the waist or from behind is generally prohibited. But it can be done under limited circumstances in the free-blocking zone. The free blocking zone is four yards either side of where the ball is snapped from and three yards on either side of the line of scrimmage.

Clipping

I discussed clipping at length in the special teams section. Here I will just remind you to teach your players to only block in the open field when the can see the front jersey numbers of the defender.

Illegal use of the hands

It used to be offensive players could not use their hands at all. They would grab their own shirts and spread their elbows like wings. That is an arcane type of block now seen only in youth football. It's seen in youth football because some youth teams are coached by middle-aged men who last played when that block was taught. Get with it if you are one of them. Offensive players can now use their hands. Nobody grabs their own shirt and flares their elbows anymore at the high school or higher levels.

But offensive use of the hands is tightly controlled. You can block the front and side torso of the defender (outside the free-blocking zone) only. You may **not** touch the defender's **head** or **below his waist**. Furthermore, when you block, your arms and hands must be **in front of your torso**. You cannot reach out to your side as part of your block. "Run, don't reach," to get your torso into position where your block is in front of your torso.

No head blocking

When I was a player, we were taught to block with our helmet. You may have been also. For God's sake, forget that. It is totally prohibited. In the sixties, coaches were enamored of the hardness of the helmet and how good a weapon it was. We now know that hitting with your head sometimes causes catastrophic neck injury. Don't teach it or tolerate it. I recommend that you get the video, *Prevent Paralysis—Don't Hit with your Head*, from the National Federation. It's only $4.

Unnecessary roughness

One last rule. Don't block guys who can't possibly tackle your ball carrier. Blocking is permitted against prospective tacklers only. It is not an opportunity to beat up on and intimidate opposing players.

In 1991, when we played the Delta Rebels, we had a tiny little boy who was assigned to me on defense. He was so small that our smallest football pants were down around his ankles. We had to teach him a special tackling technique (block tackle) because his arms were too small to wrap runners' legs.

Five different positions

I had him play five different positions to try to hide him from the other team. I'd send him in at left cornerback on one play, right linebacker five plays later, and so on. He was a minimum-play player, which meant six plays that year.

On one play, the Delta offense ran to its right and we stopped them for a loss. But a Delta Rebel tore into our tiny right cornerback way back on the other side of the field and drove him twenty-five yards back off the line of scrimmage. An angry referee threw a flag and penalized Delta 15 yards for unnecessary roughness.

You may only block to prevent a tackle or secure a fumble or some such. You may not block for the heck of it or to beat up an opposing player legally.

Little Big Man

When I saw that small boy, Will Bronson, come out for the team again the following year, I gave a private sigh of resignation, even though he had grown somewhat. But he immediately became one of our stars. In 1992, when we ran the 10-1 defense, he was the 1 in the 10-1, the only middle linebacker.

We played Richmond in 1992. For some reason unknown to me, Richmond is always the **biggest** team in the league. You can't be more than 85 pounds, but they seem to have a rule against weighing **less** than 85 as well.

In the Richmond game, which was at our field, we had fathers serving as chain gang members on the Richmond side. They said the Richmond coach spent the whole game complaining, "They got ten guys on the line and one little bitty guy in the backfield. All you have to do is break through and it's a touchdown!"

We won that game 18-6. The "little bitty guy" led the team in assists that year and was second in tackles.

Friendly side

As I said earlier, I recommend that you run your initial offensive series on the hash by your bench. Then you can easily scrutinize your blocking and make quiet corrections during that series.

If your blockers are not going both ways, the offensive line coach should meet with them as soon as they come off the field to see if there is any confusion as to who blocks whom on every play. If a play does not work, someone is probably blocking the wrong guy. Find out who as soon as possible and fix it.

The right guys

I said earlier that you must put **quality** guys, guys who would play fullback and end on other teams, on the line. You must also constantly reevaluate your original choices. Stand behind the line during offensive scrimmage. Run plays sideways across the field and video from the press box in practice. Run plays behind the stands so you can use the stands as a tower to look down on and check your blocking performance. If someone is consistently getting beat, talk to him, work with him. If he does not improve, replace him.

Patrick Walsh was named Most Outstanding High School Football Player in California in 1993. He was DeLaSalle High School's star running back. At one point in the season, he was returning punts and his nearest teammate was having trouble making a key block. Finally, Walsh told Coach Bob LaDouceur, "Coach, I can make that block." LaDouceur put Walsh in the blocking position and another player at return man and the return worked much better.

Walsh went on to San Jose State where he played football on scholarship and was elected the first sophomore team captain in that school's history.

You **must** have the right guys blocking. You cannot let your best athletes all be prima donna ball handlers.

Play calling

I read where a very successful coach was asked the secret to his success. It had to be dragged out of him. He finally said, "I don't get bored running the same play over and over."

Most coaches do. They probably have one or two plays that are working in a given game—if they're lucky. But they insist on calling ten different plays. "You gotta mix it up," they'll explain.

Run the same play over and over

No, you don't. You can run the same play over and over all day—or at least until they stop it.

Another line I've heard is, "You have to pass. If you just run they'll overplay the run and stop you."

Let me know when they do. In my experience, you do **not** have to pass in youth football. In fact, there are many very successful high school and college teams that rarely pass. The Army teams of recent years rarely passed. They were fairly successful in the Coach Jim Young era, winning two bowl games. Vacaville won the state championship in our California Youth Football League in 1990, and they hardly ever passed.

Other state champs we've played passed—but they did not have to. I've been beaten by many a running team. But I've only been beaten by a passing team once (Tri-Cities in 1990) and we had no trouble stopping their pass and beating them the second time we played them that season.

In 1993, when we had our most successful offense, I called play 1 (off-tackle) and play 7 (seam buck) over and over all day week after week. Announcers hated to do our games because they spent the whole game saying, "Sykes on the keeper."

Chart the game

I have a simple formula. I chart the game. We call a play. We write down what play we called. And after we see the result, we write down how many yards it got.

I might start a game with Play 1. It goes for seven yards. Good. Run it again. It goes for five yards. Not bad. Run it again. It goes for six yards. The other team calls time out. They make adjustments to my single-wing, unbalanced-line, warp-speed, no-huddle.

About this time my assistants start agitating to run other plays.

Why?

Well, they're gonna adjust. We can't run off-tackle all day.

We have so far. Why don't we wait until they adjust then try something else?

They adjust

After the time out, they do adjust. We run play 1. It gets stopped for two yards.

Try play 7. It goes for seven yards. Do it again. Three yards. Go back to play 1.

They stop it for three yards.

Did you see that? They crashed (slant in hard at a 45-degree angle) their defensive end. That's how they're stopping play 1. Sweep (play 3) them.

The defensive end crashes again thereby taking himself out of the sweep play and making it easy for the wing to block him. The sweep goes for 13 yards.

Do you think that was enough to cure him of crashing? Sweep them again. It goes for four yards. The contain man didn't crash this time. He didn't do anything. He just stood there until he saw where the play was going.

So now he's just gonna stand there, huh. OK, run play 7 inside him. It goes for four yards.

Note that I have not yet run play 5, our reverse. Why should I? The other stuff's working. Nor have I run plays 2 (run-pass option) or 6 (hook pass). Don't need to. Why risk a pass when we can gain yards with the run?

Work on the contain man

We mainly worked the contain man. If he minds the store on the sweep, we run the off-tackle inside of him. If he gets frustrated seeing the off-tackle succeed time and again just inside where he's playing, and starts crashing in to stop the off-tackle, we go back to the sweep. Play 7, student body forward, is another inside play that tends to succeed because of overwhelming numbers of bodies and inspires the defense to start crowding toward the inside, again opening the sweep.

So our game plan was to keep running inside until the other team overplayed that. Then we swept them. Then, when they spread out to stop the sweep again, we went back inside. Those three plays were really all we ever needed in 1993 at the 8- to 10-year old level.

And an occasional reverse or pass

Once in a blue moon, we'd run the reverse or a pass. We did that mainly to scare the bejeebies out of their players and coaches. After seeing us run inside over and over they'd start to think, "All we have to do is figure out how to stop those inside runs and we've got them." Then the wing comes flying back across the formation and goes for eleven yards on the back side and the other team figures, "Oh, man. We can't leave the backside unprotected because they'll slip that darned reverse in on us."

The threat of the reverse...

The **threat** of the reverse was more important than the reverse. Like the Nazi armies tied up in Pas de Calais before D-Day because of the threat of Patton, half of our opponent's defense was tied up on the weak side of our unbalanced line worrying about a reverse that we almost never ran. Meantime, we're sending nine guys against the other half of their team play after play on the strong side.

The **threat** of the pass was more important than the pass itself. Most youth teams have a bunch of guys spread around the defensive backfield worrying about the pass. We don't need to show it to them because they start the season worried about the pass.

Keep the defensive backs away from the line of scrimmage

But if we see those secondary guys sneaking up closer to the line of scrimmage because they're tired of seeing student body forward gain five yards a pop, we run a pass play.

"Get back!" their coaches yell. "Get back!" Mission accomplished. We need to **have** a pass and a reverse. But that doesn't mean we need to **run** them. Matter of fact, it would probably be good to run passes and reverses like crazy in the **pre-game warm-up** so they could worry about them. Then never waste a play on them during the game.

Chart and do what works

Chart your plays during the game. Go back to what works. Have your assistants assigned to watch a particular defender on each play. Tell them to tell you if they see him overplaying one point of attack. When they do, run a play that takes advantage of his cheating. When that makes him honest, go back to the other play.

Here's a table of the success probability of each of my 1997 plays after three games, all of which we won. The top lists the plays . The left side shows the yards gained.

Yards	a	b	c	d	e	f	g	h	i	j	k	l	m	n	o
-5+	0%	0%	25%	20%	0%	0%	8%	0%	0%	0%	0%	11%			13%
-1-4	0%	0%	25%	20%	17%	0%	17%	9%	13%	0%	0%	0%			0%
0	100%	100%	75%	80%	83%	100%	83%	91%	88%	100%	100%	89%			88%
1	95%	50%	75%	40%	83%	100%	75%	91%	88%	83%	100%	33%			88%
2	90%	50%	75%	40%	83%	67%	67%	82%	75%	67%	100%	33%			25%
3	80%		75%	40%	67%	33%	50%	64%	63%	67%	100%	33%			13%
4	65%		75%	40%	33%	33%	50%	64%	63%	50%	100%	33%			13%
5	40%		75%	40%	17%	33%	42%	45%	13%	50%	100%	33%			13%
6	25%		50%	20%	17%	33%	42%	36%		50%	100%	33%			13%
7	15%						33%	27%		50%	100%	33%			13%
8	10%						25%	9%		50%	100%	22%			13%
9	10%						25%	9%		50%	100%	11%			13%
10	5%						25%	9%		17%	100%	11%			13%
15							25%	9%		17%	100%				13%
20							25%			17%					13%
30							17%			17%					
40							17%								
50							17%								
60							8%								

Here's a table of how many yards you need to gain in various down-and-distance situations:

Three-down situation

Yards	Down 1	2	3	4
1	0.4	0.6	1	1
2	0.8	1.2	2	2
3	1.2	1.8	3	3
4	1.6	2.4	4	4
5	2	3	5	5
6	2.4	3.6	6	6
7	2.8	4.2	7	7
8	3.2	4.8	8	8
9	3.6	5.4	9	9
10	4	6	10	10
11	4.4	6.6	11	11
12	4.8	7.2	12	12
13	5.2	7.8	13	13
14	5.6	8.4	14	14
15	6	9	15	15
16	6.4	9.6	16	16
17	6.8	10.2	17	17
18	7.2	10.8	18	18
19	7.6	11.4	19	19
20	8	12	20	20
25	10	15	25	25
30	12	18	30	30

Four-down situation

Yards	Down 1	2	3	4
1	0.4	0.6	0.8	1
2	0.8	1.2	1.6	2
3	1.2	1.8	2.4	3
4	1.6	2.4	3.2	4
5	2	3	4	5
6	2.4	3.6	4.8	6
7	2.8	4.2	5.6	7
8	3.2	4.8	6.4	8
9	3.6	5.4	7.2	9
10	4	6	8	10
11	4.4	6.6	8.8	11
12	4.8	7.2	9.6	12
13	5.2	7.8	10.4	13
14	5.6	8.4	11.2	14
15	6	9	12	15
16	6.4	9.6	12.8	16
17	6.8	10.2	13.6	17
18	7.2	10.8	14.4	18
19	7.6	11.4	15.2	19
20	8	12	16	20
25	10	15	20	25
30	12	18	24	30

Here's how you would use those two tables.

Need 40% on first down

After a kick return, you have first and ten at your own 30. On first down, you need to gain 40% of the yards needed for a first. That's four yards. What play is most likely to gain four yards? Play k has a 100% probability of gaining four yards. But it is a new pass play that we only threw once and it went 15 yards. Probably better to try something else for now and try the k pass in a situation more appropriate for a pass.

The second best four-yard gainer is play c, an off-tackle power play. That surprised me. I did not realize that play was that good because I was looking at averages. Call c.

Need 60% on second down

It gains five yards. On second down, you need 60% of the yards remaining for a first down. That's three yards. What's our best three-yard play, aside from the k pass? Play a, our wedge. No surprise there. We run the wedge. First down.

We could have taken another attitude about that second down play. Instead of using the surest three-yard gainer, we could have said, "We have many plays that will probably gain three yards. Why not select from the ones with a greater than 50% probability the one with the biggest potential to go for many more yards?"

The ones that usually gain three or more yards are a, c, e, g, h, i, j, and k. But the one of those most likely to gain big yards is g, our counter. It only has a 50% chance of succeeding regarding the three yards we need. But we still have third down, and maybe fourth depending on our field position and game situation. We run the counter. It gains four yards. First down. Oh, well. Nice try anyway.

The 'element of surprise' usually means no gain

Now we need four again. Let's try the doggone play k. They won't be expecting it. But that's because it's dumb to run. The element of surprise is greatly overrated in football. Incomplete. The success rate of play k for all yardages under 15 just dropped to 50%.

Now we need 60% of the ten yards for a first or six yards. What's our best six-yard play? Play c and j each have a 50% success rate. We just ran c so they may react more quickly to it if we run it again so soon. Play j has equal probability in general but probably a higher probability at the moment given that we just showed them c. We run j, an inside trap. It gains nine yards. Great. Now we have third and one.

Four–down territory

Normally, you need to gain 100% of the remaining needed yards for a first down on third down. But we really have **two** more downs here because we are not going to punt on fourth and one. After all, we have three plays with a 90% or greater success rate at gaining one yard.

Let's again try one of our plays with big potential, although we need not use one with high risk like a pass. Every play but d and l have a 50% or greater chance of gaining one yard. Again, our big hitter is the counter. But we just ran it and only gained four yards. Plus, now it's fresh in the defenders' minds. Our second best big hitter is j, which we ran last play. How about h? That's an off-tackle trap? It goes twelve yards. Am I an offensive genius? Nah. The defense had some confusion and had no strong safety on the play.

Anyway, you get the idea. You should create a table like this for your offense. You generally call the play most likely to gain the yards you need. But you must keep in mind two things:

- Although you can call a play over and over in youth football, it often loses some effectiveness if you call it immediately or soon after the last time.
- The success-probability sheet you bring to the game may not reflect what's going on in **this** game.

Our counter was our best play against Benicia and Pleasant Hill but it did not do much against South Valley, where our fake sweep inside trap was best.

You need to consult **both** your what-worked-in-**past**-games as well as your what's-working-**today** table. In fact, you probably need to consult a what's-working-**this-half** table because halftime adjustments often make the second half almost a different game.

Wrist plans

It is crucial that every player know his assignment for every play. I only had 15 plays total in 1997, far fewer than most youth teams. Yet many of my first-string and most of my second-string players simply would not learn all of their assignments. Too much like school or something. So I made wrist plans. You've seen wrist plans on TV in college and pro games. A wrist plan in a sweat band with a clear plastic sewn on. You slip a card containing plays or whatever into the clear envelope and wear it on your wrist. Frequently quarterbacks wear them. I could not afford real wrist plans. They are very expensive. So I cut up Federal Express tyvek envelopes into 2 x 5 inch "baggage tag" size sheets and punched a hole in each end. You need tyvek because regular card stock baggage tags disintegrate when wet. I created tiny diagrams of each player's assignments in each of our 15 plays on my computer and printed them onto 2 x 4 laser printer labels. The labels were then stuck onto the tyvek "baggage tags" and attached to each player's wrist with rubber bands and adhesive tape. People laughed, but every one of your players **must** know his assignment against every single defense on every single play or your offense will not work. It only takes one unblocked defender to stop a play.

10

Videotape

You **must** videotape your games and you should probably videotape at least some of your practices. If you can videotape your opponents when you scout them, do that, too.

Angle

When you videotape a scrimmage or game, the camera must be **as high as possible**. Whenever you get less than about a 40-degree angle between the camera and the ground, it's hard to see the line play.

Second angle

I went to a football game at Saint Mary's College in Moraga, California in the early '90s. I was interested to see that they had at least **two** video cameras going. (They also had a movie, not TV, camera at a third site.)

One was in the usual press box location. But the other was behind one of the goal posts. Furthermore, it was **very high**, about fifty feet. It was on a hydraulic scissors lift. The woman who was on the platform had a video camera which was powered by a long extension cord that simply dangled from the platform and ran to the snack bar building nearby. At half time and at game end, the woman lowered the platform to the ground.

I presume the end-zone camera was there to give the coaches **two** angles on each play. I've felt the need for that. Often, our offensive coaches would complain that a blocker ran right by a tackler without blocking him. And I keep wondering if the two players were really that close. Or did they just **look** that close because we had a **side** view. Maybe the end-zone angle would have revealed that the missed tackler was really twenty feet to the side of the blocker who seemed to run right past him.

Two cameras at each game might be more than even the most zealous youth coaches want to bother with. If so, you might try alternating games or halves. That is, video the first half from the press box area and the second from the end zone.

Ask at your parents' meeting if any parents have access to and would be willing to let the team make use of a cherry picker or other aid in getting a high camera angle. As a general rule, your league rules probably require you to offer your opponents **equal access** to any such perch if a coach who provides input during the game is up there.

Go to the press box

Most high school stadiums have press boxes. My first year as a youth football parent, I was team videotaper. I discovered that I could admit myself to the press box at both home and away games by just acting as if I belonged there. I also discovered that virtually all press boxes have household-type **electric outlets**. No need to run your camera on batteries. Bring the battery charger/AC adapter which came with the camera and plug in.

Most press boxes have a fenced-in area on the roof for cameramen. If so, ask your videotaper to please use it. These are typically accessed by a **ladder** rather than stairs, so the videotaper's job description includes lugging body and camera equipment up the ladder. The person you ask to do it needs some strength and a healthy sense of balance. A senior citizen or unathletic person may not be able to get safely to the best vantage point.

Keep it on between plays

One of the parents who videotaped our games started and stopped the camera between plays. I don't like that approach. When you are trying to chart the game afterwards, you need to hear the public address announcer most of the time to understand all of what happened. Not that PA announcers are infallible. They often credit the wrong players with runs, tackles, or fumble recoveries.

Keeping the camera on between plays also enables you to see the chain gang moving the down marker and the first-down chains. Those markers, in turn, let you see how many yards the field position changed on the play. You also need to hear penalty announcements. With start-sop video, the ball often suddenly moves five, ten or fifteen yards with no explanation on the tape because the camera was turned off when the PA announcer explained the penalty.

When the tape started and stopped at the beginning and end of each play, I had a great deal of difficulty figuring out what yard line the ball was on. Plus the camera operator often started the camera too late and we missed a play.

I asked our videotaper to state out loud the yard line, down, and yards to go between each play. The camera's built-in microphone will pick that up. Even better, the camera person ought to give a running narrative of who made the tackle, caused the penalty, etc. The more information, the better.

You can and probably should turn the tape recorder off during **timeouts** and **halftime**.

Tight end to tight end and linebackers to tailback

To evaluate the play of your players, you need to zoom in tight. In obvious passing situations, instruct your videotaper to try to keep all players in the picture as much as possible. On kickoffs and punts, the videotaper needs to zoom back to enable the coaches to see all the players.

Try having your videotaper sit in on a video evaluation session early in the season or in the preseason so he or she can see the problems caused by doing it incorrectly. Have them read this chapter, too. At Miramonte High School, we taped wide angle for the first quarter and last two minutes of each half. The rest was cropped from tight end to tight end.

Zoomed-out video that includes both sidelines the stands, and the mountains in the background is near worthless for coaching purposes. You must be able to see what each lineman is doing.

Analyzing the tape

You can and should analyze the tape intensely. My approach was to run a play, then, having seen where it went, I'd ask myself, "Why did it succeed or fail?" Then I'd run it again to see what each player did on the play. And I'd jot down notes about who did well and who did poorly. At the first practice after the game, I'd go over my notes with the players.

I also watched the tapes more casually at the post-game pizza party and while riding my exercise bicycle. Sheer repetitions of watching reveal stuff you missed the first time or even the fifth time.

High school, college, and pro coaches watch videotapes incessantly. They call it "film," a carryover from the pre-videotape days. In his autobiography, Michigan's highly successful head coach Bo Schembechler says his house had more film than furniture. His wife, Millie, once told an audience,

> *Bo and I lead a normal life. When he comes home at night, I kneel down and kiss his Big Ten championship ring. And after dinner, if we get a few private moments, we go downstairs and look at film.*

We part-time, unpaid coaches can't afford to devote that much time to watching "film." But be advised that **real** coaches do watch lots and lots of "film." To the extent that you can do likewise, your team will be more successful.

Duplicating the tape

The tape ought to be duplicated as soon as possible after the game. Most of your coaches probably have the equipment to do it. (Many video cameras can be used as one VCR and your home VCR can be used as the other for duplicating.) And copies ought to be as widely distributed among your coaches as possible.

I have not done it, but I'd like to try the following: Each coach would be assigned to grade his share of players' performances. For example, on our team, which had 24 players, seven coaches, and an equipment manager, I'd ask each of the coaches and equipment manager to study the video tape and grade **three** players on each play. The grade would rate the player on how well he discharged his duties according to the written job descriptions discussed earlier in the book.

The coach should discuss the grades and comments with each player at the next practice. The grading sheets should be preserved for showing interested parents why their son plays where he plays or as little as he plays.

Using the tape to coach

Use the tape to **coach** your kids. They will sit still for about 15 minutes worth. We brought a VCR and TV to the stadium on occasional practice nights. We plugged it into the press box electric outlets, sat the kids in the stands in front of the press box, and showed them good and bad performance examples in the tape of the most recent game.

When we played a team for the second time in the season, we showed tape of our last game with that team as part of the preparation for the game. (Tape from the previous year is probably too out of date. The team may have all new coaches, mostly new players, or just a whole new approach.)

Frequently, players don't believe they are doing something until you show them on tape. John Madden tells the following story:

> *"...just as we started moving, [Gene Upshaw] got a holding penalty. When he came off the field, I chewed him out.*
>
> *"'I didn't hold him,' Gene said, 'believe me I didn't hold him.*
>
> *"Hearing that, I started yelling at the officials...*
>
> *"But the next day, as I watched the film, there it was, right out there for everybody to see. Gene had his arms wrapped around Ernie Holmes..."*

The video also gives them the **big picture**. They can see how their discharging their position's duties relates to the whole team's effort.

We tried taking the entire team to a meeting room for a two-hour all-video practice before our Oakland playoff game. We had stopped Oakland pretty good in the first game except for three touchdown plays which each went for about fifty yards. So we thought it would be good for the kids to see how well they played and that we only had to be three plays better to win.

Sounded good at the time. In fact, we learned that you cannot keep 24 eight- to eleven-year old boys quiet for two hours in front of even a big-screen TV featuring one of their games. We should have made a 15-minute tape to illustrate our point and shown it in the stadium in front of the press box the way we usually did.

At least one practice night of 15 minutes of video per week is probably the best amount of time to use video as a coaching tool. It could also be used in drills and scrimmage on an instant replay basis if you could set it up.

You should probably show the tape or selected excerpts to players in ten- or fifteen-minute shifts rather than show it to the whole team at the same time.

Tapes for the players

Players should be told they can get a tape of a game by bringing a blank tape to the coach in charge of video. Or maybe you can make an arrangement with a local video place. Leave them a master and authorization to duplicate it. Publicize it to your players and parents. Coaches could stop by to get their weekly copy.

Fund raising

I've never seen this done, but it seems to me a team could raise funds by videotaping each game and selling copies of the tape to interested parents from both teams. You could duplicate the tape on site right after the game if you brought a second VCR and a bunch of blank tapes. Or you could just take orders and money and get the tapes to the parents later.

Awards banquet

We used our game videos to make a year-end **highlight tape**. We showed that at the season-ending awards dinner and sold copies to interested parents. Try to get a highlight of each kid in addition to team highlights. To make the tape a complete yearbook-style history of the team, you should try to videotape related but not game *per se* activities like practice rituals, cheerleaders' practice and game and competition performances, homecoming, fund raisers, parades, pregame warm-ups, weigh in, jamboree, caravan to away games, sign-painting parties, parents cheering, post-game snack bar visits, etc.

Recruiting

We used a video tape as a formal recruiting device once at a middle school lunch time recruiting visit. My son **has** shown football game tapes to some soccer-playing friends he hoped to recruit. If you have a professional videotaper among your parents, that would be the best way to get a recruiting-quality tape made.

Camera quality

There are video cameras and there are video cameras. VHS are the low end and cost about $300 to $600. Hi-8 is the current popular high-quality consumer format. They cost about $1,000. The best consumer camera is a digital one. They cost about $2,000. The better the camera, the better the resolution of the picture. The better the resolution of the picture, the better you can see what your players are doing in practice and games.

Video tape is extremely important to a coach. And the better the quality of both the camera and the cameraman, the better coaching job you can do.

11

Minimum-play players

Where they hurt the least

Most youth football leagues have minimum-play rules. For most of my youth coaching career, I coached under a six-play rule. One year I had to give each player at least twelve plays. I found the twelve-play minimum unacceptable because I had a very weak team. With a twelve-play minimum and a weak team, I could never, I mean that literally, **never** get my first string on the field.

Twelve plays would probably be acceptable if you were cutting down to your final roster and had all relatively strong players. But it is so difficult with weak or even average players that it leaves the realm of coaching and becomes a sort of unpaid day-care duty.

Having said that, the key with minimum-play players is to put them where they hurt the least. By definition, below-average players hurt the team. To achieve maximum team success, you need to play them the least possible percentage of the time and in the positions where they do the least damage.

Warp-speed no-huddle

I invented the warp-speed no-huddle in part to reduce the percentage of the time my minimum-play players were on the field. By doubling the number of plays we ran on offense, we increased the total number of plays run in the game (on both sides of the ball) by 50%. That, in turn, meant that our minimum-play offensive players were on the field a lower percentage of the time than our opponent's minimum-play offensive players. For example, with a 6-play minimum and an average of 40 plays per team on offense, each minimum-play offensive player is in for 6 ÷ 40 = 15% of the game. But if my team runs **80** plays on offense, my minimum-play offensive player is only in for 6 ÷ 80 = 7.5% of our offense.

What offensive position?

You can put minimum-play offensive players at **wide receiver**. When I coached an 8- to 10-year old team I put them at **flanker** because it is a simpler position than **split end**. At split end they have to be on the line, which is a bit tricky. When I coached a double-wing at the 13- to 14-year old level, I needed four backs so I could not afford a flanker. I made the wide receivers split ends and taught them how to check with the referee to see if they are on the line of scrimmage before the snap.

Can you put them at any other position other than wide receiver? Not really. In theory you could put them at the following positions on offense:

- faking running back who is not filling for a pulling lineman
- tight end but only on a play where he goes out for a pass

- pulling lineman who is trying to influence a defender
- running back who goes out of the backfield for a pass

The reason these are theoretical is it's hard to both get the kid in and remember that you can only call certain plays when he is in. Plus a good scouting team will spot what you're doing and teach their players to recognize the play by the sub.

Can you put them on the backside (away from the direction the play is going) of the line? No. I've seen it tried. The minimum-play players are typically worse than you think. Watch them on video. When you put them on the backside of the line, they typically stand up and turn sideways to let the defender go by enroute to your ball carrier. I have seen a minimum-play player at left tackle bring a drive in the semi-final playoff game to a screeching halt even though all the plays run while he was in went to the right. Four plays in a row his man blew by him and sacked our ball carrier for a loss.

What defensive position?

I found I could put weak players at **defensive down lineman** in my gap-8 and 10-1 defenses. As with the warp-speed no huddle, I ran these offenses in part to create the maximum number of positions the weaker players could effectively play, namely defensive down lineman. The weak players had to be medium or heavy weight. Light weights simply could not hold their ground even on all fours. In the gap-8 and 10-1 we did a gap charge and had most players bear crawl until they were past the offensive linemen. You have to train them and discipline them with a nightly drill, but most will do it.

I have found that you can play **rookies** at defensive end or outside linebacker (contain man). But they must be highly disciplined and decent athletes. Boys who spend all their time on the football field looking for a place to hide will not succeed at contain.

As far as linebackers and defensive backs are concerned, I have found that only athletic veterans will do. Although I did have one boy who was a minimum-play player but who was too small for the line. I hid him in the linebacker and defensive back positions by putting him at a different position every time he went in and taking him out one play later. We survived that, and so did he, and he became a great player the next year. But it was scary.

Fifth Quarter

Many, if not most, youth coaches send in entire units of minimum-play players, often with a better player at quarterback. This is comparable to something our local freshman teams do. They call it Fifth Quarter. After the regulation game is over, the teams and officials often agree to stay for an additional ten minute scrimmage where each team gets the ball at the 40 for five minutes. All the weak players get to play then.

Youth programs ought to do something similar. Since game day is already full, they would have to use the **fourth** quarter. Have the regulation game last three quarters—and eliminate the minimum-play rules for that game. Then let the minimum-play players get a whole quarter for themselves.

Whole units of minimum-play players

I have been heavily criticized for my use of the wide receiver position for minimum-play players. Most coaches are very political, otherwise they would not have their jobs, and the politics of the situation is that wide-receiver positions which are staffed by minimum-play players anger the parents whose manhood is thereby indirectly brought into question. I ignore politics, and I have the resume to prove it.

The typical solution is "Orange O" or "Gold D." That is, the team has a first-string which is named after one of its team colors. A blue and gold team might have a blue offense and a gold offense. Blue is first-string and their injury subs and gold consists of minimum-play players and a back-up quarterback from Blue O.

I hate this approach. You typically only get eight to ten possessions in the course of a youth game. These weak offensive units almost always go three and out—if they don't turn the ball over. With a twelve-play minimum, you have to give these guys four of your eight to ten possessions! You can't trust them to punt. It'll get blocked and run in for a touchdown. And with all that, you've only gotten ten guys their minimum plays.

Forget defense! These guys are capable of giving up a score almost every time they are on the field. But many youth coaches divvy up the minimum-play players into half offense and half defense. That's internal coaching-staff politics at work.

In fact, I have found that you can only get one minimum-play guy on the field at a time in both offense and defense without losing the game. That means a team running the warp-speed no huddle offense to the tune of 80 plays a game has a total of 80 + 40 = 120 plays on both sides of the ball. Divide your minimum into that number to see how many minimum-play guys you can accommodate.

But when I had my super weak team in 1996, we could not get the warp-speed no-huddle to work. Too many penalties and negative-yardage plays. Furthermore, we were being forced into controlled scrimmages for the second half because the margin was 28 points or more. In controlled scrimmages, you get far fewer plays because the opposing coaches are on the field and talking to their players between plays. Try doing the math on a twelve-play-minimum rule when you have a 28-man roster, approximately 20 of whom are minimum-play caliber, and only 60 plays total in the game. You have to have five minimum-play guys on the field at all times. That, in turn, means you only get about one first down every game. Basically, it's not enough like football coaching that you would want to do it.

Decoy, D-line, receiver, crack-back blocker

In my experience, about all the minimum play-guys can do is:

- act as decoys
- play down linemen on defense
- catch a pass while they are standing still
- throw a crack-back block

That last may surprise you. It did me. But you'll be amazed at the crack-back blocks that weak players can throw. We generally have the quarterback or tailback boot out toward the wide receiver and the wide receiver cracks back on a backside pursuer. It's harder to avoid a clip if they crack on a contain man. But the backside pursuers are coming hard, facing the crack-back blocker and so intently focused on the ball carrier that they do not see the crack-back blocker coming.

I feel bad that the minimum-play guys are not better and cannot participate more fully in the game. But most are rookies and seem to me to be grateful for being wide receivers. They are not ready or full contact line play and such, in spite of what their fathers think. But the crack-back block enables them to be Mr. Macho a couple of plays a game. And I'm thrilled to death every time one of them lays out a defender.

You can practice this block with Hugh Wyatt's pancake drill. Lay a bunch of pads in a rectangle to make a sort of bed to land on. Then have a player hold an air shield while the blocker runs at him and throws his crossed forearms into the defender's chest.

Safety tip: the player holding the air shield should cross his forearms, too. That is, he should hold the left handle with his right hand and vice versa. If you hold the right handle with your right hand and the left handle with your left hand you can get your wrists injured from the impact of the block.

Coaching point: the blocker should end up lying on top the blockee. Often they will just hit the guy and end up standing over him. That's wrong. The blocker must hit with such force and momentum that he ends up lying on top of the guy who is holding the air shield.

Appendix A

What you need to teach your players

Coaching football is very complex. There are many positions and they all must master different skills. Here are lists for each position. You should use this lists to make up your practice schedules especially in the pre-season. As you teach each skill, cross it off.

All players

Tackling
- Front
- Side
- From behind
- Open field

Gang tackling
Sideline tackling
Drive block
- Left
- Right

Unsportsmanlike conduct rule (Rule 9-5)
How to carry ball on each side
How to catch ball
How to substitute on and off the field
Ball stripping
Recover loose ball
Pick up loose ball and run with it
Yell "Pass!" "Air!" and "Oskie!" at the appropriate time
Pertinent rules (Many)

Quarterback

Stance
Cadence, if any
How to take snap
What to do if the snap, hand-off, or pitch is fumbled
What to do if the play is broken (can't make hand-off or pitch)
Hand-off technique if you have hand-offs
Pitch technique if you have pitches
Drop-back mechanics if you have a drop-back pass
Passing mechanics
Sprint-out mechanics if you have a sprint-out pass
Taking a sack
Throwing an incomplete, uninterceptible pass
Throwing passes
Pass in spite of the distraction of a pass rush
How to call an audible, if you allow that
When to call an audible
How to take a safety
How to end the game when the offense is ahead
How to finish a run so as to get a couple of more yards
Down field lateral
Stiff arm

Place kicker

Stance
How to kick
When to begin approach
What to do if the snap is bad
Where to place ball for kickoffs and PATs in bad field conditions
Where to aim the kickoff
When to signal teammates to start running
Safety responsibilities after kickoff
Pertinent rules
Free kick after a safety technique

Punter

Stance
How to catch snaps
How to drop the ball
How to kick the ball
Where to cover the punt
What to do if the snap is bad
Pertinent rules
Where to aim the kick
Punting in windy conditions
Punting in wet conditions
Punting from your own end zone
Free kick after a safety technique

Kick returner

How to catch punts
How to fair catch (Rules 2-9, 6-5, 9-3-3)
Where to line up before the punt or kickoff
How to finish a run so as to get a couple of more yards
Down field lateral
How to execute any trick plays, like reverses or backward passes, you plan to use

Center

Stance

Pertinent rules (Rule 2-37, 7-1 and 2)
How to snap
Cadence, if any
All blocks which your play book calls for the center to perform
How to break holds
When to get set
Blocking assignment for each play

Receivers

Stance
How to catch
Look-in and tuck
Pertinent rules [Rule 2-5 (clipping), 7-5-7 through 11 (interference)]
What route to run if passer holds the ball for an extended period of time
Where to line up in each formation
Blocking assignment for each play
Route for each pass play
Release techniques
Stalk block technique
Keep one foot in bounds on pass thrown close to sidelines
Pass routes in the end zone
Finding seams in zone defenses
Escaping man coverage
Concentrate on catch in spite of distractions
One-handed catch (use only when necessary)
Catch the ball at its highest point
Fight for the ball
Switch ball from one hand to the other during run
How to finish a run so as to get a couple of more yards
Down field lateral
Turn upfield immediately after catching the ball
Stiff arm
Tip drill

Offensive down linemen

Stance
Where to line up in each formation
Blocking assignment for each play
Blocking technique for each play
How to break holds
Pertinent rules [Rule 3 (blocking), 2-16 (free blocking zone), 2-23-2 (line of scrimmage), 7-1-6 (false start), 7-2 (illegal procedure), 9-2 (illegal use of hands), 9-3-2, 5, 6, 7 (illegal blocking), 9-4 (illegal personal contact)]
When to get set

Running backs

Stance
Where to line up in each formation
Receive hand-off technique
Receive pitch technique
Blocking assignment for each play
Blocking technique for each play
Ball carrier path for each play
Fake technique for each play
How to respond to a broken play
Tip-off avoidance
How to end the game when the offense is ahead
Switch ball from one hand to the other
How to finish a run so as to get a couple of more yards
Down field lateral
Throwing halfback pass if he has that job
Stiff arm
Look-in and tuck
Tip drill
Catch technique

Defensive secondary

Stance
Where to line up against each formation
How to respond to motion
Pertinent rules [Rule 7-5-6 through 11 (interference), 9-3-8 (illegal contact)]
How to catch
How to bat the ball down
Job description for each type of offensive play
Pursuit angles for wide plays
Look-in and tuck
Tip drill
Backpedal
Zone coverage if you use it
Man coverage
Bump and run technique
Blitzing, if you do it

Punt/PAT/FG block linemen

How to block punts
Pertinent rules (Rules 9-4-4)

Long snapper

Pertinent rules (same as center)
Long-snapping technique
Wet ball technique

PAT/FG holder

Signal for snap
Coverage responsibility after field goal kick
Hand position

Catch technique
Hold technique
What to do if bad snap

Defensive down linemen

Stance
Charge
Blocking progression
Pass rush technique [Rule 9-4-3 (roughing the passer)]
Breaking holds
Rip technique
Swim technique
Wide play pursuit angles
Pass pursuit

Linebackers

Stance
Wide play pursuit angles
Zone pass coverage
Man pass coverage
Catch technique
Look-in and tuck
Blitzing (if you do it)
Blocking progression
Pertinent rules [Rule 7-5-6 through 11 (interference), 9-3-8 (illegal contact)]
Pass pursuit
Breaking on the pass
Backpedaling
Bump and run technique
Tip drill

Defensive ends

Stance
Trailing sweeps that go the other way
Pass rush
Contain technique
Pass coverage responsibilities if you put end in coverage
Blitzing (if you do it)
Blocking progression
Pass pursuit

Kick return front line

Pertinent rules [Rule 2-9 (fair catch), 6-1 (kickoff), 6-5 (fair catch)]
Fair catch
Blocking assignment
Blocking technique

Kick return middle line

Pertinent rules (Rule 6-1)
Blocking assignment
Blocking technique

Kickoff

Pertinent rules (Rule 6-1)
Lane discipline
Full speed takeoff before kick

Appendix B

Many of the books below are out of print. R.R. Bowker' directory Books Out-Of-Print is available for free on line at www.bowker.com/bop/home/index.html. You can usually find out-of-print books through one or more of the following methods. Ask your local reference librarian to do an **interlibrary search**. Contact **Adelson Sports** or **Hoffman Research** (addresses listed below). Contact these book finders on the Internet: www.abaa-booknet.com, www.abe.com, www.bibliofind.com.

Books

George Allen's Guide to Special Teams Allen & Paccelli. Leisure Press. 1990.
American Football Coaches Guide Book to Championship Football Drills by Jerry Tolley, self-published
The Art of Place-Kicking and Punting. Jennings, Bahr, & Danmeier. Simon & Schuster. 1985.
Attacking Football Defenses with Radar Blocking. Leo Hand. Parker Publishing Company. 1985.
Audibles, My Life in Football. Joe Montana. Avon Books. 1986.
Bo. Bo Schembechler. Warner Books. 1990.
Bootlegger's Boy. Barry Switzer. Berkley Books. 1990.
The Boys Club Guide to Youth Football. Edward M. Torba, D.M.D. Leisure Press. 1983.
Building a Champion. Bill Walsh. St. Martin's Press. 1990.
Building a Championship Football Team. Bear Bryant. Prentice-Hall, Inc. 1960.
Bunch Attack by Coverdale and Robinson. Sagamore Publishing. 1997.
Coaching the Defensive Secondary by M. Schuster
Championship Football. Dana X. Bible. Prentice-Hall, Inc. 1947
Coaching Football. Flores & O'Connor. Masters Press. 1993.
Coaching Football's Special Teams. Tom Simonton. MacGregor Sports Education. 1987.
Coaching Football's Polypotent Offense by Dick Baran. Parker Publishing. 1974.
Coaching Football's Split 4-4 Multiple Defense. Pete Dyer. Parker Publishing Company. 1980.
Coaching Football Successfully. Bob Reade. Human Kinetics Publishers. 1994.
Coaching Run and Shoot Football. Al Black. Harding Press. 1991.
Coaching Team Defense. Fritz Shurmur. Harding Press. 1994.
Coaching Youth Football Defense. John T. Reed (Same author as the book you are holding). John T. Reed Publishing. 1993.
Coach of the Year Clinic manuals, annual transcripts of clinics taught by many coaches. Telecoach, Inc.
The Complete Book of the I Formation. Roy F. Kramer. Parker Publishing Company. 1966.
Complete Book of Linebacker Play by J. Giampalmi
Complete Handbook of Winning Football Drills by Don Fuoss, Allyn & Bacon
Complete Idiot's Guide to Understanding Football Like a Pro by Joe Theismann. Alpha Books. 1997.
Defensing the Delaware Wing-T by Bob Kenig, Harding Press
Defensive Drills by AFCA. Human Kinetics
The Delaware Wing-T. Raymond & Kempski. Parker Publishing Company. 1986.
Developing an Offensive Game Plan by Brian Billick, Sagamore Publishing
Developing a Superior Football-Control Attack. Vince Dooley. Parker Publishing Company. 1969.
Directory of Football Defenses. Drew Tallman. Parker Publishing 1969.
Directory of Surprise Plays For Winning Football. Tom Simonton. Parker Publishing Company. 1979.
Ditka. Armen Keteyian. Pocket Books. 1992.
Dynamics of the Double Wing by Hugh Wyatt (self-published)

The Eagle Five-Linebacker Defense by Fritz Shurmur, Harding Press
The Explosive Double Slot Offense. Tom F. Smythe. Leisure Press. 1988.
The Fighting Spirit, A Championship Season at Notre Dame. Lou Holtz. Simon & Schuster. 1989.
First Book of Trick and Special Plays by Patrick Wyatt (self-published)
Football Clock Management by John T. Reed (same author as the book you're holding) John T. Reed Publishing. 1997
Football Coaching. John McKay. John Wiley & Sons. 1966.
Football Coach's Survival Guide. Michael D. Koehler. Parker Publishing Company. 1992.
Football Drill Book. Doug Mallory. Masters Press. 1993.
Football for Young Players and Parents. Joe Namath. Simon & Schuster. 1986.
Football: Secrets of the Split T Formation. Don Faurot. Prentice-Hall. Inc. 1950.
Football's Fabulous 40 Defense. Jack Olcott. Parker Publishing Company. 1974.
Football's Modular Defense, A Simplified Multiple System. John Durham, Parker Publishing Company, Inc. 1986.
Football's Multiple Slot-T Attack. Jim McClain. Parker Publishing Company. 1974.
Football Rules in Pictures. Schiffer & Duroska. Perigee Books, Putnam Publishing Group. 1991.
Football's Super Split The Underdog Defense. Bill Siler. Leisure Press. 1988.
Football: The Violent Chess Match. Flores & O'Connor. Masters Press. 1994.
Football Winning Defense. Bud Wilkinson. Sports Illustrated Winner's Circle Books. 1987.
Football Winning Offense. Bud Wilkinson. Sports Illustrated Winner's Circle Books. 1987.
Fourth and One. Joe Gibbs. Thomas Nelson Publishers. 1991.
Friday Night Lights. H.G. Bissinger. Harper. 1991.
The Fundamentals of Coaching Football, 2nd edition. George C. Kraft. Brown & Benchmark. 1992.
Game Plan to Winning Football. Gordon Wood. Summit Group. 1992.
Woody Hayes A Reflection. Paul Hornung. Sagamore Publishing. 1991.
The Hidden Game of Football. Carroll, Palmer, & Thorn, Warner Books. 1988.
High School Football Rules. National Federation of State High School Associations. Annual.
Hot Line to Victory. Woody Hayes. Unknown publisher. 1969.
How to Kick the Football. Edward J. "Doc" Storey. Leisure Press. 1981.
Huddle, Fathers, Sons, and Football. Andrew H. Malcolm. Simon & Schuster. 1992.
Instant Replay. Jerry Kramer. New American Library.
Just Win, Baby. Glenn Dickey. Harcourt Brace Jovanovich. 1991.
Tom Landry: An Autobiography. Tom Landry. Harper Paperbacks. 1990.
Vince Lombardi on Football. Vince Lombardi. Wallyn, Inc. 1973.
Looking Deep. Terry Bradshaw. Berkley. 1991.
No Medals For Trying, A Week in the Life of a Pro Football Team. Jerry Izenberg. Random House. 1990.
Mesa's Power Attack: Football's Winningest Offense. Roger Worsley. Parker Publishing Company. 1967.
Missouri Power Football. Devine & Onofrio. Lucas Brothers Publishers. 1967.
Modern Belly T Football. A. Allen Black. Parker Publishing Company. 1972.
Modern Single Wing Football. Charles Caldwell. Jr. J.B. Lippincott Company. 1951.
Multiple Monster Football. Warren K. Washburn. Parker Publishing Company. 1981.
The New Double-Wing Attack. Tierney & Gray. Parker Publishing Company. 1971.
New Thinking Man's Guide to Pro Football by Paul Zimmerman. Simon & Schuster. 1984.
One Knee Equals Two Feet. John Madden. Berkley Books. 1987.

Option Football Concepts and Techniques for Winning. Scarborough & Warren. Allyn and Bacon or Wm. C. Brown Publishers. 1983.
A Parent's Guide to Coaching Football. John P. McCarthy, Jr. Betterway Publications, Inc. 1991.
Ara Parseghian and Notre Dame Football. Parseghian & Pagna. Men-in-Motion. 1971.
Paterno. Joe Paterno. Random House. 1989.
The Perimeter Attack Offense. Joseph Moglia. Parker Publishing Company. 1982.
Play Football the NFL Way. Tom Bass. St. Martin's Press. 1991.
Principles of Coaching Football . Mike Bobo. William C. Brown Publishers. 1987.
The Right Kind of Heroes. Kevin Horrigan. Algonquin Books of Chapel Hill. (Inspiring story of the 1990 and 1991 seasons of the East Saint Louis High School Flyers football team which has a remarkable long-term record under Coach Bob Shannon.) 1992.
Rookie Coaches Football Guide. The American Coaches Effectiveness Program. Human Kinetics Publishers. 1993.
Run to Daylight. Vince Lombardi. Simon & Schuster. Classic. Excellent. 1963.
Run and Shoot Football. Glenn "Tiger" Ellison. Parker Publishing Company. 1984.
Saint Bobby and the Barbarians. Ben Brown. Doubleday. (Covers the 1991 season of Coach Bobby Bowden's Florida State Seminoles) 1992.
The San Francisco, 49ers, Team of the Decade. Tuckman & Schultz. Prima Publishing & Communications.
Scoring Power with the Winged T Offense. Evashevski & Nelson. Wm. C. Brown Company. 1957.
Simplified Single Wing Football. Kenneth W. Keuffel, Ph.D. Prentice-Hall, Inc. 1964.
Single Wing Offense with the Spinning Fullback. John Aldrich. Iowa State University Press. 1983. (Sold with companion video. Both available from author)
The Slanting Monster Defense in Football. Dale Foster. Parker Publishing Company. 1970.
The Smorgasbord Offense for Winning High School Football. Joe Blount. Prentice-Hall, Inc. 1965.
Spread Formation Football. L.R. "Dutch" Meyer. Unknown publisher. 1952.
Successful Multiple Offense in High School by Bob Walker. Prentice-Hall. 1957
Total Impact. Ronnie Lott. Doubleday. 1991.
Vince by Michael O'Brien. William Morrow & Company. (Life of Coach Vince Lombardi). 1987.
Youth League Football Coaching and Playing. Jack Bicknell. The Athletic Institute. 1989.
Youth League Passing and Receiving. Anderson & Coslet. The Athletic Institute. 1989.
Winning Football Drills. Donald E. Fuoss. William C. Brown Publishers. 1984.
Winning Football With the Air Option Passing Game. Rice & Moore. Parker Publishing Company. 1985.
Winning Play Sequences in Modern Football. Drew Tallman. Parker Publishing Company. 1971.

Catalogs

Adelson Sports (Sells used, out-of-print football books), 13610 N. Scottsdale Road, Suite #10, Scottsdale, AZ 85254

Hoffman Research Services (Sells used, out-of-print football books), P.O. Box 342, Rillton, PA 15678, 412-446-3374

Majestic Licensing (associated with Pop Warner), 636 Pen Argyl Street, Pen Argyl, PA 18072, 215-863-6311

National Alliance for Youth Sports, 2050 Vista Parkway, West Palm Beach, FL 33411, 800-729-2057

National Federation of State High School Associations, 11724 NW Plaza Circle, P.O. Box 20626, Kansas City, MO 64195, 816-464-5400 fax 816-464-5104

Organizations

Membership in several of these organizations includes coaches liability insurance.

American Coaching Effectiveness Program, P.O. Box 5076, Champaign, IL 61825 800-747-4457

American Football Coaches Association, 5900 Old MacGregor Road, Waco, TX 76712, 817-776-5900 fax 817-776-3744

National Youth Sports Coaches Association, 2050 Vista Parkway, West Palm Beach, FL 33411, 800-729-2057

National Federation of State High School Associations, 11724 NW Plaza Circle, P.O. Box 20626, Kansas City, MO 64195, 816-464-5400 fax 816-464-5104

Pop Warner Football, Pop Warner Little Scholars, Inc., 586 Middletown, Boulevard, Suite C-100, Langhorne, PA 19047, 215-735-1450 Fax 215-752-2879

Periodicals

American Football Quarterly
The Extra Point, AFCA
Gridiron Coach Gridiron Communications
National Federation News, National Federation
The Point, Pop Warner Little Scholars, Inc.
Scholastic Coach, Scholastic Coach
Youth Sport Coach, National Alliance for Youth Sports

Software and videos

Many programs and videos in catalogs of Quality Coaching, Championship Books & Video Productions, Gridiron Communications, National Federation, Bob Rexrode, AFCA, Syskos. See under Catalogs or Organizations.

Digital Scout, 5318 North High Street, Suite 530, Columbus, OH 43214, 800-249-1189

Offensive Line Play of the Masters. Anthony Munoz & Jim McNally, Championship Technique Video.

Official Pop Warner Football Handbook video, Majestic Licensing (See catalogs section above).

Playmaker II, B.W. Software

Teaching Kids Football. Bo Schembechler. ESPN Home Video

Techniques & Drills for Effective Deep Snapping, Shane Co.

Addresses and phone #s

John F. Aldrich, 1809 Olive Street, Cedar Falls, IA 50613

Algonquin Books of Chapel Hill, P.O. Box 2225, Chapel Hill, NC 27515

Allyn and Bacon, 7 Wells Avenue, Newton, MA 02159

American Football Quarterly, P.O. Box 3079, North Palm Beach, FL 33408, 800-556-AMFB

The Athletic Institute, 200 Castlewood Drive, North Palm Beach, FL 33480

Avon Books, Hearst Corporation, 105 Madison Avenue, New York, NY 10016

Berkley Books, 200 Madison Avenue, New York, NY 10016

Betterway Publications, Inc., P.O. Box 219, Crozet, VA 22932, 800-823-5661

B.W. Software, P.O. Box 15163, Ann Arbor, MI 48106, 313-769-8587

William C. Brown Publishers, 2460 Kerper Boulevard, Dubuque, IA 52001

Brown & Benchmark, 25 Kessel Court, Suite 201, Madison, WI 53711

Championship Books & Video Productions, P.O. Box 1166, ISU Station, Ames, IA 50014, 800-873-2730 fax 515-232-3739

Championship Technique Video, P.O. Box 1526, Brookline, MA 02146, 800-628-1981

Doubleday, 666 Fifth Avenue, New York, NY 10103

ESPN Home Video, ESPN, Inc.
ESPN Plaza, Bristol, CT 06010
800-800-662-3776

Football Camps, Inc., P.O. Box 317, Trumbull, CT 06611, 800-243-4296

Frank Glazier, P.O. Box 3421, Stuart, FL 34995-342, 303-470-8885
Gridiron Communications, 6852 Rayland Court, Pleasanton, CA 94588, 510-461-8796
Harcourt Brace Jovanovich, 8th floor, Orlando, FL 32887
Harding Press, P.O. Box 141, Haworth, NJ 07641
Harper Paperbacks, 10 East 53rd Street
New York, NY 10022
Human Kinetics Publishers (Catalog containing other publishers' books as well), P.O. Box 5076, Champaign, IL 61825-5076, 800-747-4457 www.humankinetics.com
Iowa State University Press, Ames, IA 50010
Leisure Press, 597 Fifth Avenue, New York, NY 10017
J.B. Lippincott Company, East Washington Square, Philadelphia, PA 19105
Lucas Brothers Publishers, 909 Lowry
Columbia, MO
MacGregor Sports Education, Waukesha, WI
Masters Press, 2649 Waterfront Parkway E. Drive, Suite 300, Indianapolis, IN 46214
William Morrow and Company, Inc., 105 Madison Avenue, New York, NY 10016
Mark Moseley Kicking Camps
703-339-8756
Men-in-Motion, Post Office Box 428
Notre Dame, IN 46556
Thomas Nelson Publishers, P.O. Box 141000, Nashville, TN 37214
New American Library, P.O. Box 999
Bergenfield, NJ 07621
Parker Publishing Company, Inc., no street address, Englewood Cliffs, NJ 07632
Pocket Books, 1230 Avenue of the Americas, New York, NY 10020
Prentice-Hall. Inc., Englewood Cliffs, NJ 07632
Prima Publications & Communications, P.O. Box 1260 JMB, Rocklin, CA 95677, 916-624-5718
Putnam Publishing Group, 200 Madison Avenue, New York, NY 10016
Quality Coaching (Catalog offering books, videos, and software), 10359 Haynes Canyon Avenue, Tujunga, CA 91042
800-541-5489
Random House, Inc., 201 East 50th Street
New York, NY 10022, 800-733-3000
John T. Reed Publishing, 342 Bryan Drive
Alamo, CA 94507, 510-820-6292
Fax: 510-820-1259, E-Mail: johnreed@johntreed.com, Web site: www.johntreed.com
Bob Rexrode (Highly technical videos), 1408 N. Ricketts, Sherman, TX 75090
Sagamore Publishing, Co., Inc., P.O. Box 673, Champaign, IL 61824-0673
Scholastic Coach, P.O. Box 5288
Pittsfield, MA 01203-9826
Shane Co., 4722 Campbell Road, Las Cruces, NM 88005, 505-523-7969
St. Martin's Press, 175 Fifth Avenue, New York, NY 10010
Simon & Schuster, 1230 Avenue of the Americas, New York, NY 10020
Sports Illustrated Winner's Circle Books, 1271 Avenue of the Americas, New York, NY 10020
The Summit Group, 1227 West Magnolia, Fort Worth, TX 76104
Telecoach, Inc., Earl Browning, Manager, P.O. Box 22185, Louisville, KY 40222
Wallyn Inc., New York Graphic Society Ltd., 140 Greenwich Avenue, Greenwich, CT 0830
Warner Books, 666 Fifth Avenue, New York, NY 10103
John Wiley & Sons, 605 Third Avenue, New York, NY 10158

Appendix C

Practice schedules

You can divide the season into two segments: preseason and the season including playoffs. The difference is the lack of a specific opponent to get ready for in the preseason.

In California Youth Football, we had five days without pads the first week of August, four days per week in pads for the rest of August. In Diablo Youth Football, we had five days a week until school. Late sign-ups had to go without pads for five days before they could get into pads. If you allow late sign-ups and they must wait to put on pads, you need to assign a coach to just them. He needs to use previous-days practice schedules as check lists to make sure the new players learn the fundamentals previously taught to the other players.

Once school started, we could only practice three days per week, except that teams in the playoffs could practice four days per week. All of our practices had to be no longer than two hours. Meetings counted as practice time, but equipment hand-out did not. We held almost all practices from 6 to 8 PM.

The California Youth Football practice schedule is typical from what little I know about other youth football programs. I will base the practice schedules that follow on the California Youth Football rules.

Remember that no practice segment should last longer than about five to ten minutes unless it is a competitive drill like a scrimmage. Try to have a **competitive drill** every day. These get the kids cheering and practicing with intensity. Competitive drills are a lot of fun for the players and, in certain circumstances, are excellent ways to teach techniques or good habits.

First day

6:00 Welcome remarks and orientation
- History of the program
- Safety rules
  - No horseplay
  - Keep your head up when you hit
  - Drink more water than you want
  - Protective gear must fit
  - Optional protective gear like arm pads, lip protectors, eye shields

6:03 Team organization—introduce coaching staff
- Special teams
- Defense
- Offense

6:05 Schedule
- Practices
- Games
- Playoffs

6:06 Behavior
- No disruptions
- No player criticism of teammates
- No feuds between teammates
- No loafing

6:07 Policies on
- Playing time
- Position assignments

6:08 Systems

Special teams
Defense
Offense

6:09 Warn heavy players of weight limits and pre-game weigh-ins
Put players on knees and check all cleats for compliance with league rules.

6:10 Warm-up (Taken from the *Bigger Faster Stronger Program* by Dr. Greg Shepard)
- How to line up
- Standard sequence stretching exercises to be done for the rest of the season
  - (Led by veteran players if that's how you do it)
  - Jog lap
  - Calf stretch (Push against wall or back of stadium, not fence.)
  - Achilles stretch (Same as calf only keep heel on ground)
  - Quadriceps stretch (Grab ankle and push it away from body behind you while standing until 90-degree angle between lower and upper legs)
  - Figure-4 hamstring stretch (Sit and put the bottom of one foot against the inside of the other leg then grab the toes of the straight leg while keeping it straight)
  - Glut stretch (Put right foot flat on ground on outside of left knee while sitting with left leg straight. Twist upper body so that back of left bicep is pressed against outside of right leg. Then reverse)
  - Groin stretch (Sit with bottoms of each feet touching each other. Grab both ankles. Press down on knees with elbows.)
  - Adductor stretch (Sit with legs straight and out. Bend forward and grab toes.)
  - Cobra (Lay flat on stomach. Do push up with stomach remaining flat on ground and head back as far as possible. Lock elbows.)
  - Lunge (Get on one knee with front foot out so far that you have to stretch forward to make your lower front leg straight up and down. Do each leg.)
  - Arms over head (lie flat on stomach and raised arms as high as you can. Looks like Superman signalling touchdown while flying.)
  - Arms behind back (Lie flat on stomach and interlace fingers behind your back then raise both arms as high as possible.)
  - Jumping jacks with clapping and team yell at end
  - Jock check (If jocks are required in your league, have each player pull his jock waistband out and show it to you. One coach was sued for not checking.)

6:20 Evaluations (You can have as many stations as you have coaches)
- 20-yard dash time
- Test every player for ability to be:
  - Long-snapper
  - PAT/FG holder
  - Punter
  - Place kicker
  - Passer
  - Pass receiver
  - Kick receiver

6:35 Fundamentals
- Three-point stance

6:40 Four-point stance

6:45 Rules—Unsportsmanlike conduct clinic
6:50 Fundamentals
How to recover a fumble
6:55 How to pick up a fumble and run
7:00 Rules—Need to be set for one second and need to remain motionless until snap
7:05 Fundamentals
How to carry a football (both sides)
7:10 Yell "Pass!" "Air!" "Ball!" and Oskie!" at appropriate time [Coach drops back (Pass!) throws (Air!) ball is intercepted (Oskie!) then interceptor fumbles the ball (Ball!)]. Coach-ball handlers go through these activities in front of all players who yell the correct words on cue.
7:15 Rules—encroachment, definition of being on and off the line of scrimmage
7:20 Fundamentals
How to catch a pass
Look-in and tuck
7:25 Rules—Pertaining to punt being downed on the one-yard line, going into the end zone, bouncing back toward punting team
7:30 Competitive drill
Coach tosses simulated punt to five yard line. Teams of eleven players are selected and take turns trying to down the ball as close to the goal line as possible. They cannot leave the line of scrimmage at 40-yard line or so until after ball leaves coach's hand. Keep track of each team's result and declare winner. Losers must clean up equipment after practice
7:50 Skill sprint (11 Players line up in normal offensive positions, which position does not matter. Quarterback takes snap and drops back. All yell "Pass!" Quarterback throws far downfield, all yell "Air!" when ball released, and all eleven sprint to touch the ball at top speed. Then next eleven do the same. Coach-referee enforces rules regarding getting set, remaining motionless, and encroachment.)
7:58 Wrap up
Closing comments by coach, remind of next practice
Team cheer
Handouts if any
8:00 End

Subsequent first week practices should follow the same format. You may find that something was not mastered in the first session and needs to be revisited.

Start practicing long snaps

At the end of the first day, you should have identified your long snappers and holders. You have begun to identify the other specialists. But you cannot yet exclude people. You need much more data to find the winners.

You have identified your long snappers and holders and the season is just four weeks away. The long snapper needs 1,200 reps before the first game. That's **57 snaps a day**. They get tired so you have them get those reps in three sets of 20 each. For the first week, they should just snap to each other and to the long snappers coach. He needs to teach them the correct technique and drills.

Once people start to specialize, your practice schedule becomes multi-column. Below is about where you should be by the fifth day, the last day without pads. Every player has been through each evaluation station. You have tentatively assigned all players to their positions. You still have not seen them hit which will surely change some position assignments.

Fifth day

6:00 Warm-up
6:10 Offensive specialties
PAT/FG — Long snapper, holder, PAT kicker, and kick returner kick PATs through goal posts, catch on the fly and throw back.
QB, C, R — If you have quarterback under center, he takes snaps and passes to receivers running your look-in pass from both sides
HB, R — Halfbacks throw halfback passes to receivers to both sides
OL — Stance and get off against sled
6:20 Special teams
Rules—Kickoff
How to line up for kickoff
Start, kickoff, and sprint ten yards—Coach acts as referee watching for encroachment
6:30 Walk-through stay in lanes
Run back stay in lanes
6:40 Situations
On-side kick right and left
8-yard kick
Pop-up to scout front line (Do not interfere with catch but surround him)
6:50 Emphasis time
LS/Punt/Punt return — Long snapper snaps to punter who punts **away from** returner
Passers and receivers — Work on look-in and halfback pass plays
Other players — Work on weakness that became apparent during the week
7:00 Defense
Stance and get off on ball movement
Scramble on all fours out of four-point stance for five yards
7:10 Wide pursuit angles walk through
7:20 Pass rush technique against stand-up dummy
7:30 Offense
LS — Long snappers snap to each other under coach supervision
QB/C — If you have quarterback under center, take many snaps.
OL — Get set then come to pass-block stance on snap
RB/R — Running backs throw halfback pass to receivers
7:40 1/2 team run running plays (emphasize hand-off and pitch plays most)
1/2 team run passing plays
If more than 22 players, run a third team that also runs pass plays
7:50 Switch and have team than did running plays run passes and vice versa
8:00 End

Abbreviations:
LS Long snapper
QB quarterback
C Center
OL Offensive line
RB Running back
R Receiver
PAT Point after touchdown
FG Field goal
HB Halfback
DL Defensive line
DE Defensive end

The rest of August

For the rest of August, your players will be in pads and hitting. Starting with the first day, you must find out who your best running backs, blockers, and tacklers are.

Running backs are easy to identify. You just give everybody the ball and have them run against a would-be tackler in, say, a five-yard square. Some players will do well because the player they came up against was a poor tackler. So you need multiple attempts against different tacklers. You should work toward putting the best running backs against the best tacklers. If you have several players who seem to be tied for best running back, try them in smaller and larger squares. The best will emerge.

Don't draw many conclusions about who the best **tacklers** are from this drill. Some players who tackle well in drills are terrible in games. I don't know why.

Run the pass block-pass rush competition drill with a stop watch. That will quickly show who the best pass rushers and best pass blockers are.

Run the one-against-two offensive line-defensive line drill to see who the best blockers and defensive linemen are. These will not give definitive results. You'll need to watch players in scrimmage as well.

Continue to give the long snappers 60 reps a day. If you have a quarterback under center get lots of reps of that exchange as well.

Find passers

Try every viable candidate at passer during live scrimmages. A static passing test of distance and accuracy does not reveal who your Joe Montana clone is. You need game conditions to find Joe. Run your pass plays with various passers and see who gets completions and who throws incompletions and interceptions. The guys who get the best **results** are tentatively your passers. But take a long time to decide who your passers are.

Find PAT/FG kicker

The same is true of your PAT/field goal kicker. Run a several-week-long audition for this position to make sure you are picking the right guys.

Get them acclimated to hitting

In youth football, you generally have a lot of **rookies**. They have never hit or been hit. Hitting is an acquired taste. They need to get as much scrimmage experience as possible. Do **not** have them crashing into veterans full-speed. They would be traumatized and possibly hurt. That kind of shock treatment could cost you several excellent players of the future by making them quit. You shouldn't even run full-speed hitting drills with veterans only. Run your tackling drills at half-speed all season long. Work the rookies into hitting with close-up hitting like line play and inside running plays. Introduce wide running plays and open-field tackling gradually.

Put in your offense

Assign players to tentative positions the first day of hitting. Then teach them all six of your plays and have them run them over and over. In individual and group offensive practices, have them work on the specific techniques and joint maneuvers they must perform in those plays.

Put in your defense

Assign your most prolific scrimmage tacklers to the defensive backfield positions. Find disciplined players to play defensive end and down line positions. Teach the players their defensive alignment rules and job descriptions. Have them play live against a scout offense that runs plays typical of your opponents.

Put in your special teams plays

Do **not** do as many coaches do and delay putting your special teams plays in until the week before the first game of the season. Practice special teams every day in August and for the rest of the season.

Regular Season practice

The theme for preseason practice is get ready for everything: evaluate players, assign positions, teach fundamentals and our plays and defenses. The theme for the regular season is fix what was wrong in the last game and prepare for the specific upcoming opponent. In California Youth Football, we generally practice Tuesday through Thursday evenings and play on Saturdays. Here's a mid season practice schedule for a Tuesday.

6:00 Warm-up
6:10 Specialties

PAT/FG — Long snapper, holder, and place kicker kick PATs through goal posts to kick returners who catch on the fly and throw back. Make sure first and second string both get equal reps and that each player works with all the other members of the PAT/FG team.

QB/C/R — If you have the quarterback under center in your offense, have him take snaps here and throw look-in passes to your receivers both sides.

HB/R — Have your running back passers throw your halfback pass to the receivers who would catch it in a game.

OL — Bird dog drill. Linemen face upcoming opponent's defense, coach calls out play, on snap, players take one step and point to the guy they will block.

6:20 Special teams

Kickoff

Walk-through stay in lanes one time then same thing the other way only sprint.

6:25 Live regular (the way you expect to kick in the game) kickoffs against scout receiving team. Note who is making tackles and who is not. Make personnel changes if indicated.

6:30 Situations against scout receiving team

- 1-yard kickoff
- 8-yard kickoff untouched by receiving team
- 8-yard kickoff touched by receiving team
- pop-up kickoff to front line
- TGS (Ten yards, Gap, and Star) recognition and response
- backward pass by receiving team

6:35 Kick return

"Where do you line up?" and "Whom do you block?" quiz.

6:36 Situations against scout kickoff team

- Grounder to front line returners
- Line drive to front line returners
- Pop-up to front line returners
- 8-yard kickoff
- Receive punt style free kick after safety
- Kick to middle row of returners

6:45 Regular return

Kick to back row of returners (See who failed to block his man. All others down on one knee then run play over with just kicker, returner, blocker who failed last play and tackler who succeeded last play.)

6:50 Emphasis time

LS/Punter/returner — Long snapper snaps to punter who kicks away from returner. Returner tries to catch on the fly then throws back.

All others — Work on problems revealed in last game or special problems presented by upcoming opponent.

7:00 Defense

Defensive down linemen — One-against-two drill (Defensive lineman lines up in gap between two offensive linemen and submarines through them on snap.) Also rotate each down lineman through the form-tackling drill during this period.

All others — Form tackling right, left, straight ahead

7:10 DL/DE — Versus scout team that does only running plays

DB/LB — Versus scout team that does only pass plays

7:20 all — Eleven-on-eleven live scrimmage versus scout team running all plays of upcoming opponent.

7:30 Offense

OL — Each player works on the type of block that he has to make on each play

C/QB/RB/R — Run most difficult plays, that is, passes and, to a lesser extent, hand-offs and pitches—no opposition.

7:40 OL/QB/C/RB — Run running plays and play-action pass against scout defensive line and linebackers

QB/C/R — Run look-in pass and play-action pass against scout defensive backs and linebackers

7:50 All — Eleven-on-eleven live scrimmage running all plays against scout-team defense.

8:00 End

You should vary this through the week. For example, the offensive line might do bird dog on Tuesday, chutes on Wednesday, and sled on Thursday. You could substitute pass rush and passer tackling or tackling from behind or ball stripping for regular form tackling one day a week.

Index

ability hierarchy 121
Acalanes High School 158
Adderly, Herb 60
adjustment schedule 114
Aikman, Troy 9
"Air!" 36, 57, 108
air shield 228
Alabama, University of 128
Aldrich, John 142, 170, 195
Alhambra High School 152, 158
Allen, George 18, 29
American Football Coaches Association Code of Ethics210
area blocking 197, 205, 206
Army 165
Army-Navy Game 165
Art of Place-Kicking and Punting 52
assists 102, 103, 216
AstroTurf 20, 36, 47
Attacking Football Defenses With Radar Blocking 204, 207
Augustana College 52
awards banquet 225
backed up 7
backside 227
backs out of backfield 92, 227
backup players 35
backward pass 38, 40, 41, 47, 92, 155, 176, 193, 200
bad ball drill 162
bad snap 57, 58, 61, 62
Bahr 52
ball control 120
Barnard, Christiaan, Dr. 73, 74
Barney, Lem 29
bear crawl 227
Belly T offense 147
bench route 187
Benicia Panthers 51, 108, 132, 133, 142, 200, 221
Berkeley Cougars 9, 36, 41, 68, 80, 125, 139, 157, 167, 170
Bible, Dana X. 84
big play 120
Big Ten 128
Billick, Brian 7
binoculars 133
bird dog drill 207, 208
Black, A. Allen 126, 147
blast 77, 78, 98, 120, 128, 135, 137, 138, 149
blitzing 80, 88, 89, 136, 137, 169, 171, 174
blocked punt 15, 58, 61, 62, 63, 64
blocking back 150, 163
blocking assignment 148, 202, 204, 209
blocking below the waist 101, 143, 210, 215
blocking contest 119
blocking progression 94
blocking rules 204, 205, 207
block tackle 215
Blount, Joe 83, 129, 142, 153
body composition 203
body position 203
bomb 128
bootleg 108, 127, 165, 189, 190, 191, 228
Bowden, Bobby 181
box technique for defensive ends 92, 93, 94, 95, 102, 136
Boys Club Guide to Youth Football 52
brain washing 15
broken play 100, 127, 128, 165
Bronson, Will 216
Brown, Josh 163
Brown, Tim 28, 29
Bryant, Bear 84, 147
buck lateral 119, 142, 195
Building a Championship Football Team 84
bump and run 100, 101, 192
Burnsed, Floyd 2, 3, 13, 201
Bynum, Mike 145
cadence 130, 132, 134, 135, 136
Caldwell, Charles 142
California High School 109
California Youth Football League 5, 109, 113, 132, 149, 217
camera quality 225
Campolindo High School 152, 158, 184
Celina, TX High School 87
center 118, 162, 163, 164, 178
Central Casting 5, 117
Cervantes, Artie 8
Championship Football 84
Chiarelli, Ryan 212
Chicago Bears 128
Chinn, Richard 54
choreography 23
chute 210
clipping 46, 66, 101, 139, 215, 228
clock management 132
coach hustle 108
Coaching Football's Split 4-4 Multiple Defense 84
Coaching Football Successfully 84, 147
Coaching Team Defense 81, 84
Coaching Youth Football Defense 88, 99
Coach of the Year Clinic Manual 32
code for sending in plays 133
"Coffee Table Defense" 98

College Football National Championship 81
Colorado Bump and Run video 101
competitive drills 212
Complete Book of the I Formation 147
completion percentage 5, 71, 72
conditioning 141, 142
containment 31, 35, 120, 139, 140, 154, 155, 156, 157, 158, 217, 227, 228
contain rush 100
contrarian approach 117, 128, 130
conventional offense 129, 130, 147, 159
Cooley, Jeff 125
cornerback 140
Cosby, Bill 168
Cotton Bowl 128
counter 83, 137, 138, 149, 151, 158, 159, 166, 190, 220, 221
counter option 140
coverage recognition drill 101
cover one 101
cover three 101
Cowboys, Dallas 70
crack back 120, 139, 140, 155, 156, 173, 179, 211, 228
crashing end 217
Crisler, Fritz 84
cross blocks 93, 94, 120, 136, 149, 155, 206
crossing legs 214
crossing pass route 190
Crowther sled 208
cutback 3, 96
Danmeier 52
decoy 122, 124, 179, 181, 228
deep wing 155
defense recognition 204
defensive down lineman 227, 228
defensive ends 31, 90, 95, 97, 102, 107, 115, 116, 136, 137, 138, 139, 140, 227
defensive personality 103, 181
deflected punt 1
De La Salle High School 3, 13, 14, 16, 105, 166, 190, 201, 216
Delaware, University of 147, 158, 190
Delaware Wing T 158
delayed plays 140, 157, 192
delay-of-the-game penalty 171
Delta Rebels 99
DeMonbrun, Dan 52
depth chart 2, 5, 17, 46, 117, 119
Developing an Offensive Game Plan 7
Devine, Dan 84, 137, 147, 164
DeYoung, Kyle 163
Diablo Valley Community College 16
Diablo Valley Youth Football League 102
digital video camera 225
dime defense 73, 120, 121
Directory of Football Defenses 84
Directory of Surprise Plays for Winning Plays 194
direct snap 130, 142
discipline 46
distraction drill 162, 163
Ditka, Mike 158
dive 114, 128, 149
Doerner, Cy 68
Doerner, Paul 163
double option 148
double pass 191
double reverse 128
double slot offense 91, 147
double-team block 83, 98, 130, 149, 153, 154, 156, 202
double-tight formation 91
double-whistle drill 108
double wing 54, 55, 119, 142, 144, 145, 169
down-and-distance tendencies 112
downfield blocking 213, 214
do-your-job drill 107
"The Drill" 97
drop of ball for punt 52
drop-back pass 120
Dublin (CA) High School 152, 158
duplicating 224
Dyer, Pete 84
Dynamics of the Double Wing 3, 142
East St. Louis Flyers 12
8-2-1 defense 62, 76, 86, 87
8-yard kickoff 38,.39, 50, 51
80-gap defense 86
Elk Grove 67, 80, 143
Ellison, Glenn "Tiger" 142, 145
elusiveness 118
encroachment 101, 134
evaluations 5, 7, 47
Evans, Shane 108
Evashevski, Forest 128, 147
excuses 10
expanded neutral zone 59
face mask penalty 107
fade pass route 186
fair catch 21, 39, 49, 60, 63, 66
Fairfield Falcons 78, 96, 103, 112, 113, 193
Fairfield Suisun Indians 3, 4, 77, 135, 149
Fair Oaks 46
fakes 127, 164, 165, 166, 198
fake punt 58, 61, 62, 64, 65, 131
fake reverse 38, 40, 41, 47, 157
fall on the ball 49, 50
false start 134, 137, 171
fan out on punt 56, 57
fatigue avoidance 103

Faurot, Don 142, 169
field goals 69, 184
field position 29
fifth quarter 227
first-and-third double steal 99
first sound 130, 135, 136
first step 3, 4, 148
fit and freeze 207
five-man front defense 98, 122
5-3 defense 136, 148
flag pass route 189, 191
flanker 61, 80, 91, 122, 124, 131, 146, 155, 156, 171, 172, 179, 181, 192, 226
flash cards 108
flip-flop 93, 166, 167, 168
Flores, Tom 52, 81, 83
Florida State University 181
flow 137, 138
flying to the ball 108
fly offense 119
Football Clock Management 41, 49
Football Coaching 84, 147
Football: Secrets of the Split T Formation 169
Football's Fabulous Forty Defense 84
Football Secrets of the Split T Formation 142
Football's Super Split Underdog Defense 84
Football: the Violent Chuess Match 81
Football Winning Defense 81, 85
Foothill Athletic League
Foothill High School 61, 152, 158
follow own color 57
footprints 3
formation tendencies 112
4-4 defense 148
46 defense 71, 73, 88
4-3 defense 89
Foster, Dale 84
four-down situation 220, 221
four-man I formation
four-minute drill 7, 132
free-blocking zone 215
free kick after safety 38, 41, 42, 51
free tacklers 31, 32
freeze play 177
friendly side of field 178, 179, 216
front line of kick return team 25, 41, 45, 49, 50, 51
front tackle 104
full-house T formation 47, 78, 85, 119, 120, 128, 147, 149
full-speed tackling drills 104
fumble 15, 58, 162, 164, 170, 171, 184
fumblerooski 200
fund raisdng 225
Galena (KS) High School 47
game chart 98, 114, 217, 218
Game Plan to Winning Football 42, 79, 84
game play list 7
gang tackle 21, 107, 114
gap-8 defense 73, 81, 83, 88, 89, 98, 99, 100, 116, 136, 227
gap in kick receive team 26, 27
Garland, Judy 83
gassers 142
Gator Bowl 28
George, Jeff 183
glancing blow block 214
goal-line defense 74, 75, 83, 86, 87, 116
Gonzales, Justin 49, 61
Granada (Livermore, CA) High School 60, 61, 67, 93, 109, 125, 134, 139, 141, 151, 184, 187, 195
Gray 142
Green Bay Packers 2, 60, 154
ground ball 22
Guide to Special Teams 18
halfback pass 79, 128, 149, 191, 192, 194, 197, 198, 212, 213
halftime adjustments 221
Hampton, Rodney 28, 29
Hand, Leo 204, 206, 207
hand-off 127, 128, 130, 131, 152, 157, 159, 160, 163, 164, 181, 191
"hands" kick receive team 25, 49
hand-off kick return 47, 48, 49
Harvard Business School 128
hash mark distances from sideline 34, 37
hash position 69, 93, 167, 179
Hayes, Woody 2, 84, 147, 166
helmet in hitting 215
Hendricks, Kenny 68
Hidden Game of Football 19
Hi-8 video camera 225
highlight video 225
high school's offensive system, your 146, 147
"hip and dip" 94
hit and quit 107, 209
hitch pass 155, 185
hitch release move 193
holder 14, 68, 69
holding 100, 101
Holmes, Ernie 224
Holtz, Lou 46, 80
hook block 94, 157
hook pass route 186, 199, 200, 217
Hot Line to Victory 84
hot pass 83
How to Kick the Football 52
huddle discipline 132, 133
huddle kick return 50, 51

hurry-up offense 132, 167
I formation 119, 128, 147, 149, 173
illegal formation 176
illegal forward pass 184
illegal motion 156, 171
illegal procedure 168, 171
illegal use of the hands 46, 215
incomplete pass 99, 114, 184, 185, 189, 196, 221
indirect snap 127, 128, 142, 145, 163
ineligible receiver 58, 175, 176, 184, 193, 197, 200, 212
influence block 227
initiative 83
Inner Game of Tennis 211
inside hand-off 95
inside trap 125, 151, 152, 189, 221
instant replay practice 43, 209
interlibrary search 52, 81
intentional grounding 184, 196
interception 5, 71, 72, 77, 79, 99, 108, 155, 157, 184, 191
interference 22, 60, 66, 101, 155, 184
interlibrary search 143
Iowa State University 30
Irvin, Michael 9
isolation play 77, 135, 149, 150
jamborees 113, 118, 138, 140, 141, 157
Jennings 52
keeper plays 127, 130, 137, 160, 164, 166, 181
Keller, Sam 183
Kempski 147
Kent State University 86, 87, 92
Keuffel, Kenneth, Ph. D. 130, 142, 150, 195, 196
kicker 35
kicker range 21
kickout block 93, 94, 136, 149, 211
Knight, Bobby 10
knocked-down 50 defense 95
Kroger, Matt 13
Kukahiko, Mike 61
LaDouceur, Bob 3, 16, 166, 201, 216
lane tacklers 30, 32, 40
large-split rule 4, 76, 137
Las Lomas High School 152
late pick up of punt 60
lead blocker 94, 137
leave feet when tackling 106, 107
legacy 5, 6, 17
Lett, Leon 70
line call 148, 204, 206, 207
line judge 40
Lineman of the Year 125
line splits 56, 80, 83, 130, 136, 169, 170
loafing 35, 57, 96, 141
Lombardi, Vince 2, 16, 84, 147, 154
Vince Lombardi on Football 84, 154
Lonesome polecat 91, 130, 140, 142, 144, 145, 172
long count 63, 135
long snapping 14, 53, 54, 57, 63, 68, 124
look-in-and-tuck 162
look-in pass 78, 95, 101, 127, 128, 149, 160, 161, 186, 190, 192, 196, 212
Ronnie Lott Drill 60
"lowlight" video 92, 93
Madden, John 61, 224
MagnaDoodle 133
Manteca (Delta Rebels) 83, 104, 109, 149, 185, 191, 193, 215
man-to-man blocking 42, 43
man-to-man pass coverage 4, 65, 75, 82, 86, 88, 89, 90, 91, 92, 101, 120, 173
Maryland, University of 128
McCarthy, Jack 53
McKay, John 84
megaphone 114
Mesa's Power Attack 147, 153
Meyer, L.R. Dutch 142
Miami 19, 70
Michigan, University of 224
Michigan State University 28, 164
middle linebacker 90
Minelli, Liza 83
Minnesota Vikings 7
Miramonte High School 2, 13, 15, 41, 61, 93, 95, 104, 140, 141, 150, 152, 157, 158, 160, 161, 187, 190, 198, 201, 204, 206, 212, 214, 223
misdirection 120, 137
mismatches 120, 121, 125
Missouri Power Football 84, 85, 137, 147
Missouri, University of 147, 164, 169
mistakes 203
Modern Belly T Football 126, 147
Modern Football 84
Modern Single-Wing Football 142
Montana, Joe 73
Mooney, Jason 47, 49
Moore, G.A. 87
Moore, Steve 169
Moraga, CA 222
motion 80, 81, 112, 129, 130, 135, 155, 156,

171, 172, 173, 174, 175
Mouat, Marty 142
Mount Diablo High School 41
mud 36, 47, 68, 69
muff 25, 29, 41, 45, 58, 60, 65, 70
Multiple Monster Football 84
multi-cycle offense 92, 129, 130, 131
multiple offense 119, 147
Munroe, Jim 86
Napa Saints 19, 55, 65, 78, 79, 94, 116, 122, 130, 148, 156, 185, 191, 192, 193
nasty split 137, 170
Nelson 147
nepotism 5, 6, 17, 32
Nerf football 63
Nevada at Las Vegas, University of 151
Nevada Union 190
New Double Wing Attack 142
New Orleans Saints 158
Neyland, Bob 184
nickel defense 73, 120, 121
Noon, Chris 170
Northwestern Unversity 149
nothing's working plays 7
Notre Dame box 128
Notre Dame shift 99
Notre Dame University 28, 84, 164
numbering systems for blocking assignments 204, 205
Oakland Dynamites 77, 79, 103, 120, 191, 192
Oakland Raiders 183
Oakland Saints 41, 95, 157, 163
O'Connor, Bob 52, 81
offensive line coach 201
offensive personality 103
off-sides 40
off-tackle 2, 4, 6, 93, 94, 95, 123, 125, 125, 128, 131, 138, 139, 148, 153, 154, 155, 159, 160, 174, 198, 199, 200, 209, 217, 220, 221
Oklahoma 5-4 defense 85
Oklahoma, University of 128
Olcott, Jack 84
Olivar, Jordan 130
one-crisis-allocation-of-resources 17
one-cycle offense 131
"one-exchange" mentality 79, 191, 195
one-play formation 108
134 counter trap
1-yard kickoff 1, 38, 40, 51
Onofrio, Al 84, 137, 147
onside kick 20, 21, 25, 37, 38, 41
oomph 1, 2, 13, 54, 68, 127, 174
open field block 214
open pivot 152
option 3, 14, 76, 83, 120, 130, 137, 139, 140, 181, 190
Option Football 140, 142
order of selection 115, 125
outlet receiver 3
out-of-bounds kickoff 25
out-of-bounds, running to stop clock 196
out-of-print books 143
out pass route 186
outside hand-off 159
outside linebacker 94, 95
Parent's Guide to Coaching Football 53
Parker, Norm 28
Parseghian, Ara 84, 149
Ara Parseghian and Notre Dame Football 84, 149
pass blocking 4, 197, 211
pass efficiency rating 183
passer rating 182, 187
passes that do not cross the line of scrimmage 191
Paterno, Joe 89
Pavlovian Response 46, 57, 114
Peart, Chris 49
penalty flags 102
penetration 169
Penn State 89
perfect-play drill 149
personality 5, 17, 103
Petrino, Bob 142
pitch 92, 140, 166, 181
Pittsburgh Mallards 37, 42, 179
Plank, Doug 88
Plano East (TX) High School 21
platooning 117
play-action pass 139, 188, 191, 194, 196, 198, 199, 213
play book 2, 5, 8
Pleasant Hill Rebels 221
plug offensive ends 83, 86, 99, 100
point-of-attack success chart 98, 118
pop pass 188
popsicle sled 208
pop-up kickoff 38, 39, 49
Pop Warner Football 102
Pop Warner Super Bowl 53, 131
power I formation 78, 119, 123, 128, 147, 149
power offense 120, 147
power series of single wing 119, 142
pre-game routine 218
press box 223
press defense 88, 89
Prevent Paralysis—Don't Hit With Your Head 215

protection of kicker 55, 69
pulling 83
pump fakes 100
punt formation 55, 92
"punt" place kick 68
punt technique 52
pursuit angles 96, 97, 114
quarterback 123, 126, 127, 128, 140, 152, 157, 188, 193
quarterback as receiver 92
quick kick 53, 54, 55, 145
quick receivers 100
Racely, Ed 123
rainy days 69
rapport 5
Raymond, Tubby 147, 158, 159
reach block 94, 157, 210
Reade, Bob 84
ready-to-play whistle 61, 133, 134, 141
recruiting 225
red zone 7, 74
Reed, Gregory 112
Rees, Trevor 86
release by receiver 171, 192
remedial tackling 103
replacement route 136
results orientation 211
reverse 38, 40, 47, 77, 95, 96, 97, 114, 123, 128, 149, 155, 157, 158, 159, 165, 199, 200, 217, 218
reverse pivot 152
Rexrode, Bob 87
Rice, Homer 169
Rice, Jerry 9, 73
Richmond Steelers 193, 216
Right Kind of Heroes 12
rip release move 193
River City 7, 8
Roberson, Sam 3, 77
Rockne, Knute 84, 99, 128
roll-out pass 120
rookies 102, 104, 119, 227
Rose Bowl 128
roughing the kicker 63
roughing the passer 184
Royal, Darrell 128
run and shoot 119
Run and Shoot Football 142
running play percentage 73
run-pass option 148, 149, 156, 186, 189, 194, 195, 199, 200, 217
Run to Daylight 16
Ryan, Buddy 71, 73, 88
sack 99, 184 , 185, 186
sack, taking a 196
safety (deep defender) 24, 65, 90, 101, 137
safety (two points to defensive team) 1, 36, 37, 56, 67, 108
Saint Bobby and the Barbarians 181
Saint Mary's College 16, 222
Sanford Jumbo II dry erase marker 133
San Francisco 49ers 183
San Jose State University 201, 207, 214, 216
San Ramon Bears 62, 77, 86, 87, 99, 102, 104, 106, 135, 148, 177, 185, 186
San Ramon Valley High School 15
San Ramon Valley Thunderbirds 101
Scarborough 142
Schembechler, Bo 170, 224
Scholastic Coach 47
Scoring Power with the Winged T Offense 147
scouting form 109, 110, 111, 112
scout report 2, 5, 38, 104, 108, 122
screen pass 186
scrimmage 148
seam buck 8, 123, 199, 200, 217
seams in zone pass coverage 101
Sega Genesis 81
seven-box 84, 85
seven-diamond defense 84, 85
seven-on-seven drill 71
seven-year olds 4
Shannon, Bob 12
Shaughnessy, Clark 128
shift 80, 81, 130, 172, 174, 175, 176, 177
short-punt offense 119, 142, 144, 145, 153, 154
short side of the field 93
short-yardage situations 86
shotgun 92, 119, 130, 131, 170, 192
shovel pass 186
Shula, Don 19
Shurmur, Fritz 81, 84
Siler, Bill 84
Simonton, Tom 194
Simplified Single-Wing Football 130, 142, 150, 195
single wing 53, 55, 92, 109, 116, 119, 123, 127, 129, 130, 131, 135, 142, 144, 150, 153, 155, 165, 169, 195, 201, 217
Single Wing Football With the Spinning Fullback 142, 170, 195
6-5 defense 136
6-2 defense 136, 148
60-read defense 85
six-year olds 4
skill sprints 96, 114
Slanting Monster Defense in Football 84
slant pass 78, 79, 149, 187, 190
sled 208
slot formation 80, 91, 108, 128, 139, 172
slow-down offense 132

slow motion 104
Smith, Emmit 9
Smorgasbord Offense for Winning High School Football 83, 142, 153, 154
Smythe, Tom 147
snap count 162
sneak 128
Somewhere Over the Rainbow 83
South Valley Knights 102, 221
speed offense 120
speed option 130, 148, 156
spinning fullback in single wing 119, 142, 165
spin to avoid tackle 106
split-back formation 119, 145
split end 122, 139
split T formation 128, 142, 144, 145, 205
Sports Illustrated 88
Sports Illustrated for Kids 54
spot pass 130, 160, 188, 194, 198
spread formation 53, 142, 144
Spread Formation Football 142
sprint out 120, 156, 193, 194, 199, 200
squib kick 29, 30, 34, 38, 39, 51
stack 4, 76, 205
stalemate 98
stalk block 179
Stanford University 16, 105, 128, 211
star on kick return team 26, 28
star position tendencies 112
stats 7
stemming 205
stop-the-clock play 196
Storey, Edward J. 52
straight-ahead place kick 68
straight-up punt 59, 66
streak pass route 146, 188
strength of formation 171
stripping 20, 21, 107, 170
strong backfield 80, 153
"Student Body Forward" 150, 217
stunts 56, 80, 148, 205
substitution 55, 56, 103, 179
success probability 218, 221
surprise defense 116
surprise, element of 221
sweep 2, 77, 78, 83, 85, 86, 93, 95, 96, 97, 102, 104, 108, 112, 114, 120, 123, 128, 131, 138, 139, 154, 155, 157, 164, 168, 179, 190, 194, 195, 197, 199, 200, 217, 218
sweep spots 89, 92, 107, 155, 156
swim release move 193
swing pass 157, 185
Switzer, Barry 128
Sykes, Will 69, 75, 77, 120, 125, 129, 150, 155, 217
tackling 11, 14, 102, 103
tackling drill 103, 104, 106, 107
take a knee 49, 70
Tallman, Drew 84
Teaching Kids Football 170
tendencies 5, 82
Tennessee, University of 128, 184
10-1 defense 76, 79, 85, 87, 88, 89, 95, 98, 99, 100, 109, 116, 216, 227
Texas, University of 128
T formation 128, 129, 130
TGS mnemonic 26, 38
Texas Football Magazine 87
Theder, Roger 201
Tierney 142
third-string 162, 163
31 trap 150, 151, 158
three-down situation 220
throwing-on-the-run technique 156, 157
thud scrimmage 104
thumb flick 162
tight ends 161, 226
touchback 20, 60, 63
tough love 11
trailman on sweeps 77, 95, 102, 159
trap 93, 149, 159, 189, 209, 210, 221
trap blocks 83, 94, 130, 136, 151, 153, 154, 202
TriCity Cowboys 24, 41, 78, 79, 160, 192, 217
trick plays 51, 177
triple option 119, 128, 140, 142, 145, 148, 166, 205
tripping non-ball carrier 101
trips 91
26 power 9, 140, 198, 214
26 power pass 187, 196, 198
twins 172, 176
two-center shift 177
two-minute drill 1, 7, 132, 192
two-play formations 108
two-point conversion 67, 69
tyvek 221
unbalanced line 80, 89, 109, 130, 145, 166, 172, 177, 178, 217, 218
upback 131, 172
U.S. Naval Academy 86
units of minimum-play players 227, 228
unnecessary roughness 215
unsportsmanlike conduct 9, 46, 66
unusual offenses 142
Upshaw, Gene 224

Vacaville Bulldogs 18, 77, 95, 99, 101, 120, 156, 217
Vallejo Generals 79, 98, 155, 192, 193
veer option 13, 16, 119, 129, 145, 166, 168
veterans 102, 103, 227
VHS camera 225
videotape 51, 81, 222
waggle pass 190
Walden, Jim 30
walk-through kicking plays 38, 40, 57, 66
Wall Street Journal 183
Walnut Creek Marauders 109, 163
Walsh, Bill 105
Walsh, Patrick 216
Warner, Pop 145, 146
warp-speed no-huddle offense 109, 130, 131, 133, 134, 141, 142, 143, 146, 199, 217, 226, 227, 228
Warren 142
Washburn, Warren K. 84
Washington Redskins 128
weather 3
Webb, Tremaine 104
wedge kickoff return 30
wedge play 4, 116, 137, 138, 139, 149, 150, 200, 220
white board 134
wideouts 89, 153, 173, 185, 192
wide side of the field 93
wide slot 157, 174
Wilkinson, Bud 31, 81, 85, 128
Wilmington, CA Pop Warner team 131
wind sprints 36, 96, 142
wing back 90, 95, 124, 125, 127, 128, 139, 155, 156, 159, 172, 212
wing-T 54, 55, 91, 116, 119, 128, 129, 147, 155, 158, 190
Winning Football with the Air-Option Passing Game 142, 169
wishbone 119, 128, 130, 144, 145, 149, 168, 172
Witt, Joby 129
Wood, Gordon 42, 79, 84
Worley, Tim 28, 29
Worsley, Roger 147, 153
wrist plans 221
Wyatt, Hugh 142, 228
wrap up ball carrier 107
x-twirl 187
Yale University 130
Young, Jim 217
Young, Steve 9, 182, 183
Youth League Football 52
Zimmerman, Paul 88
zone blitz 88
zone pass coverage 65, 82, 87, 88, 89, 101, 173

Your Opinion of this Book is Important to Me

Please send me your comments on this book. I'm interested in both compliments and constructive ciriticism. Your compliments provide guidance on what you want. And, with your permission, I'd like to use your favorable comments to sell future editions of the book. Constructive criticism also helps make the book's next edition better.

Evaluation of *Coaching Youth Football, 2nd edition*

Circle one: Excellent Good Satisfactory Unsatisfactory

Circle one: Too Advanced About Right Too Basic

What part did you like best? ______________________________

____

What part did you like least? ______________________________

____

How can I improve the book? ______________________________

____

My promotional material includes brief comments by people who have read the book and their name, city, state, and occupation. I would appreciate any remarks you could give me for that purpose:

____

____

____

Name ______________________________ Team ______________________________

Address ______________________________

City ______________________________ State ______ Zip ______

Feel free to leave blanks if you prefer not to answer all of these questions. I would appreciate receiving your evaluation even if you only fill out one line.

How long have you been a football coach? ______________________________

What level do you coach at? ______________________________

What part of your football team do you coach? ______________________________

If your comments will not fit on this sheet, feel free to write them on the back of additional sheets. Please send your evaluation to:

John T. Reed
342 Bryan Drive
Alamo, CA 94507